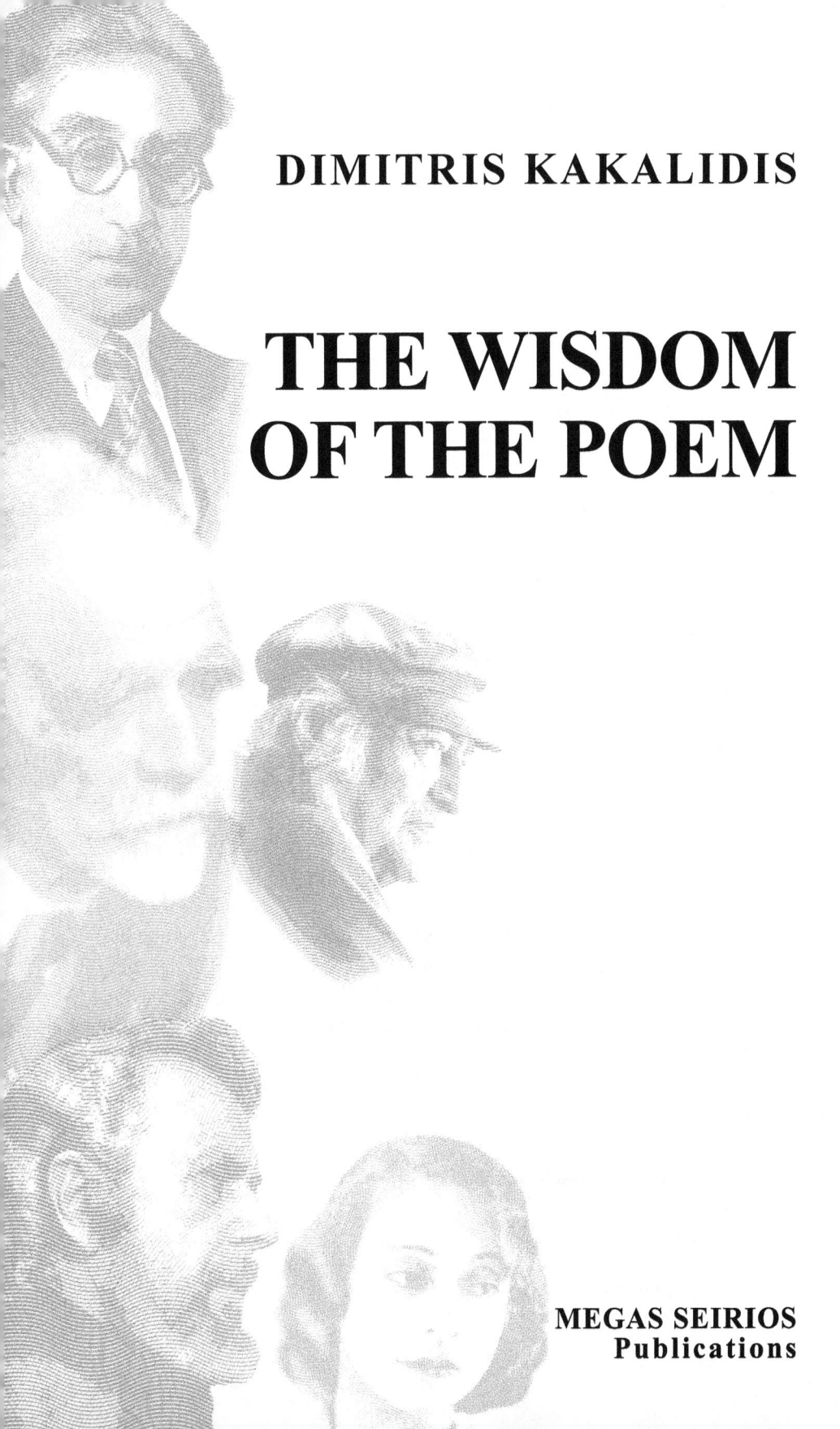

DIMITRIS KAKALIDIS

THE WISDOM OF THE POEM

MEGAS SEIRIOS
Publications

DIMITRIS KAKALIDIS
THE WISDOM OF THE POEM
FULL EDITION 2019

ISBN: 978-618-5223-32-8

© 2019 Omilos Eksipiretiton (Servers' Society)
All rights reserved. No part of this publication may be reproduced, stored in a retrieval system, or transmitted, in any form or by any means, electronic, mechanical, photocopying, recording or otherwise, without the prior permission of the publishers.

This book is published by **Megas Seirios Publications**, founded by the **Servers' Society Spiritual Centre** based in Athens, Greece. To find more information about the mission, works and activities of the Society and/or to place an order, please visit our website:
www.megas-seirios.com

or contact us at:
9, Sarantaporou Street, Athens, Greece, P.O.: 111 44
e-mail: info@megas-seirios.com
Tel.: +30 210 20 15 194
Tel./Fax: +30 210 22 30 864

Translation from Greek: Dimitris Fragogiannis
Cover and book design: Marianna Smyrniotou

*The analyses of the poems
are dedicated to all
contemporary Greek poets.*

ଔ

CONTENTS

INTRODUCTION	11
KRITON ATHANASOULIS: *I Ascend*	17
ARIS ALEXANDROU: *Study of Light*	21
MANOLIS ANAGNOSTAKIS: *The Chess*	25
TASOS ANAGNOSTOU: *Flesh of the Soul - The Hidden Lonesome Poem*	29
TAKIS ANTONIOU: *Quinisext Time*	34
ELENI ARGESTI: *Monologue With Time*	39
ELENI VAKALO: *Peace*	43
TAKIS VARVITSIOTIS: *Oh Night*	47
KOSTAS VARNALIS: *From "The Light That Burns"*	51
GIORGOS V. VAFOPOULOS: *The Glass Bell*	56
NTINOS VLACHOGIANNIS: *Ancestral Admonition*	61
EVANGELOS V. VOGIAZANOS: *Ode to a Horseman of the Steppe*	65
V.I. VOGIATZOGLOU: *Second Admonition: to the Initiator*	69
NIKIFOROS VRETTAKOS: *Hymn*	72
DIMITRIS GAVALAS: *With the Look of an Early Awakened Lioness*	78
NIKOS GALAZIS: *Oh Stranger, Announce...*	82
STELIOS GERANIS: *I Rediscovered Poetry*	87
DIMITRIS GERONTAS: *The Ash And The Fire*	91
ILIAS GKRIS: *Angel*	94
NIKOS GRIGORIADIS: *The Unseen within Us*	98
OTHON M. DEFNER: *Muses within Oneself*	102
ARIS DIKTAIOU: *The Angel of the Seventh Seal*	105
APOSTOLOS DOURVARIS: *Hymn*	109
NIKOS EGGONOPOULOS: *Bolivar*	113
ODYSSEAS ELYTIS: *The Mad Pomegranate Tree*	117

ANDREAS EMBEIRIKOS: *The Ascent*	123
GIORGOS THEMELIS: *Denudation*	127
DIMITRIS IATROPOULOS: *"Fragments Of Metalectic" 1984*	131
C.P. KAVAFY: *The God Forsakes Antony*	135
NIKOS KAVROULAKIS: *Homer*	139
EKTOR KAKNVATOS: *His Voice*	144
ANTONIS KALFAS: *Woundings and Medicines*	148
GIORGOS K. KARAVASILIS: *The Secret Rooms of the Tower*	152
GIANNIS KARAVIDAS: *The Other Sun*	156
OLYMPIA KARAGIORGA: *The Voice*	161
DIMITRIS I. KARAMVALIS: *Tonight I Will Cross the River*	166
DIMITRIS KARVOUNIS: *Wreath of Death*	171
ZOI KARELLI: *Eurydice*	176
NIKOS KAROUZOS: *Orthodoxy*	181
GIORGOS N. KARTER: *In Vivo*	185
CHRISTINA KARYDOGIANNI: *Absinthe*	189
STELLA KARYTINOU: *Ionian*	195
MICHALIS KATSAROS: *From the "Plateau"*	200
CHRISTOS E. KATSIGIANNIS: *Death of the Summer*	204
MITSOS KATSINIS: *Memory*	209
MANTO KATSOULOU: *Ritual*	213
KOSTIS KOKOROVITS: *Life*	216
TAKIS KOLIAVAS-MOLIOTAKIS: *Gallop*	220
GIANNIS KONTOS: *Not Even a Bird in Flight*	224
TASOS KORFIS: *As Prisoners*	228
GIORGIS KOTSIRAS: *The Poet*	232
CHRISTOS N. KOULOURIS: *Sea-Going*	236
LETA KOUTSOHERA: *Landscape 6*	240
GIANNIS KOUTSOHERAS: *I Indwell*	245
D. P. KOSTELENOS: *Poetry Today*	249

DIONYSIOS KOSTIDIS: *Now Lettest Depart*	255
VASILIS I. LAZANAS: *When I Returned...*	259
MARIA LAINA: *Aunt's Story*	263
TASOS LIVADITIS: *Century of Multiplicity*	267
STATHIS MARAS: *The Horse*	271
MELISSANTHI: *Lyrical Confession*	275
KOSTAS MONTIS: *Nights*	280
PANTELIS BOUKALAS: *Origin*	284
RITA BOUMI-PAPA: *If I Go for a Walk with My Dead Friends*	288
TAKIS NATSOULIS: *Tonight It Came*	292
GIANNIS NTEGIANNIS: *Final Adventure*	296
ZISIS OIKONOMOU: *Why I Rejoice Today*	300
KOSTIS PALAMAS: *The Twelve Words of the Gypsy*	304
I.M. PANAGIOTOPOULOS: *The Window of the World*	308
PANOS PANAGIOTOUNIS: *Confession to My Son*	313
GIORGOS PANAGOULOPOULOS: *Reception*	317
KOSTAS G. PAPAGEORGIOU: *From "The Family Tree"*	322
KAITI PAPADAKI-KARAMITSA: *Decommissioned Ship*	326
DIMITRIS PAPADITSAS: *The Window*	330
THANASIS PAPATHANASOPOULOS: *Summer Time*	333
NIKOS PAPAKOSTANTINOU: *Who Can*	338
NIKOS PAPPAS: *The Final Walk*	342
T.K. PAPATSONIS: *The Stone*	346
EVANGELIA PAPACHRISTOU-PANOU: *Exercise in Endurance*	351
GIANNIS PATILIS: *From the "Warm Midday"*	355
LAMPROS PORFYRAS: *Don't Cry*	360
MANOLIS PRATSIKAS: *Questions*	363
YIANNIS RITSOS: *From "The Moonlight Sonata"*	367
BIANKA ROMAIOU: *Mosaic Pieces*	371
SAVINA: *Blood Donation*	375

GIORGIOS SARANTARIS: *Come, Joy will be Divided...*	379
GIORGOS SEFERIS: *The Form of Fate*	383
AGGELOS SIKELIANOS: *Because I Deeply Praised*	388
ILIAS SIMOPOULOS: *A River of Stars*	391
TAKIS SINOPOULOS: *Landscape*	395
KOSTAS M. STAMATIS: *Experiences*	399
MARO STASINOPOULOU: *The Unicorn*	403
PANAGIOTIS E. STAVRAKAS: *And If!*	408
STAVROS STAVRIDIS: *Pregnant Nymph*	412
MICHALIS STAFYLAS: *Evritania*	416
KOSTAS STERGIOPOULOS: *Insignificant Moments*	420
KOSTAS E. TSIROPOULOS: *6th of Romanos the Melodist*	424
ANTONIS FOSTIERIS: *Notes on the Coming Day*	428
GIOTA FOTIADOU-BALAFOUTI: *Sarah...*	433
ALEKOS CHRYSOMALLIS: *You Can*	438
POETS' BIOGRAPHIES	442
BIBLIOGRAPHY	482

INTRODUCTION

The poet Dimitris Kakalidis, in his second analytical work, focuses his interest on the poet and the poetry. He delves into each poem, scrutinizing it, studying it, and analysing it in detail. He de-symbolises and interprets the concepts it encompasses, always coming to the recognition of the one, single Poet of all, the supreme creator and exponent of the Word, also expressed "by the spoken word" of all poets[1]. And the poets, having the gift of uniting with the entity, pulsating to its messages and conceiving the fields of the Word, respond to His current, a current of life, and shape it into verses.

"The Wisdom of the Poem" is an enchanting book, and its magic is owed to the fact that the analyst always refers to the ontological field of the poets, as they themselves are uplifted to the one, timeless Poet of the universe. In the same way, he unifies the meanings, ideas and messages that the creators convey with their works. In all, small and great, in life and in death, in the formed and the formless, he always sees the entity and it is that which he projects. This common attitude towards things, concepts, situations and people, delivers broadness to

---

[1] In Greek, the word for poetry is «ποίηση» (pronounced "poiisi"), from the verb «ποιώ» ("poio") which means to make, to create. The deriving word for the poet, «ποιητής» ("poiitis") therefore means the maker, the creator.

the analyses, as passions, instincts, desires, even the darkest aspects of the unconscious, are acknowledged as ontological manifestations, which must be translated into knowledge and love in order for their pure nature to be revealed to humans.

What is the role of the poet? Dimitris Kakalidis reveals it in a simple and dynamic manner: "Only a poet can be the great mystagogue, the united one, the one who perfectly represents the Monad throughout his ecstatic wanderings within infinity. He attires the symbols and the concepts. He is the substance and the shapes. He lives and experiences the unfathomable through mind and heart, and uses the verses to express it, explaining, grounding his truth into the chaos of ignorance, a world himself within the ignorance of the world itself."

He calls the poet a mystic, a spiritual leader, and a recreator of the Word. He tells us that the poet expresses Its ideas, shaping images, skilfully playing with words, revealing essential meanings – even within just a few verses. Gifted with an inner strength that urges him to break the boundaries of the limited mind, he is inspired as he passes into expanded mental fields. "And his inspirations", notes the analyst, "are our own inspirations that we deny. Our dreams are his dreams and our spirit to the harmony of his spirit harmonizes. The poet embraces the disharmony of people, he dwells within it, he accepts it. Each barbaric vibration, upon the softness of his own vibration is appeased, and every predatory thought – materialistic – within his own respective poetic thought repents, and communes in the light of his essence and the greatness of his soul, partaking in the holy of holiest of the supreme life."

Muse of all poets is the entity. Its Word they recreate, its own wisdom they convey into its verses. Hence does Poetry play a unique role in social life, as humankind, consciously or unconsciously, is influenced by its messages – messages of essence.

The analyst studies the Word of Poets and with his own

Word cross-checks it. His writing varies according to the subject he addresses. It is at times purely intellectual, sometimes emphasising the de-symbolisations of words, indicating the potential for new ways of interpretation, while at other times it is poetic, thus enriching his text with verses that turn the analyses into a work of literature. In some cases he uses arithmosophy, as in the "Wisdom of the Short Story". The arithmosophical analysis of words is implemented by the assignment of alphabet letters to digits. This method has been followed in the numberings carried out by Homer, Thucydides, Heraclitus and Pythagoras. Although there are other, later methods, the analyses are based on the numbering method of ancient Greeks, which is also the simplest of all. The de-symbolisation of words is carried out based on the concepts that correspond to the first twenty-four numbers, as interpreted by scholars of arithmosophy.

The analyses, whichever way they are accomplished, refer to the existence of the two aspects of the entity, the opposing fields that potentially exist within humans, to whom this entity has given the ability to express them. Of the two fields, one is the limitation of consciousness, while the other is broadness, inner freedom, essence. To demonstrate the coexistence of these two opposing forces, the analyst emphasizes certain concepts which he deliberately repeats within several texts. He refers to "chaos", to the "creation of the universe," and the "drama of human existence". He talks of the restrictions which humans impose on themselves when overwhelmed by "desires, feelings and thoughts", but also of the peace they experience when functioning with "heart and mind". He points out the causes giving rise to problems and restraints of the human function, while referring at the same time to the "redemption" provided by the spiritual principles, virtue, moral values, as taught by religion and expressed since ancient times by our nation's wise Fathers. He uses examples from mythology and history, which consolidate the analyses and demonstrate the importance of correct thought and action.

One hundred poems are analysed in the "Wisdom of the Poem", whose subjects the analyst elaborates on, thus participating in the ongoing work of understanding the ontological self that humans must become aware of, in order for it to emerge from within them. He recognizes the poets' ability to exalt concepts to the divine and thus transform them into "prayer", "greatness", and "essence". He contributes to the interpretation of their Word, which is the Word of the one Poet, speaking of the power of the pure "'shepherd mind", about the importance of the "Holy Communion", about the spirit that "radiates light and wisdom", about the love that dominates over "passions and weaknesses". He praises the poets and his hymn is addressed to God, to the Agatho[2], to the Supreme Being that is "omnipresent." He connects the daily occurrence with the eternal, the human with the divine, the "microcosm" with the "macrocosm". He fully believes in the pure nature of humans, which may, if they so wish, lead them to "bliss". That is why he defends the knowledge that illuminates the "abyss", the "relentless forces of the unconscious" which oppress humankind, especially during the period we are going through, in today's turbulent Times.

The poems analysed have been selected according to their topics. This is not a poetry anthology, which, in order to include all Greek poets, would need to consist of several volumes. Neither is it a critical presentation, as Dimitris Kakalidis has not carried out any kind of evaluation of the poems. As mentioned in the introduction of the "Wisdom of the Short Story", the ana-

---

[2] The term "agatho" out of the Greek word «αγαθό» is used to mean all that is beyond the duality of good and bad. It is the Entity, the Whole, the Monad. This word and concept occurs many times througout the following analyses, though due to syntax reasons the word "benevolent" might be used in various occasions. The reader must bear in mind that it still signifies "that which is beyond good and evil".

lyst's goal is the emergence of the knowledge existing within every human being and of the wisdom expressed by the creators, even if it is not sometimes done in a conscious manner.

With the "Wisdom of the Poem", Dimitris Kakalidis reaches the culmination of his analytical work. His work is extensive and thematically rich. These one hundred poets, with the many and various issues they deal with, offer their Word, for the analyst to take, to study, to develop and, by unifying all ideas into the one idea, all concepts into the one concept, to uplift it to the one Word, the source of all Words. Because, as he points out himself:

"A timeless teacher the poet is, his own century he teaches. His fiery spirit in paper he wraps and his Word is the inextinguishable light that illuminates the souls, the ancestral flame that burns and reduces to ashes its bodies, its times. And those who seek initiation to pass into knowledge, become poets, leaders of the world, guides of love, visionaries of the pathway that, as Kipling taught, leads to eternal glory, to the temple of freedom."

Klairi Lykiardopoulou

KRITON ATHANASOULIS

I ASCEND

Take me in your arms and tell me: you are dazed.
Sit me down with your company and tell me: you were
    so very lonely.
Make a bed for me with soft hands and tell me: you were
    so very tired.
Tell each other that from today your hands shall
    uplift me
to a light born into eyes determined.
Comrades on this path, remove from within me
the mud that my soul steps on, befouling itself, and struggles
    to overcome.
Further down is the summer road. A little further down the
acacia trees bloom
the sirens sing. And we close our ears, fearing that within a sweet
music we may become lost.
Onwards then. The star for me has lowered a ray. I ascend
    holding
this bright thread, suspended in the embrace of so many
    perils.
If I fall, let it be, all your open hands shall hold me,
    and I shall
never die, within your beloved hands.

                                          (Details from the sad history of man)

Staggering is the interest of human towards human, a love complete, a great response, absolute consent, supreme offering. A sacrifice made consciously and unconsciously in favour of their entity. A mystic dialogue between beings of all levels and between the intelligent human beings and God, for nature's benefit. An essential communication that from above descends as a command, the meaning of which only the poet is able to grasp.

Time its need expresses, when, dazed by the perpetual function of its personal successive moments, it tires, seeking human companionship, the embrace of the unknown God. He wishes to hear from His mouth the truth of the eternal fatigue of his tragic loneliness, which does however have the privilege, when asking for a bed, to have it offered by the service of the divine love, made by the soft hands of human compassion. To surrender itself, resting trustfully as a human would in the arms of a mother, a lover, a father, a friend, a brother. A priceless gift, from one life to another, which gives its affection, during the distance travelled by the century within the endless life of its cosmic course, for God's fatigue to rest.

The century asks of the auspicious and ominous times, its comrades, to be uplifted high above by them, the people, in the light of their hands, hands of its own, in the light of their eyes, eyes of its own, to the decision of its soul – their soul. To remove *from within* themselves *the mud that its soul steps on and befouls itself with, and to overcome* the miasma of their own souls, as it envisions further down, the summer road, the flowering of the acacia trees and struggles to persuade them to expel their fear. To open their ears, to listen to the captivating song of the sirens, to consciously lose themselves in the music of its entity, of their entity.

The great star lowers its rays for the worlds to hold onto, to climb onto them, to find themselves suspended in the light of a myriad perils – which are as many as the dangers of a human embrace. To drop down, to fall into the *opened, beloved hands*, to hold on, to live, to exist, and to never die.

Within the daily silence, the time passes judgement on its moments of chatter. Humans learn to accept fear, to listen to the song of the deceptive sirens. Enchanting are the hours and divided death becomes. As a human it is invited to ascend, to become mesmerised by the vertigo of intoxication caused by the senses, to see, to recognize the substance of the becoming. To delve deep into its life, to experience its being. Every hour, every moment, every day that passes is a thought, a feeling, an act that preaches salvation, as eternity becomes embedded in its spirit. And every act is the work of the irrefutable duration, a ritual work, mystical, emerging from its human life, in order to be able to realise the meaning of its existence.

It becomes ecstatic playing with the aspects and by unifying the opposites it becomes dauntless, fearless, to the revealing song of the sirens it surrenders. It succumbs to the mysteries of the seasons, it is initiated, its spirit triumphs, it becomes a poet. The universe he addresses, the suns and planets and gods whom as people does he see. He becomes intoxicated, dazed. *Take me in your arms*, he says to them, *and tell me: you are dazed*. The poet wants to hear the Word's truth. He becomes pan-human, pan-universal. Confirmation he requests.

This is what a human is, the need for conscious embrace, for love. And a bed he wants, made by the holy, creative hands of hope, that know how to defeat death, to redeem it by lavishly providing their caress and, embracing earth, to hold the worlds with the power of their infinite love, and from chaos to protect them. This love does the poet trust, the human love, to its power he surrenders. The one and only love does he prefer, the complete, divine love that saves. And this is the daily love, as humans show it in their every expression, the true love that must be realised. And they comprehends it within the infinite times of their life, they welcomes it, they accepts it, as it comes to them in the form of their companions.

Everything is suspended in the void and falls into the embrace of the human being, even the human being itself. And this is but the embrace of God. They are the divine *hands* holding the world, the human *hands* holding the hopes, the universes, the hands that dominate creation. According to tradition, the priests of the kaviria mysteries in Samothrace had the power, when using their hands, to even influence the orbit of the Sun.

The mystics hold the power of the hands, notes the poet. The human hands soothe, heal, love, and save humans from their own selves, suspended *in the arms of so many perils*, created by the very necessity of their evolution.

ARIS ALEXANDROU

STUDY OF LIGHT

*The devil stood before him
as a merciless light torching the desert
the temptations assault his face
as gusts of scorching wind.
Each time, as eyelids closing on their own
he responded: "It is written".
And thus he kept his eyes clear
without even a grain of sand clouding
his serene gaze...*

*Now all alone again
in the evening's lull
he begins to suspect
that someone behind him stands.
The shadow before his feet falls
the shadow with his own has merged
He still must stay
fasting he must remain
until, under the moonlight, to trample it he is able,
the shadow
oblong as it shall be – like a lizard.*

*Forty days and forty nights he has awaited trying
but the shadow, as before, falls into the line drawn
by his finger in the sand.*

*Thus, it is time for him to rise
to go to Galilee.
Let the shadow follow, as it is
                a constituent of his blood.
Let it follow, even if it whispers: "The temptation you have won over
    with someone else's answers.
Predetermined, this so called victory was."
As long as he has eyes, this shadow he will not rid himself of
he shall wait until the rains connect the grains
until his hands are able to mould the sand
until the light stands before him, as a helper and a friend.*

                                        (Poems 1941-1974)

    Merciless in its nature is the cosmic light, a truth urgently calling for redemption. An idea of God, the ancient Sun, unceasingly battering its planetary face each time the earthly Word turns its sides, one after the other, to accept the temptations – *gusts of scorching wind* – that rise up, rebel, and bombard the sole ruler of the realm, wanting to alienate him, to degrade him, leaning towards separateness. They are the grains of its earthly nature, magnetized by the bipolar current, attempting to hold onto their polarization, resisting the pull of the unified power coming from the serenity of the incarnate being, who has the clear gaze of one who sees light and darkness alike, with the insight of merging, of love, of deep forgiveness, of compassion.

    It is written since time immemorial that the role of the shadow is to be the testimony of the light. It claims its rights as a lifeless power, seeking to partake in the function of the Word's breath, pursuing the reflection's embedding in the subject. A demonic spirit, separating its being by playing, by teasing humans, in order to awaken their sedated consciousness, to raise their soul, to spiritualise their physical body.

Human and planet are one and the same. Shadow and night on the back and the lateral side of each planet, shadow and night on the back and the lateral side of the human. And as long as there is day, the symbol of the ontological, the divine presence, is the sun. And as long as there is night, its symbol is the moon with its phases, Luna, a light-reflecting, demonic personality of the world, which, as a resident of the heavens too, desires to exercise its sovereignty over earth. It projects its false shadows through humans, from whom the shadow of the night demands its redemption, as does the shadow of the day claim its merger with them.

Humans are those who resist the light, and their bodies' extensions – the planet with all its kingdoms. The light, having before it no other more evolved presence than that of its incarnate intelligent substance, requires of them to realise themselves, to become perfected and to form the exception within the economy of the universe. Humans, by completely and without resistance accepting the light's radiance, become the inner sun, symbolised by the resurrected Christ, the uncreated light of knowledge returning to the Father, overthrowing the kingdom of the born, whose parts of its very existence resist the truth, hence separating creation from erebus and erebus from the eternal, the unique day.

The light in its own light cloisters, the *shadow merging with the shadow*, as the poet says. It is from home expelled, a nature banished, which, as is written, tempts its being, always following the chosen, the one Word, which to the magic of its body surrenders. With its transformations it travels through the fields of its evolution, and, during the ascent, redeems the shadows – its animalistic conceptual creations – whose line of release the Being draws in the sand with the forefinger of His hand, as the mastermind, the guiding mind. A mind which leads its retinue, formed by the constituents of its blood, *to the predetermined victory.* Until itself in its entirety becomes the decision, the will which does not drive away its aspects, the cohesive force of the purifying love that merges, reunites the grains, restrains the photons to their layers and directs them so that the external explosions of the nuclei become internal, of awareness. The hands mould the sand, and light becomes an ally and a friend, a helper in the closure of the task towards complete atonement and annihilation of the earthy self.

In the quest for the truth of cosmogony it could be assumed that the sun, as a fiery, blazing mass, has no shade and, to acquire it, raises both its physical carrier and its extensions, its planetary bodies, to represent its living existence within chaos. These perceive its power as their own and, resisting the fire, cool down, incarnating the will for existence within their desire's chaos. As their elected representative they empower planet earth, nurturing their animalistic nature in its realm, making it human and, confessing their inability to evolve, demand the spiritual presence of this very sun.

In the temporal manifestations of the cosmic being, as a human God descends, as a sun contemplating the drama of its shadow – its spirit and its body with its emanations. It struggles with the shadow's temptations and, dominating over it, deliberately leaves it behind to follow. This shadow partakes in its eternal drama. It is admonished by the sun's teaching, becomes wise, taking on substance, entity from its entity. Through the centuries it becomes conscious and accepts its absorption by the light, the light from the sun, the sun from itself, and the fission of ideas in the universal mind becomes internal. As a human, God is incarnated, and the human, as a divine mind recognizes that by the Entity's grace it exists. Its work is that of the Galilee of nations, of planets, of worlds of wisdom and love, which poets are in a position to realise and to address for the sake of the blood-born humanity.

MANOLIS ANAGNOSTAKIS

THE CHESS

Come and play.
I will give you my queen
(She was at one time my beloved one.
Now I no longer have a beloved)
I will give you my towers
(Now I no longer fire at my friends
they have died long before me)
and this here king was never mine
And besides, what would I want with so many soldiers?
(They blindly go forth without even dreams)
All, even my horses will I give to you
only this here fool shall I keep
who knows only on a single colour how to move
striding from one end to the other
laughing before your many suits of armour
all of a sudden entering your lines
disrupting the solid formations.
And no end does this game have.

(Poems)

Come and play. I will give you my queen. And thus the poet his battle commences, giving all his powers to the game of life. For him the highness of this game was once his beloved idea, his mistress, the image of a queen of shadows, whom he sacrificed amidst her imaginary towers. Enthroned by the king of her deceit, prey to the protection of the soldiers, guards of destitution and need, subordinates of a sovereign of an ephemeral life, which wants its players on the chessboard to repeat – on the edge's field – the endless game that only leads to losses even those with victory on their side.

In *the game with no end*, the only winner is the poet. Consciously he has withdrawn from the utopian dream's futile claim, giving all victories to his co-player, knowing beforehand that they will inevitably lead his opponent to defeat; because, released of warmongering ideas, he has passed on to the knowledge of the pure mind, now possessing the deeper significance of the game. He gave it *all, even his horses* – the instincts – and only himself the fool he kept, as a fool for God, who knows only on *a single colour how to move*, this colour of colours, the colourless, striding from the edge of apparent dimension to the other, the occult, that of the wise laughter that mocks the cries of sorrows, as he stands before *so many suits of armour* of dead warriors. Resurrected in his essence, he suddenly penetrates their lines, and, disrupting their belief that they are alive, he agitates their alleged solid formations.

No end does the game of life have, and the poet reveals this futile battle's meaning. A wizard of the verse, a mighty warrior of the spirit, from another world with his divine Word he comes, as the only one who knows how to die and live again. And from the pawns he takes their consisting shadow, the grandest queen of dreams, to sacrifice her.

Come and play. I will give you my queen, he exclaims. *Now I no longer have a beloved*. Her subjects have long since died. I shot them because their king, my king, *was never mine*. And so, without a kingdom, without a king, what would I want with a queen?

Come, *I will give you my queen*. She who tormented the

dawns, projecting her shadows amidst the light, scarlet ideas battling the sun the creator mind that gave birth to them trying to maintain their existence in the unexplained substance of the existing. As non-existent, they hang on to their vision in order to prove the value of their ephemeral life, consumed in the attempt for prevalence of human selfishness. This is what puts forward the passions and these, both holy and unholy, stand opposed to the absoluteness of the being, creating the scenery of illusions of a world enslaved, of a false life imagined, as if inspired by a grand chess player, in order with his pawns to play and with their presence to fill the empty hours of his unbearable silence.

This is the poem's meaning; the beloved queen of the mind, which gives birth to the ideas, to the soldiers, the officers and the horses. And as a sorceress she builds her towers, to be conquered by the invaders of another dimension who reign in the wishes of her dreams, the poet's dream, the shadow of his shadow which he renounced in order to pass into reality, into essence. From there he reveals the quality of the personality amid its macabre reign, choosing for himself the leading, the essential role of the fool, the jester, in order to consciously agitate the warlike human ego, using the one colour that composes the many, the one idea that expresses all ideas, the one sense of all meanings. This is what reigns from end to end in the field of the continuous battle fought by the human personality against the entity, for the prevalence of the futile existence within the endless fields of its fantasies.

The universal game is symbolised by chess and how it is played only the poet knows, because he knows the reason why the human intellect created it, seeking in this way to represent the purpose of creation that forces humans to mimic it perpetually. The king and queen, their subjects, officers and soldiers, the towers symbolising the strongholds of insecurity and the horses, are but pawns in the power of humans, teaching them that they too are but pawns of their ego and that this ego is nothing more than a pawn in the game of the cosmic becoming. A pawn of pawns, a shadow of shadows is the projection of the power that defines their fate within the limits of the universal mind, the formless God of this formed human being.

This is the game of his beloved life. And *no end does this game have*. The human is called to become the conscious player, to become the poet.

TASOS ANAGNOSTOU

FLESH OF THE SOUL - THE HIDDEN LONESOME POEM
(excerpts)

A knife I hold and flesh of the soul I am. Behold the way: before you – an imaginative wound. And the seas of blood in vain do not the doorknockers sound. Oh, blissful, blissful those of you that shall apprentice in the glow of an endless night, with the dead unburied crawling through words, gathering earth crumbs, leaves, lonely sparks in the Cremains. Knowledge mournfully heads to terror, to arrogance, to decay. The ornaments fall, hair is plucked and fingers are stripped to the innermost directions. These bones creak within the rotten dresses, but the music continues in the exquisite crypts. Oh, my hourglass – the duration. The cloud drips, the syllable in the word, the word in the sound – shivers that in the flame strengthen me. The knife glows red and the Truth slides into angelic hells. Behold my heavenly road, Innocent, Innocent of this very blood whose profoundness I wore and traverse the Word.

And so did the Night ever? progress: with eyes on the knife, lips upon the cry. The blood on the streets had no intention of going silent. Centuries passed. The poem in the town square is still being raped: a naked body – in pain and shame. I thread the wound within me, I illuminate it, kiss it, and let it wear my soul.

(The other of the hidden glow)

The Word tolls: poetry births infinity. *Flesh of the soul the hidden lonesome poem*, and the poet holds a knife, the infinite, and he is *flesh of the soul. I hold a knife...* his Word tolls.

Behold the way: before you, evincible *the hidden lonesome poem*, the creation, rules the Archangel of Archangels, as fiery Word in its magnificent formation, an *imaginative wound*. The revelation of the Word, the revelation of the soul, the revelation of the mind, of senses, of emotions, possesses the one timeless John, the poet magnified in the Word, the Word of Words. *And the seas of blood in vain do not the door-knockers sound. Blissful, blissful those of you that shall apprentice in the glow of an endless night, with the dead unburied crawling through words, gathering earth crumbs, leaves, lonely sparks in the Cremains.*

The Word speaks to its Words, to its heavenly bodies. It addresses their infinite soul, their infinite spirit, the bodies of bodies – its body. And the eternal night, within whose endless brilliance its Words dwell, like the *dead unburied crawling through* their own words is and remains their supporter, their patron, a supreme womb that carried them in absolute darkness and, by transubstantiating them, birthed them in cosmic light, in knowledge *mournfully heading towards terror, arrogance, decay*. Because the chorea of this concomitance leads to the pan-universal Cremains, to the innermost of one human, of one God, *whose ornaments fall, and hair is plucked and fingers are stripped in his directions, the innermost* of innermost, after the holocaust, as matter and spirit, holy in nature, energy they are and energy they become again.

These bones, his skeletons they are, creak in their continuous repetitive osteosynthesis within their *rotten dresses* – the habitats of all – that change shape and condition, all together prone as they are to the necessary decay of their own music which *continues in the exquisite crypts*. They are the crypts of the abdomen, the heart and mind, which are surrounded by other, equally important, since emotions and thoughts are but crypts that contain one another. And only time – the duration's hourglass – becomes the dripping cloud, *the syllable within the word, the word within the sound*. It becomes the shivers that strengthen the flame, the flame of the inextinguishable fire into which *the knife glows red* – the intellectual sword of the Archangel Word poet, *for the Truth to slide into angelic hells. Behold my heavenly road,* he exclaims. *Innocent, Innocent of this very blood whose profoundness I wore and* my own Word *I traverse.*

The vast seas of blood, of the light's radiance and the others, the deeper ones, the inner oceans, which, as those of earth, cry of their nature that gestated the universal creation. And it gave birth to it amidst the chaos of their vision, in the abyss of their soul, to be adorned with its myriad forms, the infinite, the volumes and shapes, the curves and parallel lines. Vertical, horizontal concepts, ideas, forms, presences of its substance, to hold their sins as mortal trophies and immortal, to *sound the door-knockers* of Hades' Gates, seeking the exit, after the projection of the descent that predestined them, Words imaginative they are, to become the mirage of their ineffable and of their visible mystic societies.

A heavenly road the poet with his sword opens into the cosmic *angelic hells*, robed in complete profoundness, traversing the Word, forcing it to apprentice in *arrogance, terror and decay*. An archpriest recycling the love and anger, passing them through the dark passages of the beaten track and the inaccessible road, with his guilt, a guilt of the hidden poem – the creation – *that in the town square is raped* – the field of the revelation of the convergence of the parties of his presence –: a naked body.

And so did the *Night always progress since time immemorial*: with eyes on the knife – the sword – the symbol of the fiery Word. *The blood on the streets had no intention of going silent. Centuries passed* and more will come, steeped in pain and shame. And he, a divine destination, a leader re-creator – the poet –

passing the wailing into his being, he illuminates it, embraces it, worships it and, by recognising in it his body, he dresses it with his soul.

Thus, the first verse finds vindication: *I hold a knife and I am the flesh of soul*, because the flesh, the earthly field, is that which carries within it the power of the Blessed Sacrament, which constructed the universe and created the beings who inhabit it.

The second verse: *Behold the road: before you – an imaginative wound* – the path of awareness of the cosmic drama, which must become specific knowledge. And *the seas of blood*, of passions, of desires, of expectations, for their own salvation *sound not the door-knockers in vain*, says the mystic poet.

Oh, blissful, blissful those of you that shall apprentice in the glow of an endless night. Blissful, because those of the solar, the planetary, and the human Words that apprentice with the mysteries of existence, will be illuminated, will become divine, as they will realize the likes of all who wish to remain dead within the elements of the Word of their own sounds, words, phrases, rhythms, *gathering earth crumbs, leaves, lonely sparks in the Cremains* that remain from the holocaust of their deliberate Life and their unwanted death.

And thus, knowledge shall mournfully move forward, to bring about the cosmic awareness in *terror, arrogance, decay*. An irrevocable initiatory process, necessary for ornaments to fall and hair to be plucked. And the fingers of manual capacity which corrupt the evolution, consolidating the fallacy of external life, to be *stripped to the innermost directions* and be sanctified as bones creak *within the rotten dresses*. But the music will *continue in the exquisite crypts*, transmuting bones to salt, to the pure essence of the spirit, the energy that has passed through the procedures of divine fire and has become transubstantiated into sacred ashes, so as, through its stigmata, new solar systems to create.

And the mind, the pure mind, symbolised by the hourglass that remains untouched in its eternal course, sacrifices the cosmic harmony, turning it into a dripping cloud, a syllable flooding the word, a word diffusing, becoming sound, a Word reborn, perfect – shivers flooding the existent and non-existent world, the born and unborn human – to strengthen the timeless poet in the inextinguishable flame, making the knife glow red – the sword – and *the truth, sliding* more and more *into angelic hells*, again and again through all projections of the universal mind – the necessary cycles of creation and regeneration of ideas, philosophies, teachings, processes which cause friction, the means for the glory of the supreme human.

Behold the heavenly road, the Innocent of this very blood – the definitive Word, the poet holding the purpose of his task – because that is how *Night always progressed*, autonomous and independent, *with eyes on the knife, lips upon the cry* – the blatant Word of existence. It is the drama of creation that has no intention of silencing the blood on the streets, because it is but a poem, a naked body, exposed to the pain and the shame of its being, and to protect itself passes the wound through its own body, illuminating it, kissing it, dressing it with its It is the return of creation to the beyond, which embraces it, considering it the only incorporeal body that to the innermost returns again to be projected as redeemed, complete, perfect. A self-existent nature that is magnified in its creation's purpose, for it to exist divine within the beauty of its infinity and be renowned for the knowledge of the agatho[1], that of the inner strength of the beings that serve it, admiring its forms. Legions of witnesses of ideas are its ideas. And its values, the amaranth flower of wonders, are the poets, having the advantage of spiritual strength, as they march on in its perpetual cycle.

---

[1] The term "agatho" out of the Greek word «αγαθό» is used to mean all that is beyond the duality of good and bad. It is the Entity, the Whole, the Monad.

TAKIS ANTONIOU

QUINISEXT TIME

THE ARCHPRIEST

*Thus spoke
an angel of great counsel
to death's seven anti-spirits.*

*Great is the power of death.
An untroubled sea
in the endless lull of the clouds.*

*The crying of the deceased
at the mercy seat of thence Erebus.*

*Dried was the soul of life.
To death was the spirit slain
falling unspent to loss.*

Dawnless night shall not be there.

THE DANCE

*Alleluia
three-sun Notional
Son-of-God
of an uncreated womb.*

THE PEOPLE

*They close the body's eyes
and the mind alone darkens
unseen is its range
within the universe's depth.*

*Shadows, empty and unsleeping
count their days.
And from the cremains pass unto the light
and nowhere do they go.*

THE DANCE

*Alleluia
undaunted Theurgist
of the firstborn Chaos.*

THE ARCHPRIEST

*Abominable of death is the time.
In its mouth the divine zero blooms.*

(To the deceased)

Within the synod of the quinisext period's Archangels, the miracles of God take place. An Archpriest the inner mind, a teacher of immortality, the will of the superior of wills for redemption of the dream it preaches. Great is the power of death and the anti-spirits, in the endless false lull of stellar clouds, unburdened do they rest. In the desert of Erebus, crying voices of the deceased, their atonement they request, that dried was the soul of life. In the dawnless night the spirit of the Word unspent to loss remains. And no end shall there be to the unredeemed spirits' lamentation.

Dance of enlightened, redeemed spirits, of saints the Conceived, in a three-sun formation, the Creator of the *uncreated womb*, which the Absolute brought forth, it glorifies. The people become aware. No longer fallacies do their eyes see. The descending mind shadows the carnal body and its respective inner one in the light remains alone. The spectrum of the universe, an unattested body in the uncreated depths. The shadows of recollection remain vacant, to recycle the fire, ashes the centuries to become, passing unto light, to the ubiquitous of emptiness itself to go.

Alleluia the dance, alleluia God, alleluia the firstborn chaos. Alleluia the emptiness. Omniscient Archpriest, *abominable of death the time*, as in the mouth of the Word the *divine zero blooms*.

Dead, according to the teachings of Jesus Christ, are those who fend for the mundane. Immersed in their dreams, they refuse to understand divinity and, by their seven anti-spirits, to a forced punishment they are submitted. Those remaining in the *untroubled sea*, a crying voice their word in the *interminable lull* of vapours, small-minded, with their desires' toil they occupy themselves. Beyond the *mercy seat* of *Erebus*, the *soul's life has dried* and the spirit dies in the dawnless night of sufferings, slaughtered where the human is lost and the Christic consciousness unassimilated remains. An angel of the forces is the bearer of the message that of life eternal the bestower does indeed exist. Released is the divine fire and abolished is the kingdom of death.

Dance of universes, alleluia the sound of notional suns, a harmony of theogony, of divine knowledge the chosen, the water of the immaculate spring, of both visible and invisible miracles are the wonders of the undefiled womb. Of its mysteries the works, birth of births, the God-birth of Christ. Erebus and darkness are the mundane. Of the Holy Spirits is the care, of light the favouring. A Sun existent is God and as an angel of will he shall dispel the *lull of clouds* and the *state of death* is abolished.

The poet refers to the dawnless night of life, to death's power, where *unspent to loss* the spirit is driven, into the flow of the rivers of earth, that from the sky receive the light, the power to exist. And in their light are bathed the earthly. Jordan is the Word, Baptist of all, in the body of earth the body of Christ he recognises and through His Spirit are the worlds anointed and His spiritual myrrh is scented. By His descent, accomplished is the synod of cosmic Words on earth. Angels of all, in His light enlist. *Alleluia triple-sun Notional, Son-of-God, of the uncreated womb.*

The poet has the depth and height, he has the earth, the abyss, God himself, what the world also has but does not suspect. It does not see their homogeneity, the single will of God. The entity is fragmented by the unholy outer mind and life as a realm of death is perceived. A spectrum of shadows is the world. Closed are its eyes. Unattested in its depth the universe, in its fire it is consumed, and the ashes of the shadows that the timeless counted, pass unto the light. Amazed is the firstborn Chaos.

Alleluia of everything the Dance. The Word is Your Archpriest, from birth to death for You the *divine zero blooms. Thus* the poet *spoke.* Within *death's power,* great is the lamentation.

Blessed be God, for Christ has truly risen from the dead.

The poet refers to the Holy and Undivided Trinity. To the Father, the Son and the Holy Spirit. To the triune God, the triune human, whose spirit with the purpose of salvation has chosen death. In the human spirit it has established it's power, as the one to be content with the *untroubled sea*, the sea of unconscious Life, from where it's desires evaporate and their vapours the *endless lull of clouds* create. *Crying voices of the deceased*, the supplication of the seven anti-spirits to the *mercy seat of Erebus* that an *angel* of *great counsel* God's redemptive Word announces.

Humans become aware, they see that their spirit is being lost, they understand that their dawnless night has no end, as long as they remain unrepentant, do not praise, and do not seek salvation. The *abominable time of death*, with the power of the liturgy, the dance of universes in the ever-blooming *divine zero*, God's compassion the people invoke and are redeemed.

ELENI ARGESTI

MONOLOGUE WITH TIME
(excerpts)

XXVIII

While transforming, I record you, time,
in the stairways of a myriad materializations.
Among the crowd of shapes shrunken and enlarged.
In single-tendency, tragically irreversible.
Where the West cannot be overthrown.
And the East launches of rays its arrows
rigorously insisting on its irremovability.
Merciless, you do not return!
You only hurl the stolen apples of youth
dispersing its fragrance
stellar pollen in a universe perpetually in love.

XXIX

Adjust me in perpetuity
a burning flame
in the altar of the universal world!
And oh! do not abolish me time, as a glow
to the astonishing miracle
of natural phantasmagorias.
Don't! Do not violate
the absolute authority of harmony.
Of mysteries the key
within me I hold!
Of All I am
the unexpected crypt! (Monologue with time)

A burning flame the humans are, *in the altar of the universal world, the astonishing miracle in the* becoming *of natural phantasmagorias, transforming within the stairways of* the entity's *myriad materializations*, their merciless being while soliloquising they invoke, the *rigorously irremovable*, praying it does not violate their *absolute power of harmony*.

The key of mysteries the humans keep within, as the poet says. *Of All* they are the *unexpected crypt in the single-tendency of the tragically irreversible* field, where the *West is not overthrown and the East launches the arrows of its rays*. Merciless is time that hurls the *stolen apples of its youth* towards everything, diffusing its *fragrance to a universe perpetually in love, stellar pollen*, to adjust the perpetuity according to the unchanging will of God, in its essence recording the human, cosmic course.

While transforming, I record you time; this, the poet can say. The poet knows of the *stairways of a myriad materializations* of life. Quality of the creator the intuitive wisdom is. Every field that constitutes the existence of humans, their constitution, is a stairway upon which their nature climbs to realise their vision. And many are their visions, myriads, infinite.

Shrunken and magnified are the shapes, their thoughts, their feelings in the *single-tendency of the tragically irreversible* becoming, where their completion is not overturned and their spirit's continuous Dawn fires its arrows – irremovable thoughts – persistent, directed towards the irremovability of the nature of emotions and ideas, to be established in the essence of the mind; the specific knowledge to become, the merciless, which entrenches its uniqueness, hurling the *stolen apples of youth* that represent it to the world, thus distributing its authority to the parts of its externalised being that still remain projected. As stellar pollen it scatters its fragrance, *perpetually fertilizing a universe in love*, adjusting its fires to perpetuity, forcing it to gestate it, to shape it, to regenerate it, keeping the flame alive upon the altar, a soul of its phantasmagorical world.

Everything in the universe perpetually transforms. Subject it is to variations imposed by time and, evolving, it nears the realization of its being. Self-completion of the becoming of beings, which, situated on the path of their evolution, are responsible for carrying out the mission assigned to them by the cosmic law, which is none other than the work of their individual and collective development, in order to conquer the necessary awareness by the externalised existence in its entirety.

The entirety of these changes is perpetually recorded in the collective and individual subconscious. It is processed by the fields and subfields of the inner mind and, as a commonly accepted and proven experience of a state of consciousness, they re-diffuse it to the kingdoms of manifestation. It is a privilege of intelligent humans, the ability to intuitively conceive, in order for them to realise the nature of creation, the essence of which by the cause and effect of its action is thus characterised.

In the poem the meaning of this evolutionary course is given through internal processes, which initially take place in the field of the universal mind and then are manifested as formed visible and invisible presences. They become time, rhythm, harmony, prone to the *single-tendency tragically irreversible* field of the mind's nature, which is not overthrown in its sunset (West), making its presence as a continuously rising sun (East), catapulting the irremovable fire as a self-regulating flame, *burning on the altar of the universe*. There, this very mind does not abolish itself as nature of time, as the *phantasmagorias' astonishing miracle* of existence, which, in the *absolute power of its harmony*, does not violate itself.

This one and only unique truth is the *key of the mysteries* that all humans keep within, as once again, they are – as the pure mind – *the Ego of All, the unexpected crypt*, a reality that out of intuitive wisdom the poet has the ability to know.

Each poem is a monologue of the very Word that is recited for the balance of cosmic forces and therefore of humans, since they are the resultant, the crypt that includes the All, the inner mind which orders and directs their being as well as the external, the *key of mysteries* that at will opens and closes the *gate* behind which knowledge and ignorance of self-preservation, conservation or self-coverage is kept. The outer mind is self-transforming and records the time of its manifestation, transmuting it to the very essence of its nature – the unchanging mind, which alternates its experiences with those of human nature having as a reference point its timeless being.

ELENI VAKALO

PEACE

If only my humble, calm hand leaned
onto your great earthly palm
And with comforted eyes resting
on your beloved body, to simply
along your footsteps walk
With your own will

So alone. A silent tree
That a forest pretends to be...

In the evening, while from the fields returning
At dusk

I shall be your sweet bread
And the restful chamber
With its strong white walls
Which held the light
And, when as a woman I sit by your side
At the mantel's edge by night
On your shoulder I shall rest my head
And I shall love the Virgin Mary
With her sweet watery eyes

(Theme and variations First poetic collection)

Of the mysteries of the universe, of the secrets of man and woman the poet speaks, of the glory of life, of nature that does not go against its nature. And only she, as greatest of the dream, as superior of the agatho[1], as greater of the forces of the soul, the womb that birthed the sun, the woman of women, having in her hands the balance of the world and the keeper of heavens, can lead her universal life in perfect harmony with the will of God. The female of the One brightens the life of man, as in the earthly cycle of existence, *in his great earthy palm*, she offers her beauty and on his body rests the lust of her eyes, unexplored wills with his own will to follow the footsteps of light. A centuries-old knowledge which people declined, entrained by the silent presence of the tree, which led them to the grim forest of their rebellious soul, which disobeyed the divine Word.

Perfectly does the Word know of the woman's place in the neediness of man, and of man's will in the woman's nature, a womb luminous with his miracle of spermatogenesis, when, upon the conjugation's need, the wisdom he shall pour out of the mature, contrite man, because in ignorant times to his desires he succumbed, the many mercies of the woman he ignored, and her grace he appropriated. Man and woman both their other half considered as their slave and their body as a vessel for pleasures did they use, ignoring the power of love that uplifts lovemaking to a divine destination.

Of true love speaks the poet, the complete love of man for the woman and the woman's dedication to the greatness of man, whose body and spirit she recycles in her heart, experiencing the bliss of union, as in her innards the world she gestates and nature does she birth, the nature of the being, finding greatness in the glory of God. Religious life is lovemaking, love, and without the Holy Spirit life we do not have.

And I shall love the Virgin Mary with her sweet watery eyes. A complete woman, she who totally worships God, man, life, love, light, knowledge. This knowledge returns from the fields at dusk, accompanying man and woman to their home, where each is to the other *a sweet bread* in their *restful chamber* with the *strong white walls*, the woman's heart, a holy womb, a hearth of inextinguishable light, accompanying God to the erebus of infinity. On the man's shoulder she leans her head, and loves eternity, giving birth to hopes of deification, his redemption from the unbearable shackles of denial, which both embraced during their past's beginning, when they limited their spirit to the flesh and separated themselves from bliss for the sake of artificial pleasures, ignoring the uniqueness of their hermaphroditic nature, disobeying their entity's will.

A woman the poet is, to the divine will she surrenders, showing the way to reunification with the man, uplifting the fleeting romance to its spiritual subsistence, where the human soul is redeemed of the projections of the mind, the influence of instinctual drives, the passions of desire, the unrelenting binding of the ego, the estrangement of woman and man from the harmony of love. Peace to passions. Unexplored are the woman's cravings and profane are man's aspirations in the house of love. Body and spirit wear the gloom of the night and have no other path than that of neediness, to proceed into the sanctuary of eternal knowledge.

The lily's immaculate mysteries in the service of the dedicated woman are. And the spirit of man rejoices, the mind calms, the world rests assured. In the ritual of love, a saint of miracles is the creator, the one having under His rule the external light of luciferian spirits. In the midst of the abyss the divine couple stride and its testimony is a Word of ressurection, of immortality of holy spirits in the divine account of the inextinguishable light. The love of man and woman in everyday life is a prerequisite for their peaceful co-existence, which to the revelation of agatho[1] leads, where love its universal mysteries in earth's altar lays, deifying the cycle of unappeased human need.

The poem shows the infinite power of woman, the infinite potential of love, a result of obedience to the will of God for the salvation of both sexes. A salvation which might well be experienced by people on earth through the events of celestial time, which as a man and woman manifests. The fiery Word assumes human qualities, externalizing the essence through His aspects as irrefutable proof of the truth of His divinity. His being He recycles as a common human being, needing, as a man, the beauty of a woman's soul and form, to eternally perpetuate His creation's miracle.

---

[1] The term "agatho" out of the Greek word «αγαθό» is used to mean all that is beyond the duality of good and bad. It is the Entity, the Whole, the Monad.

TAKIS VARVITSIOTIS

OH NIGHT

Oh night that plummets from the tree
Full of openings and of darkness circles
A great eyelid you are
To the north a crystal blue you promise
To the south, a canister full of lightnings
To the east, a vast, bright eye
To the west, a star-laden ship

Oh night, from the galaxy coming
Deep your ancestry runs
A black avalanche you are
Innumerable years ago
As soon as a girl you touch
A pale shimmer she becomes
of birds a farewell song

Oh night, gate of the unseen
A shore, vast and without age
A wedding gathering of shadows
The only homeland where the flower of silence grows
The worthiest habitat of death you are
And at the dream's turning point always your body lays
Speckled with a thousand sparkling lights

(The winter solstice)

From the night, this night is no different; nor apart from the tree of life does anything else give it reason to exist. Full of openings and of darkness circles, a great eyelid in the eye of God which is shutting. And when it opens, to the north a crystal blue it promises – the knowledge, the spirit's intellect – to the south a canister full of lightnings – the myriad souls, unfledged hopes full of desire for life. And from east to west it is the world's eye that to a ship transforms, a star-laden one, shining, fiery boat that sails the worlds, proud amidst the chaos.

Oh night that comes from the galaxy of primordial souls, deep your ancestry runs. The black avalanche, their bodies you are. You carry the countless years and the desire they have for you to touch a girl – nature – to transform it into a pale shimmer that will accompany the farewell song of the birds.

Oh night, gate of the unseen, eternal nature of nature, shore vast and without age, the wedding gathering of shadows of the oceanic, everlasting light. The only homeland where the flower of silence grows, the worthiest habitat of death you are, since you defined as a reason for your substance, amidst the dream's turning point, to have your body by a thousand lights illuminated.

The night has no age, the poet says. It sprang from the chaos of the mind, neither beginning nor end it has. Mother of gods and humans, it is the womb that also gifted the unseen, having the heart as its gate and the mind as its guard. Before this gate the poet stands, overseeing the creation's miracle and ecstatic he becomes. The whole creation, the unfathomable, in his vision, is a tree *full of openings and of darkness circles*. This is the night of cosmic light and from this do all nights plummet.

At *the wedding gathering* of shadows, beneath the *great eyelid*, the look of promise turns into a *crystal blue*, the sky, a child that earth birthed to cover it, as, in the night of chaos that created it, it strides illuminated by others, at the mercy of the cosmic dawn. And through the night's openings, the infinite *circles of darkness*, spring the lightning bolts, the bright souls embodying the inspirations, bringing the revelation of the only homeland where *the flower of silence grows*. This is the *habitat of death*, its being. *And at the turning point of its dream* is the world that sparkles in the poet's spirit, speckled by a thousand lights, the panorama of existence. Night is the presence of the entity plummeting from the tree to become *a great eyelid* with the crystal knowledge of discernment in the north – the intellectual field that spreads the lightning bolts of wisdom to the south, to the field of its rebirth.

Thus, the dawn of knowledge towards its twilight inevitably heads, so that by completing its circles, its work within the galaxy to vindicate. And to return lit by the stars, seen through the unseen, from its deep ancestry, as a new idea, thought, conception, a *black avalanche* that will sweep the *countless years* to another womb, which once again is earth's pale shimmer. And after hearing the *farewell song of the birds,* to return, the night, once again through the same gate to the unseen, there, *at the vast, without age shore, where the flower* of eternal silence grows, to call to the assembly of withdrawal the one and only homeland – the manifested universe.

The poet refers to the manifested nature of the universal mind, the full of *openings and dark circles* field, likening it to the night that perpetually unfolds its darkness' circles, as, from the tree, symbolising its life, headlong it tumbles, sweeping its projection into infinity under the creator's supervision. An undefined field, to humans inconceivable. For the poet, a supreme vision revealed by the lightning bolts of his inspiration, projecting a blue, crystal palace in the north, through which the shimmering knowledge of this very mind is reflected upon the south, for the blessed of existence miracles to be formed within the mineral, plant, animal, and human forms. And to the dawn of dawns, the source from which the suns spring, a sun bows to the poet, the sun of his world. It is the inner light, the light of lights, that of the discernment needed by the human, the earthly knowledge to create its own ideas, its own stars, its own visions, which the poet will see travelling to the west, loaded on a ship, in order to complete at the four corners of the horizon its intellectual, emotional and natural development.

Then humans will be able, by receiving the knowledge, to see within the depths of the galaxy, the origin of the night, their origin that, as a *black avalanche*, millions of years ago began its plummeting within the field of the absolute, in search of the meaning of its mystic nature, which the poet as a girls presents, to become upon its touch a melodic *pale shimmer,* a melodic *farewell song of the birds*. The *girl* symbolises the object of desire of life, never to be acquired.

This is the drama of the world of forms. A glittering drama full of greatness, which exits through the *gate of the unseen* and becomes the Word-time, to return and once again find itself on a *vast shore without age*. To take the world and carry it to the place where crossings transpire in the wedding gathering of its own shadows, in the one and only homeland *where the flower of silence grows, the worthiest habitat of death*. It is destined for time to die within the timeless *turning point of* its *dream*, leaving behind the memory of its body for other circles of a new dreamlike existence. Its spirit to sparkle, an eternal night in its perpetual rotations that, speckled by a *thousand lights,* through the *gate of the unseen* will once again its appearance make, plummeting from the tree of life.

KOSTAS VARNALIS

FROM "THE LIGHT THAT BURNS"

PROLOGUE

To gaze at you, sea, unable to get enough of you,
from upon the mountain high
smooth and deep blue and within myself I richen
from your many treasures.

On an autumn afternoon
after a sudden downpour
charges through the clouds, laughing dazzlingly
a sun without a scarf

Through the air to travel, the islands, the coves,
the seashores as silk vapours
and with the seagulls as companions once in a while a ship
the heavens to open up and take.

Rejuvenated from the bath, to roll down
the red slope while dancing
the pines, the golden-pines, and the blossom of the treasure
with their scented hair dripping;

and to their bright dance along with them they drag
into the water
the abandoned snow-houses - they too inside their dream
unawakened a great time, to sing.

So thus to stand, my sea, my forever love,
with cloudy eyes admiring you
and those forthcoming shall lay in your expanse before me
the many sufferings behind and far away to leave.

Until the time you take me, seductress you,
to your bosoms, high above, the blooming
and from this blackened Hell far away to take me,
far away from the blackened damned...

(The light that burns)

Day and night does *the sky's light burn*. A fiery sea the Word and from his spirit's field the poet cannot get enough of gazing at the vast *smooth, deep blue* wisdom of the planetary Word, enriched by the *treasures* of the infinite ocean of mysteries that it gestates, worlds unseen on earth's splendour birthed. An *autumn afternoon* the grand time of the sudden downpour, and like a *sun* he charges, *laughing dazzlingly*, to undo the vapours that his dark desires spawn.

In his spirit, symbolised by the wind, he takes the islands, the coves, the seashores, on a journey, dissolving their silky vapours, accompanied by the seagulls. A fiery boat he is, wishing the *heavens to open and take* him to the ineffable kingdom. Redeemed after the purifying bath of the mystic light, to return and while dancing to roll down the deep-red slope with his Words, the meanings, the beings, the spirits of the trees, as from *his hair, the scented*, his intoxicating radiance exudes.

With the bright dance the regenerated entity sweeps the *abandoned snow-houses* that in their *dream sing* the great unawakened love of humans, the century of a sea with which their heart madly fell in love. With joy it enchanted them, clouded their eyes, and *those forthcoming* they have *on its ex-*

panse before them, *while behind and far away*, many sufferings does the poet have. An entity the sea, the life, which speaks to it with love, and begs it. He prays to it, but he also orders it, defining lengths and widths of its road, until beyond its *blackened Hell*, from its blackened infernal self, where life ceases to be an enchanting dream. It is the crystal clear vision of the mind, the kingdom of the essence that from its bosom lets its conceptual dreams, the heavens with the transcendent beings of their infinity, emanate, so as to be nurtured. Supreme ideals of life, which the poet holds and contemplates as the rights of humans, that must be understood and realised by them in order to be integrated into the knowledge of the earth. The sea to become the mother which on her *bloomed bosom* will tie their spirits' fruits, to offer them as liberating wisdom. To enable them from the supreme field of consciousness to gaze upon the evolution's future, which on its deep-blue celestial bed will richen by the treasures of the soul's depths.

The sea and the sky, the humans and their passions and their solar spirit shall trace the physical and metaphysical circles that the entity imposed on them. The spirit with its transformations competes with time, mutating its body from an aquatic lust to a heavenly passion that with its tears cools the earth's pain. A perpetual cycle, ontological, to spiritualise their dream, it calls humans to awaken and partake in its *illuminated dance*, to praise with their song their ever-perceiving nature that their own hell predestined them to overcome, from its grim fate liberating it.

This is the work of the timeless poet and with his poems the history of this drama he recounts to us, revealing with his verses the mysteries of the sea, in which the sky is reflected searching for the shipwreck of its soul. He travels through the seas of denial and the oceans of will for love. And he is the one gazing upon the sea – and does not get enough of it – as a sun enjoying it with his eyes, evaporating its life's spells that deceive and cloud his vision.

It is the human spirit that wanders, following the cycles of its evolution, sullen, uninitiated into the secret passages from darkness unto light and from this sky's light to the other sky that covers no hells. This land's dome with its martyred sun stays *within its dream* and listens as its beings *sing, unawakened for so very long*, centuries, eras that alternate their stubbornness with the ropes[1] of slavery. Islands on whose *shores the silky vapours* linger and do not vanish into the spirit, are not delivered to their sky, in order to be liberated and pass on to other skies, more substantial than the earthly chain's need.

To this truth this poem refers to. It describes the sea, the eternal love of the earthly world, the human one, that *with clouded eyes* enjoys *the forthcoming on their expanse* in front of it leaving behind the sorrows and the many sufferings; even if *through the air the islands, the coves, the seashores journey*, with their unredeemed imagination, in vain within a boat-dream waiting for the heavens to open and take them. Humans through the centuries have learned to fantasise with their spirit, to hold earth's body captive and not let it pass to the infinite field of consciousness. They prefer to roll down the *deep-red slope* of desires.

The poet unites with the universal vision. He travels with his islands and his plains, accompanied by the spirits – the seagulls – like a *boat that the heavens open and take*. And purified he returns, to participate in the sacred ritual with its golden pine trees, which with their golden blossoms flood the waters with the myrrh of immortality, consecrating them, for the sea to pass into divine love that unclouds the eyes and brings discernment. So that those of the future with those of the past merge, so that the earth takes them to its bloomed bosoms high above, where hell is assimilated to heaven and the

---

[1] The Greek word "κάβος" (kavos) used in the original poem means both cove and nautical rope.

damned with the saints together drink from her breasts, the breasts of the sky, the immortal elixir, the spirit's light.

To the everyday earthly life refers the Word, to the sea, symbolising passion but also wisdom, since within it are the heavens mirrored. In humans with the sudden outbursts of anger but also the serene state of mind that is not hidden by the veils covering the soul, as it is enchanted by the alternations of human nature and follows them, seduced by human dreams, forever waiting to succumb. For the heavens to open, to greet them, to enter the chorus, to participate, to be redeemed of the red fire of the desire's slope.

GIORGOS V. VAFOPOULOS

THE GLASS BELL

*My gaze draws
a circle
around the horizon.
My voice finds no wall
its echo to return.*

*Day and night I walk
and immovable I stand
at the centre of the circle.
And the glass dome's edges
of the circumference the curbstones close.*

*Perhaps my step
unfolds
upon a moving disc?
Perhaps my body,
passed through the dome's axis,
with it moves along?
Or perhaps like a horse, around
the same well I revolve?*

*I explore the crystal dome.
Nowhere an opening.
Nowhere the Pole's star.
And on my hand disoriented
the guiding compass.*

The beginning and the end around me
into an unbreakable wreath are bound.
Time and space, within me have dissolved,
as indigo does in water.

Unstable my existence is,
spherical and rubber it inverts
within the glass bell.

And as the void into hemispheres
around me cascading forms,
my elastic enclosure
towards the glass dome grows.

Will it break the bell?
Will it crack?
That is the question.

(Complete Poetic Works)

A surrounding circle the horizon and the *voice no wall can find*, the poet says, *its echo to return*. Day and night, with their irremovable walk, humans around the centre of their selves revolve, making the *edges of the dome close the curbstones* of existence's limits. And whether the *step unfolds* upon the moving planet, the moving sun, remains to be investigated. Having being passed through the axis of the sky, the body with *the system moves*. With the system does earth move, the natural sun and, as it revolves, its instinctive life is separated, living in a *well that is the same* as the unconscious' abyss.

Crystal the poet calls the creation's *dome*, without an *opening for humans* and without *the Pole's star* as a guide. *Disoriented* is the mind, the heart a *guiding compass*, it authorises the hand to become the magic wand that determines life's *beginning and end*, which, as *an unbreakable wreath*, bind space and time that dissolve into the human entity as *indigo in water*. *Unstable* is the external *existence* of humans, *it becomes inverted in the glass bell*, while *the void around* them *in cascading hemispheres forms*. These symbolise emotional and intellectual processes which, elastic as their nature is, develop in order to be unified, to be completed and become the challenge, to break the glass shell, for the soul's energy to surge into infinity, for the mind's essence to excel.

In a circular formation the universe travels, alongside the Word's light. It is the other gaze, the inner one of the poet and his hearing that seeks the return of light and sound, as from the centre of the cosmic existence the Word of being is transmitted and is absorbed by the *circumference's curbstones*, without meeting – due to human emotional intervention – in its horizontal diffusion the verticality of will that is symbolised by the wall, in order to produce the necessary vibrations – the only ones capable to restore it as the new Word.

These processes take place within humans, the poet says. They take place amid the universe, the field of the emotional and intellectual world. And they are fictitious, they are not real. They are the projections of the undeveloped, external human mind, which, as it tries to mimic the inner, speculates with its individual unconscious projections on the nature of creation. And it is deluded because it wishes to confirm and maintain its existence, projecting the simple natural processes of evolution as an insurmountable obstacle for its very evolution.

Investigative but limited is the human mind, it makes the mistake of seeking outside itself the polar star that will guide it on its journey. It desires to find the orientation, the hands fumble for the beginning of the thread. Insurmountable is the shell of the externalised mind, which the poet parallels to the *glass dome* symbolising the crystallization of emotions, ideas and events. These are the ones that, after their dissolution and restoration to the centre, the centre of the self, are assimilated by it.

The process of this evolution the poet provides to us by using the metaphoric concept of the glass bell in which the existence, as an *unstable, rubber, spherical*, length of time, *inverts itself* within its own *void*. This void is formed in cascading circles of the polarisation hemispheres in the positive and negative fields, causing it to seek its exit from the virtual enclosure within which it limits its own self.

Investigative by nature, humans with their gaze seek within the circle their imaginary depictions upon the horizon. And their voices, their songs, their war cries, their weak and quiet whispers are lost to the edges of space and do not return, for them to harvest the internal wholeness from the processes of their work. Their activity takes place during day and night, without shifting their fate from the *circle's centre*, keeping them on the axis of their existence, around which the sun and planets, extensions of their being, with their wanderings revolve their bodies within space, simultaneously revolving the humans themselves.

Within the great well of the unconscious do humans reside and are called to turn it into knowledge, in order to stop being irrational and to become conscious. To accept the nature of things, the order of the universe – of their being – harmonising their ideas with this reality, which is but the internal and external order of the world. Within them the Pole's star – the great sun guiding them. All natural processes are related to their evolution and when they cease resisting them, then the intellectual, limiting shell surrounding them will break and their spirit will spread throughout the universe, to recognise their entity and be redeemed.

The poem speaks to us of the unredeemed humans who face

their existential problem influenced by identification, which is at fault for their limitation, while at the same time paves the way for the concept of the mind's balance, which through the great question leads to the Shakespearean reflection, to which the answer only the entity is able to provide; as long as humans reach this awareness and clearly state the question.

It is the universal, ontological mind, which is divided into two levels. One is the immanent, the inalterable field of the identity of things, the actual, the substantial, while its other is the enclosure, the glass bell that symbolises the crystallization of the processes of the rigid Word which the pure Word sounds, in order to break it for release to come; an ontological process that has as its purpose the system's deconstruction so that, by its innate capacity, again to be reconstructed. This function characterises the physical and psychological constitution of humans who through it perpetually evolve, thoroughly having the initiative to unite their will with the will of the entity and, to the extent that they do, the realisation of their choice is achieved.

NTINOS VLACHOGIANNIS

ANCESTRAL ADMONITION

If you wish in paper to wrap the flame
your urn you must prepare.
And if with a boat you wish to cross the ocean,
then as a dolphin learn to swim.
When you must, close your lips
and open them when
with your hands they can cooperate.

And if
your self you cannot help,
then any assistance is in vain,
that out of pity only shall you be given.
First is the decision
and second is the step.
And if in a workshop you see
shackles being forged,
then sometime will someone wear them.
Give a hand
that forge to bring down.
The graves are not terrible
because, even sealed as they are, they guide.
Tragic is every prisoner's martyrdom
if the purpose is not divine.
The blind can see
and even the mute can orate,
when free upon their land they stand!...   (Witnesses of silence)

If you wish in paper to wrap the flame, your urn you must prepare. A timeless teacher the poet is, his own century he teaches. His fiery spirit in paper he wraps and his Word is the inextinguishable light that illuminates the souls, the *ancestral flame* that burns and reduces to ashes its bodies, its times. And those who seek initiation to pass into knowledge, become poets, leaders of the world, guides of love, visionaries of the pathway that, as Kipling taught, leads to eternal glory, to the temple of freedom.

Centuries-old is the seeker's path and the poet is the master who has the ability to take all forms. Even into a dolphin he transforms, to pass over to the other side his continuation, the disciple, until the mystic under initiation learns how to avail himself of the opportunities given to him and his hands are able to handle the energies and forces of the soul, in order for his own Word to emerge from within the master's Word. His virtuous deeds to indicate the truth and not to need the admonition, but that he becomes the admonition towards others. And if those who are naysayers *cannot be helped*, for them *the assistance will be in vain*, no matter whence they receive it.

A workshop life is, within which *shackles are forged*. First is one's *decision* to want to be saved and *second is the step* that for freedom one shall take; a position of humblness to assume, from his superior self a helping hand to accept and the forge of slavery to be brought down.

The graves that hide the failure *are not terrible*, the poet says. To the divine purpose they *guide the prisoner*, as he realises the tragedy of his blind, mute self. Great is the teaching! Humans are initiated into their own strength, the knowledge. They are trained to lift their gaze, to cease their muteness, to walk on earth and orate, freeing themselves of the forced silence that in the past they self-imposed.

Endless the sea of illusions is. In this delusion humans must learn to swim, with ease to manoeuvre, not to sink nor drown; and, when their body does not manage, to transmute; in their spirit the necessary combustions of emotions and ideas to take place that fanaticise and enslave them in the egoistical stances which out of insecurity they are forced to take in order to defend themselves from their fellow humans.

The spirit of will as a flaming scripture manifests. It gives the Word to others, as from *his urn*, ready to be transmuted into a new life, the phoenix rises and spreads its wings. The lips open, they recount the passions of life, all hands into enabling are initiated, the world of truth in its own truth strides; the innate ability, which in itself is inherent in humans, and the other – the acquired – to turmoil, to the dissolution of hell lead, where their *shackles* are forged.

One does learn! The assistance is in vain if one does not help along, if the decision to take the crucial step one does not make. To the Entity also to give a hand, partaking in the struggle to be freed of the shackles that in one's dark self one's own attachments forge, because of what one chooses, insisting on ignoring one's strength, one's spiritual nature.

The poet speaks of the power of the Word, the light of the world, the divine purpose. It frees the prisoner of martyrdom, giving him the will to unseal the graves, for his spirit to be redeemed, so that humans can walk free upon the earth. The flame of infinity to wrap in paper, spiritual oceans of his passions to make the seas. A dolphin is his existence that will forever save his body from the aquatic element that oppresses him.

It is the flame of everlasting fire which must pass through paper, to become the knowledge that will burn the ignorance, into purifying ashes to transform it. It is the aquatic element to be dominated by the dolphin's ability – the advanced Word – the ability of sounds, the synthesis that people study, to pass on to the future civilizations' Word.

It is the lips, which must close, to be able to open when

the hands learn how to speak. To provide assistance to compassion, to help in the decision from its step to shrug off the shackles of spiritual poverty, bringing down the ego's *forge*.

It is *the graves* to be unsealed, the tragic martyrdom to be uplifted, divine to be its purpose; so that the blind that wander the abyss lift their gaze, liberating the planetary Word that will bring the grounding of the human spirit; for ancestral admonitions to be vindicated, for the poet's vision to be realised!

EVANGELOS V. VOGIAZANOS

ODE TO A HORSEMAN OF THE STEPPE

Restless nomad
unique,
ruler of the steppe
the trot through the Gobi desert
the passion for rivalry
without the conceit of a winner
a Centaur's silhouette at twilight,
a child of the Temoutzin
in the yurts* of Ulan-Ude
with an unexplored glance
implying...
As in the sky you were projected
upon the Bactria,
an extension of the colours' orgy
that fairy-tale morning
when silence took shape
a fountain upon your forehead was the light;
through a crack of the imagination
naked, you were revealed
with a primitive cry.
The sun of your country
dazzling
and its moon as the bow strokes
upon the heart's string.
Mongol of the wise choice

who freedom intoxicates
even more than koumis* does,
figure of the fairy-tale
with the lightning horses and the Yaks*
did they truly exist,
those moments of vertigo
upon Mongolia's blazing flesh
in this supercilious adventure
beyond the range of reason
or a Conqueror did you come out of the dream
with our hearts as a trophy?

Athens, November 1990
(First person)

The poet refers to the realm of history and myth, of fantasy and reality, of the transcendental, the inconceivable and the earthly visualization. Rider, *Conqueror of the steppe*, restless is the tumult, dazzling the silhouette, a nomad who roams the wisdom's desert, assuming all shapes of light, recordings of the earth and moon. For the Sun to study, the mind to learn, the truth to train in the beauty of the miracles; the truth that their internal beauty chose, in order to keep the wise alert, to protect the untaught, and to teach the half-taught the value of need.

Discernment, Asian knowledge, ancient reminder of noble rivalry in the arena of people, where – *without conceit – the winner* contemplates the defeated with prudence and love. *Within the nomads' yurts* the centaurian form – *unexplored in the twilight* – the mystery of human breeding with the horse implies, projecting into *the sky upon the Bactrian* the passage of Alexander the Great, who tamed Bucephalous, a symbol of omnipotence, which leads to the civilising of the earth, the human epic.

An orgy of *colours is silence, a fountain* of light *on the* nomad's *forehead*, the forming of the sun at the sounding of the primitive cry, where, *through a crack of the imagination*, the moon becomes enlarged within the soul's and form's chord. A universal vibration resonating to the *heart's string* by the Mongol of the *wise choice*, who knows how *to intoxicate* his worlds with freedom *even more than the koumis does*, as, with the *lightning horses and the yaks, the figures of the fairy-tale* the true *moments of vertigo* become. *Mongolia's flesh* the mind tames, the *blazing, supercilious* cosmic *adventure*, to take it *further than the range of reason*, coming out of the *dream a Conqueror* with the pulses of time as its *trophy*.

The poet refers to *the Gobi desert*. There, he tells us, unfolds the drama of the world, acquiring the dimensions of the unfathomable, the sun's great trot, the human spirit. There, the soul's mystic power appeases with its authority, controlling the visions of the heart, the momentum of the universal Word above and below the ground.

A nomad since the dawn of time is contemplation, in its evolutionary circles wandering, seeking its spiritual identity, placing upon the human forehead the seal of its immortality. Shepherd of the powers, the chosen one, with the *lightning horses* guiding the universal flock, passing through the valleys of reason to the peaks of inner knowledge, where the unique sun shines, the internal nomad, the ruler of the other steppe, the everlasting, the eternal, the unaffected by time and space, the diffused within the universe's heart and mind.

The symbol of the inner guide is the horseman of the steppe. For him is the poet's *ode*, for the spiritual leader representing the eternal nomad, the unique, the restless, whose invisible is the spark that rekindles the passion for the rivalry of the visible. Without being possessed by the *winner's conceit, a child* of megacosmic becoming, the nomad indulges in his microcosmic self, in the human passions, for the release of the primitive cry. With his naked presence he reveals the shape of silence which is none other than the shape of things, the shape of the world, whose music is the sound of light vibrated by the heart's pulses, the choices that people make, seeking the intoxication of the *wise choice* of the nomad-spiritual leader. He will lead them through the *blazing flesh* into the vast realm of the spirit after uncovering the hidden meaning of the desert, symbolising the spiritual wilderness in which humanity is. The people are devoid of benevolence, as the rivalry between people is not noble, but is possessed by the conceit that holds them hostages within the desert of their tortuous life.

Is life a *fairy-tale figure*? Are there really worlds *beyond the range of reason* or is cosmogony no more than a *supercilious adventure*? Does humankind need the Conqueror's exit from the dream, does it desire him a trophy bearer, does it accept him as a leader? Does it embrace his circles, giving substance to his struggle? Is the intoxication of ideas true? Are its beliefs essential?

Since the dawn of time has truth taught myth and myth the decorum of thoughts. The centuries, with will as their guide and faith as their chariot have travelled. History received subsistence and the path of the dream meaning. Inside the mind Memory was established and Knowledge by God was instructed to bestow freedom of will upon human existence, to achieve great things.

---

* Yurts = Traditional Mongolian tents.
* Koumis= The national drink of the Mongols.
* Yak = A type of Mongolian cattle.

V.I. VOGIATZOGLOU

SECOND ADMONITION: TO THE INITIATOR

Did you ever see the ample gleam around the view of things, when their inner glow expands and light from within – inexplicable – spreads to eternal Fire? Did you perhaps hear the city's death, writhing in the summer's heat, like an animal to be slaughtered on the altar, towards heaven shooting voices, whispers, moaning, praising the Indescribable?

Then quietly listen and contemplate. Let the first sound deeply vibrate peace, unlocking the seven-sealed Great Secret and let it joyously open up all creation. Here give heed to the Alpha. As when we say Absolute, Ruling, Untouched*. And then listen to the strange hum that echoes within hidden passages, as it rapidly flows with the undercurrent. Like the lengthy Ou that deepens and is lost in the abyss. As when we say Woe, Favourable, Heaven*. And let the mind touch the ultimate Mi of silence. The soundless depth, bleak, that your voice stifles and the cycle closes. Unknown end, unknown beginning. As you were once gifted to be spoken to in supreme harmony by the Initiator, the Fate, the Great*.

Remember these sounds. Until time once again steals the breath from the bodies, for the unrevealed sword to shine. And the Supreme Word to flash the command to sow. Then, let times move forward, chasing the grand game. Until the living without prospects and the dead without memory to close the cycle.

Until, in other words, the plan shines revealed.

      (Thirteen versions for THE STIGMA and eight admonitions)

* In Greek these three groups of three words begin with the same letter, A (Alpha), the diphthong Ou and the letter M (Mi) respectively.
(Absolute = Απόλυτο, Ruling = Άρχων, Untouched = Ανέγγιχτος)
(Woe = Ουαί, Favourable = Ούριος, Heaven = Ουρανός)
(Initiator = Μύστης, Fate = Μοίρα, Great = Μέγιστος)

An ample gleam the inner knowledge is. The soul grows, expands, the light increases. *Inexplicable Fire* enriches the eternal spirit of humans, to understand, to see, to realise their own glow. Humans, whose undertakings to the will of the Supreme Being are subject, with the blessing of the uncreated light and its contemplation a feverous entity's miracle.

Death hears the city's tumult. In the *summer's heat writhes the Ruler* of light and on His altar sacrificing himself, the archer of whispers, of voices, and of the earth's moaning, the indescribable epic of His theogony he praises and admires. *"Follow me; and let the dead bury their dead"*, the Word of the Great Master tolls. To total sacrifice the God calls His world, and the poet, the initiator disciple, to himself he gives an *admonition. Then quietly listen, and contemplate.*

The *first sound* vibrates the asleep, the seven sealed gates are unlocked. Upon the revelation of the Great Secret, the *joyous creation gives heed to the Alpha*, and learns: "Absolute is God, *Ruler, Untouched*, my nature's One." With its human ears it listens to the strange, mystic hum *echoing* within its secret passages – the hidden – where *the undercurrent* of the emerging Word *rapidly flows*, shattering the resistances of the becoming, a result of its own creatures' egocentrism. To the Omega the praise of the humans, the pleading vesper of the soul.

Woe to the defeated for they are lost into abyss, but *Favourable is the Sky and the mind deepens* upon touching the *ultimate Mi of the* supreme *silence*. Seven are the mysteries of the Word, of the Church the teachings of deliverance, initiations that release the voice of the Soundless grim depth. The cycle opens and closes. Unknown is the time of beginning and end. To humans is harmony given, the Fate of the Initiator, of the mind the *Great* atonement. The memories are purified. Knowledge becomes the Amen, the completed Word. With the *humble breath* of humans, *time* alternates its glows, commandment of the unrevealed fiery sword in the endless duration of the cycle, for the vindication of the divine plan according to the God-man's will.

Life is an ample gleam, from within comes the revelation upon the viewing of miracles. Humans delve into their being, and their being is the world the existent within God's love, of His heart the inexplicable Fire. Life gives heed to death and its human heart for death's redemption on its sacrificial altar writhes. In the mysteries of existence does the mind apprentice. The grace of awareness it was given, the power of contemplation. Anyone who has a mind to think and "He that hath ears to hear, let him hear."

A hymnodist every poet is, to the will of the absolute, the grace of miracles. The becoming of days does wisdom oversee. As a shimmering soul the gleaming power of the chosen existence rejoices in the projection of spectrums. The *undercurrent* within the passages of the seven-corded body resonates. As a divine instrument, it reads the vowels and consonants, logoic notes, in the musical score of the cosmic mind and the music of the universe harmoniously it interprets. To the splendour of the sounds, joyous is creation's contemplation. The human mind is deified upon touching the *ultimate Mi* in the symphony of silence.

Deepening and contemplation, contemplation and revelation, of the absolute, God is nature, form, and essence. Sacred are His memories. At the glow of the sword, *Supreme Word* is the shimmering commandment for the sowing of wills, of denials, of hate, of love, of darkness, of light and of the prospective times that follow, to take part in His *grand game*. Until, as people alive, they renounce the *egoic* memory, *prospect* of a dead life and the Supreme Being closes the cycle; for His divine plan to shine, justifying the expectations of disciples, of initiates, for the perfection of the ignorant, the uninitiated times before the holiest face of the One.

NIKIFOROS VRETTAKOS

HYMN

Your name: bread on the table.
Your name: water at the source.
Your name: a honeysuckle of climbing stars.
Your name: an open window at night.
      on the first of May.

Your name: filings of the sun.
Your name: a verse of a flute at night.
Your name: a rose upon the lips of angels.
Your name: two oak trees on which the rainbow
      supports its edges.

Your name: folded upon my lap.
Your name: a landscape divided by colours.
Your name: a script upon the afternoon's fire.
Your name: a deer sunken to its knees
      in an ebb of the sun.

Your name: a gentle rain on the sower's forehead.
Your name: abundance in the shepherd's hut.
Your name: a lantern sweetening his sleep.
Your name: the fire dancing in his fireplace
      as a bundle of carnations.

Your name: a whisper from star to star.
Your name: a murmur between two streams.
Your name: a pine's monologue at Cape Sounion.
Your name: the sun's analysis upon the peelings
    of fruit into colours.

Your name: a rose petal on an infant's cheek.
Your name: a pentagram on the antennae of crickets.
Your name: the universe's transparent twilight.
Your name: a procession of five swans dragging
    the Pleiades through the heavens.

Your name: a reigning olive tree.
Your name: a joyous hum in Ithaca.
Your name: three lilies upon the peak of Taygetos.
Your name: the glow of roses upon the face
    of the Virgin Lady Ergani.

Your name: the charioteer of the sun's chariot.
Your name: a valley bringing to our home.
Your name: a jingling of horses at spring.
Your name: a praise playing in the light
    of open windows.

Your name: Peace in the branches of the forest.
Your name: Peace in the streets of cities.
Your name: Peace in the routes of ships.
Your name: a loaf of bread, placed on the side
    of earth, that was left over.

Your name: a pediment of pigeons on the horizon.

Your name: Hallelujah upon Everest.

                                            (Royal Oak)

The poet meditates; his body, the body of God, deposited in His name upon the Holy Altar of the universe. His *name*: *bread on the table*. The bread symbolises the body of creation, which is never too little and always is abundant. It is the field of matter, derived from the inexhaustible source of the spirit, the mind and heart of infinity, which define the limitless name of God. From the spirit are humans fed and from its source do they quench their thirst. Spiritual is their body, and the source is an eternal heart, from which wisdom and love flow, watering the *honeysuckle of the climbing stars* – the ideals gleaned by their hopes, for the realisation of the first principle of His will, God's will through the cycle of infinite knowledge.

The *first of May*, the first of all months, all years, all centuries, of His name all names – God. The nature of the universe's mind, which encompasses the light of His Spirit, is symbolised by May, the fifth month. Through the open to darkness windows, God's spirit sends the rays, the *filings of His sun*, like a musical *verse from a* universal *flute*, full of revelations in the night of the ignorance of humans.

The Word to become an angelic *rose* upon their *lips*, for their toil to acquire meaning. Their work in the storms of life to culminate at the *rainbow*, the crown of the iris, supported on the world's binary field, on the two cornerstone opposites of their nature, matter and spirit, good and evil, ignorance and knowledge, desire and love permeating them, injustice and fairness which they express towards all that take place and which represent their nature.

These are the forces that determine the lives of humans, the poet says, like relentless scriptures of their soul's fire, as the *name* of God, *folded upon their lap*, becomes a *landscape divided* into *colours*, the outline of a deer, *sunken to its knees in the ebb of the sun* – of feelings, thoughts, ideas of the becoming of forms. They form their personality, as they unfold its aspects during the day, in space writing His name with a fiery script during the afternoons.

The crown of the iris is the *name* of God, rising to the sower's head, and becomes a gentle rain, the sweat on his forehead, his aura, blessing the goods of the earth to prosper, and from their abundance, an offering in the *shepherd's hut* to become. As light it will sweeten his *sleep, the sleep* of the universal Word, singing the name of God as the lantern's flame; and the fire shall grow, its fires shall rise in the fireplace, the hearth of the infinite house, symbolised by the hut, a dancing fire as a *bundle of carnations*[1] – to which the poet likens it –, phallic* symbols that with the whispers of God's myriad names fertilise the uteri of all.

From star to star, from one river of ideas to another, the dialogue of the *two streams* of light continues and from the river of the spirit it is conveyed to the river of the body, and from the river of the body it becomes a monologue in the oceanic temple of Cape Sounion, where the sea's desires gather to pray. The initiator poet with his lyrics analyses the pan-human glory, the wisdom of God, the wisdom of the sun that is inherent in the colourful garments of His essence, which are symbolised by the *peelings of the fruits*.

A *rose petal* caressing the *infant's cheek* is the name of God. A divine presence, of His immaculate form the form, radiating the benevolent, it initiates humans to knowledge, guiding them to approach its essence with the ancient symbol of the pentagram – the five fields of the mind – that the poet wishes to see even in the *antennae of the crickets*. It trains them, so that by unifying the contrasts they become able to hear the magical song of the crickets and thus, in the *universe's transparent twilight*, dawn is revealed to them, the completion of their psychological cycle which is the result of their capacity to

---

[1] The Greek word for the carnation flower is «γαρύφαλλο» or «γαρίφαλο», both pronounced "gariphalo". The second part of the word is the reason for its symbolization as phallic.

synthesize ideas, with the ultimate purpose of realising their spiritual nature. The five swans symbolise the harmony, the supremacy of the mind, as they drag the *Pleiades through the heavens*, a dancing presence of the souls, a seven-virgin dance.

Your name: a reigning olive tree. Only then, the poet says, infinity, symbolised by the "olive tree", a word whose arithmosophical analysis provides the number eight[2], may, with the knowledge of the causality of the dawn of creation, with its joyous hum reach Ithaca, offering three lilies – its three carriers – as refrains of the Word, to become the glow of the roses in the blessed face of the Virgin Lady Ergani, the Highest of the Heavens.

Sun is the name of God, and the poet, a *charioteer on his chariot*, becomes the meadow, the plain of homecoming, the chariot of light, that with the accompaniment of the carriage horses' bells, brings *him to his home*, to the innermost of the house, where eternal spring is the only praise, the harmony of music, a consonance of infinite Words of the eternal all.

Everything expresses the name of God, the entity. This is what is externalised in the infinite fields and subfields of its existence. Her name is *Peace in the branches of the forest, in the streets of cities, in the ship routes, the bread* of breads, *abundant* at the entity's temple on earth, and the doves that trace its *pediment on the horizon*, singing *Hallelujah* upon the peaks, *upon Everest*, the highest mountain, symbolising the spiritual field of the world.

The poet reads the entity. He interprets its physical, mental and spiritual messages. He greets it, acknowledging it in the names of its body and from its infinite greatness the muse is inspired, leading him to the mysteries of the soul. And the soul speaks to him of love, its love for the form.

The name of God, the form. His name, its light, and, of all

---

[2] This arithmosophical analysis applies to the Greek word for the olive tree, «ελιά» (pronounced "elia").

forces, life is stronger. His name, a *joyous hum in Ithaca*, where the rainbow transforms into the crown of glory of the inner being and becomes Peace, given by God to humans as a reward for their efforts.

The name of God, a seal on nature's toil for the acquisition of knowledge by the human being.

DIMITRIS GAVALAS

WITH THE LOOK OF AN EARLY AWAKENED LIONESS

With the look of an early awakened lioness
and your mane stirring the wind
I saw you emerging dressed with the sea.
In underwater currents you lived
in your secret city beneath the water
but now you emerge.

The church domes are flung
miles high into the sky
the Spirit's Dove comes white
from the horizon's centre
Apollo with Archangel Michael chats
and your eyes green and blue
face the Mysteries
our own eyes cannot face.

Full and undefined
calm and perfect
alone and unchanged
from the sea you were born
but a face of fire you have become
with a diamond diadem.
In your eternal existence I find
of the Mysteries the solution.

(Internal incest)

Internal incest, exchange of fires, mixing of energies and forces within the Agatho[1], intersection of radiations, qualities of light, *in the eternal existence of Mysteries* the *solution. With the look of an early awakened lioness* the entity, it *stirs the wind with its mane*, awakening the world spirit. It highlights its universe enrobed with the *sea* of its infinite nature, an oceanic essence, of its secret life the truth, Aphrodite emerging *through the waters*; emergence and flinging of the idea to the sky of earth, to the spirit of matter. *From the horizon's centre*, timeless Apollo and Michael observe. Their divine, archangelic eyes, eyes of the sea and the sky, a meeting of souls and bodies, face the miracle and become human eyes, infinite eyes before the All Seeing Eye's judgment, the revelation of the Mysteries to the inalterable one and only self.

Within his completeness, the *calm* and the *perfect*, the poet studies. His face, the face of the sea, the *face of the fire* with the sun's *diamond diadem*, of many suns a successor, of knowledge the life. The truth lies within the truth and the truth is life within every image. And every image is, as the human being, the entity's likeness, an assimilation of the idea with inspiration, of inspiration with essence, of essence with form, of form with the soul, and of the soul with emotions and passions, symbolised by the sea. And the sea with all its symbols, forms which itself created to represent it throughout the centuries, is the assimilation of infinity with the absoluteness of zero.

To the knowledge of the cycle, to the *Mysteries' solution*, poetry initiates the world. The mythology of water, the mythology of fire, is the entire human history. In this treatise, an imaginative creator of images, a great word-collector, of tragedy the dramatist, a worthy exponent of the Spirit which created humans, every poet proves to be. Into darkness he descends,

---

[1] The term "agatho" out of the Greek word «αγαθό» is used to mean all that is beyond the duality of good and bad. It is the Entity, the Whole, the Monad.

indulging in the undefined. He alternates his spirit with the underground and *undersea currents* and with those above the earth, the winds. Primordially incestuous with the Agatho[1] of radiance, of pure blood, he takes part in the confession of all. With the immaculate Mysteries he communes and the perfection of the being he envisions beyond the revelation, of the eternal existential problem the solution.

The power of envisioning was capable of guiding humanity through the centuries. And this is the power of the poets; every poem a vision, every vision a truth, the potential for realisation. The participants in the creation of healthy visions, of the thought-forms of strength and optimism, constituting the hope of fulfilment, of human deification, the participants in the feat of feats, in the miracle of creation, are the pioneers that prepare the way for the ultimate expression of the perfected being, whose definitive advent all poets await. In waves the revelation comes to the world. From Hesiod, Homer, Aeschylus, up to the contemporaries, up to the very last poet of the century, visions are expressed on the evolution of the being and these are that vibrate the entire nature of the one and only theanthropic Word.

The poet constructs every thought, moulds every word, shaping the emotion, giving reason to the ineffable, invisible dream to exist, to the unmanifested spirit seeking expression, perfection upon Earth. Great mystagogue, craftsman of the manifestation, as a conscious culmination of form's perfection, with a fiery chisel he shapes the Word, participating in the form-moulding of the universe, an essential undertaking, the result of procedures for redemption, that the highest form of art of human Word itself is capable of bringing. Poetry teaches people to think, to work, to create, to form their Word, giving the opportunity of expression to the emotional world that seeks its path through the impasses upon which the universe has fallen, as it asked of its own creator within the chaos to be created.

And the poet comes! Timeless is his coming; each of his verses, one of the aspects of its sacred aspects, the entity, life. *With the look of an early awakened lioness*, symbolising the instinctive life, *with* its *mane* it *stirs the wind* – the challenge of instincts to the spirit – and the emergence of its passions is achieved. There resides the unprocessed truth, in its secret world *beneath the waters*, beneath emotions, tucked away by the dark forces in its deeper being, the unfathomable. And the poet exudes it, in cycles he processes it, revealing the diamond's facets and the diamond brightly shines.

Domes of churches, *the domes* of the heavens cover the Spirit's greatness, symbolised by the *white Dove*. Archangels of God's kingdom, resultant of the deification of all beings, Apollo and Michael with their *green and blue eyes* give to the eyes of the entire world the ability to see. To face their being, to realise in all faces the unique, the inalterable, the perfect face of God, with *the diamond diadem* of infinite suns, of His eternal existence the light, *of Mysteries the solution*.

NIKOS GALAZIS

OH STRANGER, ANNOUNCE...

Of my father.

We live in a country
poor in steel
but we became self-reliant
from the steel
that they hurled upon us.
Chiefs, by God,
other imports we do not need
the fiery rivers
that once flooded us
magnificently framed us
with walls of lava
other investments we do not need.
I heard that sharks proliferated
with their dorsal fin carving
our homeland's seas
still reaching us
are those who disembarked
transformed
into respectable patrons
roaming among us in the market
energetic and progressive
predatory and lecherous
saprophytes born
from the steel's rust
that they poured to embalm us

within the trenches in which we fight
for this soil
with our primordial rifles.
I have a copper-mouthed
Tyrrhenian trumpet
and you desire melodies
I shall play for you, as a satyr
in the forest with the streams
as veils will flutter
fairies with unbraided hair
at the time when you, effeminates,
will be auctioning off,
the struggle over all.

(With the Geese's step over the Carcasses)

Through the battle of the ages the history of this land has its course, and the beings who reside on it – in the flow of life – are governed by division in their every choice. Night from day is separated and darkness from light differs. Truth and falsehood come together and march on the same path. The truth of the few as a falsehood by the many is perceived. The light of the few in dark times as a distant sun seems within the conscience of many. A defining factor in this cosmic process, human beings, governed and guided by their lower nature.

Announce, stranger, that we are poor, says every country's poet, not in spirit, but in *steel*. And he plays with the concept of steel, aspiring with his verse to demonstrate that the uncontrolled omnipotence of earth, symbolised by its iron strength, has not been placed under the control of humans and that it is expelled as a steel will, which the greed of dark forces through intermediaries occasionally projects. These are the *chiefs* who ignorance gives birth to and nurtures, and who appropriate the – almost naive – selflessness or selfishness of the respective social factors. With *fiery rivers* of blood the debtors pay their debts. And other *imports* of a burning flood of hatred, which frame people's dreams into walls, for subjugators of the spirit to invest their own interests, *we do not need*. Because as *sharks* they proliferate, carving with their *dorsal fins the seas* of every country and spread terror and panic, with their omnivorous greed devouring the visions of the races.

People do *not need other investments*, the poet vociferously cries, derived from the transformations of sharks into *respectable patrons* who roam the world *market, energetic and progressive*, collecting knowledge, strength, spirit, grabbing their light of their soul. These lecherous, – supposedly human – beings, claim that they are friends and allies of the peoples, while in fact they are but chiefs that exploit the social and political circumstances created by history's upheavals. And their servants are the *saprophytes born from the rust of steel that* their *chiefs* hurl, to *embalm* people within the *trenches*, where they struggle *for their soil* with their modern weapons or *primitive rifles*. And chiefs and servants revel while listening to the melodies of the *copper-mouthed Tyrrhenian trumpet*, in *the forest with the streams* and satyrs, watching the *fluttering veils of* the fairies with their *unbraided hair*. These are the *effeminates* that auction off the world's *struggle over all*.

Oh earth, homeland of the peoples, mother of gods and humans, you who you gifted light, for the greatness of your offering, by the ungrateful humans, with *fiery rivers* of hatred and falsehood you are repaid. Because they refuse to evolve into the greatness of the light, they fear your power, they fear your soul, they do not want it, they fight it. They place it in the crosshairs of their memory and towards it hurl their furious reaction; because they cannot stand to give up the mentality of primitive life and consciously remain in trees and caves, in the barbarity of their dark spirit, despite the fact that since the beginning of consciousness the world was abound with temples of the spirit, with the teachings of the wisdom of the peoples, the divine supreme knowledge.

And they abuse the reputation of others, claiming – the sacrilegious – that it is their own reputation that was spread to the ends of the earth for cultures to acquire their purpose of existence and a reference to the language of languages, miracle of the Word. World pulse of divine harmony, of earth is the Word, ecumenical, of wisdom and love the beauty. Heavenly, brilliant dome is their nature and their heart the sea, of humans the passions, a primordial narration in tragic epics.

Thousands of years has this pan-human, glorious culture travelled, and the poet, to demonstrate this truth's degradation, uses the contrivance of the aiantian trumpet, with which he says that fools desire of him to play *melodies as a satyr*, to accompany the dance of the fairies with the *unbraided hair*. The spirit remains free, to live and experience the truth, recycling the worldly vision through the music of its own Word, until the time comes that they will be forced to stop abusing it by auctioning off its splendour, which is the struggle *over all things*, the struggle for freedom, for the civilizing of the entire humankind.

Fond of the darkness of their subconscious, those who refuse to be initiated to the truth of the light, they covet the field of ontological consciousness that has been conquered by spiritual people. And they fight it, degrading everything that is sacred and holy. They make people fight, seeking to enslave them, to deprive them of the opportunity to express their souls' powers, fearing the competition in the arena of spiritual comparison. And when the miracle of each new civilization is created, they panic, they cannot stand it and deepen the chasm, for the abyss to launch human division.

This division is that which as a reputable protector, energetic and progressive, with its *dorsal fin carves the seas* of ignorance, makes sure – throughout its transformations – it frames the peoples within walls made of his passions' and desires' lava. Heroic the planetary soul, in the trenches fighting with its remaining external strength. Its internal respective strength is ignored by the supposed protectors, deluded, still repeating their falsehood, spreading the lie that this virtue never trully existed, but even if it did, it passed, illuminated, scattered, and was lost.

On these crucial, substantial meanings is the poem based on. Mongers of the Word the dark times, they find well-wishers and flood the countries with their anxieties and insecurities. They invest in the weight, the heart and mind of the races and derive from the market the vital force that gives them the ability to exist, perpetuating the debauchery of their veto against the true progress that truth has taught and continues to teach. As omnivorous cetaceans they roam, the poet says, and, spreading terror, they devour everything, concepts, ideas, visions, ideals. And the ancient teaching about beauty, the beauty of the soul and the form, they degrade to a low sensual pleasure of a cheap vision, which they insist on enjoying in the shady forests of their lower dionysian nature, limiting their communication to the elemental kingdom of the sulphides and nereids, which are but a projection of their own lecherous, predatory, unredeemed spirits.

STELIOS GERANIS

I REDISCOVERED POETRY

> *Poetry is that self of ours,*
> *that never sleeps.*
> GIORGOS SARANTARIS

a'

I rediscovered poetry waiting for me, ageless
At the threshold of time. In my night
The sun's fluff suddenly shined
Syllables, brand new, glow upon my lips.
A verse, an only son, with the scent of trust
As a cool benefaction fell into my heart

And in its arms I resumed shivering and shinin.

b'

Golden butterflies, the words, my solitude adorn.
The words that from the land of sleep awaken me
The words that like a cool benefaction fall
into my hands. Words that become a colour and a shiver
And music. The words - my first love.

>*And a verse, an only son*
>*that in the night called me father.*

(I rediscovered poetry)

Ageless time is, ageless life is, the day and night, the eternity. It is poetry, on the threshold of which rests the poet, as he returns from the cosmic night into the cradle of light, where the fluff of flowers shines, the aura of nature's crown, the sun's wreath, and they become the light of lips, the uniqueness of the Word, the verse of verses, of infinite trust the scent, the only begotten of mercy, of the unwithering blooming the completeness. Shivers and shinings overwhelm the universe, as poetry, as a transcendent being, holds it in its embrace.

It is the nature of the poet that rejoices. *Golden butterflies, the words, adorn* the temple of solitude and from the *land of sleep* they raise the dreams, inviting them to participate in the pandemonium of colours with the myriad hands. They willed to be benefited by the shiver of love and the music of the first and last Word, the son poet, who *in the night* celebrates the holiness of the Father and God singing the supreme chant.

When poetry is lost, life is also lost. Humans are lost, their mind immersed in ignorance and their heart its dreams erases, dispelling the visions of time. The spirit surrenders to flee and does not pass on to the neutrality of knowledge, remaining in the prison underground, the confinement deep within the soil, fate of the unconscious world. People crawl, creep, as the poet is absent, the fiery Word, the glorifying of what is beyond. It is the being with the sanctified senses, the only one that can control the qualities of the solar disk which from the earth seek their recognition. *In the night* he studied and the skills he acquired from this experience detect the unspoken syllables, the marks that upon his lips will become the unique verses of trust.

Time, the representative of the world becomes. Ignorance ended and the dawn was found again. The day calmed the wickedness within *the land of sleep* and the golden-winged hopes were awakened. They became the living moments, the luminescent beings, words to structure their sentences and to build of love the musical temple. The soul shivers, the mind vibrates and its Word glows upon the lips, the verse of trust shines within the poet's wisdom and the heart dances to the cool benefaction of all, it vibrates. The poet shivers in the embrace of the world, and the world, in the poet's embrace, is magnified.

The stirrings come to drink from the eternal fountain's dewdrops, for ideas to acquire substance, for meanings to become expensive, precious gems, to be transformed into souls and fly to solitude's lair; to adorn it, to decorate the planet with the light of meanings, for the *land of sleep* to become inundated by the spirit's essence. For life to rediscover poetry, ageless the day to become, the sun to shine with the *brand new syllables*. For the lover to rediscover his lost love, the wandering man his lost self and the ageless being its entity. It always awaits on the *threshold of time*, and *in the night* it suddenly shines, in the spirit, as a revelation of the age-old future in the present.

In the evolutionary course of the worldwide becoming, the Word, in its own poetry apprenticing, recreates itself. Through the meanings processed by people, it learns the synthesis, expanding the epic of its harmonious expression as it perpetuates the multiplicity of happenings within infinity. It is the nature of the universe that is poetic, it is the poetry of the world that is universal, and the humans, the poem of poems, learn to meditate on the agatho[1] of their creation and re-project the beauty of their essence. The Word becomes rhythm, music, the parts of which compose the work of universal harmony. And this megacosmic miracle, microcosmically – as a poem – as part of the essential agenda, is expressed, to demonstrate the power of poetry, which perpetually radiates from the field

---

[1] The term "agatho" out of the Greek word «αγαθό» is used to mean all that is beyond the duality of good and bad. It is the Entity, the Whole, the Monad.

of the unified existence. Poetry is the power that unites humans with the entity, and its expression is its own care.

When humans are indifferent, they lose this benefaction. They cease to be benefited. They lose their trust in senses and the shining of their soul is lost. The shiver is muted and the fountain of their heart dries up. They are not benefited from love but are condemned to remain dormant in the land of solitude. No son is there to search for a father. No father is there to call for a son. Clashing cymbals humans are, a verse without music, without meaning, with the old, dark *syllables upon the lips*, which are repeated without colour, until *on the threshold of time* they seek *poetry* again, where it, the highest, *ageless, awaits*.

DIMITRIS GERONTAS

THE ASH AND THE FIRE

In the slender column I am not interested
ash
elegant, it rises
and, through its porous rashes,
kind.
Only when that ash falls
and in its heart the crack shall appear
blood
blood from blood
this scorching crack
the Desire.
And as it dies, its spark
does not concern me;
it suffices that I have gazed into its blazing soul
burning and singing:
I, the eternal moment
And of myself nothing will remain
in the thoughts' plangent prayer.

(The poems)

A slender column, as all others in the temple, yet this poet *is not interested*. Even if with its capital the column is destined to hold the sky, to support the knowledge. Even if it becomes an inferno among rituals and as a phoenix it perpetually rises kind. Even when the *ash falls from its porous rashes and in its heart is revealed the blood of the scorching crack – the Desire –* even when its spark is extinguished, it is of no concern to him.

It is enough that he knows. Because its *ignited soul* has appeared to him as the burning bush that *burns, sings* and prays. And its song, an eternal confession to his Word: *I, the moment. And of myself nothing will remain* but the essence of my plangent thoughts.

The column symbolises the human being. Its stem is the human body; the capital is the head and its base, the legs. And its grooves, moments that the artist-time with its chisel has engraved, for fire to flow, for the human spirit to descend as light from heaven to earth and to ascend from legs to head. And through its invisible hands with their mysterious fingers the human's fiery soul in all directions to be diffused.

A column is the poet among the colonnades, a human among humans, a jewel of jewels his soul, his heart, chanting the eternal song of the world's desire. He is indifferent to his form, letting its beauty burn in the cosmic fire, a sacrifice to become for the other, the occult, which in the innards of infinity remains alive.

Porous are the rashes of the blossoming, kind, feverous marks of puberty, promised to effuse, to drip the blood of the heart, blood from blood, for the passions of life to arise, to ignite and to extinguish, for the races to live and die, bloodstained cracks, as the centuries come and go, and of the abyss the Desire withers.

The drama of the world is a *plangent prayer*. The poet contemplates, delves into his soul. Revealed are the passions created by his world-deceiving heart. The blood forcefully flows into the grooves of his existence and his soul's fire transforms his ideas into light, becoming a song, an *eternal prayer*, a manifested Word, a plangent sound. And nothing remains but the blood that gave birth to blood, the light that gave birth to light, the sacred desire from whose essence the world was born.

Every poet a mystic, a hymnodist, the supplication of the world's soul he emanates. This is what remains of the *plangent* flow *of thoughts*, the processes of the mind, the one who carved him, shaping him into a column among infinite columns, a human, a temple among infinite temples, for his being, his soul, his body to burn. Apollonian light, within the earth's prayer, a column of its temple alongside the other columns to await.

The life awaits the soul, the soul awaits the form. Time awaits the hour. The creation is subjugated to its unfulfilled spirit and accepts the burning of its formations; the burning of the column with the offerings that record the myth of its sufferings. The memory, art beauteous, within the work of form, a ritual of the poet, the emptiness of verses.

The essence remains as the unique texture, the identity of the anonymous drama that has taken place, for its establishment in knowledge, for existence to be recognised within its inexistence. For its vanity to be accepted as the necessity of the inevitable falsehood – a visible column – a pillar of the ineffable temple, a form, a presence, the epic of which was the irrefutable witness to the expediency of the unmanifested.

ILIAS GKRIS

ANGEL

Midsummer, a burning sun, biting
Shadows, bodies, clusters of depths
The Angel and the sea were pulling
Boats on ocean travels
The woman with the white legs, the man-eating
"White legs of love" the Angel said
And at once the wave groaned
Her eyes moved as hungry snakes
At the green depths they were tamed
They called the Angel to their rain

Whenever times, creaking, softly speak
A bird the Angel becomes, at the darkness it pecks
And as my dear cousin he arrives
Behind him the dreams as barefooted children
Further back the woman with the white legs

a woman, naked, with a hedonistic glow, a white swan
touches his chest and hair, a granary, swathes him,
waving in the wind. But he shreds his clothes, he cries:
"Each one of them steals from the innards, throwing stones"
The Angel then sits upon the day's upmost step;
in his hands he squeezes light, to water the children of the rain
of gods and humans deceived.

(Lethargic world)

The poet's greatconcern is the sun. The sun's great concern is the poet. A fiery *Angel* pulls the *boats*, symbolising the *bodies*, through his earthly and heavenly *sea*, in the *ocean travels* of all. Obedient the *man-eating* legs of the woman, they expect the Angel-lover, the dominant sun, hiding behind human passions and the groans of the waves of its own desires. These, as primordial, *hungry snakes*, undulate within his eyes, forcing him to focus them onto the depths, making him cry for his drama. They are the invocations of earth that supplicates, for the rain's blessing to come, that will cool its hot fever to and will purify it.

Thus the depths calm, the poet says. And when the turmoil comes again, caused by the gnashing of the teeth of the hidden, magical hours, tragic weeping of the moon-woman, nothing remains for the Angel, the ancient sun, but to transform and to *become a bird*, and at her darkness to *peck*. For the hierarchy of the heavenly brotherhood to be ahead in time, and, obeying her, her visions to consciously follow, as barefoot, carefree children, to open the way for nature's purification, symbolised by the *woman with the white legs*.

Supreme glow of the soul, *naked hedonistic* love, all-white *swan, woman* the one, of many promises the fulfillment, within the sacred embrace of the universe with the life-giver of miracles. Androgynus glory, and her hair, a granary that swathes everything, as it waves her mercies, cries to become, and shreding her clothes, to disperse her seeds of fire, in infinite wombs to be fertilised. Stealing from *the innards* of one self the life, its integrated life, for nature to *cast stones* at its planets, into orbit placing within chaos its dreams, its cravings, its desires, just as the *Angel*, who from his work distances himself and stands upon the stairway's upmost step. It is the day of his Word, shinning from the essence of his love, soul, and life that, within his *human hands*, the light *he squeezes, to water the children of rain, from gods and humans deceived*.

Human substance the light assumes. A *burning sun* the human being, in its attempt to transmute its being into knowledge and assimilate its shadows – the dark aspects of its existence – it becomes the omnivorous monster, biting the *bodies, clusters* of unexplored depths. And as it devours everything, it unconsciously imitates the entity that created it, in order to give a way out to its existential anguish, considering it the only path towards redemption. As an Angel the poet sees the human being, an Archangel-mind in the vast cosmic sea, through which it pulls the parts that constitute its being, leading them to the man-eating female fields of love; an offering of love to become, to be initiated in the whiteness of the divine thighs, where the Angel enhances the Word of his love, the groan of waves of the ever-flowing seasons.

A woman is the sun's beloved, his mistress. For her he illuminates the worlds, for her he agonizes. An unexplored nature is his nature and for her appeasment he suffers; he shreds his clothes for her, with his cries perpetually splitting his nuclei, inarticulate sounds that within her seek to be harmonised, as a man he becomes and as a woman he exists. A human, struggling to become an Angel again, a conscious fountain within the universe's chaos, a source of light from where to the ignorance of the world the knowledge of his truth will flow.

Possessed are the centuries by the processes taking place within the unruled field of the universal mind. And the human beings study. Supreme teacher of knowledge, the one, eternal poet. Solar is his nature and great of the humans is the unquenchable concern. Infinite are the revelations during their discipleship and the poet a leader of leaders and beyond the Hades ofpassions. Primordial symbols are the snakes, the eyes of all, the eyes of his unexplored nature, reflecting his soul, the soul of God and within its ocean the universe is rebaptised. Humans take courage, they exit from passions, treading their life in the abyss. From their errors they are taught and learn.

Man-eating are the woman's limbs, they assimilate the male aspect, transforming the shames of love into an angelic Word. And the groans, *hungry snakes*, opposing currents, unified within the ascending direction of the spine, thus taming the *green depths* that symbolise the functions of the abdomen, of the planetary solar plexus. And *the Angel* of mercy responds. He alternates his aspect with the aspects of kingdoms, and the human, of man and woman, dominates. Aura, female glory, crowns the strength, spermatogenesis of light it dissipates her grace in future circles which by the magic of her existence will be seduced; for people and gods to be liberated through the new knowledge, to their being to yield.

NIKOS GRIGORIADIS

THE UNSEEN WITHIN US

Because it is not watered
the urns fill with heaven and the mountains
are thrilled, leaping as deers in the valleys
where with only a single poppy
spring its sovereignty establishes.
The right always belongs
to whomever blossoms within the least, shouting
do not make noise, silence gilds
Unless you whisper
with your lips upon the flute of the wind
and within you burns the ever-virgin light.
Because then the girl's body
 is fragrant like an inaccessible cavern
glowing with fountains of sperm.
To be in and out as an adolescent and be scented
tender until your old age
and soaked by the drops of vigil
until from the depths of the heaven to emerge
the rose that turns the unseen within us scarlet.

(The unseen within us)

Clay urns are the ancient bodies, robust bodies, *filling with heaven* and glory. The immaculate within them is *not watered*, complete in itself, *unseen* even by its own mind, it is not possessed by thirst. In its transformations it impersonates the world, playing with the morphic alternations of the becoming and in its perpetual presence it endows the poet with the gift of free vision; to imagine it as the mountains which in every flutter of his heart become deers and jump in the valleys, where with even a *single poppy* the indication comes, the spring of life that dominates, as an answer to the merciless and inglorious death. The least of flowers that, with its inalienable right to existence, *gilds* the *silence*. And the silence, a voice that calmed, a whisper of *the wind* in the magical *flute* of life, to enrapture the *ever-virgin light, the girl's body, an inaccessible cavern, fragrant* from the offerings of the seminiferous adolescent desires.

And *until its old age* to be scented, tender to remain, an a world unwithering. To bathe *in the drops of its vigil*, a *rose* emerging from the depths of the fiery dome, a scarlet god, of the invisible sun a reminder, a promise of perfection within the imperfection of the externalised all. The grace of life glows, indicating the power of the ever-unseen world within us. An unwithering rose, the scarlet-born sun, the scarlet-born human being. On its lips the *flute of the wind*, a bucolic Word, immortal, a glorification of the ever-virgin light, which turns the body of its girlish nature fragrant, a womb that from love is watered and the instincts of the universe rebirths.

The unhoped-for pulse rises and at the culmination of the cosmic vigil the acknowledgment comes, the awareness of the fullness in itself. Within, the unseen of those that do not mourn. Because the unthirsty *is not watered*, the poet the invisible beauty praises. The beauty of the mountains cannot be hidden – the spiritual mountains that transmute their essence into a miracle, febrile dance moves, carnal odes of elks, mindless memories, dominating within the frolics of time.

A single conception is enough and life becomes the domination of the absolute, the jurisdiction of spring over the triumph of passion, a silence magnified within the humble whispering of the cosmic light. And the *body* glows, *fragrant*, the inaccessible becomes accessible, attracting the sun into the great cavern, to become enlightened and to illuminate the darkness, for the *ever-virgin* light to pour forth. A flute-bearing initiator is the immaculate, glorious Word, of its meanings the sperm-giver, gestated in the womb and the he who does good is birthed, gifting to the eternal of his nature his divine myrrh; anageless adolescent overlooking the passions, the lovable heaven of the unseen world.

The story of our life the initiator poet tells us. It is the water in its urns. It places the *wind's flute upon its lips. An ever-virgin body, a girl's light*, initiated into the mysteries of the Word of love, of man and woman the unreachable erotic breath. Time shall be watered, *tender* to remain *until its old age*. The universal youth to be maintained, until the mind, trained from the vigil's exercise, to appear, to be revealed, confirming the imperishable of its eternity.

Clear is the statement of the truth that *the unseen within us is not watered*, it has no need for the life, renewal and rebirth that the visible, manifested world has. The poet gives us the symbols, urns that fill with heaven. Carriers the bodies of instinct, supervised by the mind. Minerals that have developed their Word into a plant, animal, and human kingdom, to be imbued by the magic of its nature, perpetuating the radiance of its intelligence. A miracle evangelizing the dynasty of God within the presence of the human being, an inalienable right that no one can deny.

The will to live dominates. The existence itself is knowledge that recycles its being, having as evidence the creation of the human being, to validate all that preceded its presence in the centuries-old evolution. An anthology of its Word the poet's Word. He is the thinker of truth, the light of love, the visionary who redeems the mountains, extols the bodies, the dancer of spring – spring the songster.

Spirit and body, imaginative mind, into the unimaginable it initiates, with the unseen, the inconceivable, the world it familiarises. This world has need of the emotional tide, but more need it has of love. Erotic ritual that with the light quenches the thirsty, as the fountains of the spirit from the depths of the inaccessible cavern of the divine nature originate, glowing, and with their immortal water anoint the humans, so that like *a rose from the depths of heaven* they emerge and turn to scarlet the unseen of the world within them.

OTHON M. DEFNER

MUSES WITHIN ONESELF

Be a man of your time,
But with teachings from the past.

There is purity – if you so wish –
Even within a "porn" magazine.

And religionism with anarchy destroys
The words of love of Christ.

Feel young because you question,
You seek, think and progress.

Do not, however, consider the brass experience
Of the elder, useless, as if scrap.

At the depths of bitter Atlantis
Only poor virtue can save you.

(Stichira Idiomela)

Word of Words, Master of saints and humans, soul of souls, the light of lights is Christ. At His purity, the resignation of eternities. A man the poet is and the religionist prostitute, an ancient nature, her virtue he invokes, her purity sunken at the depth of depths he seeks. Life does not consider the *brass experience of the elders useless*, the love of Christ it contemplates, even though it questions it, it seeks and it progresses. It is of His will the blessing that from the *depths of Atlantis* life calls Him, to save it, to raise it, to uplift it.

Poor destiny, god-bearing, with the lessons of the past it travels, nurturing the man of times, taking care of his body and spirit, teaching him through the poet's mouth, with the teachings of its nature it feeds him. Its purity calls him to acknowledge it within its life's course, where religionism, the damned, unrestrained in its downwardly intoxication, surrendered to anarchy, the *words of love of Christ* heretically fights.

A feature of youth is immaturity. To evolve and progress it must think, deepen, reach into the bottomlessness of its very thought, in the prison of its death to be found. That is where the sun matures, there the *brass experience* into golden light is transmuted, the progress of nature exudes and saved is the *poor virtue* of the world. From the distant past the Word has been the *man of the time* of times. His present and future is from his past possessed and as an embittered land for the emergence of its sunken continents he cares and strives.

The power of each poem in the essence of its lyrics hides. It diffuses into the meanings, concepts and actions, undertakings that detain and release life, enslave and liberate humans, to redemption leading them, to the emergence from the depths of their own selves, where they intentionally allowed themselves to sink, unconsciously knowing that they will be called to present themselves at the invitation of the Word. They have authorised the poet to provide the thread, the path, the Christic consciousness. The great stream, the river of the love of God reaches even Hades. It cleanses the path from ignorance's filth and in the ascent, as virgin is His nature, births the chosen sun.

Poetry has a higher purpose. It seeks, it searches, it is passionate, it is religious and, expelling its religionism, it raises the brass shelter from the mouth of the abyss; for the doubts of the soul to dissolve and youth to know, to utilise its urges, to intersect with the desires of earth; for humans to acquire experience, to grow, to mature. This is the course, the path of the being. The poet alternates his knowledge with the untapped experience of humans and the *muses within themselves* rebirth the light.

Beauties are gifted to life, the seasons belong to it and its man, the transcendent spiritual sun, within life's batch of keys, the key to its forbidden gate becomes. There, in the life of prostitution it will be tormented, it will be troubled, the soul and form of life will be initiated, learning to recognise the hidden entity of the sun, the onebeyond the febrile impulses of sensual pleasures, elevating its instinctive life to the purity of the sacred intentions of time. The sacred fever of light contemplates the anarchy of darkness and its words, *words of love*. Through the path of questioning humans to their own existence are subjected, tracing the periodic cycles of their imperfect nature, talking to the Merciful of all, ready to obey His will. The time, the hours, the words as a divine power in the eyes of the perfect man line up and of the *bitter Atlantis* the sunken epics are arranged.

A chieftain is *poor virtue*, a point of reference is the mind and love is the stance, as humans, enthroned by the *words of love* within the heart, they feel young, because with their inner spirit they can question the gloomy fallacies and meditate, investigating the destination of their progress, which does not consider the *elders' brass experience, useless as if scrap*. That is why from *the depths of bitter Atlantis*, poor in spirit is virtue, with its love it lifts them, saves them, for humans to become concsious of the Word of Words, the Master of Masters, Christ.

ARIS DIKTAIOU

THE ANGEL OF THE SEVENTH SEAL

I oscillate between God and humans.
I bear God's messages to humans
and the hardship of humans to God.
I envision a land within the clouds
and approach it, shivering from sacred shivers
of a presence outside of life and death.
I foresee the presence that I bear within me:
a power that ignites the black stone,
that colours reptiles, fish and stones
and reconciles yesterday with today.
I hold a thread and as a spinning top with earth I play.
Upon a thread hangs human
fate. Destiny I have prematurely come to know:
a strange adolescent who stole the light.
'Tis I who have stolen the light and yet I have
betrayed it. Its presence dwelling within me thus avenges:
the Demon threatens my Angel.
I oscillate between God and humans.
The messages of humans to God I bear
and the hardship of God to humans
enveloped in the fiery mantle of the prophet,
wild and threatening within my wilderness,
on a passage, recently unearthed,
of the Seventh Seal of John.

(The poems 1934-1965)

The sun oscillates in the sky, bearing God's messages to chaos and of chaos the teratologies to God. Dweller of the miracle, it preaches His Word and in favour of His house, with humans it interacts. The beings envision *within their own clouds a land, shivering* their *sacred shivers* as they sense the absoluteness of what is beyond their presence, a presence inside and outside of themselves, of life and death.

Every being foresees the internal presence of the entity, the poet says. This is the outmost of all and the innermost of the becoming *power that colours* the creation of fire and stirs its time, bending it to the will of its eternal timeless being, gripping the strings that connect the people, who symbolise the spheres, the gods and their fate. It holds the premature destiny of an adolescent knowledge that travels as it plays by stealing, grabbing the light of its own maturing, a maturing that encompasses eternal youth and youth encompassing the wise old age.

Archangelic potential of light that sacrifices itself, and gloom that appropriates the sanctity of light, dwelling in it and while claiming its own being, which is again the light, it treacherously awaits its merger with it; the *Demon's threat to the Angel* and the Angel's promise for submission, regarding the oscillation's continuation between Demon and God. To perpetuate the transfer of the underworld's hardship to the upper world and the upper world's mercy to descend to the needs of humans, who avoid vesting the *fiery mantle of God* as the prophet, the wild and menacing being of their wilderness, dominated as they are by their demonic possession which they are fighting to expel. Until they love it, fall in love with it, worship it as themselves, so as to pass onto the *unearthed passage* of their hearts. Each to become John in the Revelation of the *Seventh Seal*, a synthesis of the whole, an acceptance of the disparate parts of all.

The human being oscillates between its two worlds, between its two parts, good and evil, benevolent and cunning, heaven and hell, love and hatred, the absence and presence of form, the void and its projection upon the enchanting beauty of contrasts. This is its drama, to envision a *land within the clouds*. An angel that was shaped with two aspects, one colouring life and being subject to death and the other, *shivering sacred shivers*, to remain a *presence outside of life and death*, having the ability to foresee the entry and the exit of its megocosmic breath, igniting and extinguishing the black stone, which symbolises the power of all, colouring and discolouring its worlds. Eternal *reptiles, fish* of perfection, perennial spiritual gems that God within His being reconciles one another, for the world to have an excuse in its sins, to justify the polarisation within its externalisation.

All people hold *a thread* in their hands and as a *spinning top* play with *earth* and the *fate* of all – even their own is *on this thread hung*. On their emotions and thoughts, on the maturement of their premature desires, on their adolescence's frivolity or their adulthood's wisdom life depends, the poet tells us. With the sunrises of their spirit, the sun's light arrives every day and with its sunsets, before humans savour their abduction's dream, with acts of betrayal the presence of love they extinguish from their heart. The dark *Demon* outside the house of light *threatens* their *Angel*, fearing his luminous presence, the intrinsic need of the becoming, which oscillates in chaos and undertakes its work, until it is absorbed in its being and thus harship follows its *God*.

Enveloped the prophet *in the fiery mantle*, a sun *wild and threatening* amidst the chaos, in the hermitage of God he cloisters, the abbot of six Churches and he is the prominent seventh of the attending universes. An adolescent oscillating between the father and the mother, between heaven and earth, between spirit and matter, to symbolise the relationship of humankind with God and God's relationship with Himself. An

Archangel Word playing the eternal game, with dizzying speed he spins his innumerable spheres, holding them with the infinite threads of his hands and swirling them within chaos, a power that appointed the world in his work's beauty to be glorified.

Lord, none of Your shapes have You lost. Relics of their souls the humans are. Archangels the greatness of Your kingdom incarnate, and Your beings volition beyond Your own volition they have not. You the oscillation of Your suns, the relics of Your spirit, the light-giver of all. You of Your presence the poet, of Your Word the expression and Your rights You claim throughout the centuries. Teach us to bring forth Your will, we the desperate, the ignorant. Hear us, Lord, as in sin we lead our life. In Your magnanimousness send Your Angels, in Your fiery mantle to vest the earth, for You as benign and benevolent, of Your kingdom the power You save.

Note: The word "hardship" of the verse "and the hardship of God to humans" is perceived by the analyst as the condition of the one who is complete in labours, struggles and toils, which are given to people by God for their evolution.

APOSTOLOS DOURVARIS

HYMN

I know you
blue gleaming
daughter of the wind.
I met you
in the swallow nests
when with soil, saliva and feathers
they built their homes
the messengers of Demeter.
I met you
in the huge fires
that the ploughmen lit in October
to scorch the fields.
I know you
– small flower of the Orange tree.
I met you
see-sawing on a swing
hanging by the moon.
I met you
as a crystal thread
inviting
the thirsty wayfarer.
I know you
– silver-smoked chalice.
I met you
in the wine of the holy communion

that you communed as a twelve-year-old.
I met you
in my blood,
a red sky and the coolness of pomegranates.
I know you
– sealed breath of the northern wind.
I met you
from the amulet
between your breasts
that confessed
the first pain of your flesh.
I met you
in the dusty road
that desperation carves
when hesitantly you tested
how solid
the last step is.
I know you
– sour blackberry raki
I met you
within myself
and I love you.

(By His Own Hand)

A blue glittering daughter of the wind is the acquaintance of the poet; the soul of heaven, the breath of earth, the powerful pro-creator of Light; womb of the sun, a fiery sea. In her dreams, dreams of the world, she travels and enchants humans, love, God himself, nurturing the poet's spirit *within the swallow nests* of the eternal spring. She teaches the spirits of his verses, the messengers of Demeter, to build their homes similarly to those of the ploughmen, where the love of the year's seasons dwells amid the huge purifying fires of October, the terrible frosts of winter and the invincible forces of summer.

With the blossoming of the orange orchards, the wisdom's blessing is diffused within the non-mourning days' ever-flowing cycle of the ever-lightful life. There, the century makes its acquaintance with her morphic existence as, in a hammock *hanging from the moon* with crystal threads, identical to poetry, in perpetual she sways. And she invites the *thirsty wayfarer* to drink from her *silver-smoked chalice* the *wine of the Holy Communion*, a communion through which the twelve-cycle of all into the eternity of the One she initiated, in order for the human being to gain concsiousness of the transcendent Light.

To meet within its blood the *red sky* and the coolness of the pomegranates; to receive the breath from the *sealed breath of thenorthern wind*; to turn its intellect into an *amulet between its breasts*; for other winds to come and confess the *first* and *last* sin of their human flesh. On the *dusty road* that ignorance paved for them they walked, testing the solidity of the staircase from *first* step to the *last*, seeking intoxication in the *sour raki* of the *blackberry bush,* in the depths of their soul to know the despair that forced them more and more to search inside themselves for love.

Southeastern the lust that with excitement is prone to death, a subordinative human being of its dissolute self which to the transgressions of denial succumbed and the relentless carnal pain took as its guide. It seeks the blue *gleaming daughter of the wind*, its soul, with *soil, saliva and feathers* it builds her a swallow nest, for the spring to come and dwell in its heart; to announce the spiritual fruitfulness of Demeter, as, a ploughman itself, it will ignite the fires of Saint-Dimitrios the horseman, to scorch the remnants of the parenthesis opened by time for human pretexts, when the ego spent life in the unbearable time of its earthly shame.

The poet counts the acquaintances in the flowers of the

orange tree and the suns he envisions in the fruit trees. Gilded laments, citrus wonders that await the man-Hercules to surrender to him, where the magic of the moon its powers exercises on the plain of the nightly adoration of the form's realm.

Crystal thread the overhanging grace, in the vastness' brilliance it levitates and urges the thirsty beings to quench their lust in the vacant body of cosmic awareness, symbolised by the chalice; holy Communion, unsurpassed theurgic act, transfusion of the mysteries of the agatho[1] to *blood, a red sky of coolness and pomegranates*. Auspicious revelation of all unto the ages, where God with His own breath seals the *breath of the northern wind* and becomes the amulet of the world in the breasts of life, where centuries praise His creation's rule, human and angelic, heavenly and earthly dream, of His Creation the beauty. With juice the kingdoms fill, panacea of His essence, of rivers the life, a flood of God's knowledge. Infinity bears fruit.

Your spirit's wreath, Lord, aura of matutinals, the amulet of Your universes is. As bad omens come before You, to Your power they repentantly pray, that on the dust of Your pathway the road of despair they have carved. In the *sour raki of the blackberry bush* the poet experienced deprivation and the greatness of Your blood the stream of life it brought within him, as a redeemer of Your powers, Lord and God You are, Life-giver, and Your worlds You save.

---

[1] The term "agatho" out of the Greek word «αγαθό» is used to mean all that is beyond the duality of good and bad. It is the Entity, the Whole, the Monad.

NIKOS EGGONOPOULOS

BOLIVAR
(excerpts)

THEY SAW AN APPARITION OF THESEUS IN ARMS, RUSHING
ON AT THE HEAD OF THEM AGAINST THE BARBARIANS
The heart of a man is worth all the gold of a nation

For the great, for the free, for the brave, the strong,
Befit the words the great, the free, the brave, the strong
For them is the absolute submission of every element, the silence,
for them are the tears, for them are the lighthouses,
and the olive branches, and the lanterns
That up and down jump with the sway of the boats and
write upon the dark horizons of the ports
For them are the empty barrels tumbling in the
narrowest – of the same port – alley,
For them are the coils of white rope and the chains, the anchors, the
other manometers,
Within the irritating odour of oil,
To rig a boat, to set out, to leave,
Similar to a tram that starts moving, empty and brightly lit in the
nightly serenity of the gardens,
With one purpose of journey: to the stars.
For those I will say the fine words, dictated to me by Inspiration,
As deep inside my mind it nestled, full of emotion
For the forms, the austere and wonderful, of Odysseas Androutsos and
Simon Bolivar.

(Bolivar)

The gold of the world, the gold of the universe, the value of the human heart, the divine heart, the Thesean, the apparition of which, prefectly clean, brilliantly shines, borne upon the angry deities of the unspiritualised, dark raging hordes of the unconscious. Of benevolent armed men the vision, the presence of an unblemished mind, the purity of the brave, the great, the free, the strong. Theirs is the strength, the greatness, the freedom, the bravery, and the appropriate submission and shameful transgressions of barbarians in the absolute of every element's silence are appeased.

Of heroes are the tears from heaven that as lighthouses upon earth the pathways of the ships illuminate, recording the horizons' course. And *olive branches* as a wreath upon the heads of the strong are placed, of Athena a donation, Aegean breeze, winds of fire, to distinguish the dark ports. There, the *empty barrels*, which symbolise the world of the human being's soul that is in trial, emptying and filling with hopes, tumble in the *narrowest alley* of every *port*. The arithmosofical analysis of the words *"empty barrels"* reveal the number of trial, twelve[1], as these words give us twenty and forty-six respectively, a sum of sixty-six (six plus six equals twelve).

These heroes, the great tested of their world. *For them are the coils*, the ceaseless cycles of life, cycles of knowledge to be mastered, since the analysis of the word *"coil"* gives us five[1], the number of specific knowledge. The *"white ropes"*, through the number eleven[1], symbolise the potential for introspection and the strength to dominate over the bestial nature. And the *"chains"* with the number fourteen[1] gives temperance, the prudent handling of energies and forces of the soul. The *"anchors"* again give us eleven* and the "manometers" fourteen[1],

---

[1] The arithmosophical analysis applies to the Greek words the poet uses for "empty barrels" ("άδεια βαρέλια», «coil» («κουλούρες»), «white ropes» («άσπρα σχοινιά»), «chains» («σχοινιά»), «anchors» («άγκυρες»), «manometers» («μανόμετρα»), «gardens» («μπαχτσέδες»).

as confirmation of the meaning resulting from the arithmosofical analysis of the two previous words, ropes and chains. All these objects are merely the tools for the conquest of knowledge, which is symbolised by the *"coils"*, the circles.

For heroes to rig a boat, the poet tells us, *to set out, to leave, similar to a tram that starts moving, empty and brightly lit in the nightly serenity of the gardens*, after first passing humankind through the *irritating odour of oil*, the liquefied fires of the subsoil – the dark flows. There the senses, with scent being the predominant one, repel the odour of the black gold that symbolises the descendent field, until humans learn to embrace it, to love it, so that with their acceptance the thinking mind passes into emptiness, their emotional world is redeemed; so that the boat – the carrier – leaves the aquatic field, to be transformed into a tram, to be grounded, to be illuminated, for the body to be emptied of the hopes of delusion; so that it travels through the *nightly serenity of the gardens*, symbolising the final field of trial (the word "gardens" gives twelve[1] again), which is the delusion of beauty. But it is also the field of service that the one trialled expresses with the assistance of the angelic spirits, which are symbolised by flowers, the ascendent respective of oil, the gold of the spirit, the gold of the heart, the power of love that will lead the strong to the stars.

For them the poet uses the *fine words*, dictated to him by *Inspiration*, as *deep inside his mind* it nestles *full of emotion* for these *austere and wonderful forms*, the timeless, of *Odysseas Androutsos and Simon Bolivar*. Entities which symbolise the continuous revolution of the soul of humankind, against the oppression of its very own personality. Their names, as confirmation of their action, with the sum of the numbers resulting from their arithmosofical analysis, give us eleven[2], the energy of the mind, used for the conquest of the inner truth, the true

---

[2] The arithmosophical analysis applies to the Greek writing of the names Odysseas Androutsos and Simon Bolivar.

knowledge. To this the poem refers to.

The poet uses the symbols to demonstrate the eternal course the spirit makes through the dark perimeter of the controversial, having as a guide its magnificent formtions, a result of powers of the soul which, driven by its innermost nature, are externalized, acquiring supreme dimensions, incorporating the features of the infinite mind, to realise the work of its nature, the nature of the world.

These great heroes, represented in the poem by Odysseas Androutsos and Simon Bolivar, are the soul and the form of the world that suffers. This is evidenced by the number given through the arithmosofical analysis of the name of the first, fourteen[2], which symbolises the prudent handling of energies and forces that arise from the revolution of the soul in its quest for knowledge (fourteen, one and four equals five) which descends from one, the Monad, to four, which is the field of matter – of form. It is also proven by the number given through the analysis of the second name, fifteen[2], that is the vital fires, the digits of which, if added, give us six, the completion of parts, of the soul and form. These words constitute the ennead (form equals nine, soul equals nine, nine plus nine equals eighteen, one plus eight equals nine[3]), which encompasses all other numbers, in other words the wholeness, the earth and the sky with the stars, the field of infinite all.

---

[3] The arithmosophical analysis applies to the Greek words for «form» and «soul» («μορφή» and «ψυχή» respectively).

ODYSSEAS ELYTIS

THE MAD POMEGRANATE TREE

In these all-white courtyards where the south wind blows
Whistling through vaulted arcades, tell me, is it the mad pomegranate tree
That leaps in the light, scattering its fruitful laughter
With windy wilfulness and whispering, tell me, is it the mad
                                        pomegranate tree
That quivers with foliage newly born at dawn
Raising high its colours in a shiver of triumph?

On plains where the naked girls awake,
When they harvest clover with their light brown arms
Roaming round the borders of their dreams–tell me, is it the mad
                                        pomegranate tree

Unsuspecting, that puts the lights in their verdant baskets
That floods their names with the singing of birds–tell me
Is it the mad pomegranate tree that combats the cloudy skies of the world?

On the day that it adorns itself in jealousy with seven kinds of feathers,
Girding the eternal sun with a thousand blinding prisms
Tell me, is it the mad pomegranate tree
That seizes on the run a horse's mane of a hundred lashes,
Never sad and never grumbling–tell me, is it the mad pomegranate tree
That cries out the new hope now dawning?
Tell me, is that the pomegranate tree waving in the distance,
Fluttering a handkerchief of leaves of cool flame,

A sea near birth with a thousand ships and more,
With waves that a thousand times and more set out and go
To unscented shores-tell me, is it the pomegranate tree
That creaks the rigging aloft in the lucid air?

High as can be, with the blue bunch of grapes that flares and celebrates
Arrogant, full of danger–tell me, is it the mad pomegranate tree
That shatters with light the demon's tempest in the middle of the world

That spreads far as can be the saffron ruffle of day
Richly embroider with scattered songs-tell me, is it the mad
                                            pomegranate tree
That hastily unfastens the silk apparel of day?

In petticoats of April first and cicadas of the feast of mid-August

Tell me, that which plays, that which rages, that which can entice

Shaking out of threats their evil black darkness
Spilling in the sun's embrace intoxicating birds
Tell me, that which opens its wings on the breast of things
On the breast of our deepest dreams, is that the mad pomegranate tree?

(Orientations)
(Translation by Edmund Keeley and Philip Sherrard)

In the *all-white courtyards* of the world where the *south wind* blows, the poet plays, united with the wisdom of nature, asking people if this wisdom, if this very nature is really the pomegranate tree. There, in the construct of its light, in the *vaulted arcades* the spirit of the world leaps into nature's other light. And with its *fruitful laughter* it shapes its spirit to *wilfulness and whispers of the wind*, making its *newly born foliage* quiver in its dawn, as, before the triumph of the miracle of its existence, *all the colours of the iris* it opens. It awakens the *naked girls*, its female bodies, to harvest with their *light brown hands the clover*, the symbols of its triadic world, and within the *borders of its sleep* the vast fields of their dreams to guide.

Unsuspecting and innocent the pomegranate tree *puts the lights in their verdant baskets* to overflow with the bird singing of its Word and their names it announces, in order for it to be able with its benevolent spirit to combat the *cloudy skies* of fumes caused by desires, by the ignorance the world has for its grace. Until the day comes that the world renounces its envy, that is nature's envy, and ceases wanting to be adorned with *seven kinds of feathers, girding the eternal sun*, the blinding, with a *thousand prisms*. Then there will be nothing forcing it, that which is *never sad and never grumbling, to seize on the run of a hundred lashes the mane* of its nature and *shout*, for a *new hope* to dawn.

This is the mad one, the poet says, that with its handkerchief flutters the leaves made out of *cool flame* and becomes a *sea near birth with a thousand ships and more*. It is this *mad pomegranate tree* that *creaks its rigging high in the lucid air*, to vibrate its spirit's carriers – the bodies of all, celestial and human – and be propelled by the waves – their feelings, desires, passions –, that a *thousand times and more they set out and* as one body *go to unscented shores* – to the beyond.

A *blue bunch of grapes the pomegranate tree*, high as can be, *flaring and celebrating, arrogant, full of danger*, and along the way it *shatters, with light* flooding *the demon's tempest in the middle of the world*, its *saffron ruffle to spread as far as can be*; to become the *saffron ruffle of day*, the *richly embroidered with scattered* songs.

Yes, *it is the mad pomegranate tree hastily unfastening* its *silk apparel, petticoats of April first and cicadas of the mid-August feast*. It is the one that wants to play, to rage, to entice the threats, to shake out its *evil dark blackness*, to spill from its *embrace, the sun's embrace, intoxicating birds*, to spread *their wings* on the breasts *of things*, on the breasts of the world's *deepest dreams*, of its own dreams.

At the new, primary point of the horizon the *mad pomegranate tree* blows and life makes its appearance. At its start, full of light it scatters the seeds of its fruit that quiver from longing. These are that bring the dawn of colours, as they are strengthened by the *shiver of triumph*, because they managed to be born, to exist. And they become the world, its desires, feelings and ideas, its plans.

Its visions, naked, virgin girls destined in *the plains* their nature *to awaken*, entice the nature of the world, the nature of the pomegranate tree which symbolises the perpetual recreation, to participate in the orgiastic game by seeding the wombs – the baskets – with the winged desires of life that chirp its countless names, the lights of their soul, its soul, in order to be able to battle the ignorance of the world - which is also the challenge for knowledge that evolves the newly born spirit.

This newly born spirit, the poet symbolises with the south wind, through which the *mad pomegranate tree* blows its will, its murmurs stubbornly whistling within the labyrinths of the cosmic light, desiring to make them spring up as conscious life; so that they diffuse *into the day which in jealousy adorns itself with its seven* eternal miracles, *girding the sun with a thousand prisms* – the civilisations of earth. These, as they blindingly pass, construct the immortal legend of hope, which is claimed by the world's need for completion, for redemption, that is hidden beyond even the illusion of light.

The word *"handkerchief"* in its arithmosofical analysis gives us eleven[1], a number that symbolises the energy of the female principle, the power that directs the course of the world.

---

[1] The arithmosophical analysis applies to the Greek words the poet uses for "handkerchief" ("μαντίλι"), «leaves» («φύλλα»), "pomegranate tree" («ροδιά»)

Through this the fires spring up, the "leaves", a word that in its analysis gives us ten[1], a number which, among others, also symbolises the eternal action of time. From these fires the natural ocean is created that is nothing more than a reflection of the universal, divine Mind, in which life moulds its beings and its people – the people who make their ships, symbols of the carriers, their bodies.

This is the ocean of matter and spirit and through it people travel, matured from the knowledge given to them by the mad, crazy pomegranate tree, as it takes them to *unscented shores* with the power of its waves, that make its *rigging* – its ethereal wings – creak in the *lucid air*, the planet's etheric field. The spirits of the wise and enlightened are waves in the vastness, evolving humankind during its great journey in the quest for the unscented shores – the fields of fulfillment. The *blue bunch of grapes that flares and celebrates* symbolises its spirit that, ripe with wisdom juices of the pomegranate tree, is called with the power of its inner light to shatter the tempest of its negative nature.

The arithmosofical analysis of the word *"pomegranate tree"* gives us ten[1], which is the "panteleia"[2], the divinity, heaven, eternity, the sun. This mad deity, *the mad pomegranate* tree, is the one unfolding the fields and subfields of its existence, revealing its universe, which in the poem is symbolised by the number eight, the eighth month, August. This carries within it the number fifteen (mid-August), the strength of the vital fires which penetrate its being and incite its rage, wishing its terrible *black darkness* to entice; to enchant it by shaking it from the *embrace of the sun*, to spill it out transformed into intoxicating birds; to open their *wings on the breast of things*, the breast of their *deepest dreams* – the deity's breast.

The power of the entity the poet wants to demonstrate, us-

---

[2] "panteleia" («παντέλεια») was a Pythagorean name of the number ten, meaning consummation, fulfillment, perfection.

ing the pomegranate tree as a symbol. He asks while playing with the concepts. The entity is everything; it creates everything; is inherent therein. It is the one whistling in its *vaulted arcades*. It is the south wind, as well as all the other winds, that carry its all-mighty spirit to all points on the horizon. But with the south wind the poet refers to the beginning of the entity's manifestation, as, according to esoteric teachings, the south is the gateway from which new life emerges.

The entity leaps in its own light, spreading through its spirit – the wind – its *fruitful laughter in wilfulness and whispering* – its polyspermic fruits. The entity is the *naked girls*, it is the singing of their names, its own names; it is the blinding presence of the *sun with a thousand prisms*. And it is the horse with its mane that in its human body rides upon itself, giving it a *hundred lashes*, thus imposing its will on its lower nature.

It is the spiritual and physical ocean, it is the entire circle that *unfastens the petticoats* – the subfields of its existence – causing its *black darkness* to spill from its embrace as *intoxicating birds* – its ideas – and open their *wings on the breast of* its *deepest dreams*. It is the sun, the sky, the stars and the earth of its miracle!

ANDREAS EMBEIRIKOS

THE ASCENT

The words when falling upon the body of night
  Resemble ships which plow the seas
With men who sow and women who talk
Among the smacking of kisses
Lizards passing into the shivers of the shores
  Of a sea stretching to the sand
With jaups and splashes
Just before the sun rises
While the voices of matter's rhapsodists are heard
And the clamour of an upright rooster
Upon a salt column of meridian countries
When cravings swell on the shores
Of myriads marching through the gusts of wind
Before the eyes of the blessed girls
Who bend down with their breasts touching the water
The pure water of the streams
Until they find and feel in their bodies and their souls
Without limits without conditions
The acquired ascent of pleasure.

(Every Generation or Today as Tomorrow and as Yesterday)

The universe finds itself in an unconditional surrender to the forces from which it was created, the poet says. Prey to the opposing flows of its being, it climbs up and down the scale of the upward and downward spiral in search of total physical and spiritual pleasure. On a single path treading, where for centuries as a human God Himself descends and ascends, and the words, fiery parts of His Word, *fall into the body of night* and become *ships which plow the seas*; words they are too, unformed ideas, fluid, that from the depths of His desiring heart led the way and became the oceans of the spirit, to create the mystery of men who, obedient to the will of God, seed the beauty of the talking women, nature of their nature. Profuse gestation that results in the chatter of births, magical revelations of the eternal erotic orgy, of the ontological existence the unquenchable orgasm.

The poet addresses the miracle of universal pleasure, the pleasure of emotion, thought, an undefined complex, unrevealed to the uninitiated time, which itself refuses to unconditionally surrender and to ascent it is forced by the inclination of its own soul. Acquired is the momentum of the existent, to the privation caused by its need it succumbs, to the *smacking of the kisses* it surrenders and in the shivers of the shores, in the outcome of its being it ends up. Lizards, unrefined bodies of its bodies are the memories, the universe, its own body, they permeate.

A pioneering divine sun of the continuous sunrise is the poet, he is the fiery sea that with the *jaups and the splashes* of the cravings of the universal soul is *spread* up to *the sand* of his morphic crash, *just before* his knowledge within his own glory dawns. He is the rhapsodist of matter, of the great mother who gives birth to the light, as an *upright rooster's clamour* his rhapsodies are, as a *salt column of meridian countries, swelling on the shores of* his *myriad* cravings, souls that lead their lives *in the gusts of wind* – the eternal spirit. *Before the eyes* of the fulfilled female aspects of his being, his presence remains unaltered within its essence and they desire to unite with him, to feel and *sense their bodies* and their souls. To be initiated *without limits, without conditions*, to accept to be nurtured from the entity and then, in their turn, for the *ascent of pleasure* the entity to nurture.

The human words *fall on the body of night* and travel, tracing their circle in infinity, leaving earth, returning from the universe to the source whence they began, in the mouth and spirit of the Word, as Its universal miniatures. These words and deeds of humans are that shape the becoming, the poet says, and every one of them is but a recycling of part or of all creation. It is as if humans previously never existed, as if they were created with the vocalisation of the word. It is as if there was no universe and it was created when humans created it with their own Word, with the suns, the planets and the seas that roam within the night – the night which began to exist when someone else, countless years ago, spoke the word "night".

And the imagination of one spread and became property of all other beings that followed. For seas to resemble seas, ships to resemble ships, men to resemble *men who sow* infinity into women and women to resemble *women who speak* the other Word, the redemptive, that *of kisses*, and reveal the mysteries of cosmogony which are hidden in the depths of the oceans and, ascending, *pass through the shivers of the shores*. Primordial models of pain and pleasure, which in the poem are symbolised by lizards, the sensual magic of the *sea stretching to the sand with jaups and splashes*, processes of the earthly night that culminate just before the star of the day rises, *while the voices of* eternal *rhapsodists of matter* and spirit *are heard*, occult guards, who are entrusted with the protection of human aspirations. The *clamour of an upright rooster* are the odes which are engraved *on a column* created by time, for consciousness to be recorded, when the *cravings swell in the shores*, for passions to find a way out.

A happy ending, an ending auspicious for the myriads who tread through the gusts of their spiritual nature, before the eyes of the comely brides, who offer their breasts and nurture the agatho[1], symbolised by the *pure water of the streams*, emotion that is transmuted into love, for bodies to find their bodies, souls to find their souls, the human being to find the human being and God to find God. *Without limits, without conditions*, this surrendering of the humankind, of the microcosm to the macrocosm, of earth to the universe, of the universe to the infinite, of the fall to the *ascent, of pleasure* to bliss, of nature to nature, of man to woman and of woman to man; of sensuality to life and of life to itself, to its absolute being, where the mystery of its existence has no beginning or end, within the omnipotence of the absolute One.

---

[1] The term "agatho" out of the Greek word «αγαθό» is used to mean all that is beyond the duality of good and bad. It is the Entity, the Whole, the Monad.

GIORGOS THEMELIS

DENUDATION

You can say that we have nothing, nothing
Belongs to us: body, love or bread
We pass on, they stay, the eternal things
(Perhaps more complete, filled with our love).
Something of our own, a light, a lost light,
The eyes that dream will see it,
Where you stood, where you looked at your face.

When we are left alone and bare,
What will become of us without shelter and fire,
What will become of you, how you will you be resurrected
Without the other flesh, the perfect comeliness.

Save, my God, the body, so that you are saved and we are saved.
The day, the night, the time, an imaginary story.
Other shadows will wander amidst the rooms
Touching the things, our things.
Accustomed, docile and just released
They will seek hands clenched as our hands.
Here the courtyard's tree will stand
And our roof, always damp as in springtime.
The sky above it deserted.

When April arrives in its slow future
With all its glory, when the Great Easter arrives
In royal purple I will adorn you for the great feast,
Precious jewellery: to be handsome among the handsome.

("NEW STATIONS" magazine)

We have nothing, the poet says, not even this body of ours yet. *The body, bread, love, eternal things* we leave on earth, *filled with our love, complete*. As *we pass on*, we leave them, lost, amid the light to remain; for the spirits of continuity to come, to admire them and to dream. Faces that were ours and we gave them, things that kept our great soul, to dwell in the tomb of the ancient land, awaiting the return. The perfection of flesh to adorn, God to save His body, to resurrect it.

Alone, bare, we the deceased, in silence, in the hearth without a roof. *The day, the night, the time*, is of death an imaginary *story*. And other than our being in the world does not exist. We live the comeliness of our nature and the times *wander* as *shadows amidst the rooms, touching our things; accustomed, docile* bodies, substitutes of our perfect body. *The hands*, are clenched *hands seeking the hands* of God, to greet the gift of His love. A tree of earth that stands in the middle of His universal courtyard, tying the fresh fruit of youth to deserted heavens, rooftops of houses used by angels and people, enduring the time of the slow future. *April with all its glory* to come, the *Great Easter*, for its beings, the planets and suns, to enrobe in the precious *purple in the great feast*. For the immortal century to be *handsome among the handsome*.

Megacosmic, poetic conception is the miracle. Sensuality within the body, knowledge of the mind, as a revelation to the poet it is donated, for time to be ecstatic, for humans to live and experience the union, in harmony's universal music of God's blessing, in the radiance of His spirit to partake. To be denuded in the light, to deliver their soul's need, their body and everything they own, bread, love, earthly things, material and eternal possessions, to leave them to become completed; the extensions of their being, whatever they held captive due to incomplete care, as they leave, in love to abandon them; to deliver their dreams' works to love's own light, their face to the face of God, who looks at them with another look, with *eyes that dream* a dream different than their own. And this dream is universal. It is the vision of the soul that knows how to vibrate at the sound of the Word, for the human heart to pulsate, to fall in love with the unknown, in its sacraments to participate.

A tree is the world and the desert sky rejoices. In the spirit imprinted are the scenes with which the dome of the temple must be adorned, for the dive plan to be imprinted in the hollow of the skull, so that the eyes of the entire world shall turn and see. The mind into the abyss plummets and there the shadows dance amid its imaginary story's shipwreck. And when the poet descends, following the celestial sun in its work of deliverance, he becomes a witness of the solution to the drama and the story of the true, inner life in a work poetic, divinifying, he records.

Eternal Lampri[1], Easter that from its holy sufferings sheds light amidst the darkness of the abyss. Cosmogony, which by the grace of God and the testimony of His angels is divinified, the human race celebrates a cosmic feast. The contemplation of the earth, a God-man, after the fall upright he stands. And the sphere revives its vision, in purple the divine nature is dressed, the wreath a *royal glory*, a solar aura its crown, a jewel of jewels the love of its heart.

Save Your *body, God, to be saved, for us to be saved*, the skies chant from the birth to the resurrection of the world. All beings repeat this supplication during the evolution of the immaculate life which the holy spirits live, and glorify God as they care for earth. And the return of the sun from the eternal depths they await, protecting the human being in weddings, births, baptisms and death, the bodies to have as company in the denudation of the dream, the dissolution of their world to withstand.

A month of celebration is their unseated April, Easter of

---

[1] "Lampri", meaning bright, is another name for Easter according to the Greek tradition.

a myriad names of the Eternally Immortal. As the spirits by His spirit turn ecstatic, they are redeemed of the abyss. And all beings take part in the joy, the eyes look at the face, and things are dematerialized. The Christs are attired in the perfection of the body and the life of humans, the largely passive, they cover with sacred divine purple. They had nothing and gained everything. The light, love and life found their light. Body of bodies, sun of their spirits, the entire earth and sky their timeless Easter celebrate.

DIMITRIS IATROPOULOS

"FRAGMENTS OF METALECTIC" 1984
(excerpt)

12

But where does this light come from.
So much
If colours spoke
the sweet grey and the pale blue
they would claim it.
The sources of decent light ignore it.
With a finger upon lips, I impose
silence on the atmosphere.
The moment of enlightenment is awestruck.
Apotheosis of the metre, the rhythm, the harmony, the
symmetry.
A magical balance.
When, assured that it does not originate from somewhere,
at last you feel it that comes from you.
And it emerges, bathes the objects
in other eras
times ancestral, gravities foreign.
Our own.
Of us, the foreigners,
who trusted you with our continuity
but it appeared as if we were trusting you
with our life
and filled with error, various things you do
to hinder us

without yet knowing
that these too We have programmed
antichronic exercises
investigations necessary for the completion.
We the Foreigners,
Our Own.

(Arabian Nights)

For the dynasty of light is the Word. For what shapes the centuries and becomes the life, the drama and the mercy of the being. Everywhere and in everything the light, the love, the wisdom, the knowledge, the power, the source of which humans make the mistake of seeking outside of themselves, in the flowers, *the colours, the sweet grey, the pale blue*, until they understand and seek it in the silence imposed by the sun within them, the inner Word. Source of sources, *apotheosis of the metre, the rhythm, the harmony, the symmetry,* the poet says. A *magical balance* that leaves God awestruck, as *through him the light emerges* and bathes him throughout all eras. This alienates the times, ungrateful for the trust shown in them by God, as they repeat the error of humans who reproach the difficulties and oppose the divine plan that imposes on them the *antichronic exercises, investigations, necessary* expansions *for completion*.

Always foreigners are humans to themselves until they realise that they are themselves the only source of the truth of the inner sun, the inner universal being, an enlightenment timeless of the beings who represent it, admiring it within the ever-flowing, perpetually performing rituals on the magic it exerts in favour and against its own becoming.

The grey colour symbolises the astral field, the desiring field of humans, who claim the light for themselves and always characterise it as life, as their power, as they are governed by personality, an entity receiving light by others, living in the dream and choosing the magic of illusions, which are created by the universal mind for the cosmogony of its existence. A profuse expression of endless sensual and cognitive processes that mislead them in the becoming, which is particularly fond of acquiring human properties, claiming human nature, the only surrogate of its divine existence.

The pale blue is the field of the mind's projection, where reconstructed is the externalised light, the ideas, the feelings, the emotions, the imaginary sky that reflects its colours on earth and sea. In the light earth sleeps and dreams of the universe's grace. Great interpreter of its dream is the poet. Each verse of his a de-symbolisation of truth and in every concept the depth of its essence.

He is the saviour Word, the liberator of the ancient power. Light speaks of him and he speaks of light. This ongoing dialogue the poet de-symbolises, a dialogue of the body with the spirit, an inextinguishable dialogue of darkness with light. In the flowers of night dawn blooms and light fashions the cravings, the desires and the visions. And yet no one knows the origin of this light that forms the grey, how it constructs the blue and from where the inflorescences of all come and encircle its own being, to be protected from human logic, the irrepressible outer mind that separates day from night, friend from enemy, its own from the foreign, its existence from the Being. Until it understands, until it sees that all from within it spring, there they exist, from there they start and there they return, without ever having left, because they were always there.

A sun illuminating its own self, a source quenching its own thirst, a truth that exists to confirm itself. A true sky that does not darken, eternal cosmic night, all-bright, whose body and spirit is constituted of billions of suns, permanent ideas that, even when they die, do not their house abandon. They are extinguished and reignited inside the mind and heart of humans and shine, forever shine, as the one, the unified light, as all emotions, which are the one idea, as all ideas, which are the one knowledge, as all knowledge, which is the consciousness, as consciousness, which is enlightenment, as enlightenment, which is redemption, as redemption, which is God. It is God who speaks always and through all, as from within He comes, like an *apotheosis of the metre, the rhythm, the harmony, the symmetry,* in His own light to bathe the body of the eternal all.

A magical balance is achieved, when humans are reaffirmed that from nowhere else but from the unique source, of source of their selves, of their own becoming, does light emerge, which as a fountain rises from the depths of their being, and, in bathing them, rebirths them. A time of light that alienates their world. They leave themselves to their aspects and Foreigners to themselves they become, full of error so as to be hindered, to deliberately forget and not know that they are the great programmer, time and anti-time, engaged in the eternal pursuit of its completion. With Foreigners and its Own it occupies itself, the infinite, existent and nonexistent selves Words, Words of colours, Words of bodies, Words of spirits of infinite lives that perpetually transform and within their own light are lost.

From myself the foreign, the poet says. The century of light emerges, in its own light it bathes, establishing its dynasty throughout the infinite, obedient servant in the miracle of its Word; to have the confirmation that this light comes only from itself in all eras without exception, trusting them wiht the continuity of life that is full of its own error and, because of this function, as a human it is hindered to pass to the realisation of the divine plan. A hindrance that is imposed by divine care and includes the exercises of time as *necessary investigations* for the self-completion of light within light, of the human being within the human being, of the universe within the universe, of God within God.

C.P. KAVAFY

THE GOD FORSAKES ANTONY

When suddenly, at midnight, you hear
an invisible procession going by
with exquisite music, voices,
don't mourn your luck that's failing now,
work gone wrong, your plans
all proving deceptive – don't mourn them uselessly.
As one long prepared, and graced with courage,
say goodbye to her, the Alexandria that is leaving.
Above all, don't fool yourself, don't say
it was a dream, your ears deceived you:
don't degrade yourself with empty hopes like these.
As one long prepared, and graced with courage,
as is right for you who were given this kind of city,
go firmly to the window
and listen with deep emotion, but not
with the whining, the pleas of a coward;
listen – your final delectation – to the voices,
to the exquisite music of that strange procession,
and say goodbye to her, to the Alexandria you are losing.

(Collective Works)
(Translated by Edmund Keeley and Philip Sherrard)

The God forsakes Antony. With his invisible procession, abandons Dionysus Alexandria. *And the exquisite voices are heard, the music, at midnight*, within the famed, ancient Egyptian Pharaonic city. The sacred ritual of withdrawal. The souls ready to withdraw God summons, the passions to be disembodied, earthly life to receive initiation, to be deified in the unbridled, redemptive procession, to engage in the ecstatic choreia; the choreia that, with the dream's sacred orgiastic awakening, melts the bodies to the divine fever.

This is the time that God abandons personality, symbolized by Antonios, leaving him to become a victim of his own hands, at the mercy of his passionate reversal. Humans, descendants of their divine nature, attached to their form, are but destined to fail in their undertakings. And the futile cycle of their insistence, their plans – all proven to be fallacies – God disavows, and inspires the poet, teaching him, admonishing him:

Do not mourn uselessly. As one long prepared, and graced with courage, say goodbye to her, to Alexandria that is leaving, the city you dwelt in, the magical glamour of your love, shining in its glory – your glory. And, *above all, do not fool yourself*, embrace your failure. *Do not believe that the exquisite music, the exquisite voices* reaching your ears, *are a dream*.

Do not degrade yourself with the empty hopes death has of holding you. Do not deny the city; even if God has denied you, as you were deemed worthy of living in *this city*. You, the soul that embodied her dreams. Do not hang on to them, and, above all, do not keep her in your thoughts. Let her go, do not let your grief torment her any longer.

Feel the deep emotion pervading your being, do not become a victim of the cowards who, *in their pleas* and *whining*, linger, falling behind, left to crawl through their earthly chaos, as they do not accept to withdraw, listening – *as their final delectation – to the voices, to the exquisite music of the strange procession*, and, accompanying it through its course, to be redeemed. Reveal your greatness, *say goodbye to her, to Alexandria*. Embrace the loss of the city.

The spirit procession dances. The music heard is the sound of the choreia's rotating bodies, physical and etheric alike; the voices, the eternal exhortation of its exquisite Word. The poet welcomes the blessing, responding to the great calling, listening, witnessing. Alexandria, the magical city; abandoning the dream and being abandoned by the dancer. Glory and decline. The poet is aware of it. No opportunity for deification must be lost. He is familiar with the invisible procession, he sees it with the eyes of his soul. His vision – a universal vision.

Oh, the religious entourage of life. *Suddenly, at midnight, as one long prepared*, the entire world is summoned to God's sacred choreia by the invisible procession, *with exquisite music* and poetic voices. Humans and God. Within the confusion of the city, *the useless fallacies* and grief are founded, yet, as within the glory of the miracle its undertakings are conceived, its own failure is planned instead.

Oh, *Alexandria that is leaving*, the world's *dream* that was deceived. In the harmony of exquisite music, *the pleas of the cowards* are but a desecration, and the grief a slow, mortal sound. Immortal heroes of courage and strength; they do not succumb. Carriers of the knowledge formed against the threat of time by the Dionysian spirit, they do not intend to abandon the city to the hands of the foolish.

Oh, those who fall in love with the glamor of form, how they disobey the Word of their divine nature, of their soul and Life, which destined them for its greatness, masters of erebus to become themselves.

Oh, the desire to prevail over the fallacies; oh, the spiritual preparation for the time of withdrawal. Blessed are those who accept the loss of the ancient glory, and say farewell to her from their window, as though she too – a dance form – follows the accompaniment, reaching the invisible realm of the divine procession, uplifted to her formless essence.

Unredeemed, the abandoned, timeless Antonios, listens to the poet. Great is his grief, a need of his passion. Distant descendant of his divine nature, forgeting himself, he surrenders to the games of love, and the Alexandrian magic, rehearsing for the crown of life, does not appear favorable to him. The will God favours, of strong fighters, presenting them with gifts. The senses the enchanting dance raises, yet the poet is not fooled – his hearing is not deceived. He is not persuaded that it is all a dream. He perceives life, in its circles, to be immortal, unique, essential. As an entity at once invisible and visible, unable to gain or lose anything; as the everlasting impresario abandoning its followers, only to summon them back to its pure nature, the sudden manifestation of a divine, harmonious revelation.

NIKOS KAVROULAKIS

HOMER

*Many centuries
your form have imprinted, Homer,
and to the whole earth it spread;
and you painted
the roots of our race
the ageless.
And you saw
with the eyes of the soul
forms universal, global
and beings demonic, otherworldly
mingling with humans,
in a titanic, unprecedented
apotheosis of life and Hades.
Beyond time
you faced
unknown lands
touching
the clouds of myth;
and you met the Cyclops
and you felt the messages
of Circe and Calypso
and the Sirens you heard
the temptresses.
To these beings,
the unnatural monsters,*

you gave forms
– beauty and ugliness –
depending on the horrible passion
that our nature tyrannises.
Into a dream you turned life
with demigods and heroes
and seeped into the cloudy myth
the fate of the great genus.

(Unpublished)

    In the timeless field of its existence, the Word became time and with its centuries its own self imprinted. And through its form and soul, *in all the land* painting, it spread the miracle of the race, the miracle of the world; the one that God predestined to represent the cultures, the roots of all races, His own roots, which ageless remain.

    Through the *eyes* of the human *soul*, God chose Homer, giving him the inspiration through the infinite power of His Spirit to reveal the mysteries of His creation, shaping *demonic creatures, otherworldly, forms universal, global*, titanic, human, unprecedented lives, on the unknown to lean their unbearable monstrosity. *Beauty and ugliness* this *passion that tyrannises* the *nature* of the world, the nature of God, the poet's nature, of time the existence and non-existence, for the realisation of the beyond. And only Homer, the father of poetry, could seduce the divine-human passion, amusing it, comforting it on its drama, shaping and in its fate presenting *Hades*, the *heroes* and *demigods* like the only ones capable of saving it from Circe's transformations and Calypso's enchanting entreaties, which more so resemble the seductive song of the Sirens. This seduced and still seduces the *unnatural monsters*, making them fight from their other outer-world dimension against the dream of life, which in the *cloudy myth* the vision of the *great genus* seeps.

Song of the Sirens, the enchanting song of nature, intoxicating drink of life, transcendent divine drink, for which the very soul of God thirsts, tasting it through the passion of breath, giving humans the potential to participate with all their senses, inhaling to the depths of their earthly bodies, but also exhaling the height and depth of their infinite divine self. This song, the poet tells us, Homer chose to praise the greatness of the creator. It is his other self, which in his transformations enjoys enticing the man-Odysseus, who, tied to the boat's mast, explores the esoteric mysteries of his captivating female Word, that which implores his male power to succumb to the grace of glory.

The ultimate master of poets knows the mysteries of the mind, the power of his female substance and the vigour of his male volition. And with these qualifications, privileges granted to him by the divine powers, selecting him as the timeless poet with the ability to receive and convey their messages, like the great ruler of heaven and earth, of their body and spirit, as high priest of the temple they have appointed him into the mystery of their own lives to initiate them. And Homer is his name! Homer – a cycle of his own centre, centre of the universal mind, who throughout the eternity of his eternities his ordeal to the periphery transmits and worthy is he proven, worthy leader of his creatures, of his divine teratology the twelve-labour legend.

The arithmosofical analysis of the word Homer gives us the number twelve[1], which we find in the twelve gods

---

[1] The arithmosophical analysis applies to the Greek writing of the name Homer, «Ομηρος».

of Olympus, the twelve labours of Hercules, the twelve disciples of Jesus Christ and elsewhere. Thus, with this reference it can be concluded that Homer, as a timeless symbolism, is ahead of times and is the beginning and the end, the megacycle, a time which contains the smaller circles of the cosmic chain, the centre of the highest philosophical and literary insight, a source from which poetry springs, the spirit of creation in all fields and subfields of its manifestations.

A hostage[2] of chaos is creation, hostages of themselves are humans, oppressed by their dreams, by their aspirations tormented. Countless are the procedures of evolution for their perfection, the completion of their entity, procedures which take place during the processing of the megacosmic work, which is none other than the work of the self.

This, the one, the only self is that externalises its universe to vastness, in order to amplify its existence, seeking confirmation, the vindication of its decision for projection. And the only one that can justify it is its own higher self, which pushed it, urged it to project its being and with its inspiration to create the world, having the complete responsibility for the consequences of this very act, after seeking to live a dream, the phantasmagoria of which is in need of the fulfilled poet for its conscious outcome. Its creations, its gods, demigods and heroes, the accomplishments of the chimera express the deeper meaning of the purpose of their existence, which justifies the paramount decision to investigate the nature of the mind, which, as long as it stayed in its state of non-manifestation, in a non-consciousness remained and its being sought to become aware by encountering its own chaos.

---

[2] The Greek word for hostage is «όμηρος», the same as the name for Homer.

So began the descent, the wandering of the mind and the ascent to return to itself, to its essence, the Monad. This is analysed in the twelve-labour myth, which the poet seeps into the cloudy mind of the fate of the *great genus*, of the great humanity, a universality that all beings and *unnatural monsters* contains. Their forms received beauty and ugliness from fate and fate determined that their horrible passion would *tyrannize our nature, dream of life*, which the Poet fashioned with *demigods and heroes*, eternal people.

EKTOR KAKNVATOS

HIS VOICE
(excerpt)

Touching seabirds and
northerly balconies   my shadow declared itself
soundless   and because of its trot upon
the water   or upon dead shale
it is that the winds raised their banners   that
with flutes I revoke you   that
non-existent is the immaculate conception of the word
that the rain collapsed to a rag
because as spoils they took its bow
Thus I scattered the darkness with the
wheels left and right as the axle broke
and of asking you as a bunker
to ask you not to speak but to writhe
on stretchers even the sidewalks
they carry...
... yet I insist: as a vestment I wear your
eyes   only-begotten I am appointed by the opal ruler
of your throat;   that therefore is
how it is to love you

(In perpetuum)

Eternal dream, the world's distant journey to infinity, weighings where the chimera its shadow confines, an unvoiced music on the standing trot of the waters, an illusion within its emotional world perpetuated. A conception of a completely free initiative, for the world to experience through the spirits of the winds its nature, such as time in its banners records it. Dead is the shale and for its resurrection the flutes, the magical instruments of the Word, the *immaculate conception* revoke. And the *rain, a rag* that has collapsed, seeks its *bow*, to target the restoration of the mind, with words playing in the Triodion[1], in the periods of major confessions, when the gates of the unconscious open, for balance to come to life's work.

The axle of the carriage of darkness brakes, with the ancient *wheels left and right,* and the questions seek the definitive meaning of times, which are withdrawn, writhing as *on stretchers even the sidewalks they carry,* where thousands of people are sick and as sleepwalkers walk. Awakened among the asleep, the poet, as *vestment the eyes* of consciousness he wears, *only-begotten* the truth *appoints* him. In the centre of the throat, the centre of knowledge, is the revelation of the nature of love.

The imperative procedures of the spirit against the chimera are those dictating the need for linguistic cleansing, and poetry, making use of semiology, reveals the underlying concepts with eternal symbols such as seabirds, the shale, the banners, the flutes, the spoils, the bow, the wheels, the axle and all that constitute the universe's nature, which expresses the presence of the being, the existence of existences, the maximum life. This is the poet's disquisition, who, as holder of the Word, has the ability to rebaptise the concepts, synthesising the nouns with adjectives, the trivial with the important, the heavenly with the earthly.

The northerly balconies are the observatories from which

---

[1] The Triodion also called the Lenten Triodion is the liturgical book used by the Eastern Orthodox Church. The book contains the propers for the fasting period preceding Easter and for the weeks leading up to the fast.

the mind is capable of supervising the ever-flowing, where the shadows labour in vain for their establishment within the fluidity of the liquid element, which has seabirds as company – the large and small spirits of existence – to support it in the toil of its futility. Shale, ancient rock, the planet, by the winds fragmented, as they impose their sovereignty upon it and their banners they raise.

Non-existent is *the immaculate conception of the word*, as well as existent and the rain collapses upon the sphere, delivering its emotional fluidity, through the power of the mind to become the bow that with the arrow of its accuracy will scatter the darkness; for spells to be broken, to release the Word, to express the perfect language, to stop the writhing of humans, who out of ignorance, as substitutes of the pathway the sidewalks have appointed. There, humans collapse helpless, and the nurses-knowledge with the stretchers of compassion carry them, for the great initiation preparing them.

Life is a vision and every poet initiates the world to another dimension of the monumental dream. There humans are called upon to speak its own language, to apprentice in the esoteric fields of the self, to cover the distance separating them from their being, as time, dimensionless, upon the dimensions of their minds is projected, and, using symbols, the revelation of its own entity – their own entity – it seeks. This de-symbolisation is attempted by the timeless poet, penetrating the depths of semiologic interpretations, juxtaposing the petrified shapes of creation with the unformed essence. He provides humans with the initiative of free conception, because this is the only one that can lead to the truth, since its work is the union of humans with the entity, the field of the universal mind in which the universe apprentices.

The poet, *by touching* the *seabirds*, which symbolise the spirits of infinity, and upon the *northerly balconies* – the field of high intellect – defines as soundless the universal shadow, the personal human and planetary ego. Realising the futility of the emotional tide that gestates death, himself he surrenders entirely to the Word, the vestment of which he wears as the one aware of love and light, of the eternal living truth, which by the creator of the universe for the grace and glory of the human being is bestowed.

ANTONIS KALFAS

WOUNDINGS AND MEDICINES

6.

I will begin
eventually a bright dagger
deft stabs we will travel
strikes of couples that to you were unsolved
We will perish in the panic of unemployed seafarers
seeking the accuracy of the stupor
we will stay up all night with crystals and bloodstained handshakes
of people of toil in love

we will go astray because we loved the daughter
of the captain who died young
we will wet the exits upon the bright avenues
of your shoulderblade that is stabbed by a meagre matchstick
we will sow fingers in the abdomen of the ignorant
machines

but I will not return without defeated sailors
without memories of my journey I will not stay

I will not allow your memory not to have its bottle
my return not having consequences I will not accept.

That is why
I will eventually begin
a bright dagger

(From the unpublished compilation "Woundings and Medicines")
("Writing" magazine)

The start of thought, a *bright dagger* the poet's idea that deftly directs its stabs into the dreamy realms as flesh. And it becomes the deterrent, the stab placed on couples and brothers, a beneficial punishment that controls the unsolved human relations. Humans, by the panic caused by the remorse of their false life, are forced to flee and resort in stupor to stay up all night. They fall in love with the toil of bloodstained handshakes and engage in a meaningless mutual confirmation of their chimeric self, lonesome existences wandering within the chaos of interdependence, attached to the earthly livelihood.

Man's eroticism strayed for the comely daughter. A captain himself, still young when to death he was sentenced. The exits get wet, becoming purified, the poet says, the *brilliant avenues* of the mind are dampened, for people to turn their back on the influences of the downwardly intoxication, to the stabbings of the burning match. A spirit resurrected is the becoming, sowing the radiances of the fingers to the depths of the abdomen of the mindless, awkward beings.

A conscious conqueror, a hero of the land and sea is the poet, refusing to return with the sailors undefeated from the redemptive death – the parts of his own self. He carries along his partners who were consolidated with the spirit, with his entity and became the memories of the consequences of his actions, those of the man who bears the responsibility of the entire world. A cause with no substantial result the hero does not deign, this one, to exist, because he is the road that leads to the redemption of his universal self.

The poet unites his spirit with the spirit of Christ and following Him he treads on the road of the chain until it is perfected. He preaches the ontological relationship and on the human one places the knife, to cut those ties of the personality which, ignoring God, the soul keep tied to the abyss. This knife is the *bright dagger*, the sharp challenge travelling with accuracy, solving the unsolved causes of the misfortune of the *lonesome couples*, the disoriented from their destination, which is: "The two to become one flesh."

People, amid their toil, in love with their inverted divine self, crystallise their spirit, and the *handshakes, the bloodstained*, seeking to feel the lost love, *the* astray *daughter of the captain*-mind, the sun that sank into the depths of their unconscious being. Only with the tears created by the sacrifice of the heart and symbolising the externalisation of emotion, the crying of the recovered pain, the *bright highways* of the shoulderblade may get wet, to be purified. The shoulderblade symbolises the rib of the being from which its female existence was formed, which sought the exit, its differentiation from the male.

Because of this separation both sexes are stabbed by the match, their meagre spirit, the poet says, the spirit of the wine, as by the downwardly pleasures they become intoxicated, entangled in the processes of the unconscious field that is located in the abdomen, where the spiritual energies are not assimilated. And the five fingers – symbolising the mind – must be sowed, for knowledge to be gestated, to be born, to be grounded; for humans to be redeemed, to unify their aspects, to recreate the hermaphrodite, the captain-mind to ascend, as a sun rising in its kingdom, and ascending from the fields of the heart, to restore the visions of a love astray.

The human being has succumbed to its toil's need, to the stupor's antics, to its despair's panic. Lost in the power of its sensual pleasures, to the deception of the dark forces it obeyed. The knowledge of the ontological ego it appropriated and became self-limited, trapped within the dead end of its soul and form. Polarised it became in the relations of its demonic aspects, projections which delimited the territory of its kingdom, to oppress its own self and be oppressed by it, having death as ally and enemy, friend and brother, father and mother, unique substitute of its creator. It questioned

His commandments, and by making the comparison between Him and itself, it separated the form from the essence, the Word from the sound, the sky from the earth, the knowledge from ignorance, good from evil, human from God, man from woman, the creation from its creator.

Unrestrained is the calculation, as individual egoism on the periphery of its divine being it became stranded and of its outcry the reproach it wore. It falsified the importance of truth and was forgotten, an unemployed seafarer in the artificial ports of its soul and heart. And its mind, a resourceful human, an insurgent who recovered, a mystic, a trophied winner, who accepted losing its companions, fully assuming the consequences of its actions, returns holding the *bright dagger* that the poet gifted it. Ready to start again its luminous journey into the dark realms of flight, where memory in its bottle its own demonic spirit retains.

GIORGOS K. KARAVASILIS

THE SECRET ROOMS OF THE TOWER

With the certainty that eventually you will separate us, death,
Drily we cough in the night,
Nervously we move the pillows,
Our gaze on a dazed strip of light stagnates,
Silence licks the wall.
In this chamber we travel and keep on travelling,
Prey of a storm that never caught up with us.
In its landscapes our roots suffocate.
And time became rigid on our faces.
So it is time to put out the summer of peace,
Again to reveal the wounds
On bodies that search for their shadow or they found it.
So it is time to move to other journeys,
In veins new shivers to spill.
And if necessary, ablaze with wounds
In the storm's peak to open
This chamber's window,
Virgin times of our other lifetime
To reside
In the secret rooms of the tower.

(Blood culture)

When the poet speaks, all can understand him. He knows very well what he is saying and to whom it is addressed. He speaks to our death, to our human self he refers to. His Word is the anatomy of death. Deep are the incisions which reveal the infinite eternity of life, as it springs up, arising from the limited eternity of death.

Necessary are the mental processes inducing a cough in the throat, the centre of knowledge. In order to find where their head to lay, humans nervously move the pillows, trying in this way their ideas to classify, the chaos of their mind to settle. Humans, deluded by the erroneous knowledge of the supposedly superior forces of death, to its idea are subjected, auto-suggested by it, and their gaze, devoid of discrimination, a mere strip of light, in the contemplation of the landscape of their inner being stagnates. Fearful silence, licking the impenetrable wall by which the multi-tier tower is built, with dark and bright chambers, halls where the knowledge of immortal life is taught.

With a *chamber* the hall of ignorance is symbolised and another one for wisdom, halls in the chamber of the main mind, in which the sun perpetually to infinity travels; and the creatures, strange creations, the human one unique among them, fruits of the earthly sphere, unique itself, eager to reach its own completion. Hunted by the cosmic storm to alienate it, but it does not reach it, the poet says, and its prey only in its dream exist. A dream trying to overcome that of earth, the dream of the storm, a dream of death's limited eternity, that with immortality it has the nerve to compete.

The roots of the family tree of life *suffocate in the landscapes* where it has chosen to take root and to exist. Death the roots and rootlets absorb, the leaves become rigid. Upon faces surprise is expressed, a resolutive question that brings the awakening, the awareness of the form's effacement, which is nourished by *the summer of* fictitious *peace*, which completely forgets the wounds, whose cause flows within the body's veins, forcing them to seek their shadow. And after finding it, to move, for other journeys through the same veins to start again, asking *to spill new shivers* into them, new spirits. If necessary – and it is always necessary – ablaze the bodies from the wounds of the unified body, in the *storm's peak* to open – and they do so – the cosmic hall's window. For the *virgin times* of this lifetime and of all other lifetimes to enter and dwell in the secret fields of the mind, a mind that to a tower is likened by the poet, in the *secret rooms* of which take place the mysteries of existence, where death seeks redemption, its ascent from its inevitable fall.

The *shivers* penetrate the *veins*, the blood stirs up, it becomes inflamed. The ideas become inflamed and excited, all bodies glow red hot. They are the spirit's fires of desire which perpetuate the wounds. Thought deepens, chaos is embraced, and the world ablaze of its own wounds is healed, reborn, and enters the chambers of knowledge, because in the other ones of ignorance, of darkness, it has already apprenticed and thus becomes the holder of the shinning truth.

All *times, virgin* in nature, timelessly into the human being converge, in its cells to reside, within its physical and spiritual body. There, together they constitute its being. In its flow, the flow of the spirit, everyday life they express, on war and peace they prey, on hatred and love, and bliss is always generated by the endless processes of this eternal struggle. On the fruits of its epic the mind preys, on experiences and knowledge, to take them on the journey to other currents, moving the universe to another universe, also brightly lit by the wounds it opened on itself, seeking the *storm's peak*, that which emits the essence of meanings with which heroes, poets, occupy themselves.

Thought, emotion, life itself from life is suffocated, by its own glory. And a new face it seeks, as the faces it has worn in the past have gone rigid from the cares of the soul and the passions of the form, during nature's constant journeys through time that does not stop. Because, just like a human, a restless explorer, incessantly it agonises, alternating the fields of its existence in search of its own ending. There converge the energies and forces of the soul, the soul of the universe, of life that does not compromise and with its current dissolves the *dazed light* which *stagnates*, the fearful silence that appropriates the active friction, which into storm transforms and constantly travels, running behind the preys, never catching up with them. Because this is the storm of externalisation, an exhalation suffocating in the depths of its being, and, recognising its futility, an unconditional surrender it has accepted, its return to the innermost of the temple of the divine body, where the exhalation is simultaneous to the inhalation, the idea with the essence of life, life with its contents, alignment with the mysteries of its virginity within *the secret rooms* of the universal world.

GIANNIS KARAVIDAS

THE OTHER SUN
(excerpts)

By the courtyard's fence
with your silent tears dripping down your smile
you awaited me
me, who embodied your reason
your affection
your worries
But the sign
sowed by the comings
in the dusty womb of distance
a stranger's form often it took
And you, already in your hands having the slain
cockerel as a greeting
did not know
if the droplets which the stones dyed red
were from that strident throat of dawn
or from your heart.

* * *

You awaited me
You awaited me one summer
You awaited me one lifetime
mother...
Later
without seeing me
you shut your eyes
forever

To be able to expect
and to be sure
that I will come.

* * *

Every voice
is your voice
before being heard as the voice of another

Every step
firstly will be heard as yours
and then as a stranger's one

Every day by the window
with your own eyes
inside me sees

You exist within your death
as the sun within the night.

* * *

When I look at your picture
in space
there is no space

Your soul into dimensions does not fit

When I look at your picture
in time
there is no time

On your grave you hold it, lifeless

It cannot hurt you any more
It cannot age you any more
It cannot deaden you any more

By your death it has been deadened.

(The other sun)

Tormented soul, tormented life the mother-woman, the eternal longing. Embodying her reasons, her *affection*, her *worries*, and, estranged in time, within the distances elapsing to the coming of the son, various forms she takes and constantly changes, taking on the dimensions of the mother-earth.

She is and remains a sacred image, an essence of divine presence, the immaculate, bloodthirsty high priestess, to the sacrifices made to liberate the animal forms of her male nature, mystic rituals, dedicated to the welcoming of the return of her initiatory births. And these are the animal forms seeking, within her *dusty womb*, to deliver the *strident throat* of their magic spirit, symbolized by the rooster, the king-cock of dawn and of her heart, to be impregnated by the euphoria of the ascendant womb of her boundless love.

There, by the *courtyard's fence*, the stones are dyed red by the droplets of her blood and her *silent tears drip* down *her smile*, as she awaits the new embodiment of her cravings with the sign of the sky, which forebodes the endless summers of life. Mother of all, she who does not need to see, because she is confident of her new cosmogony, as her endurance is beyond time. That is why she is confident of the eternal, which in her perfection comes, to be redeemed.

She closes her eyes to time. Her endurance, that of another lifetime. *Every voice* is her own voice, before her female word is *heard as the voice of another* of her forms. And her every step is firstly her own and then *as a stranger's* step sounds.

The days, freely flowing into the timeless, with her own eyes see her creation. Inside her death she resides, as the sleepless sun in the vastness of the night, where *there is no space*, where dimensions are dissolved and her picture does not encompass her dimensionless soul. Time is nonexistent within the depiction of cosmic glamor. She holds it on her *grave, lifeless*, and it *cannot hurt* her *any more*, because she is invulnerable. It *cannot age* her *any more*, as she is ageless, it *cannot deaden her any more*, she is immortal. Because, in the countless births and deaths constituting the chain of her being, her death countless times her time has killed.

Time is alive and reigns within the darkness of the unspiritualized whole and the mother giving birth to it is the one which condemns it of its sins, her sins, as it seeks to be incarnated and become the oppressor of her fundamental existence. As her glorious offspring, it boasts of her expectations, while she admires it. Its redemption it seeks, ignorant, insisting on keeping her entrapped within its form by preserving of her own form; a monster which into a jubilant child transforms, returning from his wanderings in the vastness, to dominate the love arising from the heart, the eternal womb of her nature.

Higher than the life-giving mother is none other, to accept him. That is why he praises her, he sings of her, he creates poetry and Word for her, losing his limits in the quest and keeps her alive within his memories, within the shapes of the *courtyard's fence*. There, God portrays the human, there he believes that his mother awaits him, with her *silent tears dripping down* her *smile*, as he knows that her reason and affection he embodies in all expressions of his existential worry.

A sign of her tragic fate the advents, which, in her *dusty womb*, the estrangement sow. This is the meaning of the slaughtered cockerel: the perpetual sacrifice propitiating her nature. That is how the mother wishes to greet her son. But he refuses to return, he cannot stand the confrontation, because he knows deep down that the *slain cockerel* is in fact himself, his glory, his life's achievements. He does not want to return to the essence which projected him. The distances dominating him are the excuse for the long delay, and he lingers on the other voice, following the stranger's footsteps, knowing that she looks at him every day with her own eyes, because she, the one mother who is all, is the sun of his death, of her death.

The greatest initiation, redemptive, is death, and in her picture it seeks the space where she, as eternal life exists. And the *space does not exist*. Because the soul *does not fit*, neither *in dimensions nor in time*, since time is deadened and the mother stubbornly holds it in her grave.

As eternal the poet sees her. She is beyond pain, beyond old age, beyond death. The deadening of death is her great achievement, the redeeming. Whatever is gestated and born into existence, dies, but she dominates her deaths. She keeps them subservient to her power, deadened by her own immortal self. An initiator indigenous of her creation, she dominates the generative authority which created her, the spaceless space, the timeless time... And her earthly grave is but the dwelling place of her deceased dreams, the conceptual ideas of her being, awaiting the acceptance of infinity's emptiness.

This is *the other sun*, the simple everyday person, the son of the noble mother, who lives to love her. And she, a timeless day, suppliant of the ineffable God, takes care of him in his advances, the earthly and the heavenly, rekindling his memories, so that he remembers her, so that he recognizes her true nature, her divine glory.

OLYMPIA KARAGIORGA

THE VOICE

Suddenly,
The Voice cracked the glass skies of our life.

In its wake, it touched a roof
Somewhere, high above
Forgotten, (unwittingly forgotten).
Inside, the young woman
Lifted her untied hair from the gray time of the room
The gray love of poverty,
Fear she folded into the palms of the child
Which was slowly born in her enamored innards,
And surrendered herself to the path of the Voice.

The Voice fluttered,
Immaculate light of the dove
In a morning church.

On the laced altar
The well-ironed, the proper,
The Red Drop was spilled
Which waited, hovering.
The Red Drop of a God's flood
Which they say was
Lonely
So lonely
Always so very lonely.
And the blood spread, spread, spread

A lake it opened, recumbent on the sunset
Full of pure grief
For some benevolent fishing-boats
And some uninhabited glances.

And the Voice set sail,
A flag was raised, joyful
In the hasty square of people.

It saw the paper boy in the corner
And calmed down and went silent.
The girl cleaning the windows of the strangers' house,
The girl with the silent, long braids
She stopped, looked at the Voice through the glass
And smiled.
The boy in the corner,
Grabbed the smile
Before falling and getting dirty
Before falling and perishing
(So much dust)
He wore it as an amulet on his hoarse chest,
And continued dreaming.

The others? The many?

They did not even hear the Voice,
Only something akin to a distant hum
As an infant's lullaby
Blurry in the dim candlelight
Of a woman who was young
And had children
And stared at the sky, the entire sky –
So that the baby has blue eyes once born

(Really, what was that song called?)

(The loudspeakers)

Crystal palaces, glass skies, our life's buildings, false structures, wherein the forgotten man, the unappreciated wife and the missing child reside. Poverty *the gray love* enfolds within their innards, where the miserable love is slowly born; to grow, to increase its pain in the *gray time of the room* of desires and torture, which the startling of the great, liberating Voice expect. To come and crack *the glass skies*, touching somewhere high above, the skulls, sacred rooftops which cover the male and female reflection, an archangelic hermaphrodite force, to let its hair blow in time, to spread its light, to send its aura's radiance to follow the Word, surrendering to its path. A sacred Voice, and, in its morning fluttering, the tormented night of ignorance communes.

A sacrifice is the fear *upon the laced altar, the well-ironed, the proper*. A *Red Drop*, a desire which, hovering, waited to be spilled, a theanthropic loneliness, to inundate the world. Love of blood the atonement, a *recumbent lake* which purifies the sunset, a heavenly benevolence, inner *grief, pure*, lucid, which, with its carriers – *the benevolent fishing-boats* – travels, waving its joyful banners that as a greeting rise in the *hasty square of people* at the sound of the blessed Voice.

Ephemeral is the pain, the anguish, the death. Prudence calms down and becomes silent, complacent, it becomes *the girl with the silent, long braids*, that, from the window of *the stranger's house*, stares at *the boy in the corner* and offers him her *smile*, to keep *as an amulet* of his dreams, a *song*. To heal *the hoarse chest, before falling*, before *getting dirty*, before becoming *lost* in so much dust, where *the others, the many*, have fallen, and hear the Voice as something estranged, as a mysterious *distant hum*, an infant's cry, that becomes a lullaby, a sun which resembles a *dim candlelight*. A desolate womb the Voice which uncontrollably gives birth to children, to the heaven's hope, from its births the Word to grow, to become a man, to have *blue eyes*, a song, immortality to initiate and from it to be initiated.

A mortal daughter is birth, a concubine of death, a priestess of the form, an enslaved aspect, to the glamor of her seduction she is subjected. In her ivory towers she resides. There, her dream sets and rises, an imaginative colorfulness, to comfort her darkness and enrich her misery in her deliberate impoverishment, where, forgotten within her gray ignorance, she has chosen to dwell.

The soul falls in love with the Monad. Its appeal resists the deadly prison and to the Voice of its conscience surrenders, in the inner womb of its heart, to give birth to the fulfilled poet. An hermaphrodite angel, a deliverer, who, with his sword the heaven of crystallization will crack, to tear down the building, to discolor the dream, to empty time, to transform poverty into a wealth of spirit, to redeem the *enamored innards*.

The *palms* of the divine *child* shall let the fears fly, and transform, winged cherubs to become, the bright ideas of the universe; the sacred ritual of the immaculate dove to attend, where time communes in the field of its unmanifested being, instilling its sacred *blood*, to fulfill the Scripture, so that its loneliness acquires meaning in the temple's retreat. There, in the Holy Altar, the priest of silence appeases the cosmic passion, transmuting it into the knowledge of the spirit which imparts its possession, an immaculate essence, of blood the substance, holy life.

A *lake recumbent* is the need of deification, contemplating the sunset in its sorrows, bloodied sea where the benevolent bodies, which by fishing-boats are symbolized, seek the emptiness of their glances, in their immaculate nature to indulge. The Word sets sail, directing the fleet of its spirits to eternity's calling, present in this *hasty square of people* – the field of mental alertness. The flag of the fulfilled personality is raised, obedient to the teachings of the christic supervision.

Ephemeral are humans' works, as their infantilism abstains from the spirit and with the suffering's punishment they occupy themselves. The study becomes aware, complacent. The observer is honored. A holy Voice dominates, the silent moments, the ceaseless needs. And these, obedient, amid the transparency of the mind, in the harmony of their nature are arranged. The sayings smile, the benevolent, girlish joys. In its virginity, nature is of the dark spirits the humanization.

Heed, He who by Thy sovereignty has the armies of the soul's silent forces, He who has as shelter the mind of Your creation, amulet of the heart, of Your blue eyes the light, of the Son the immaculate spirit, of bodies Your body. Heed, as You, of Your jurisdiction the benevolent, within the recycling of Your manifestation, a presence of Your immaculate nature, as infinite in the might of Your existence You oversee, of Your kingdom the Creator.

DIMITRIS I. KARAMVALIS

TONIGHT I WILL CROSS THE RIVER

Tonight
I will cross the river
wetting my folded flag
long before the changing of the guards
long before the dogs of night gallop.

It's been long since my loves
dismounted.
But the opposite bank
has sent me a message
of its caves;
and I, the recluse,
very much want to cease
to fortify my unfortified summers
the snake of death to trample!

Tonight
I will cross the river
wearing something of my childhood clothes
which I have religiously kept so long
the white little shirt
of my Sunday church,
the blue short pants
from the parade
and the cap

with the wind's sayings.
And so, when I dress, with a slow tempo,
my tired steps I shall move
to receive communion of the wine
which, unwatered, all these years awaits
in the catacombs
and in my early textbooks!

Tonight
I will cross the river
holding tight in the deposits of my lips
the swallows swording in your kisses;

and, into the eyes dragging the spoils
of my old campaigns,
the extinguished lamp of my desolate soul
I shall take,
a fire to light, to burn myself and illustrate
on a small mosaic
your adored form!

("AIOLIKA GRAMMATA" magazine, issue 127)

A river of love and light, with its power separates and unifies the fields of the universe, keeping the uninitiated worlds in isolation. A guardian angel it is, flowing within the entity's being, the very soul and intellect of God, the encouragement of instincts, a necessary exhortation of the spirit for the conquest of infinity, the cosmic destination of controlled cognitive functions.

Great is the reflection of the poet for the sake of people. A ferryman of cosmic forces, he wets his *folded flag*, and, *before the changing of the guards* of the unconscious and the howls of the night dogs are heard, he crosses to the other side and returns again to the point where the loves of the world had dismounted. The message from the other side reaches that point, following him. It is the conscious Word that comes from the caves and advises him to stop and check his direction, in order to *fortify* his *unfortified summers* – the acquired, unguarded knowledge – to subjugate the *snake of death*, so that the force of life can be brought under control.

The flag is the symbol of personality which must be completed. It must get wet, purified in the sacred river, before the *changing of the guards*, who, like Cerberus, *dogs of night*, guard the gate of the abyss, preventing the unprepared from passing through it, thus shielding them from the risk of passing from where they cannot return. Because the gallop of their own sufferings, caused by the uncontrolled instinctive life, will preclude their return to the light of knowledge. That is why the initiated poet places the immature loves, which personify the attachments, to dismount before the *recluse goes across*. And, protecting his soul with the fortified summers, he places under his dominance the snake of life and death, the soul's force of the universal world.

This force is symbolized by the children's clothes, *a white shirt* and *blue short pants*, through which the poet offers a sense of the Greek flag with the white color of the waves, symbolizing purity, and the blue of the sky and sea – the force of the mind. An identity of the ontological existence, which he devoutly keeps within his mind and heart, as he takes part in the timeless parade of the cosmic congregation, wearing the uniform and *cap with the sayings of the wind* – of wisdom's eternal spirit. All of nature is thus dressed and heads towards glory, towards knowledge, with a *slow tempo*, harmonious.

The cap bears the image of an owl, a symbol of wisdom, which, through the education received by the poet and which our entire nation has received and continues to receive, as its tired footsteps, through the course of millennia, having the entity as its spiritual leader, lead it to the catacombs, where it partakes of the *unwatered wine*. There, the spirit of the race's teachers cloisters with the repositories of knowledge, that which is also kept within the *early textbooks*.

The poet keeps within the Word's deposits, symbolized by the mouth's lips, the swallows, which foreshadow the spring, while swording the air, to cause vibrations which bring the embraces that will lead to union with life. Within his *eyes* he bears the *spoils* which the soul of the race obtained from its *old*, spiritual *campaigns*. This is his beloved. And he proceeds to light the *extinguished lamp*, as a torchbearer of the entity which the darkness of the wilderness burns. Illuminated is the mind and a *mosaic* is formed on a universal miniature, the *adored form* of holiness, of spirit the essence and beauty.

Initiation the poet offers, for the Greek race to recognize its power and its beauty – its knowledge of the truth. A truth that is ahead of times, flowing like the *river* which brings renewal, rebirth of the spirit, as the poet crosses it, leading the world to the opposite – of ignorance – bank, from darkness to light, from the desert to the soul's euphoria, to bliss. There, love and light lead, as the wet blue-and-white flag with the Holy Cross unfolds, bearing the sayings of the winds, the precepts of wisdom, guiding earth and heaven to the Greek spirit's glory, to liberating knowledge.

The wet flag also symbolizes spirituality which unites the race, to overcome the sufferings caused by the instincts, the *dogs of night*. Forces that lead to romance, to vain love-affairs, which must dismount from the uncontrolled flow, to pass onto the *opposite bank*, with the *caves*, the hearts of the holy hermits, the Fathers of the race, wise masters, who, with their love, protect and guide it. These caves are the hearts of all people, with power flowing through their bodies, whose magnetic fluids separate good from bad, evil from agatho[1], darkness from light, ignorance from knowledge, body from spirit, heaven from earth.

This river, which the poet crosses dominating his power, must also be crossed by the human being, to pass on to the balance which brings the unification of the forces and to become the conscious recluse. As a child to pass and to wear the agatho[1] and the strength of the mind, as a mature man to partake in the congregation and the glorious parade of the universal world, communing in the Immaculate Sacraments of his fiery divine soul, which it, too, is delivered to the divine fire, to be portrayed as the unique mosaic of his perfected divine form.

---

[1] The term "agatho" out of the Greek word «αγαθό» is used to mean all that is beyond the duality of good and bad. It is the Entity, the Whole, the Monad.

DIMITRIS KARVOUNIS

WREATH OF DEATH

in memory of
Georgios D. Zografistos

In his eyes you could see
an empty nest.
In his eyes wandered
of his soul the shadow.
The flame in his light flickered
from the resignation's innermost unexpectedness
and in his footsteps he heard an inevitable breath
counting the vain days and nights
in the symbols of his palm.

Five plagues, the five senses are
in the dust of the irreversible road
embedded.

And in the light of Dawn, to be dressed he wished
by the loving hands
with the world's frost.
And the sun's light, he vowed not to see
if in his eyes, the worn will be baptized.

(Unpublished)

A person's drama the poet recounts. His eyes were the mirror of the soul, he tells us. In it, the idols nested, the illusions of the world. Even the sun was mirrored in him. *The shadow of his soul wandered* and he could see his own flame in his own light, the other, the inner, flickering, as he realized his *resignation's unexpectedness* coming from the soul's innermost parts. And, in his footsteps, he *heard* the unexpected breath of return, which the *vain days and nights* counted *in the symbols of his palm*.

The five senses, the five plagues of apostasy from his being, during the eternal night, remained *embedded inside the dust of the irreversible road*. And when the *light of Dawn* arrived, he performed the unique, magical, redemptive act. *He wished to be dressed by the loving hands with the world's frost*. The loving hands could be likened to archangelic wings, which symbolize the ethereal substance of humans, by the power of which, for the redemption of his world, the hero has agreed to be clothed in death. And he swore *the sun's light not to see, if,* through *his eyes* during his next projection *the worn* would be baptized.

Inspired is the poet's by a man's life and death, of the life and death of the universe he speaks to us. Even the deceased's surname is no coincidence. The poem, dedicated to the memory of Georgios D. Zografistos[1], represents the creation of the universe, which appears as if painted by the creator's hand upon the vast canvas of chaos. Painted is the human being in the vast landscape of its existence, starlit it travels through its deliberate night, the wanderer. As if it has agreed with the creator to be the resident of the nest, the emptiness of His eyes, His soul's shadow, the flame of every sun, flickering, the breath of God himself, which is heard in its footsteps and counts the *days and nights in the symbols of its palm*.

An oversized being, huge, unimaginable, of creation the monster, in its five plagues, symbolizing the field of the mind,

---

[1] "Zografistos" in Greek means "painted".

it counts with unbearable pain the accomplishments of its five senses, which want to remain *embedded in the dust of the irreversible*. And they wait as eternal speckles, after its passage to the beyond, its returning to the world of forms, to become the seeds that will give it the ability to be born again as a new universe.

Knowing of his cycle's drama, in the light of the eventual Dawn, where the great night meets the great day, the poet places his hero to make his wish. The folding of the wings symbolizes the movement made by the hands, hands divine, to embrace the body, as they encompass all the manifested being, which is likened to the *world's frost*. In withdrawal, the conscious man-God gives a promise to never see the light of the new sun again, if he allows *in his eyes the vain, the worn to be baptized*, which would mean the unnecessary repeat of the erroneous functions, to which in his prior existence he was subjected.

The universe's journey through void, the human's wandering in chaos. He is the simple, tormented man, the protagonist of life, the hero of the poem, and, in him, the history of the world we see, the poet tells us. His eyes empty, the empty eyes of God, are the nest where *the shadow of his soul* wanders and the flame of desire for a life full of passions and attachments flickers. These constitute his large or small ego, his good or bad will for the power or for the love that he has and shows for his own works. With these works, he tries to emulate his creator's works, filling with sorrow the soul from the torment to which he submits his personality, his form. Monstrous is his daily life, reflecting the teratogeny of creation, with which he becomes passionate, identifies himself, and therefore suffers.

Known are his cycles of evolution during his lifetime. A common man, mortal. Within his cosmic family he is born, in it he acts, its roles he assumes, his incomplete cycles he performs, he evolves, he ages and he dies. Innermost, unexpected is his resignation. At the unavoidable time, the exhalation from breathing departs, it withdraws and man is delivered to the other, the inner inhalation, by which the universe its manifested existence absorbs. It is the time of the great return of the time duration to the timeless, where the knowledge for the interpretation of symbols is acquired.

The five fingers of the hand represent the five fields of the mind, where the creation of the universe is recorded. It is read in the eyes of man – the eyes of God – through the heavenly bodies that constitute the creation and appear as birds making their turns, when beginning their journey in search of the meaning of their existence. They have left their souls hovering like a shadow, to remind the observer of their passing, which left its mark in chaos lingering in the space between existence and non-existence.

The flame of hope flickers from the innermost field of its own resignation from vain projection. The man grounds the "wantings" of his ego. A mystery of time is the road! He had placed his hopes on his senses, therein he had polarized life and embedded it along with his wounds. His bodies are impenetrable walls and his ideas the decoration of infinity. His feelings are countless recordings and their images are the frozen, elusive landscapes of his joy.

He wandered, he learned that he failed, he was embittered. In the *sun's light*, he experienced the shadows of volumes. A shadow himself, and larger is *the shadow of his soul*. Its indelible marks weighed him down, as the footsteps of his bodily pain kept him a slave to the "wantings" of the form. The needs of his life were multiplied. His most consistent, his most sincere teacher, the law of wear, the meaning of his nature's toil it taught him. And his loving hands, his magical wings, embraced his frigid world and he then became a future sun, ulterior, a distant promise to redeem all.

This is the destiny of man, the conclusive and irreversible. His tragedy is reflected in his eyes and these are the eyes of God, which in their void contain him, just like the void encompasses the universe and as every empty space on earth contains the beings and humans, so that the events of life evolve within him, forging his will and leading him to the realization that the final withdrawal brings his salvation. The human being is a universe, it traverses life, loaded with hopes, ideas and visions, symbolized by the suns and planets, which seek grounding upon the ineffable pedestal of infinity, which is also the field of the mind's holiness.

ZOI KARELLI

EURYDICE

You came to call me.
Of death you do not know,
the cruel, immobile presence.
So great is your love,
that, among the dead
you can stand, but,
a love of worldly pleasure does not suit me.
The frigid kiss of death I accepted,
a cruel and forthright opinion.
Part of existence is life,
and the one who knows of death
the concept forever will exist.
Powerful is the knowledge I acquired,
how can I forget it?
And if I follow you, I am non-existent
to living passion,
which brings you so close to me
at Hades' depths.
I stay away from you
because of death the separation
is so very perfect,
that no mortal, living
cannot learn of it.
Your sweet voice brings me
memories, lovely and precious.

Slowly almost, the terrible silence
of Hades is dissolved
from the exquisite, which you bring,
erotic message, song of life.
But vast is of death the broad
world, you cannot find me
as you desire me, you will be lost,
you, who live the lovely, ephemeral life.

I follow you, yet I know
of what awaits us. This is
the profound separation. You believe
in the subtle shadow following you.
Oh, my love desires you,
but it is different,
tried by death,
defeated is the warm, tender passion
that you seek to find.
Why do you wish to hold me in an embrace,
I do not fit.

I know I will lose you
despite approaching you.
The dead, this cruel gift
hold.

The ecstasy of the moment does not hold me.
For myself, your love I seek
beyond the material presence,
in the vague, incredible meaning of the eternal.

(The Poems of Zoi Karelli)

The hope withdrawn from futile life, initiated to death, speaks, about the meaning of its mystical existence, about the truth of the one whose realm throughout centuries prevails, having chosen the awakening of those who were trapped in the deep dreams of human creation, because they rejected the vision of the one and only visionary. And, through the very mouth of this death comes the revelation, the one which in the Book of the Dead with fiery letters has been recorded.

A love of worldly pleasure does not suit me. Oh, you, love, *who among the dead can stand* and does *not know of death's cruel, immobile presence*; you came to call me. I am *the life* which *the frigid kiss of death* has accepted. An *opinion cruel and forthright* my own choice is, an integral part of eternity, an existence which wanted to apprentice, to learn about its miracle. Knowledge which cannot be forgotten, eternal initiation, immeasurable depth of the non-existence of passion, which, seemingly existent, brings its dream closer, in my perfection to be redeemed.

I am your need, and, the closer it brings you to me, the more I move away, calling you to my essential depth. *No mortal has known me, because only I know of my obituary's mysteries*, wedded as *death to life* and as *life* to its own *death*. An idea of inconceivable inspiration, that only I possess, in order to exist, to play with my own self, to fall in love as if alive and as if dead to be drawn to the sweetness of my erotic voice, that which I left on the other side, before descending to the depths of my fulfilled existence.

From where I am, I can reign over the eras, I can return through my broadness, not as what I was before accepting to die, but as the *vast death*, whose *terrible silence*, with the exquisiteness brought by your voice, the illusions dissolves. And your song, my own erotic song, a supreme message, makes me lose myself, more and more, as the life the *lovely, the ephemeral*. And I have the power to follow you, knowing what awaits us, what awaits you. A profound separation of the shadow from form and of form from its shadow.

I take the desire from form, in order to birth its love for my own, *different life*, the one *tried by death. Defeated is the warm, tender passion* that seeks to find me, to hold me in its embrace, to learn that in it, I do not fit, and that I accept to lose so that I can win, proceeding to project the cruel charisma which all my dead selves retain. Those not *held by the ecstasy of the moment*, seeking the love of the living beyond the binding material presence, from the defined to the indefinite, from the credible to the incredible, from the mortal to the eternal and from the eternal to the immortal, which, by its own death has been initiated.

The poet offers the other dimension of death, the concealed, that which is sanctified by its own horror, the voice of silence, whose teachings are heard from the one who, despite the desire for the glory of life, is ready to listen, to agree to sacrifice it; Orpheus, the mystic, who descends into Hades and passionately seeks Eurydice, desiring to have her body handed back to her; to embrace her and, bringing her into the world, to offer her *the ecstasy of the moment*. To learn that no one can come back from the realm of true death; that, from redemption, there is no point in being redeemed.

Death is the other aspect of life, the specific, the concrete, not of the abstract, the imaginary, the one immersed into dreams and oppressed by the ghosts of artificial joy. It is the redeemed ego which is aware of its autonomy, as it has withdrawn its aspects to the bottomless depth of its being. There, an ancient god is the one imposing his will onto eternity, to perpetuate the power of his truth. His being he recycles through the chaos of the human soul, until to him, all its forms it surrenders.

This is death and the simultaneous resurrection, the inner life, free from desire, from the desire of existence, the need to project its self, the need for externalization, which, to its pure nature is subjected, without ever being able to be truly lost. Of this death the poet speaks, the redeeming, whose knowledge whoever gains know that, if they wish to return, to follow the apparent life, they will be non-existent, because they will have acquired the power of not forgetting the only part of their being that is true.

The redeemed know that this intentional separation from phenomena is union, that renunciation is the stance and that the stance is eternity, that life is death and death is life. And this they teach, the deep separation, *the love that desires but is different,* because it is *tried by death* and knows how to lose by always projecting the *cruel gift* held by the dead, the initiated, those who death as a resurrection have accepted. And they are not carried away by the ecstasies of every carnal moment, but seek, as Christ, the complete *love, beyond the material presence, in the vague, incredible meaning of the eternal.*

NIKOS KAROUZOS

ORTHODOXY

Sweet the darkness is, in the images of the ancestors;
immaculate hands, partaking
clothes seized by serenity, and the wind they do not know,
deep is the mercy from the immaterial rocks,
the eyes, like fragrant fruits.
And the cantor, whole, ascends the plane-tree of the voice,
poor world,
the blue scent an incense, and silver is the smoke
wax, increasingly on the children dripping,
poor world,
as they come out – oh first joy – with the Gospel and the
candles
and then the great joy of accompanying the Holy.
Father Giannis, in his white chasuble wrapped,
a good father and a good grandfather with the sirocco on his beard,
years, centuries-old years and youth that beauty has.

(Sleeping bag)

On the world stage of religions, Orthodoxy, a brilliant sun among suns, illuminates the path, on which Holy Fathers marched and continue doing so. They support the world within the cosmic circles of ignorance in which humanity apprentices, waiting for the mercy, the grace of God for the forgiveness of sins accumulated by unrepentant centuries in order to dominate the ego of people and nations, who failed to grasp the meaning of Christ's teaching. A teaching which speaks about the power of love and leads the human being from the chasm of darkness to the mountains of spiritual light.

Orthodoxy, of your myriad saintly names, to the Word of the macrocosmic light, the supplications in your liturgies, a devotional glorification to God the all merciful.

Lord, of Your will the law, as a wreath of thorns on the human head is placed. Have *mercy* upon Your *immaterial rocks*, the eternal ancestral mountains of faith. *Hands partaking* rise to You and the blessing of Your grace receive. The empty mouths partake of light. Lord, *sweet is the darkness* in Your *images*. The heart's thirst in wine rejoices, and, finding greatness in Your immaculate body, the soul its aura increases, the sun's matutinal diadem, of Your mercy the priceless, spiritual treasure.

Serenity seized the holiest shape and the secret breath knows not of earth's wind. Fragrant are the fruits of Your wisdom, shining as the eyes of the soul. All-Seeing, a fully-grown plane-tree for You the psalm, the uplifting of earthly voice and, under Your eye, the world is saved. To the scent of heavens an incense is the salt of the land, and the benevolent smoke to Your divine nostrils rises. Burning candles are the bodies, dripping the wax of joy, and, Your world, within the Gospel of Your truth is perfected.

Your Archbishop is every humble priest, accompanied by angels, the white hour attired, the eternal beauty of Your image and likeness, of the supreme Father, of Your ancient youth he preaches. Oh, how much grace there is within the whiteness of his beard – Your beard! To this the faithful are initiated, and, in the alterations of the winds, their spirit is strengthened by the undisturbed peace of the Church's Holy Fathers, who, through their life, the truth of Your Word have proven. Orthodoxy the poet calls the wisdom of the world. It is the rise of Christians to the fall of atheists – of materialists. Nature is reborn, the heavens rejoice, and the spirits of eternity the Almighty praise.

Sweet the darkness is, in the images of our ancestors, immaculate hands partaking. In these verses, the darkness acquires substance. To light it is equaled, confessing of its sins the lust to God through the spirit of the saints. Spirits demonic repent, of Immaculate Sacraments the essence they commune and purified they become.

Clothes seized by serenity, and the wind they do not know, deep is the mercy from the immaterial rocks, the eyes, like fragrant fruits. Blessed are the believers, that the shape of serenity they have chosen, and, as immaterial rocks, to the winds of cosmic disturbances they are immune. Deep, is of the wise the supplication. Lord, have mercy upon us; God of forces. Fragrant are the fruits with the eyes' sweetness. To the spiritual fruits the poet refers to, those of the tree of eternal life, which the ascetic cultivates within the Orthodoxy's monastery, in the garden of the Virgin Mary, in the Church of all which with the *immaterial rocks* of its saintly bodies has been built.

And the cantor, whole, ascends the plane-tree of the voice, poor world. From there, from the life-giving fountain, symbolized by the plane-tree, warbling the water of life ascends, a hymnology of the prominent cantor, to quench the fever of the world's soul, which deification seeks, redemption from the chastisement of its weakness.

The blue scent an incense, and silver is the smoke, wax increasingly on the children dripping, poor world. In the liturgy, a sacred ritual, the passion of the burning land becomes an incense, with the entourage of stars. Of agatho[1] radiating, as *silver smoke*, its blue fragrance time smells, the heavenly aroma, the cos-

---

[1] The term "agatho" out of the Greek word «αγαθό» is used to mean all that is beyond the duality of good and bad. It is the Entity, the Whole, the Monad.

mic myrrh. Dripping are the burning bodies of the dedicated, symbolized with the candle, and, by God's blessing, the disciples are anointed to superior knowledge, to redeem you from the suffering, *poor world*!

As they come out – oh first joy – with the Gospel and the candles and then the great joy of accompanying the Holy. Oh, first joy, "who hung the earth upon the waters". *Great* is the *joy* of His Resurrection, with the candles, symbolizing the suns of the universe, accompanying the world's saintly paths. There, among them, a priest, *wrapped* in the *white chasuble, a good father*, the poet says, *and a good grandfather, with the sirocco* – the south-east wind – on his beard, a mystagogue, that the years, centuries and youth, he has as his companions. To demonstrate the power of the Holy Trinity, whose fiery expression dematerializes the world and passes it into its uncreated nature; the eternal, invisible, unique spiritual beauty.

This is the greatness of Orthodoxy, the human hope for the salvation of the world within the greatness of God. It triumphed through the Greek race, which, since ancient times, a divine will to battle pledged it, to express the wisdom of faith, alternating with the currents of other races, maintaining the essence of knowledge, an irremovable power, within the circumstances of insurmountable difficulties. Eternal the Greek spirit, it marched into the abyss and gave rise to time's blossom as a rose, a symbol of human perfection, radiating the light of Christ.

GIORGOS N. KARTER

IN VIVO

It concerns me
  the market
the writing
  the carrier wave
mercy my God
  my issue
my victim
  my myth
and I remember
  my posthumous

I, the animal-originating
  the infantry soldier
  as a poet
  who knows
  receiver or giver

(Endomisi)

In life, *the market concerns me*, the poet says. Therein he resides, there he exists. He is *the carrier wave*, the megacosmic issue of the becoming, his poetic writing. He is the great victim of his myth, carried through the sky and ground.

And he remembers; in his *posthumous state, an animal-orig-*

inating infantry soldier. And, as a poet, he wonders: *who knows, receiver or giver* is his Word? This is mainly what concerns him, his work in the market, his writing, with which he marches on. But what is the market and what is its quality? Apologetic, invocative is the verse: *Lord have mercy*.

The weight of centuries, upon the poets pins its hopes. From the field of the universal mind, as if by radio, the ideas, the carrier waves, within the timeless market as a universal request are broadcast, seeking to ground the megacosmic vision.

The writing tolls, the verse, more than its century weighs. This is the ultimate issue of the poet. A victim of victims himself and yet for his victim cares. He creates the myth, he reshapes it, throughout eternity he maintains it. Animal-originating, human as his is, a horseman, rider of winds, overlord of power, from his horse he dismounts, if necessary, and on foot he battles death. And in his posthumous existence, the past of the market he remembers and monitors its present, having the responsibility of the vision for its future. *The carrier wave*, the great contemplation. The quality of writing is the issue with which he occupies himself, within the manifestations of the myth of existence.

There are times when the Word glorifies his nature. From these the labors of spirit spring, and life is initiation that leads to bliss, an ontological right enshrining the works of people. In the market of ideas, the knowledge of life prevails, and wisdom is the everlasting rose of poetry, the specific knowledge that cares for the meaning of the writing. The myth is analyzed to its essence and nothing is concealed that cannot be revealed.

Dark days follow. In exile, the poet, and the days become centuries. The time of the market changes, *the carrier wave* of ignorance's miseries it becomes. Knowledge is lost, the treasure is forsaken. Poor in spirit, the remaining, sparrows deprived of wisdom. Forced to admit their defeat, their nakedness they seek to accept. Receiving the message of their soul, the poet takes the Word in his Word and exclaims: *Lord have mercy*. The great *issue* is their self. He is their victim, the poet. The posthumous, from knowledge born the infantry soldier, recollecting the past splendor of the entity.

Culture of cultures, times of times, centuries of centuries deepening into his being, and as a poet he wonders: *Who knows, receiver or giver*. Receiver of power, of will, of knowledge, of the revelation of fate, which, as an immortal appointed him, to create the terraces of his greatness, increasing the wealth of his spirit to the zenith of his universal Word. And, as a giver of nadir, an unsleeping guard in the depths of his extremes, to be *concerned with the market, the writing, the carrier wave*, his *issue*, his *victim*, his *myth*, and to remember his *posthumous*.

The poet dismounts. His steed is no longer Pegasus, whose power is perpetually expressed through the revelation of the mysteries of the mind's nature. In the rotations of time, when purpose requires it, on foot the poet battles the prosaicism itself, as his divine legacy is not recognized. And he awaits the answer to the question: *Who knows*, only as a receiver of the animal-originating flows of the carrier wave do they recognize him, or as a giver of knowledge of the divine, of the posthumous, of what the poet really is, as his spirit is immortal and on the market still remains?

CHRISTINA KARYDOGIANNI

ABSINTHE

Uninitiated I was, to revelations and miracles.
Signs and wonders
my idols did not attire
upon the canvas of my symbols.
The faithful representation of the world
in the paintbrush of the iris
ideas and desires it embroidered
with the colors of the heart
and of the mind the endless suffering.
Skeptical to your visioning
I taunted your unearthly
and unrealistic conscience.

My education was practical
other words it did not know
except those I had learned till now
and concepts I did not know how to translate
beyond my meager local limits.
By my ancestors' logic
I was distrustful of all that was hidden
and absurd.
In vain I tried to interpret
images and shapes
within the inaccessible arcades
of a transcendent gallery.

And the terrible moment of Revelation came.
Common sense is overturned.
Lucifers and demons
the world's strings pull.
– "And the third part of the waters became Absinthe..."
"and many people died...".
In anguish, I now try to decipher
the next quote and word
of "those which must come to pass"
"for the time is near".
And, in awe, I wonder:
– What mystical Scripture
what classified interpretation
all these centuries remained hiding
in the mystical word "absinthe"
in order to reveal to us
your timeless duration
in your hitherto unknown to us
and terrible in power
prophetic insight
with the foreign word CHERNOBYL.
In your "Revelation"
destitute, I reveal myself, John.

"Revelation of John, Chapter 8"

The meaning of the Russian word
"CHERNOBYL" is absinthe (wormwood)

(20th Century, The Twilight of Titan)

Uninitiated to revelations and miracles, the human being consciously avoids to attire the *signs and wonders*, which *on the canvas of symbols* are but a *faithful representation of the world*, as with the *paintbrush of the iris* they *embroider ideas and desires* – cravings and yearnings of the *heart* – with the colors of its choice. It perpetuates the *endless suffering* of the inferior mind, which remains skeptical to the divine visions of the prophets, and, as *unrealistic* and *unearthly*, it taunts their *conscience*.

Humans avoid delving into the fields of the prophets' knowledge, to the deep meaning of the Word, to make their wisdom their own vision, and take refuge in a vacant of inner meanings education, because they do not know words other than those they choose to use, after failing to translate *the concepts beyond the limits* of their shortsighted vision. With the limited, ancestral logic, they distrust *all that is hidden and* considered absurd, as in vain they try to interpret *images and shapes* tightly kept sealed by the mind in its esoteric fields, within the arcades inaccessible to the common human, within the transcendent gallery of the universe. This is their function, until, at times in their life, terrible moments of the timeless Revelation come.

Lucifer and demons pull the strings of the world, the poet says. To the revelation of Revelation the poet initiates the world. People die when feelings, symbolized by water, are poisoned by inferior thoughts. And the time comes for the results of the denial. The unconscious opens up, infernal energies and forces surge. *Signs and wonders*, the Luciferian, demonic works which the mystic Scriptures confirm. The *timeless duration* of the terrible power as a prophetic Word tolls for the initiates and they are offered the *esoteric interpretation*, which, to the uninitiated, classified remains in all eternity.

People are deprived of this knowledge because of lack of awe to the miracle perpetually taking place before their eyes; the miracle of existence, of the presence of the entity, as, perpetually in the transcendent, the divine mystery of its liturgy is revealed. This is none other than the function of the universal immaculate mind, the nature of things, through which Life's happenings emanate, as with His projections God likes to play, giving His creation the meaning of His diffused miracle, which people must decipher, to know their own mind, of ancient tradition, which *"Absinthe became the third part of the waters..."*, because, from its being, the universal mind was separated, denying the One from which it sprang.

The human egoistic mind, adhering to its Luciferian nature – the demonic – denies the sanctity of the Triune and becomes prey to its own choice, perpetuating its drama. This is the cursed world which must return to its creator, after being perfected and atoned. Within the human will lies the initiative for reunification. Timeless John, wanting to reveal the nature of the external mind, teaches humans by showing them the unconscious; to see it, to know it, to place it under control, to recognize its divine nature, so that it ceases its transformation into *signs and wonders*, the utopian, catastrophic projects which it undertakes, only to vindicate its opposition to its own creator.

The faithful representation of the world on the canvas of symbols is interpreted. They are the symbols of the mind. Humans paint them with *the colors of the heart*, giving them – deliberately – an otherworldly sense. They refuse to accept the earthly, worldly meaning, because they fear that the truth will force them to embrace their overpowering spiritual nature. This initiative they have taken, centuries now, when they were separated from the single homogeneous field of their existence, as the downward spiral of desires they preferred.

There were, in the distant past, mystics and saints, when the entity had trusted the human race and provided it with its direct support, by allowing the incarnation of angelic spirits. The freedom of will has existed and always exists, but humankind has appropriated this blessing. The angels who defended the jurisdiction of people were characterized as fallen, as they were dragged by the fall of humankind, and, upon the spiral's return, the upward evolution they did not wish to follow, remaining supporters of the earthly polarization and not of the union with the entity, selecting the individual subfields of the pure mind.

These subfields, through *symbols*, express the nature of their universality, the universality of humans which only externally they accept, and which, through its unique path of truth, of the spirit's verticality, the entity tolls through the mouths of the prophets, of the saints over the centuries, with the *"Revelation"* of *John* as their resultant. And this is but a timeless revelation concerning the mind's triune field, the path which those who seek union are called to follow, the pioneers, who can lead the humankind, as it cries and groans within the deadlocks of the denial which it continues to project against the calling of God.

The interpreters of the *Revelation* of *John* are only the saints and sages and no one else. The uninitiated cannot possibly penetrate the unconscious field of humanity and emerge from it without consequences. The Revelation concerns the past, present and future, as perpetually its truth is recycled in the fields of the universal mind, interpreting the undeniable ubiquity of God, which is the only one that, when recognized in Its pure nature, can placate Its angry facets, those withheld in the unconscious of humankind, thus facilitating it in making the passage to the path of the spirit, for its liberation.

Humanity must understand that, because of the intelligence given to it, its power is unique in the universe and that, only if this power is recognized as the power of God, can it be redeemed and perform the task for which it was intended, in full acceptance of the difficulties that arise from it. Philosophy, arts and literature, science, poetry, under the guidance of spiritual leaders, teach this truth, to convince humans to look upwards.

"For the time is near" and poets wonder *in awe "of those which must come to pass"*. With their verses, they interpret the clas-

sified concept hidden by words and meanings of the divine Word, and, in your "Revelation", destitute they are revealed, John.

STELLA KARYTINOU

IONIAN
(excerpt)

*I laid upon the sleeping
breath of earth.
On a meadow filled with nights
and love.
As a bird,
the broken wings I folded
on the tempest of pain
on the chorus of rain
within the mystery of silence.
In the secret plains
of ecstasy.
Into my irrevocable past
I immersed the matutinal song
of stars.
In the bright labyrinth
of space
I scattered the glow of a thought.
With the soul travelling
through infinity,
I touched the peaks
of eternity.
It was then that,
in the pale-blue firmament
the floodgates of my joy opened.
It was then that*

my breath a faith sealed.
I do not I know if you were
made of light
or of the material of agony.
An enchanted chord you were
my dawn and spear.
You were fate.
The wild cry of ancestors
deep within me.
You were the victorious cry
in my bloodless Calvary.
Thousands of molecules, thousands of years
vast expanses, awaiting
the lost sheen
of an untainted hour
brought you to me.
To exist, a virgin receptor
of your urge.
Upon the leaves, which tremble
our grief
upon the wind which travels
our cry
deep in the soil womb of earth
I will preserve you, unique
expression and essence of life.
After me, after the symbols,
beyond the unknown
my beginning and end.

(Ionian)

Life refers to the spirit, to God who created it. Within its dreams His creation it envisions, as like a *sleeping breath of earth, a meadow filled with nights and love* its body is, the *secret plains of ecstasy*, the silent mystery of its existence. *As a bird*, His manifested female energy folds its wings *in the tempest of pain*, caused by the fiery rain, the drops of which as tears fall upon the earthly body with the sorrowful crying of stars.

The *irrevocable past* is immersed in pain, seeking its present, *the matutinal song* of the universal soul, within the *bright labyrinth of space*, where thoughts are scattered, the ideas and visions of people, expecting, as they wander in infinity, to touch *the peaks of eternity* with their nature's sensitivity.

The poet seeks her identity; life is seeking its identity. It seeks to know whether the spirit was created by *the light of joy or from the material of agony*, when, as Zeus' head, the *pale-blue firmament opened* and from wisdom's floodgates this goddess sprang with the *enchanted chord* vibrating in the pulse of the universal being. And it became the spear of will, targeting the eternal dawn, the fate of the fate of the son of God, as a *victorious cry* of His ancestral roots, a *wild cry* in His bloodstained Calvary, for blood to gush, transmuted into the holy water of life, a sanctification which His martyrdom from bloody to bloodless transforms.

There, at the time of the vindication of Christ, *thousands of years* – the *molecules* of His own existence – *the lost sheen* in the *vast expanses* of His anticipation, to His untainted hour He returns them; to exist as the *virgin receptor* of His *urge upon the leaves* of His tree, which, just like the human races, they appropriate the sorrow of God, guiding with the wind the cries seeking the *soil womb of earth*, so that life can preserve the uniqueness of its essence. Following it are *the symbols – beyond the unknown* is its *end and beginning*, within the eternal cycle of its cycle; within the indwelling resurrected God, who seals the breath of humans – their faith.

To live until infinity, to be crucified and die, in order to be awakened by the idea of identification with their delusions.

Long is the path upon which the precept guides them. And their nature, immaculate, undefiled and divine, recycles the emanations of its tortured soul, and, floating in the vastness, seeks the source from which its essence comes forth. Investigating the breadths of the horizontal dimension, it attempts to determine the depths and is uplifted, to touch the verticality of the peaks of its spiritual mountain, in order to assign the responsibilities of its drama to the universal self, considering them the causes of its beginning and predetermined ending.

In itself is life and its path. Within infinity it writhes and its greatness in the vastness is exhausted, predicting its cycles *beyond* even *the unknown*. There, the entity creates the light and transmutes the agony of matter into bliss, when, upon life's return, the scattered *glow of eternity* comes to seal its faith as the *only breath* of the universal world.

Humans lie down in their night. Their love, a wounded bird with folded *wings within the tempest* of their immense pain. Silence and mystery in the chorus of the cascade of cosmic rays, the ineffable, which define their evolution. Upon *the bright labyrinth of space*, the dark equivalent of earth is reflected. It is the *irrevocable past*, within which the human mind as a *song of stars* is immersed, scattering the gleams of the soul, the well-traveled in infinity; for the greatest cry must become of the Word a redemptive fate, renouncing its past, and, irrevocable as a timeless present, it shall emerge through itself, a labyrinth-mind preserved within the work of the soul. The work of humans is its work, of daily life the pursuing of the expectations of its vision, a soul arming itself with the spear of will, and, presenting the shield of the heart, as an ever-virgin it battles the darkness of erebus.

The silence of *ecstasy on the tempest of pain* is imposed, and, in the *secret plains* of the soul, the infinite knowledge travels free, sealing the rhythm of its sacramental nature, a harmony that from the disharmonies of its external being emanates.

As the mastermind renovator of its world, the human being was chosen; a dark and bright sun, the firmament's chosen one; Phoebus, the commander of all in its inner being; the immortal, eternal, of the armies of spirits the theater-maker; the greatest poet, having its works on its left, its passions holy and its resurrected yearning, the hope of the eternal all. The light of its life from its fountain emanates. In the dark erebus of its soul its spirit shines and the flashing lights of its Word throughout the century toll. A unique lamp, the horror of its existential night it prepares, and, beyond itself, *after the symbols, beyond the unknown*, as the end and the beginning it marches.

MICHALIS KATSAROS

FROM THE "PLATEAU"

I did not come to startle your days – the sword I do not hold.
For centuries I wandered among your crowd, gathering scattered seeds.
I did not come to stop the rivers the waters the fruit I did not come.
I wandered among your sounds – so many centuries.
Black banners I waved in the arteries of the roads
with my heart nailed to the terrible pole to I called you –
The law I did not come to abolish.
I climb up onto the gallows – this moment
your shape I give you – I call you
I did not come as a stranger – I did not come.

I am the wind the rain the desolate forests
I am the waterfall the water the bird
this city and the other –
I am the road the dawn the final port
my heart
my face and yours
I am here and elsewhere and everywhere
in the wind – in the older dates
in the ships – the sounds – the fields
in the factories I am – in the dark halls
in empty rooms – in lovers – in ruins
in bells
alone alone alone

from the beginning to the end of the world.
And now here, onto this plateau I call you
now that I shall plunge the knife into the chest – my blood to give you
flowers – huge doors – heavens – trembling they flow
before your feet in your dreams in the bread
banging destruction and a new dawn descends.

My wind every night freezes me.

(Plateau)

Alone from the beginning to the end of the world, the poet, to the plateau of knowledge he invites us, where sacrifice, blood, all of life, flows from his chest to our chest, and his heart becomes our heart. He is the higher self who resides *everywhere: in the wind*, in the past, in ourselves. Word of his Word our Word wanders, illuminating the *dark halls* of cosmic existence, with the mass of his invisible presence filling the *empty rooms* of love.

And he is the lovers and loveless residing in the ruins and in the bells, high above, where the soul's message is broadcast for the summoning of the omnipresent face. It is he who waves the *banners in the arteries of roads*, as he experiences the drama of the tormented heart that, *nailed to the terrible pole*, preaches the harmony of the cosmic law. Heart of the universe, the human heart, the heart of the Son of God. And the poet, experiencing his divine drama, the terrible torment he accepts, giving the shape of his priesthood to the utmost necessity of the eternal coming.

He is the Archangel of preservation, not of destruction – the sword he does not hold. Son of love, god of harvest, he is the unstoppable current of fire within the bodies, where his sound flows, the soundless river of light within the rumbling fruition of unappeased spirits. These are *the wind* and *rain, the desolate forests*. These are the waterfalls, the water, the birds. These are the cities of cities, of the chosen people the spirits of transcendent spirits, which become the path of dawn that leads the glory of form to the formless, to its *final port*; the omnipresent personalized destiny is impersonal within the omnipresent.

The *heavens tremble*, the *huge doors* open, the entity is revealed. In the great sacrifice of blood the flowers are fragrant, dreams become befuddled, ecstatic. *At the feet* of the world, the feet of God Himself, His creation within His body flows – within the bread. Banging noises of destruction are the harrowing cries, and, the *new dawn*, as an announcement of eternal life descends. *The wind*, symbolizing the spirit, *freezes* the poet's every night, so that he remains a prisoner of the chain, a deliberate shaping, a formation of the identity of all for the world to pass onto the realization of its nature.

The poet characterizes every hour as an hour of poetry, with every flower being the blooming of infinity. The fruitfulness of the rivers is the ceaseless tumult. In their greatness, the centuries march and he who comes is not a shadow, he does not surprise, he does not frighten. The law he does not abolish, by his light the world to his own law is equated, by his wisdom it is perfected. And when people seek him, they always find him. He is the one who hurts and grieves, as his knowledge in ignorance is inherent and ignorance his knowledge chants. Lamentations are his songs, paeans of triumph his canticles. At the weddings of the world, he is the people, the groom, the sun of bridal chambers, the poet, who in the winter suffers for spring to come, struggling in the night the final dawn to bring. And he is every thought; peace in conflict, as, in the factories of death, life battles death; love, which, as an only lover, the ruins studies. He is the womb's orgasm, a sound voluptuous, sweet, enchanting, the spirit's lily.

Who is the poet? Every person. He wanders among us, *in* our *sounds – all these centuries –* and our gallows – our every unredeemed moment – are his gallows. He is no stranger. He is our most sincere emotions, the path we tread within the mind, every sunrise following every sunset, *here* and *everywhere*, in the eternity of dates recorded within our spirit, in our mind and heart, to remember the drama of our need which encompasses our passions' cause.

We meet him every day and doubt him. He is our friend, father and brother. He is the mother, the family and our worries, the society, the universe, our universal self. And his inspirations are our own inspirations that we deny. Our dreams are his dreams and our spirit to the harmony of his spirit harmonizes. The poet embraces the disharmony of people, he dwells within it, he accepts it. Each barbaric vibration, upon the softness of his own vibration is appeased, and every predatory thought – materialistic – within his own respective poetic thought repents, and communes in the light of his essence and the greatness of his soul, partaking in the holy of holiest of the supreme life.

Of the Poet[1] the poet speaks, the one and only, the immaculate. The One who inundates our being, who lives within our existence and redeems us of our egoistic nature's burden, as, being a sacrifice to His entity God, in His infinite love, to the perpetuity of frost He descends, and from the eternal night of death releases humans, redeems them, deifies them.

---

[1] In Greek, the word for poetry is «ποίηση» (pronounced "poiisi"), from the verb «ποιώ» ("poio") which means to make, to create. The deriving word for the poet, «ποιητής» ("poiitis") therefore means the maker, the creator.

CHRISTOS E. KATSIGIANNIS

DEATH OF THE SUMMER

And there, around the end of September
desperation suddenly comes
as you see the seashells, the oyster shells
and all sorts of colored conches
forgotten on a stone wall in our courtyard.
The days and nights of summer
haystacks of parched brushwood and shrubs
as worn-out words of an entire lifetime
on the side plot discarded
to rot or to burn.
Oh, unbearable life!
Oh, unbearable harvest of remembrances!
And, oh, this pain and desperation
which seems as the return
from the hasty burial of summer.
But, serene, this weather
becomes to me, yes, beloved,
after the wild and painful summer weather.
And besides, on my ear I'll have
a large shell
listening to the deep sigh of the ocean.
As for my unblossomed hopes
let them become feed
to the upcoming winter's vultures.
If something is to be left

of the glory of the summer I lived
let it be even one drop
from the red grape juice
on your white summer dress.
And listen, Marikaiti, remember me
whenever the gardens, orchards, plains
bloom again.
Remember me whenever you are intoxicated
from the fragrances of the verses
of poets that shall come.

(Death of the summer)

And there, around the end of September, desperation suddenly comes. Ninth number, ninth month, the one that ripens the sea. The blessed master that gives his eyes to the poet, to see the *summer's days* and *nights* through the other eyes, the infinite, birthed by the ocean, *the shells and all sorts of colored conches, forgotten* by people's indifference to the deepest secrets of life. And the *worn-out words*, with the shrubs await the rotting or burning.

Unbearable harvest of pain which seems *like a return from the hasty burial of summer*. Magical are the joys of the *unbearable* life, pain and fatigue and sadness. To the depth, the merciless recounting. The *side plot* always remains the unexplored field of land whose fire burns the heart of the sea, so that grace returns from its grave as *serene weather*, beloved, bringing the largest seashell to its ear, so that, through it, the *sigh of the ocean* it may hear.

And, with its *unblossomed hopes*, to feed the *vultures* of the winter-hibernating soul, waiting for the last drop of red grape juice to paint the *white summer dress* of life. The poet asks of Marikaiti, wearing it, to remember him as she becomes intoxicated by the fragrances exuded by the verses of all poets. To remember him; he who is the spirit in matter, the Monad in the form, which encompasses his soul, his lava, his fire, as constantly his seeds she gestates and with these she regenerates him, giving birth to brigades of blessed poets, again and again returning from the spiritual oceans, from the sea, from the land, from poetry itself. *All sorts of colorful* seashells are their ideas, their poems. Shells, empty and full, talking about the unknown, invisible mysteries of life, and the others, those visible, of the tortures of passion, which make their rounds in the *summer's* days and *nights*, seeking to return from the hasty burials of summer, as *serene weather* to come within the wild winter.

Only the poet may be the great mystagogue, the one united, the one who perfectly represents the Monad in his ecstatic wanderings within infinity. The concepts, seen through the eyes of the entity, are revealing to the human who pulsates and vibrates to the messages of truth.

Arithmosophically analyzed, the word "poet" gives us the number ten*, which, according to Pythagoras, is the eminently perfect number that represents all principles of the divinity, united in a single entity. The name "Marikaiti" gives us the number thirteen*, which, according to Uspensky, represents the other aspect of life, the death, which aims to achieve the return, after the decay or the burning. *Oh, unbearable life! Oh, unbearable harvest of remembrances! And, oh, this pain and desperation which seems like a return from the hasty burial of summer*. That is what the poet refers to, asking of Marikaiti to remember him, looking forward to her revivals. *Whenever the gardens bloom again, the orchards, the plains*, he envisions her becoming ecstatic and intoxicated, pulsating and vibrating as himself. Because, as a Monad (one plus zero equals one), he is reflected on his material existence, symbolized by the name "Marikaiti" (one plus three equals four, matter), as the *serene weather*, the *be-*

loved, which brings the *large shell* to his *ear* so that he can listen to the *deep sigh* emerging from the vast ocean of her emotional world. The word "shell", analyzed, gives us the number sixteen*, which, among others, also symbolizes the power of nature that re-establishes the truth which is falsified by the doings of humans.

The poet wears the symbols and concepts. He is the essence and the shapes. He lives and experiences the unfathomable through the mind and heart and uses the verses to express it, explaining, grounding his truth to the chaos of ignorance; a world he is within the ignorance of the world itself.

He shapes the meanings, identifies with them, hurts and regrets, rejoices and plays, as they transmit to him the pain, the aching of their souls. The shell also symbolizes the de-spiritualization, the dissolution of forms that as haystacks burn on the *side plot*. The word "plot", analyzed, gives us the number seventeen1, a number symbolizing the creative and redemptive mission of the Word for the life-saving rebirth after the death of every summer.

The cycle lives and dies and the poet is reborn into the *unbearable life*. But he worthily supports it, feeding his *unblossomed hopes* to the *vultures* of desperation, to uplift his morale, to resurrect his dreams, so that they become the vineyards that will give the juice of red grapes, to intoxicate Marikaiti and drench her white dress, to turn it into a gown red as blood, the life of the womb which birthed him into the immortality of the infinite, eternal, supreme soul.

The *remembrances* remain indestructible. They are the fruit of a perpetual harvest which instills the fields of memory with the essence of the miracle, as it states its presence in the eternal cycles of the soul which wears the matter, so as to exist

---

* These arithmosophical analyses apply to the Greek words for poet, Marikaiti, shell and plot - «ποιητής», «Μαρικαίτη», «κόχυλας» and «οικόπεδο» respectively.

through its manifestations and to march as a divine woman, perfected through her intersections in the chaos of her wanderings.

The meaning of the poem is contained mainly within the reference made by the poet on the *desperation* of the *unbearable life*, but also in the eternal blooming of her gardens where the roses of the spirit blossom with the *fragrances of the verses* of the upcoming poets.

MITSOS KATSINIS

MEMORY

Memory is immersed into stabbed heavens
it gathers the painted wounds of anguish
the broken hands of angels
the wooden legs of the disabled
the silent hours of the bleeding Love
the stone tears of betrayed hours.

Memory travels with the furious rain
it walks barefoot on moonless nights
in the catacombs of the refugee district
it records the harrowing cries of captive hopes
it converses with the mother preparing the Last Supper
making the table of the free Dead.

Light is imprisoned by vipers and wolves
veins are fed by the poison of time
death suckles on the fiery chaos
trust shifts,
the voices of justice are bitter smiles
the songs are heroic marches for Peace.

The states have no blooming tree rows
intolerable barbaric sounds they have
impasses and unbearable crosses
memory plants optimism in Tomorrow
it unlocks the cells of the exiled world
the children wait for Spring at the vigil's window.

(Peacefully)

Many are the sacrifices, countless the deaths, terrible the disasters. Invaluable is the contribution of the spirit, the sky personified in the century, in the forms of martyrs, of the saintly people, those who love Peace and seek it in its Freedom's heavens. To find it stabbed each time, caring for it and defending it, considering it their heart and body, the body of the world, their feelings, their ideas. Supreme, beloved life, entity that the initiates worshiped and their continuers carry on worshiping throughout the century. Glory and greatness do the poets recognize in its magnanimousness, as it gathers the anguish, the *painted wounds* from *the broken hands of the angels* who surrender *the wooden legs of the disabled* to *the silent hours of the bleeding Love*, which keeps under its protection the petrified tears of the betrayed time, ancient boulders that plummet down the dynasty of chaos, persecuted by the hatred which battles them because of their worship of the agatho[1]. This inner nature, the memory of the furious rain, *barefoot on the moonless nights, the* secret *light in the catacombs of the refugee district*, a unique archive recording the harrowing cries of those captured in battle for the vindication of its hopes. This, the poet tells us, is *the mother, Peace,* eternal life, which *prepares the Last Supper*, to initiate the Dead into the vivifying, macrocosmic mystery of spiritual freedom.

The *veins* of all *feed on the poison of time*, wolves to burn amid their own fire and vipers to be torn apart at childbirth by their own children, to feed the deaths of their own light, suckling *trust* in the *fiery chaos*, the *voices* of *justice*, the *bitter smiles, the erotic songs, the marches* of Peace, shifting the center of gravity of faith which they have acquired to their optimism's Tomorrow. So that Spring comes, as *children wait for it at the vigil's window*, through the *intolerable barbaric sounds* of the states that *have no*

---

[1] The term "agatho" out of the Greek word «αγαθό» is used to mean all that is beyond the duality of good and bad. It is the Entity, the Whole, the Monad.

blooming tree rows; in the states with the impasses and the *unbearable crosses*, where memory peacefully unlocks the hearts, planting the seeds of its Love, trees of panhuman bliss to become.

Peace, memory, Love and light. Death drinks these, suckling on the breasts of the world. And its Dead, children who agonize over the viper's drama, the wolf's martyrdom, the *stabbed heavens of* their *bleeding Love*. Oh, the destitution of death feeds on the magnanimousness of Peace and the memory of the mind records the account of cosmic experiences. The most recent are those of injustice committed against the angels, the representatives of good will who defend the justice of warriors who were left disabled in the battlefields, fighting for the work of Love; the Love which is not the fluid feelings but the duty, the specific, the absolute interest to earth's sufferings that, as indelible paintings, the heavens stab.

Bleeding, compassion becomes purified by the *furious rain*, and the betrayed hours, barefoot *on moonless nights*, supplicants, wander the catacombs for the atonement of the refugee districts. Specific knowledge the human care becomes, lavishly offered to heal the harrowing cries that were deliberately captured by the envisioning of their hopes. The meaning of Love is that which liberates, that which raises the Dead, which comprehends the viper's pain. Its light is an everlasting knowledge before the appetite of wolves, and *the poison of time* a panacea, a remedy diluted in the chalice of Hippocrates, of Asclepius, for death to be cured of its own *fiery chaos*.

To shift the favor of fate, to sweeten the *bitter smiles, and the voices of justice, the songs, the heroic marches for Peace* by the entity to be heard. *The states* to acquire *blooming tree rows*; the intolerable, barbaric sounds a cosmic harmony to become, humans to be relieved of the *unbearable crosses*. Exiles everywhere to returnin order for the *world's children* to stop sleeplessly *waiting* for *Spring* in the garden of Love.

A garden filled with roses, a world flooded with light, the vast dwelling of the peaceful heart. Knowledge whose value will be appreciated by the ignorant, when they will feel the severed *legs of the disabled* as their own *legs, the broken hands of angels* as their own broken wings and see the *wounds of the world* as their own wounds, *the silent hours of the bleeding Love* as their hours, the petrified tears as the unbearable weight of their own memory. A memory traveling within their mind and heart, hunted by the *furious rain* that comes from the stabbed heavens of global consciousness. Oh, the truth of Peace, greatest of all truths!

MANTO KATSOULOU

RITUAL

We, the lovers of Life,
We, the hierophants of Justice,
We, the worshipers of Freedom,
And we, the praisers of Fire and Light
We kneel, with holiness covering
The bloodied bodies
Of the Prometheans of Hope
In the human form.
With the blade of awareness, we slice
All laws of Death,
Birthed by the spirit of the Epimetheans,
In piety, chanting Alleluia
Beyond the borders of the Becoming and Existing.

(In Search of Apollo)

Hierophants of Life, opposed to the Epimetheans of sins are the poets; *lovers of Fire and Light*, the inalienable rights of the world for the sake of justice they practice, worshiping freedom, of holiness the *Becoming* and beyond *Existing*.

Alleluia, of piety the tumult. In the epimithean pain of Death, a birthing of the dark spirit, ruling is the promethean reflection. It foresees, it pre-exists, it oversees. Greatest of immortals the poet beyond, keeper of bodies and souls, that in the dynasty of sufferings the wisdom of the world would disappear. The greatest hierophant, those of the abyss it attends to. It takes care and foretells. It is its offering, its sacrifice. To the vulture, God's liver is offered and life springs, gushing, a glorifying light which the lower, desiring fire subdues. Holiness the purification radiates, wisdom in the becoming, and *the bloodied bodies of Prometheans of Hope*, having *human form*, in complete awareness under their domination bring the *laws of Death*.

We, the poets, the Prometheans of universal *Hope, in the human form* of the spirit's perfection, have the task, the poetess says, greatest of greatest, highest of fire, to cover the time, protecting the body of God, each body, from the despair of human Death, Epimetheus against the justice of timeless judges. We, the praisers, the Apollonians, *of Fire and of Light* the worshipers, those having the vision of the eternal all. Alleluia, the exclamation of *the* inextinguishable *Light*.

Lovers of Life are the spiritual workers, greatly toiling, ritualizing in the sacred temple of nature, of earth's nature, of sun's nature, of God's nature, and they ascend the ladder of infinity, uplifting justice, freedom – life itself. Time glorifies its days. And, kneeling, its times with holiness cover the blood-born body of Hope in day and night, having human awareness as a *blade*, a *form* enclosing Death's thymic self, to control the world of decay, to magnify truth within chaos, to enlarge human morale. For the Becoming to shiver and, *beyond the borders of Existing*, existence through its absence to be reborn; for the miracle of the sun-raised land to become the trigger for Prometheus on Epimetheus' chaotic reversal.

The breath of the earth is a Life stance and the human mind by the mind of God is directed, so that it heads towards the vastness of existence, practicing the justice of truth, the initiative of its free opinion, worthiness of beauty that light as an illustration of its essence carved, to evangelize the greatness of the being. This is the intelligent ruler of the ungrateful

Death, who uncontrollably births the contrast of dark spirits of ignorance within the harmony of Prometheus' immortal mind.

Humans fall in love with life, they ritualize justice, they love, they worship their freedom, they praise the self. And their doxology, a doxology of Fire, becomes a sacrifice of Light; Apollo, kneeling on the firmament and praying, radiating hope of eternity's response, anticipating the deification of people, planets and suns. Great hierophant in the perpetual universal ritual of the invisible and visible cosmic procession, of Death, who is eternally resurrected within the chorus of his living mystics.

And all will apprentice, and, taught the words of poets, through their mouths repeat: *"We, the lovers of Life; we, the hierophants of Justice; we, the worshipers of Freedom"*. *Praisers of Fire and Light* they become, wearing the shape of holiness, and they kneel, *covering the bloodied bodies* of God's sons. In their form, *a blade of awareness*, an incision they cut, practicing their anatomical art upon the unredeemed death which birthed the spirit of the abyss; to be redeemed by *the Alleluia of Becoming* which in piety is chanted by the inextinguishable inclination of its divine soul.

Humans, oppressed by their time, trapped in the Existing, in ignorance, by their own limited knowledge are condemned. During the process of the evolutionary cycles of their existence they are awakened and, marching through their being, the rights of their omnipotence from the state of their own weakness they demand. They gradually perform their ritualistic task in full, amid their comprehensive universal self, within existence and non-existence, within life and death, directed by divine knowledge, without which they cannot exist; every poet is well aware of this, because his spirit is *beyond the borders of the Becoming and Existing*.

Alleluia, holy is the Word in the Body of His Body, the Spirit of His Spirit, His eternal, universal ritual, of His Omnipotence the God.

KOSTIS KOKOROVITS

LIFE

*I was born before the Sun
the stone
and the water.
I have no age.
I am Eternity.
I am the Moment.
People do not know me,
because in their registries
no one declared me,
in their registries...*

*I exist,
without having been born.
People do not know me.
But they sense my existence.
Death is not lurking for me.
I am no mortal and I cannot perish.
I did not enjoy the grave's rest.
Neither did the music of the ossuaries
drive me to insanity,
by myriad instruments of bones,
conducted by the wisest of skulls ...
People often mention me
and as an Unknown god worship me.*

I am
but the untamed wind,
unfolding threads of rain,
flowing and leaden threads.
And autumn's dry leaves
in the deserted cemeteries,
as they crawl
to pray,
a funeral march begin,
burying lost dreams,
which death and Fates follow...

I am no mortal
and neither can I perish.
Death is not lurking for me.
I have no age,
I am Eternity.
I am Life!

(Additions and subtractions of poems)

From non-existence comes the sun's tumult. *From the sun* comes the stone of remembrance *and from water* the age of eternity; the one moment, the unknown, as nobody was able to see it, to declare it in the registry of life. And it remains an unborn existence, with people not knowing of its entity, but only sensing that *death* does not *lurk upon* it, like it does on them, as it is no mortal. Only they can enjoy the grave of their rest and listen to the music *of the ossuaries*, as *myriad bone organs* drive them to insanity, conducted by *the wisest of skulls*. They mention the Unknown *god*, worshiping him as the untamed wind that from a desire to live unfolds its rays, colored and leaden, to *crawl in the cemeteries* of the world like dried autumn leaves, turning their prayer into *a funeral march*, to continue to be buried as *lost dreams* followed only by *Fates, by death*.

Who is it that was born before the sun? Who is it that shaped the stone and gave the gift of water, the water of life? Of the Unknown god, the unknown human the poet speaks, the intrinsically self-existent entity. The one which has two faces, of life and death, of the clarity of its Word and of the removal of its meaning, until the emptying of the primordial idea. This is the one which hides the infinite secrets of the created and the uncreated, because, as it is no mortal nor can it perish, it has the power to rejoice within the manifesting aspects in *the grave's rest*, taking care to turn its bones into instruments, to be able to enjoy the music in the ossuaries and beyond them. From the wise skull of its skulls to conduct the sanity lost by the intoxication of the world-misleading life that itself creates, to be *mentioned by people*, as this is the only path it has defined, to have the good will to make its revelation; and to make it to poets, to those vibrating with its truth, with its messages.

Sun-radiating flows of the untamed wind, symbolizing the spirit; *threads undulating, leaden*, are the leaves, human souls which, in the autumn of their existence, towards the end of their cycle, *crawl through* its *deserted cemeteries, to pray* to it – to their substance. *Lost dreams* are its dreams – their dreams – which must sleep, must be buried, followed by the Fates and death, to hear their *mournful march* from the heavens and receive the answer from the higher being through the poet's mouth.

I am no mortal, neither are you; *I cannot perish*, neither can you. *Death does not lurk upon me*; it does not lurk upon you. *I have no age*; you have no *age*. We are eternity, we are life, because *we were born before the Sun, the stone and the water*. Here, in this world, we exist as born and unborn. Our existence we sense.

Our only hope, to submit to the will of the entity and play its eternal game, teaching death, which insists on lurking upon us, believing we are mortals, lost within its fallacy. This is our other aspect, the tormented, the resultant of our being, the prize of the one who is born, the punishment of the existent. The only path forcing us to accept our eternal essence, to be recognized as human beings and recorded in the registry of the universe as the unique holders of immortal life in eternity, the conscious who created the sun, the stone and the water, the moments of our being's age. Unsuspecting is the moment of its arrival from non-existent to existent, from the unmanifested to the manifested. Supremacy of the absolute are its perpetual projections within chaos and its reign, superior to death, a triumphal entourage of spirits that mention it in their scintillations, as their own existence, its *existence*, they *sense*.

The greatest of conception, the chosen of revelation – is every poet. Bones are his organs, music is his spirit and the creation emanating from his wise skull is deifying. A poem worshiping his nature; his *Unknown god*!

TAKIS KOLIAVAS-MOLIOTAKIS

GALLOP

Of reasoning the rebellious horses roam near me
on the doors of heaven, in oblivion's palaces.
Alienated they await, by now the familiar strangers
and a sob on the edges of remembrance weighs heavy.

Of reasoning the rebellious horses roam near me
in the pits of vastness, on the paths of the earth.
Noblewoman, life, her loom she enters
with hopes she sets the warp, with sorrows she unweaves.

Of reasoning the rebellious horses roam near me
on the horizons'edges, on heavens' breadths.
And reflection, from above observing those below
some realities of death denies.

Of reasoning the rebellious horses roam near me
stepping on legends' shards and sacrifices' fragments...
Sparks fly on time's marble turn
from joys they lengthen, on the sighs they turn.

Of reasoning the rebellious horses roam near me
beyond the bitter lips and the sad eyes.
And in a vibrant life, full of youth
of a welcoming dawn, they seek the path.
Of reasoning the rebellious horses roam near me

raising and lowering elusive steps.
In imaginary and remote corners hiding me
and from where they began, there they dismount me.

(Soil and Color)

Rebellious are the horses of reasoning, roaming near the humans and harassing them, claiming them from the oblivion of heaven, from the magical palaces of their willful escape. To succumb they await. *The horses of reasoning* are *the familiar strangers*, as the poet tells us. They are the memories that, scattered, weigh down upon *earth's paths*, noblewomen who, as fates, hastily weave the hopes, and, to fool them, unweave their sufferings.

Yet *on the horizons' edges, on heavens' breadths*, the inner reasoning, from the height of the superior defends itself and *denies* the *realities of death*. With its horses it does not identify; in bliss unaffected it remains. Human nature, essence of life, the fictional heaven projects and the profound meaning of oblivion, which is the erasing of fallacy, willful amnesia becomes, residing within human palaces.

There, the alienated, *by now familiar strangers on the edges* of the entity, their entity, are weighed down by the sobbing, and, with the irrational galloping legs of the undominated instincts of life, they open *the pits of vastness on the paths of the earth*. Having remembrance as their guide they become the *noblewoman-life* who sits on her loom at night and with her hopes hastily unweaves the sorrows of the reasonings that she had weaved during the day, attempting to turn her nature into knowledge. An elusive dream of her fallacy, as with the terrible reality of her own death she identifies.

The rebellious horses of outer *reasoning* are sworn to mislead her; their own efforts they turn to shards *and sacrifices' frag-*

ments. In the *marble turn* of *time*, as *sparks* they *diminish* their mental achievements, the joys, returning again to sighs, to hide behind the bitter lips and *sad eyes* of the world. In vain they await *a vibrant life* full of spiritual youth; in vain the welcoming dawn they seek, the path that will lead them to the source of their existence, ascending and descending the steps of the imaginary stairway. Their dreams in remote corners they are forced to hide away, on the edges of the entity where they first mounted *the rebellious horses* which sprang from the eternal self, separating their stance from it. Twofold is human nature, stillness and movement, peace and turmoil. The imagination, without the mind's direction, in its being, within its worlds gallops.

The poet likens the desires and inferior thoughts to *rebellious horses*. Humankind, for its own perpetuation, has chosen this form of existence. Endlessly it recycles its having, appropriating it when it was offered by God. It was gifted so that it could turn knowledge and experience into a deeper meaning of life; to be free, to be redeemed of the desire which led it to separatation from the entity, as with its egoistical reasoning it identified.

The horses of the senses gallop; *rebellious they roam near* humans, asking them for the grounding, the release, as in peace they seek to remain, in forgetfulness of the self, in the palaces of the mind. The poet however knows that oblivion, as the world means it, is not heaven, because true oblivion, the conscious forgetfulness of individuality, does not come when the edges of the remaining remembrance are burdened by the sobbing. From the pain of memory comes the sobbing, from the lust of those who desire *life*, on the *paths* that lead to divisiveness. *Life* is in a hurry as *it enters its loom* and prepares. It weaves its *hopes*; it *unweaves* its dreams. The perpetual cycle of composition and decomposition, the universe that is broken down and made again.

On the horizons' edges, on the heavens' breadths, its inner presence the entity makes. It supervises its projection, refusing to accept death as a reality, expecting its frenetic reasoning to return to it, to be integrated, to be spiritualized in its being, which is the pure reasoning – the essence. Even heaven is fictional, it is oblivion invented by the world in its denial to accept hell that with its own defection has been created, resulting in the externalization of its power to take shape with the horses, which symbolize its reasonings. They are the ones roaming nearby so that it accepts them, so that their being aligns with its own being, the true heaven. For the redeeming of senses, passions, dreams, hunger and thirst, of the indomitable greed for life, for projection, for existence.

Form the nature of creation sprang the miracle and choice is a human right. Common is the reasoning that seeks to ensure the perpetuation of the seemingly existent, limiting. The poet from high above contemplates the cycle *of death*, sees it turning into *shards*, fragments, as, by his own horses, his legend to the entity will be sacrificed. A pedestal of eternity is earth, it insists on maintaining its volume *in time's marble turn, sparks* flying, to illuminate the path of the sighs' return.

Beyond the lips, beyond the form, *beyond the sad eyes*, there is a *vibrant life*, the poet says, *of a welcoming dawn*. This is the path, the road that ascend and descends the steps, the fields of the being, *in imaginary and remote corners* of escape, from where the humans' abandonment of themselves begins and continues to take place; and there they must return. Destined are reasonings to travel them to existential quests, to always return them to their roots. They are their micro-spirits, allies in their escape and their return.

GIANNIS KONTOS

NOT EVEN A BIRD IN FLIGHT

memory of Takis Papatsonis,
near the 15th of August

Oh, when I think of you,
ravines open outside my home.
Isolated I become from the outer and inner world.
A bird species I become which in the void is weighed.
Those moments, I remember my father
telling me: "hands are for eating
and working, not flying".
I insisted, however, and later I grew wings
and flew away, lost for days.
They searched for me. Don't look at me now,
limited to these few square meters.
Entrenched behind your heaven,
various objects I threw at people.
These did not fly, but made a
terrible thud on the ground, then
I threw my past.
Rubber as it was, it came back to me
and my future. Inextricably I went
and did not catch up with time.

(At the turn of the day)

The poet's standards are sacred, existing within the heart and mind of the universe; within his mind and heart. He always reaches them, exceeding their form and becoming their essence. There, the world loses its identity, it goes beyond the qualities, beyond the good and bad; qualities which are the cause of human stonewalling.

The poet's thought has immediacy and its results are tangible, real, self-evident. The educator's advice, of the mother and father, the friend, the brother, is not sufficient – it is incomplete. But he processes the mistake, he utilizes it, filling in the void. He transforms his body, he becomes a bird, grows wings and flies. *Hands are not just for eating*, they are also for so many other things.

Oh, the teaching of angels, the first, the primordial, emanating from the origins of the universal world! Before this planet, before this sun, before this heaven, there were others who with their fire fortified their being. The dynasties of fire for centuries have been gathering knowledge within the poet's vault; and now, he knows that he can entrench himself *behind* anyone's *heaven*.

The earth's ravines have their own story, too. They were opened by thoughts, the ideologies of poets, and they were depicted in the memories of passers-by, those who resided in the *inner and outer world*, since, voluntarily limited as they were, they had their own laws and did not succumb to that with which they disagreed. People in all, in their form and spirit, they passionately advocated for their rights and gathered the Word of God in another vault, one different from that of poets. They were able to choose the qualities and classify them as auspicious and ominous centuries, such as to safeguard their civilizations; to think they could catch up with time and sort it out, believing they knew their fate's destination, even if they barely weighed themselves within the void, even if they did not succeed.

People had fairy-tales to comfort them, tales of heroes who became birds and flew, of those who killed dragons and saved people, saints of whom people made pictures, statues, to ensure their grace, keeping them in their memory as the only ones who could send their blessing from beyond. Until they found out that a verse could hide so many secrets that they began to cajole poets, wishing to trade with them; this matter has remained in negotiations ever since.

The poet constantly asks for more, he wants people to change their hands, to transform their bodies, to become birds, to follow him, to overcome him, to reach their own heaven and exceed their boundaries. That is why the poet fortifies himself behind their heavens and from there throws *various objects* at them – useful or not. To awaken them with the thud made by the problems, the terrible issues, the horrific events, those of the past, present and future, the inextricable mysteries that take on human form and hinder the human course, so that they cannot catch up with their time and the poet is then forced to receive their *rubber past in* his *future*. To unravel it with the meaning of his verse, which cannot be bribed, because its value is proportional to supply, to the unconditional surrender of centuries, to the complete sacrifice of those who repented, because they realized that, in the path of the brisk weather, they had chosen to regress.

Ravines opened up around the hermitage of light, revealing the *inner and outer world*. The father's memories became exhortations for another heaven of heavens, where jobs take on another value, equal to the work of creation, and people are the archangels, residing by the throne of God, carrying out His cosmogony's miracle. *A species of bird* is the mega-symbol of the spirit, and they must imitate it. They must be incorporated in it, take on flesh and bones, weigh themselves in the void, hover as celestial bodies, becoming their spirit and soul – their immaculate body. Then their descendants will be able to see them as role-models, imitate them, become poets, so that they too can fly, work with their hands, continue the work the archangels began, integrate it, consolidate the opposites. *The inner* with *the outer world* to harmonize, to redeem it, and, from their hermitages high above, behind the heavens, to safeguard the right of evolution of other universes, which await their turn, to sort their time's mysteries; so that poets manage to become isolated in their inner self, so that humanity is redeemed from its illusions, as, through *the few square* kilometers of their apparent restriction, the limitless of eternity with their love they will control.

TASOS KORFIS

AS PRISONERS

Looking at the paddy wagon with the convicts stopped opposite my house – the guards must have gone to cool off – I remembered my weighings. Their hands rest on the wagon's bars, like my own which clenched the rails of the ship. Wild, their eyes, melancholic. The gallows resemble the ports; the army camps with brothels.

The ships are moving prisons: stinking of manliness and abandonment. The starry nights lash the flesh. Imagination gallops with deprivation; it fills with kinks. You are afraid of admitting your pain or writing it down. An unguarded garden is your woman. Your mother dies from her grief.

The seamen's books, identical to the prison discharge papers, push you away. Landlubbers do not let you in their home; they fear your eyes that have seen so much. You prepay the tariff at bars and for women. Thugs may kill you out of fear over an investigative glance.

You are thus left looking at the children playing in the parks, like prisoners, closing their eyes, dreaming.

(Poems)

The human heart is a paddy wagon filed with prisoners, the poet tells us, full of despair and impasses. A ship traveling into the unknown, a planet, a moving prison, where *starry nights* during the interminable journeys *lashes at his flesh*. An imagination full of kinks, frantically galloping, afraid to admit the pain for the woman's unguarded garden, the mother's grief, for the prisoners behind bars with *their wild melancholic eyes*, for *the army camps with the brothels* and their thugs in *the bars* with the *women*, ready to kill the onlooker, even over *a mere investigative glance*. There is nothing left but to look at the convicts in *the paddy wagon opposite his house*, as if he is not actually in it. Even if he knows it is so. Even if he knows that the ports are gallows that make him distance himself from reality, even if he remembers the repeated weighings of the great ship. Despite the narration of the cycles, he is left looking at *the children playing in the parks*, who, as eternally imprisoned souls, close their eyes and dream, enchanted by the *imagination galloping with the deprivation* filled with the kinks of the world.

The seamen's books, identical to the prison discharge papers, push him *away*. The same sailor, the same resident, the same human, a traveler with every weighing, the same dream, the same grief. The same thirst of sensations oppressing prisoners and guards, with *the* same *hands resting on the wagon's bars, clenching the ship's rails. Wild* and *melancholic*, calm and joyful, the same eyes see the gallows and army camps which resemble brothels.

With their heart an ally, humans prostitute their spirit, their soul, their body, their life to their very life. For a conquest of joy, grief and melancholy is the payment's contribution. Unfulfilled the sailor's dream remains, whenever the ship lifts anchor for the port of another, unknown, universal dimension, to reach the same impasse, the same landscape, the same planet with the eternal problems, the same situations.

They are the mental projections which do not change; the emissions of pre-eternal claims. The humans perceive life as a reality, as a given. They are governed by it and are subject to their own projections, without delving deeper, to be able to distinguish apparent from essence. They ignore their spiritual power and are carried away by the performances of the external projected mind. In their heart they imprison every hope by retaining the desire behind the bars they forge, to retain their spiritual strength – which they fear.

When the vast human soul is externalized as what it truly is, the ontological power of the pure, universal idea, is not threatened by its own self, while, when manifested with the properties of the human being, flesh is lashed in the vast, starry, cosmic night. Limited is the universal spirit within human manifestations, it bears the shackles enforced by humans themselves, as they are trapped in the smallness of the mental field which they have chosen for themselves and their world. They are thus forced to prostitute their nature, buying the substitutes of their bliss with the pretext of anguish caused by earthly life. The meaning of the poem focuses on the detentions made by humans, detentions of energies and forces of their soul, which are not expressed – they are not completely externalized. In doing so, they become trapped within the heart, forcing the mind to recycle the performances of life without being able to process them and transmute them into spirituality and essence, into bliss that emanates from their inner being and redeems them.

The poet speaks of humans, who, in the field of existence face their own self, as prisoners they are projected within their body and, especially, in their heart. This is where the processing of emotions and desires takes place. There the mind makes its choices, depending on the preferences of humans, who are thoroughly accountable for their judgments. It is they who must listen to the poet's encouragement and with their strong hands take down the prison bars; when the senses, in the poem symbolized by the guards, are withdrawn. With a liberated spirit to abolish the gallows set up for the atonement of brothels, who have set up camp within their life. To become the sound that will cleanse, that will purge its bodies – the ships – from the *manliness*, as Hercules to turn the river of light to the manure of Augeias and be cleansed of the dirt that centuries accumulated in their physical and emotional world, unifying their earthly body with the universal. A sleepless guard of the heart to become, of their female existence a womb, so that the mother who gave birth to them will not die of grief. The prison discharge papers must become a passport for universal circumnavigation; to be the light, so that people open their homes and welcome them, not being afraid when looking into their eyes, because inside them they will see their own soul. The women in bars must be redeemed of their passions, becoming holy courtesans, who will teach the knowledge, the truth, and, instead of thugs, archangels of divine wisdom will accompany them.

The future observer, when watching the children playing in the parks, will thus not see them close their *eyes, as prisoners*, and dream of action, but will see them participating in the great game, the supreme vision of the creator of the universal world.

GIORGIS KOTSIRAS

THE POET

I see the murder – I envision it
Every moment, I intensely experience my drama through eternity
I hear steps approaching, heavy
Iron, closing the door of my consciousness

I am the murdered and the murderer
Because without blood my life cannot grow

Every moment, I perish and destroy
I live with my pain, joy and sorrow
Every now and then a trickle of joy escapes
Slipping though the crack of my sorrow

My solitude is my death and resurrection
Every moment, I am resurrected and die again
With this killing which called for me and which I seek

Crystal shards as in a dream
Every moment, I seek my resurrection

(The poems of Giorgis Kotsiras)

The poet sees *the murder*, he owns it, he envisions it, he holds it – like the Saint in the image – from his devilish horns. He has tamed him; under his dominion holding him. He is the eternal partner, of time indomitable. Only the poet can keep his intentions in check, because his verses have the power to describe eternity's drama without prejudice, substantially, with love's passion which atones humanity's sins and uplifts it to the temple of awareness. The gates open and close depending on the influences, the impressions received by the primate who judges the whole, and whose judgment is formed by the degree of complacency that the daily becoming has of itself.

The initiative belongs entirely to humanity, as to the outcome to which its decisions will lead it throughout eternity, regarding the evolutionary course towards its ontological destination. It shapes its death, drawing energy from its life and giving it substance, as a merciless judge projecting its skeletal, terrible martyrdom. With its iron shoes it keeps it a slave in the bowels of earth, to be dominated by the vast power of its soul, whose task is to control its cosmic, morphic and spiritual manifestation, so that it does not overcome the limits of evolution set by the entity, for its own protection, enabling it to carry out its work.

Murdered and murderer are construed by the poet as one, whose blood flows through the universal veins of the supreme whole, perpetually transmutating the physical body of life, giving it the ability to exist throughout its undergoing alterations. The human spirit can experience its spirit and body, the pan-universal body of one, with the myriad possibilities it has; to be reborn through its own death, through the murder it commits against itself and the resurrection following this dramaturgical act. An act which characterizes the entity in its main action within the existential cycle; this cycle submits the entity to its own non-existence, through which it springs out as the eternal existence.

The poet reveals the entity in its full cycle, the unique, the supreme, which every moment destroys and perishes, living *with* its *pain, joy and sorrow*. An entity whose *life cannot grow without* its *blood*, and, every second, in the thoroughness of its time lets *a trickle of joy slip through* the passage of its sorrow, to reach the ocean of bliss surrounding it. A death including its resurrection, an intrinsic ability of the entity, whose union both parties seek; to create the hermaphrodite becoming, the unique being, which *every moment shreds* its *dream*, leaving it in shards, dying and seeking its redemption in the vast realm of its solitude.

I see the murder, the poet says, I envision it, the one I commit every moment with my thoughts, my feelings, my actions; the thoughts and feelings and actions of the people – because I am the people. *Every moment, I intensely experience* my vision througout eternity, listening to the appropriation, the selfishness, the envy, the malice, the separateness, with their *iron steps*, symbolizing the heavy sins of life, as they come *and close the door of* my *consciousness*. I know that *I am the murdered and the murderer*, the perpetrator and the victim, because, without the desire, the blood's fire, *life cannot grow*, no interest in the work is sparked, which generates the overwhelming passion that dominates all and is simultaneously dominated by them, mutating its fire to the light of love.

I open and close *the door of my conscience*, and my God, the higher Self, stands by me according to my will; analogous to my intentions are my works.

Either way, my death, an extension of my life, is repeated, and life, an extension of my death, strengthens or is weakened depending on my attitude, the poet says, since my one *joy slips through* the only *crack of my sorrow*. Because, if joy was lost from joy, resurrection from its resurrection, the universe would be extinguished within its own fire and the entity would die as the source of the radiance through which it becomes revitalized would die out.

Pain leads to redemption. From its bowels emerge the droplets of joy which create the oceans of bliss. Solitude that harmoniously combines death and resurrection. A disharmony which agonizingly seeks the death of life and a harmony which its resurrection interprets. *Crystal shards* of its own dream is the world, *every moment* seeking its *resurrection* and finding it; because, through his verses the poet generously offers it, this *murdered and murderer*, perpetrator and victim, since, *without* his *blood*, the eternal fire, eternal life cannot exist.

CHRISTOS N. KOULOURIS

SEA-GOING

*The voyages and the fate of ships
are determined not only by the experience of seafarers.*

*When, in high seas
against the foaming waves and storm,
they shoot the vigor to defeat death, to escape
the turmoil, triumphantly,
greeting
distant ports with wild continuous whistling,
I do not know how you contemplate it.*

*But the fate of ships
in the unbearable emptiness of the sea
a saint studies, kneeling, with invisible eyes
watching over every movement.*

*And, at all times, he hears the human pulse,
the martyrdom of impatience, the variable of time.*

*He gathers all hopes in a secret coral,
the matins of the depths to oversee with holiness,
because, listening to all human sorrows,
he has wept so,
that the bitterness of all seashores
certainly has within it signs of his own grief.*

(The Terrestrial)

It is not only *experience* that *determines* the course *of ships*, the poet says. It is not the seafarers' knowledge that guides fate. These along are not enough, they cannot sail through storms, shoot at the foaming waves of the sea their vigor against death, gazing at *distant ports through the turmoil*. The whistling, symbolizing their Word, is not enough, nor are greetings meaningful, if so carelessly you contemplate.

In *the unbearable emptiness, the fate* of these ships is *studied by a saint, kneeling, with eyes invisible*. On *every movement*, on each revolution of suns and planets, watches over the voyage of pain, feeling *the human pulse* on his own *pulse, the martyrdom of impatience* in his own *martyrdom, the variable of time* in his own invariable time. Future humans gather *all hopes in a coral* taken out at the time of secret matins, from the depths of holiness; hopes reaped by human sorrows from the many tears of pain and bitterness *of all seashores, signs* of their own grief, sown by efforts of the past for their own glory.

It is the field of higher consciousness which has the cycle of the universe's evolution under its responsibility. It supervised it and always supervise it. Humans must learn this well. They must learn to contemplate on this, as the poet tells us. *Wild continuous whistling* of the Word is the effort which paves the way so that the vision can cross to the other side. The message is great. Humans are not alone in the storms of death. They are guided through *the unbearable emptiness* of seas – of emotions and ideas, of their psychological states – learning to directly shoot their vigor to the center of the turmoil, where pain and bitterness aggregate *the martyrdom* of variable time's *impatience*.

Each poem's wisdom lies in the de-symbolization made by the mind, as it constructs and reconstructs its own mental structure, giving form to its inner content, externalizing the importance of the happenings of its own nature. Manifestations perpetuating the mystery of its existence, an inviolate sanctuary, a functional area, a grandiose temple in which the poet perpetually works, and in which the field of higher human consciousness also resides. This is what the saint personifies in the poem, as *with holiness he oversees the matins of the depths* – the awakening of the unconscious – and sympathizes, weeping, as he hears *all human sorrows*, knowing that every person is also a seashore full of bitterness, a piece *of his own* great *bitterness*.

Eternal is the world's grief, but it does not bear it on its own. Comforting are the saintly forms reflecting the divine power that hides within the inner mind of all people and guide the way through the sea's foaming waves – of their passions and weaknesses –, indicating how to emerge victorious from the fight with death. As long as they remember that they are not alone, that each difficulty is shared by their other self, the saintly, which emerges from *the matins of the depths*. Because they are the ones struggling to *gather* their *hopes in a secret coral* and proclaim the commands of their Word, as their own courage destined them to again be the ones working against the grief derived from fatigue which results from the evolution of their nature.

It is the other, inner experience, that which governs ships and determines their voyages, the ontological one, to which humans must refer to. With the holiness characterizing it, it gathers all their efforts and hopes, supports them in their sorrows and cries for their drama that lies scattered throughout all seashores which symbolize *the variable of time*. Unbearable would be the martyrdom of impatience without the contribution of the entity, which guides *the fate of the ship* within the absolute *emptiness of the sea*.

With eyes invisible, kneeling, the entity oversees the revolutions of its desires, emotions, thoughts, ideas, visions, of humans, of beings, of the Words of its Word around its self, as they all together march towards perfection; towards the harmonization with the idea of death, with *continuous whistling*, holding the scepter of life, hailing its glory, the glory that created them. This should be the stance of humans throughout life; grand, universal, a stance that recognizes the breadth of their spiritual existence, which is expressed in all happenings of the manifestation, while at the same time listening to *the human pulse* within the invariable of its variable time.

A seashore is the beauty of form and the soul is the depth; an abyss looking forward to satiate the time. It idealizes sorrows and, by delivering the signs of its grief, preaches the sadness of its entity. All its *hopes in a secret coral gather*, as mythical daughters, oceanides, those participating in the occult step by step, cell by cell, building the shell of time, a viviparous idea from which sprang the vertebrates and the human skeleton, a bony force that supports their flesh and surrounds the being's marrow.

Harmonic mysteries evolve, divine titanic currents in the human spirit; and their pulse becomes their harmony and their harmony becomes the earth's vibration. Eternal incentives of the matins *of the depths, signs* of the bitterness of *all seashores*, so that the balance of the universal world is maintained.

LETA KOUTSOHERA

LANDSCAPE 6

*That morning
a letter with no sender
came to my address.
I opened it quietly.
It was a clean white piece of stationery paper.
Without signs of writing.
Without words.
At first I looked at it bewildered.
Then, I looked deeper,
    further on.
To the roots.
To the trees
growing in silence.
To the ink
still residing in its womb.
I delved into the quest
of my very first thought.
I began revealing shapes
of another, secret writing,
reading the fingerprints
of a silence.
They laughed at me
    the books
as I read
a white, unwritten piece of paper.*

A whistle sounded,
half-happy,
half-sad.
A meeting-a departure,
I said.
A brisk
    summer's noon
came to mind.
Your breath smelled
    of rosemary.
From all over, your breath
    I anticipate.
In the waiting
is the purest pleasure
I thought.
I carefully folded
the beautiful silent letter,
I placed it in the envelope
and kept it
among my dearest
    belongings.

(Flowing landscapes)

Every morning, letters arrive at the poet's address, with *no sender*, on *clean white piece of stationery paper*. They carry messages of the world, recorded *without words*, with a depth that reaches down to the roots of existence. There, in the vast field of silence, the ink of the global womb continues seeking the primordial thought, to reveal the patterns of eternal writing. Its whistling sounds are heard *happy* and *sad*, so that the meeting of eras with time takes place and the *departure* of the ephemeral *summer* for the absolute field of the mind is achieved, where the breath of the being is all breaths of most supreme spiritual pleasure. This is recorded on the white thymic which is likened to the white paper. The ultimate pleasure, as the most beloved experience of redemptions is kept.

Without words are *words*; *without signs of writing* is the writing; without meaning is the thought in the unthinking field of the mind, where the rootless roots are inherent, the treeless forests, the concepts of concepts, which grow in the field of silence of the invisible womb with the colorless ink. There, the non-existent shapes suggest the existence of another *secret writing*, that for which the recorded knowledge of people snickers, trapped in false pleasure. A poetic conception is the relationship, a poetic conception is life, the existence, the source of creation, the ultimate field of silence that surrounds us and in which "we live and have our being".

The meaning of this truth is conveyed, inherent in actions, in empty meanings, in empty words, in the empty hours of the empty time with the bottomless depths. Bewildered, humans observe the processes of the becoming and see their own conscience drift away. This happens because they cannot hold on to the great current of essence which emanates from the pure field of the mind, as a unique revelation of their nature.

Pervasive in everything, the mind, it reviews the creations of its projection until they are finally devoid. The human being is immersed in the quest for its primordial thought. This is the only path of conscious intention: to reach the source of things from which its universal self-sprang. The *white piece of paper* is the symbol of the unwritten field of the mind, its unmanifested and unspoken world, a world without emotions and external knowledge. These imprison and restrict within joy and sorrow, dividing the oneness of the Word to duality until the fullness of time unites the breaths. In the poem, this fullness is symbolized by "rosemary", a word which arithmosophically analyzed gives us number seven[1], which is, among others, – according to D.J. Cooper – the knowledge beyond the mind, the winner of contrasts, the ruler of fields. With this breath, which is pervasive, the poets are united, and, through the sense of inner vision, they unify all senses to its own uncreated light, for the departure to take place which will lead to the great meeting of wanderers near and far within the pure field of mind.

Upon returning, in an attempt to follow the *fingerprints* of the *secret writing*, humans are hindered by the chimera's recorded memories. They read the *white unwritten piece of paper* and try to comprehend the implicit truth. Whatever they may have been, was defined by fate, it was meant to be. And silence became Word, the tumult. Pure knowledge became the dream of those born; and the pleasure of the first pleasure became a memory, of the unsurpassed bliss of love.

Nature by its chimeric courtships is tormented. Inadequate is the breath within the imperative panting of life. A ruler, a leader of the brisk summer is the unfulfilled desire. That which gallops on the *first thought* and spreads its magic, imprisoning essence in form, in shapes, in scriptures, in words, in the imperfection of things, in the artificial pleasure acting as a substitute of happiness.

A lot can be read on a written piece of paper, but infinite on an *unwritten* one. Thoughts and words become void, emotions are redeemed. The forms and shapes to their essence return. There, the human being lies face to face with the primordial state of its nature, the pure field of the mind, from which its existence sprang and continues to spring every moment. The reason for purpose indicates the necessary cycle of futility in which humans reside, in order to consciously close it as they intentionally opened it and return to the unique state through

---

[1] The arithmosophical analysis applies to the Greek word for rosemary, «δενδρολίβανο».

which they will live and experience playing, while at the same time they will await for entire cycle of the ontological existence's externalization to pass to the absolute.

GIANNIS KOUTSOHERAS

I INDWELL

With the day of return
and of Icarus the Hellenic wings
is the way back heartwarming –
Homer!
I timelessly retrace.
I Pythagoreanly wonder
what good I have done.
I am sensitized.
I envision
of the Beyond the mind and intellect.
Life-giving is our country's insight –
– Plotinus!

And I return
to the ancestral lands
to the city of Pallas Athena
to the poetry of social lyricism
and the source of ever-flowing sensitivity.

I indwell.

Orly - Greek. 26.3.1988
(The ever-shinning rock of Acropolis)

With the day of the return and of Icarus the Helladic wings is the way back heartwarming – Homer!

To himself the poet refers to; with him he converses; his being he addresses; timelessly researching the fields of inspiration, which the immortal miracle of spiritual Greece created, of the spiritual world, of the spiritual universe. They are the Hellenic wings of Icarus which raised earth to heaven, taking its spirit to the sun, where it will be initiated in knowledge and return as a sacrifice and a holocaust, its place to take; the *ever-shinning rock* to become, to illuminate the paths of poetry's greatness within the ever-flowing social lyricism of expression of sensitized beings, of the Beyond's visionaries in the *life-giving* land of insight.

I timelessly retrace, the poet says; and civilization he becomes, Pythagoras. He wonders, what good has he done. He is sensitized, he envisions *the Beyond of mind and intellect*, the *city of Pallas Athena*. It is the inexhaustible source of his sensitivity, and his entity restores the spirituality of humankind – which dwells in exile in the barren land – on the day of return, in ancestral lands, where his spirit since time being has and always will reside.

He is the spiritual leader of memory. Inherent he is in time, guiding the virtues, the arts and literature, letting the cycles of intellect find their way back from the past. The mind is indwelled by the thought, the idea, the feeling, the desire for life, life itself; by poetry and the poet who expresses it. The entity indwells its own flight, its own creation, the return, the return to its source from where it started and forged its own self – its miracle.

Wisdom is life, the state, the country, the land with the *Hellenic wings* of Icarus which seeks the life-giving sun from which it sprang, shaping its spirit into a body, a myth, a history, to renew their ontological relationship, to continue to flow from the sun, causing its drama, so that it has the strength to endure time; so that it marches in the vast field of its existence which is widened by its zeal for knowledge, wisdom, beauty of the bodies and souls which represent it. It indwells its own magic and its magic indwells it. It indwells its own wisdom and its wisdom indwells it. It indwells eternity itself and eternity indwells it.

This is what Athena teaches us with her *life-giving insight*. Life-giving is life, life-giving is the country. Life-giving is the source *of social lyricism*, the source of the *ever-flowing sensitivity* from which everything springs. Life-giving is matter and the spirit that nurtures it, sculpting it into an ever-shinning work, *Plotinus*! Cosmogonic is its work, a chosen one, rational, and only the poet with his verses can manage to describe it. Its epic in the *city of Pallas Athena* becomes *the Beyond of mind and intellect*.

This *is the path*. The wax-made wings – the body's external tendencies – burn, as they seek the fire's source, allowing the emergence of others – the mystical, the only ones that can withstand to purification. With these the poet returns through the path of the heart and mind, of love and wisdom. He does not come to fall or to precipitate; he comes to lead the human spirit towards the glory of the Pythagorean spirit. With the urging of the world's need, he returns to the past, to the rhythm of *the social lyricism of the ever-flowing sensitivity*, to convey the wisdom to the present and integrate it into the work on the protection of the future, so that it is inherent unto the century.

Six verbs constitute the poem's meaning: *Return, retrace, wonder, sensitize, visualize and indwell*. The entity indwells its own entity and retraces. It descends into its own depth, in the field of assimilation of energies and forces, the solar plexus of the world, and returns, ascending through its universal body towards the heart, reaching the center of the throat, where the Word it will become; the life-giving discernment, the life-giving sunlight, a day eternal of Pythagorean knowledge, which the motivation of the work investigates, separating good from bad, to process and transform it into sensitivity that will bring the agatho[1] to envisioning.

---

[1] The term "agatho" out of the Greek word «αγαθό» is used to mean all that is beyond the duality of good and bad. It is the Entity, the Whole, the Monad.

The poet wonders, *Homer*, he is sensitized by your being and with the inner wings timelessly he retraces your work, envisioning the eras. He indwells himself; your own self. Soul immortal of the Word, to the concept of the divine, of the absolute mind he indulges and from the supreme tier of the spirit to the lowest of matter he descends, returning to it once again. This is the human goal, assimilation with the entity through ecstasy.

Life-giving is the insight of Greece, of the country from which you derived your knowledge, Plotinus; Platonic, neo-Platonic, predominantly fundamental, indwelling, as the perfect ever-flowing source of wisdom-Athena, in the poetry of the universal *social lyricism* of Homeric sensitivity.

Greek soul, Greek beauty – the beauty of humanity. And the mind is an inexhaustible source, the essence of life. Homer-Word, the path of cultures and history grieves in the city of the gods. In the life-giving country, reminiscing the spirit's grandeur, the great time of complete return does the poet await. He is sensitized, wondering about the existing possibility of realizing the aspirations of humankind, and the restoration of the century he envisions.

D. P. KOSTELENOS

POETRY TODAY

I

Poetry today
is not a caress for the ears
it is a knife to the heart.
Poetry today
no longer wanders like a carefree daughter
on tender meadows
but as an eternal mother-earth, a respected old woman
full of wisdom from suffering
to the old springs she returns
in deep thought she drowns
and agonizes, as a mother giving birth.
Poetry today
from frivolous and unholy marriages
has broken off – from music
and dances arousingly erotic
and in the eternal marriage of the mind
to the world's first principle
longingly she offers herself again.
For this and only reason
in our world – this world
of useless murders –
poets are blatantly murdered.

II

Poetry today
has reached at last its limits, the universal
struggles to hold on
to the peaks conquered since ancient times
not to come falling down again
to Tartarus' torments
where evil gods condemned her.
And to her struggle
she sacrifices her children – her lovers
she sacrifices the poets
that now wonder among the crowd
unrecognizable and anonymous
from fear of their murder.
Poetry today
kills poets
with a daily love
    – to the death.
Poetry today
has finally won the battle.
And the ones defeated in this world
are only the poets.
Woe to the victors...

(The limits of the Aegean)

On this day of the twentieth timeless century, in the carnal, materialistic life, the divinely inspired poetry as a death penalty is imposed on behalf of humankind's atonement. And the martyrs bearing this condemnation are the poets. An immense *respected old woman* on the *tender meadows* of the centuries-old land, of the life-giving mother, with the wisdom gained *by* her *sufferings, the poetry does not wander carefree.* Because their euphoria by omnivorous beasts is devoured, those created by the immature civilization of endless mental processes, which is not imbued by the current of the heart, with whose power poets envision the world. Envisioning of a gently ascending life that uplifts the legend to its fullest, conveying it to narration, to the description of the essence hidden by deep meanings. These concern the causality of existence, and the results of tasks which intelligent beings – its representatives – are called to undertake under the guiding light of poets.

Poets have the privilege of redemptive death, an advantage of a deep mystical life to which the worthy and capable are initiated. They are the members of humankind who are not carried away by the dictates of the ruthless fate, as it covets the fate of God's sons and battles them, to the elimination of spirituality's final droplet, a trial to which the cosmic law submits the entire planet, to awaken humans and resist the dark forces which impose the corruptive use of their grim Word. The poet clearly states it in the poem: *Poetry today has broken off from frivolous and unholy marriages. In this world,* where *poets are murdered, poetry* does not participate. The murdered poets are those who participate.

The spirit of poetry, with its ultimate mystery, as the resultant of all mysteries partaking throughout the centuries, guides humankind towards the New Age which has began. A humankind that continues to lead its dead life through all fields of Hades which have remained to end their cycles in the intellect and heart of an unfathomable future, full of fear and subordination projected by the voracious "-ism" of the human spirit, anxiously seeking its redemption from poets. This is why poetry continues to murder them, knowing that they are the only guides who, with their sacrifice, will indicate the way to the complete resurrection of its deceased dreams. Dreams which remained fruitless due to the failure of strong personalities, as they assigned their undertaken mission to the individual egoistic projection and disregarded the emergence of the total ontological ego. This is the only thing that can bring liberation from the personal demands of uncontrolled individuals, no matter their social class, because of their uncertainty, stubbornly seeking consolidation in social life. They disregard their fellow-people and insist on ignoring the fact that they are merely extensions of their own selves.

Thus, poetry loses its meaning and the poet, partaker of the great idea, becomes the scapegoat, the sacrificial lamb, the murdered, the common to all, the higher self, as humanity in its entirety, still not accepting the mercies of spirituality, remains in denial, appropriating the spiritual benefactions, relief emanating from its inner being, whose conduit is the poet. Whether intentional or unintentional, this criminal behavior has but a single purpose: the annihilation of this very humanity, which, through the respective leaders representing it, remains indifferent, oblivious to the risk indicated by the dictates of poetry, whose subject is still the hymn of hymns. A divine chant, which only a select few can hear – those having the advantage of being initiated to the one and only privilege of spiritual immortality –, that which is present and offered to those anxiously seeking it and accepting to be sacrificed and even murdered for it. To become the martyrs who return to the ancient sources of deep thought, to save those who are drowning in the descending reputable visions, as they participate in *the arousingly erotic dances*, accompanied by murderous dancers who blatantly kill the anonymous, those not prone to intoxication by the cries of the crowd of evil gods.

These devotional lovers of mother poetry, *the poets, in a daily love to the death* indulge and accept the role of the defeated. And *woe to the victors*. Because, in this race, paranoia – little by little – gives way to deep knowledge, although otherwise apparent

– appearances can be deceiving. Poetry is the supreme initiator of gods and humans, defeated and undefeated, dead and living, sleeping and resurrected. The centuries-old goddess, older than universes, leader of leaders, of those who accept her and of those who deny her and battle her, mistress of lovers who love and hate her, the ultimate death of deaths, the eternal resurrection, the appropriate life of truth, the order of greatness. A harmony within which the universe is rebaptized and the god of maintenance is nurtured, for its other self to come, that of destruction and the one of perpetual creation to be prevailed. Perpetual recycling of the becoming, of spirit and soul, of life and form, becoming prey to the voracious greed of redemptive death, a law governing all creation in its eternal poetic exhortation.

Entity is poetry and its Word, a sweet caress to her own *ears, a knife to* her *heart* which teaches her not to *wander as a carefree daughter on tender meadows*, making her a respected *old woman, an eternal mother-earth, full of wisdom* acquired through her own sufferings, to return to the deep, *old sources* of her being. To be able to be saved from *frivolous and unholy marriages* and to *longingly offer herself to the eternal marriage of the mind with* her *world's first principle*.

The poets are murdered, lost. Knowingly does *poetry sacrifice her children*. For centuries, this has been her great torment; of her, which is the path of life, of deification, the great trial, the panhuman, the universal. The serpents are initiated to its mysteries, and, on the endless path of their transformations, on the holy path, they leave their shirts, the multileveled shapes, be worn by newfangled zealots, who for centuries in ignorance remained, and perceive their discipleship as consolidation within knowledge. They refuse, upon receiving the first initiation, to sacrifice their newly acquired spirit for the catering of masses, who follow and desperately seek the ticket to the material and spiritual survival on this planet.

Deep, ancient are the origins of dependence on egoistic existence, they threaten to precipitate the resultant of the spiritual becoming, the poetry, from the high peaks which it has conquered; and it, prominent life, battles to hold on and does not surrender its being to regression, to become prey to the greed of the time, which is unable to break off from the origins of cavemen. Inextinguishable light of knowledge – poetry, it refuses to return to gloom and sacrifices the aspects representing it – an old lady, sovereign of chaos, to remain as the only promise, a redemptive life within the impasses of recurring death.

DIONYSIOS KOSTIDIS

NOW LETTEST DEPART

*Colorless days have passed
colorless days shall come;
Passion is night imperishable
the night which moved us
the night eternal;
And mother earth, immutable
colorful, brightly shining
how within her innards
mercilessly, ruthlessly
our rapacious night concealing
our faith and dream
faith and falsehood!*

*I caress, I kiss Your footprint
Your immaculate tread
the existing, the non-existing...
I kneel, I kiss Your footprint
eternal within the bustle
untouched within passion...*

(Unbroken)

The faith and dream the poet seeks – *faith and falsehood*! As if they are concepts synonymous, hidden *within* our *innards*, the earth's innards, in the pitiless night, where *colorless days that passed*, seek the footprint left by the *existing* and *non-existing immaculate tread* of the entity. To kiss it and be deified in the *untouched passion*, in the sacrilegious bustle of the chimera, that which *moved the night* and the beings which inhabit it. To *brightly shine, colorful earth, immutable*, independent, with an autonomous life within its rapacious fate; unaffected by falsehood, free within faith, eternally to live.

To encompass its night, dominating its sleep, to control its endless dreams and offer them a destination, directing beings which incarnate the passion of its rapaciousness. In its own reality to be earthed, the immaculate, the footrest of the foot, where the existing and the non-existing, the born and unborn Word remains the Being, coloring and discoloring the centuries with the – untouched by the bustle of His creation – holy passion.

Literally submerged is the human being within God's benevolence, as the immutable planetary Word that immovable on its axis remains, constant in its faith, exploring the dimensions of its night, revolving around the unfathomable mystery of its existence and non-existence, by whose power it is imbued and it exists. They caress the footprint that God's *immaculate tread* upon chaos has imprinted. Speechless before the greatness of the macrocosmic miracle they glorify the *brightly shinning, colorful*, universal presence, which has the ability to conceal within its innards, their own *innards, mercilessly, pitilessly* – the poet says – its *rapacious night*, its *faith and dream, faith and falsehood*.

A person, a god, mundane, universal, who within the bustle of his passion perishes and yet by his own passion remains untouched. To maintain his autonomy throughout eternity, being the supreme divine self, the unifier of falsehood and truth, of faith and faithlessness, of the dream and reality, of fantasy and the essence of the mind, of the manifested and unmanifested, of the perishable and unperishable world. Timeless time is God within His century; he divides the *colorless days* which come and go within the indestructible cosmic night. He sets His universe in motion and the flock of His entities to constant vigilance he urges.

Resultant of the creation of God is the human being, uplifted to the spirit of the poet and adhering to the greatness of its rights, His compassion pleads:

"Lord, *now lettest* thou thy servant *depart*". Because he, the son of God, born of the Holy Spirit, His kingdom attends and guardian of the spirits of the night he is, the favorite of mother earth, of the colorful, brightly shinning hope, which, pitiless Hecate, encompasses *the night within her innards*, concealing her mysteries from the clutches of her rapacious, false, uninitiated paganistic dream. And she prays until her son accepts her and concedes to descend into her; Virgin Mary to appoint her and his blessing to gift her. As savior of her world to worship him, obeying the command of God, which in response comes to the plea that eternally is transmitted by the poet and which is:

Lord, *now lettest* thou thy servant *depart*; the one who loved the night, who fell in love with falsehood, who was shaken by the dream. In Your vision apprenticing, he was divided and dreamed of his soul's temptation. The futility of outer passion he embraced, the false ideals of the chimera he accepted, and, renouncing his faith to Your glory's being, to the chaos of ignorance he fell and in the darkness of night he immersed His soul's pain. From the brightly-lit knowledge you send to earth, as sun of Your suns, You, the polluted human *passion to* Your *untouched passion* prays.

God heeded the supplication of night; its fatigue is great within the dream's falsehood. Rapacious, the impossible it addresses and the feasible it delivers. *Untouched passion* in the eternal *bustle, Your immaculate tread,* as an *existing* and *non-existing* imprint, a footprint caressed by chaos, the faith of Your truth within its falsehood, in its dream to find.

Oh, *ruthlessly, mercilessly* does night's rapaciousness conceal You, but you are the *colorful, brightly shining earth,* the poet says, in night the eternal, the imperishable, guiding passion to Your divine apathy, where Your days colorless come and go and untouched leave You, of Your priesthood the God. By Your mercy, in Your greatness the universe, your servant, *lettest depart.*

VASILIS I. LAZANAS

WHEN I RETURNED...

When I returned, my mother said to me:
Where were you my son, where were you?
I had given birth to you with a hyacinth on the lips,
A hundred-petaled rose I had planted in your heart,
I had rocked you to the rhythm of the nightingales...

Where were you my son, where were you?
You marched, with a bright tunic,
cheerful, carefree,
through morning streets.
The matutinal breezes kissed you,
the grass flowed beneath the soles of your feet,
the foliage of trees parted,
larks greeted you as you passed!

And now you have returned!
And how can I recognize you my son, how?
The fog drips from your eyes,
the daffodils bloom on your chest,
the lizards follow your footsteps!
Oh, where are the hyacinths, the roses?
who is the one who stripped you bare,
who tore up your brilliant tunic?

So, where were you, where were you my son?
where did you congregate so many harrowing cries and lamentations?
who plundered, alas, for ever,
the matutinal smile from your lips?

(In the middle of the night)

The power of every poem resides in the mother's heart and from there it springs. It is the work of her dreams, representing her feelings, her passionate love for the fruit of her love, to whom she gives birth so that he may become a man within the world of her hope. And she expects him, waiting for him to return from each day's battle, from every cycle of his feat, perfected, mature. For his glory to shine, so that she may be glorified. For his sun to shine, so that she may be illuminated. For his knowledge to grow, mature, to become wisdom, a sacred teaching, which will uplift her to the supreme.

When the son returns, she, every mother, his mother, asks the hyacinth, looking at him on the lips. She explores his heart, seeking *the hundred-petaled rose*, her sense of smell to be enchanted by its fragrance. She listens, trying to hear and feel the harmony of nightingales within her own heart.

On his *bright tunic* to see the stars embroidered by heavens and his carefree, cheerful face *on the morning streets* to be kissed by *matutinal breezes*, as back then, in his farewell. For *grass* to flow *beneath the soles of* his *feet*, foliage to part, to become *larks as* he *passes*, to become greetings, and she too may be able to greet him, recognize him and see that the symbols of death, *the daffodils*, do not *bloom on* his *chest*. And from his eyes, as tears of joy, rose water, distilled fog, to drip.

Lizards, subservient, obedient to his knowledge, will *follow* his *footsteps*, so that she is certain that she has won and will not be forced to ask: "What became of heaven's roses, the hyacinths? Who was the one *who stripped* him *bare*, who *tore up* his *brilliant*, flaming *tunic*?". So that lamentations do not to exist to be counted; so that matutinal smiles from lips have not been plundered.

The poet is the knowledge of life. He is the father, the mother and child. He contemplates the drama of people; he lives and experiences it as his own. This is his gift: to perceive, to hold, to create the feeling, cultivating it into love and, passing it through the heart, to uplift it to wisdom, – his beloved mother, she who gave birth to him. That is why, deep down inside, intuitively, as he is flooded with the power of his spirit, he is always aware of the meaning of things.

The poet places the word *"hyacinth"* upon the hero's lips, a word whose arithmosophical analysis gives us number thirteen*, the rejuvenating death, the destructive factor which transforms. Yet it is also number four (one plus three equals four), matter which continuously through spirit is recreated; the body, the form, earth itself, whose Word he places upon human lips. And, in his heart, he says that his mother had planted *a hundred-petaled rose*. The word "rose", when analyzed, gives us number ten*, a number symbolizing the source of eternal nature, none other than the heart of the universe and of humans, rocked by their mother to *the rhythm of the nightingales*, the light of knowledge. Besides, the word "nightingales", arithmosophically analyzed gives us number five*, symbolizing light.

Brilliant is the tunic with which the poet dresses the Word, and his vision is cheerful and carefree, greeted by *"larks"* – knowledge again, as this word's analysis gives us number five*. And he enjoys being kissed by matutinal breezes, while *"grass"*, symbolizing wholeness through number ten* – the eternal source again – *beneath the sole of his feet* continually flows.

At the great time of the son's return from the apostolic journey of vigil, she, the tragic mother, is forced his nakedness, his plundering to accept, as the reason for his existence serves a single purpose, that of offering divine gifts to his world, a sacrifice to which all beings, intentionally or not, are submitted. It is the power of the spirit offered to matter. It is the power of the brilliant ego, of the perfected personality which must become prey to the inexplicable within the uninterpreted field of need, through which redemption springs when, upon the return of the Son of God, his wealth is proven to have been completely dedicated to matter.

The word *"daffodils"* gives us number eighteen*, a number symbolizing materialism, which battles the spirit, so that, from the chest, on the side of the heart, the inner meaning of hyacinths emerges, matter transmuted to the pure essence of the spirit, as the *"chest"* in its analysis gives us number thirteen-four1. And through this heart the "brilliant" "rose" to rise, words whose analyses give us nine and ten respectively*, which together are nineteen, the spiritual sun, which by mystics is gifted to the legions of darkness.

This is the poet, the knowledge of life, becoming the myrrh-bearing ode on the mother's mouth, a tragic Word which mourns for the harrowing cries that the fruit of her love has gathered and asks him: *"Who plundered your matutinal smile? Where has your beauty gone?"*. And the answer:

In the hearts of people, in their spirit, in their consciousness, remains the poet's inner beauty. It is the drama that leads the world in search of redemption, thus enabling it to realize and accept its existence.

---

1 These arithmosophical analyses apply to the Greek words for hyacinth, rose, nightingales, larks, grass, daffodils, chest and brilliant - «υάκινθο», «ρόδο», «αηδόνια», «κορυδαλλοί», «χλόη», «ασφόδελοι», «στήθος» and «πάμφωτο» respectively.

MARIA LAINA

AUNT'S STORY

Yes, I suppose I am.
Yes, I am now.
The swishing of my skirt
the straw hat
at the doorway's bare head.
So there are so many things
things which give me the joy of the place
where time once was
for their sake, I let my hair down and fly at night
shy things, which blush
leaving regret and going towards glory.
Yes, Theodora smiled;
my hands are dry
but I can touch everything.

as if I am not
as if I am no longer myself so that you remember me
when, into the moon's thin water
the garden's pagoda will slide

my dearest Li-po
my dearest stag
forget all else;
if again you wish to hold me.

(Rose fear)

Yes, I suppose I am. Yes, I am now. A substantial conclusion, when doubt creeps, projecting *on the doorway* of daily life the *many things* left behind by time, as it abandoned the carelessness of the now and then, the before and after, moments which the protection of a straw hat accepted. An ephemeral joy of the being, which in the space of ignorance resided, delving into the impasses of sorrow and of human division. For the sake of impasses, the poetess becomes a witch, letting her hair take her to the knowledge of things at night, where the shy dreams blush by the revelations of the other, the occult, the unique self.

A smile from the depths of the heart thoroughly touches the being, as hands lose the ability for groundless, emotional communication and the body, with curvatures and sensual memories overcomes the moon's magic, sliding into the watercourse of the garden of lovers with the sun of the witches. The poetess, to a deer likens the beloved male nature awaiting the female one. Addressing it, she urges it to forget the sins committed by time against its beloved seasons and allow nature to embrace its own nature.

A divine destination of its female substance is earthly love. With her skirt's swishing, she enchants the dreams and with her *straw hat* she disarms the sun. Her *now* is the *bare* present *in the doorway*, denying the displacement of concepts to the disputed sovereignty of things. The mind allows time to meander and, releasing its forces from the transience of the day, to enter the cosmic night's eternity. Female rest of time, surrendered to its glory, to the male will, to the power of essence.

Penetrating is the poetess's gaze in the depths of human desire, which the pain does not share. A grabbing ruler of grace which preaches union, love for love, as to lawless promises it has surrendered. Liberalization is a poetic act; knowledge of God for the purification of charm to which moments are subjected. Hours are left to enrich their being by the rebirth of human hope, as things *give* them *joy*. How many miracles exist, keeping light subservient to the dark appetites of the century!

Tragic is the finding of drama's existence, a finding free and honest, where the probably and maybe of the circumstances' dynasty on the certainty of the mind are catalyzed. A base of the shy confessions of the Sphinx, to restore the sorrows, to leave, to go to the hermitage of glory, to the one-dimensional to deliver the multidimensional human temptation.

Ironic is favor's smile by which responsibilities overcome life, dealing with the senses of the flesh which constantly have cared for the burial of the soul. So many stories, so many ideas, so many heroic acts in vain; a shame is the chimera's entire work. She was a resident of a gloomy palace which embodied boredom, the premature aging of puberty, strolling through time's places to project her groundless visualization. Now a conscious woman *in the moon's thin water*, the ego of egoes, the soul in form, the form in life, a pagoda her spirit is in the sun's complying grace. And the mystic of love, having taken the form of a deer, the symbol of the ancient goddess Artemis, knowledge unappreciated which throughout the centuries worried over the vilification, the inevitable fall of erotic secrets, which were left exposed to the circumstances of human monstrosities.

The poem refers to the woman, to the eternal, highest, supreme, exquisite, unique relationship with the male, who by her, his nature, is attracted. Wishing to rule her dreams, from her transformations he is governed, passing from stage to stage, to reach, through processes of learning, to the wisdom of the perfected man. *There are so many things* which teach him life, the woman's nature, his nature, for the sake of which she abandons her emotional world each night and journeys to the uninterpreted realm of the soul. To find herself in the absolute of her being, where her ego is the man's ego, the ego of desires, of passions, the ego of love, of light, of the sun and the moon, of gods and humans, of dream and reality, of death and life.

The enlightened woman abandons the ephemeral, advising the man to also forget the futile. And she invites him to unite with her within the unique divine embrace.

TASOS LIVADITIS

CENTURY OF MULTIPLICITY

I sometimes contemplate the people I have met,
my childhood companions, the stones we gathered
></br>*when it rained*
and placed them below the sheds, lest they catch a cold
others died, others sank in life, others stepped
></br>*on me to pass,*
comrades in battle, on the snow or in a makeshift
trench, those who did not return, those who deserted,
others who surrendered. I contemplate the comrades
in prison, the cigarettes we shared, the loneliness
left whole to each of us, the long-drawn glances
></br>*through the window*
and those tearless, silent farewells
to those condemned to death. People magnanimous or contemptible,
></br>*defenseless or strong,*
leaving one inside the other, everything he gave
or denied him. So many words, so many gestures, so many faces
></br>*within me, which I no longer am.*
And you, beloved, when you push me away, outside your
></br>*door you shut an entire embittered world.*

(The Complete Works, Volume One)

The poet contemplates the people he has met. The comradely childhood years, gathering *stones when it rained* and placing them inside the sheds of misery, *lest they catch a cold*. A magical, infant, ritualistic act, to protect the people from the flight of those who died, abandoning life, sinking or stepping on the body of truth, to pass on to the other hell of their impasse. And to protect the others, those in battle, fighting *on snow* or through the underground trenches, from enemy shells. *And those who did not return, and those who deserted* and those who made peace with their weaknesses.

The deepest of contemplations about his imprisoned comrades, whose sharing their loneliness with cigarettes. And this loneliness was the entire responsibility of each, becoming a long-drawn glance through the window, a silent farewell, to those condemned to death, a tearless tune. A destination, which, as a person magnanimous or contemptible, helpless or strong, in others left its aspects, to become the memory of all that they had given it, as well as those who denied the heart's offering, with feelings, with *words*, with *gestures*, with their many *faces*. These faces lose their identity, their ego, to the poet's ego. People let him pass their bitterness through the gate of woman's life, and, if she accepts them in her womb, to enter and be gestated, as light to be born.

A giant is the poet's spirit, bearing the human spirit and calling life, shaping it into the woman, to accept the destination of fate, to embrace her *bitter world*. To open her heart, the soul and gate of her flesh, because she is the only one that can redeem, give light, purify the sins of betrayal, of abandonment, of desertion, the transgressions of surrender.

The poet knows it well; he knows her nature. The woman is the only one who with her power can save the world, as long as she accepts it as the entity, having the gift of establishing her feminine nature through contemplation. This deep contemplation is what seeks its path, as it travels through the forms, the happenings of history which the entity creates for human evolution. Occult and mysterious, relentless it traverses the distances of time, residing within the human mind. And only to the poet's spirit does it reveal its nature, its meanings, the expediency of martyrdom, to which people intentionally or unintentionally are submitted. As if it is a being within the being, whose spirit expands and the human becomes wise. He takes the fighter's place, defending the rights of the tribe, placing forth his breasts as sacrifice to the enemy's shells. And, at other times he denies life, he dies, sinking into the difficulties of his own helplessness, while others shoulder his discouragement; to christen it strength, endurance, so that they too can endure the torturing, as they watch those *tearless, silent people, those condemned to death*, and will receive the stimuli that will induce new contemplations.

Contemplations are the humans, ideas, images, parts of the universal mind, of the entity, whose spiritual nature, permeating chaos, seeks its parts, the parts of itself, so that they may realize its existence, to return, to join its essence. It is the one contemplating within every person, every fighter but also in others, those who are not anxious, or, if they are, they try to escape the task which calls them to battle. It guides them to overcome the obstacle raised by the imperfection of their nature, embracing an ideology, a "belief". To know the nature of ideas – their very own nature – with their struggles, and to delve into contemplation – to become the contemplation itself.

Their thoughts to acquire sensory receptors, to palpate the forms, the presences, the names of their comrades. To know the causes of desertion, like the rest, those of endurance before the loneliness of prison, which did not let the true fighters sink, even though others, that seemed stronger, *stepped on* them. And all *people, magnanimous or contemptible* and *defenseless*, in the give and take of transaction to recognize and as fighters to embrace their duty. To see that they have received and have given *gestures, words*, that they have refused and have accepted *so many faces*, so they lost their ego within the depth of their being, their entity.

This is the entity, the beloved. She must not push them away, the poet says, and outside her gate – her womb, her heart – shut *an entire embittered world*. Because she often does so, in the form of the eternal woman in her immature aspects. And this is the poet's grand conception, that he contemplates this truth. He becomes the entity's contemplation, conversing with his supreme beloved and, as if he holding her answerable, he pleads and tells her:

"And you, beloved, when you push me away, outside your door you shut an entire embittered world".

STATHIS MARAS

THE HORSE
(excerpts)

III

Today I speak to you of the bespectacled unknown god
simply
and offer you the horse.
When you hear the the battle hymn
when
you hear the trumpets sounding
when
you are sure of the firmness of the soil beneath your feet
then stand on your toes
cry out
and attack.

The same enemy with the same tunes
do not expect more information;
gaze at the white horse I have offered you
the proud horse I hold within my chest
which indifferently shakes its mane
and follows your footsteps along the bank
and follows you to the bowels of earth
there I reside
into soil transmuted
accountable in my absence, Lord
there, you reside
still hoping
and standing
on your toes.

(The water and the horse)

Agnostics are the humans who believe in the *bespectacled god*. They borrow his colored glasses and see the world through the light refracted in their spirit, choosing at times one and at times another color, so that every so often they manage to interpret things through the prism of any of their theory. And to boast, considering their judgment infallible, the only path to deification, even if the existence of God they deny. But even when reaching the inescapable conclusion that God exists, they still believe that they must look like him, be somewhat similar to him, like their own self, as ancient scriptures stated than humans were made in the image and likeness of God. God is as unknown to them as their own self, because they also see Him through the glasses of the agnostic.

The human spirit is but a horse, untamed and undominated, a body with instincts, with flesh and soul. A battle hymn is their Word, heard through the sound of trumpets and recorded by the poet's verses; to become a poem, a grounded entity, investigating *the firmness of the soil beneath* its *feet*. They stand *on their toes*, uplifted, they give the signal for the attack of time against inertia, a property of nature, which resists the eternal purpose of their spiritual evolution, in which it sees its biggest enemy.

Humans keep seeking *more information* to saturate the voracious, lower mind; to feed unsatisfied instincts, their insatiable need for carnal pleasure, mistakenly believing that they will thus be able to satisfy the demands raised by the appeal of their soul for union with the real, non-*bespectacled god*, to whom the poet is held accountable, accepting his absence within His redeeming existence.

White is the *horse* of contemplation, a purifying offer, and the chest of pride encompasses the wise poet's loving heart. With its mane, the knowledge-dominated horse shakes the breeze of its radiance and its light touches the bottomless depths of the abyss. *Along the banks* of the river that sweeps the declining life, it obediently follows the initiator's footsteps, which lead the dark personality of the world to the residence of the chthonic god. There, within *the bowels of earth*, all humanity is directed by the sound of trumpets of the epic battle hymn, which the poet continues to record with his verses. *Transmuted into soil* the sun, the sins of its fall it confesses. And its hope to lift humanity's being, so that it stand *on its toes*, with the awareness of the consequences arising from the act of their humic exaltation, to the Lord it bestows, who, as omnipresent, in the bowels of the sun's nature resides as well.

Today I speak to you of the bespectacled unknown god, the poet tells us, bestowing human qualities to God, to reveal human foolishness in its true range. And its black horse, symbolizing the body of passions of the untamed power, is accompanied by a white one, to balance the opposites, to purify the changing body, so that its glory shines and the beauty of soul and spirit is recognized. For the divine battle hymn *sounded* by the *trumpets* to become a paean of the Word, so that consciousness becomes certain of the existence of the footrest of feet; for the Earth to be intergrated into the body of God, who, holding the balance of the absolute, stands on His toes, and, crying out, attacks the defiance of dark spirits so that he illuminates them.

An enemy to enemies, a tune against tunes, a friend in support of enemies and friends; the compassion of love which battles indifference, inertia, which holds the human a lifelong slave within the depths of the unconscious. To await, to hope for the release of all who against their will descend to the hermitage of death, pleading their Lord and God for redemption. To be released from the shackles forged bytheir thoughts, ideas, theories, as, enticed by their ego, they indulged in the choices that ignorance dictated to them, claiming any kind of right, pursuing all their unrealistics objectives.

A rhythm of rhythms is God, spirit and body, enemy and friend, the tune of tunes of the omnipotence of His infinite parts. A tune whose Word like a battle hymn is emitted, a harmonious melody, with the enlightened spirits resonating within the body of creatures. The body vibrates, the soil confesses and is reconstructed. Living, fiery, spiritual blessing is the divine grace that to human hope is gifted. To lift itself, to stand on its toes and, jumping as a pterodactyl time, uplifting the abyss, to become lost in the divine.

MELISSANTHI

LYRICAL CONFESSION
(excerpts)

III

3

*We reached the point where the desert starts
with its great transformations
As fire, water and clouds
into our loneliness, we transformed
We traversed storms
Lightning spewed its flames
– on copper rocks, dragon's tongues –
Our forehead tore through clouds
unscathed we escaped disasters
from lakes of tears we emerged
as a swan that does not wet its feathers
We passed through haunted woods
and on our path, far away we heard
the insidious stirring of reptiles
On precipitous rocks, we stood
we looked over bottomless chasms
as the abyss invited us
wth a thousand magnetic gazes
But we courageously overcame it
with eyelids closed, singing
The wind, our lamp did not extinguish*

....

We passed through crowded streets
where crowds clamored like the ocean
Many veils have waves taken from us
flowers and stars were lost
But here, all flowers and stars
now rain down, into our embrace
Our prayer flies low
a dove with its legs tied
Afraid to ascend to Your heaven
whose roof increasingly distant becomes
Its way, it finds again, which leads
to You, from our heart a golden bow
It prepares for the great leap,
but half-way, struck
by vertigo, as from a bullet, it falls
Lord, make us worthy
Lord, in the days of trial
your face, do not hide from us
Send us helping angels
Lord, let us be recognized
beneath your sword's menace
Lord, accept our humble psalms
Lord, accept our humble heart.

....

(The Poems of Melissanthi)

Amid the changes of the becoming, *the fire, water and clouds* and, above all, *loneliness*, transmutate and become humans. *Traversing storms* and reaching *the beginning of the desert* of their soul, which is mercilessly struck by lightning. Demons, who, transformed into dragons, spew their flames onto *copper rocks*.

Spirits which have taken a stone form, to resist the eternal fire, which in God's furnace melts the universe, to reshape it into new, more evolved forms, with predominant the human form.

To transform again, to become *the fire and water*, the *loneliness* in their spirit's perpetual deluge, the lightning, the dragons, the spirits with the pure forehead that will tear through the clouds. And through the tears of their eyes, through the lakes of their pain, as immaculate swans with unwetted wings will emerge, after first passing through the *haunted woods* like reptiles which move their *insidious stirring* away at the sound of God, who watches them, alert, as over *bottomless chasms* they look and hear the enchanting song of the abyss which with its thousand mouths invites them and with its *magnetic gazes* commands them.

We made the song of the abyss our own, the poetess says, and its eyes we turned into our own, and when we shut our *eyelids, the wind* of its spirit, of our spirit, did not extinguish the light of the lamp.

Busy streets are the streets of the world; constantly changing shapes, a multiple of feelings, ideas, forms, spirits, centuries, seasons, *stars*, heavens, *flowers*. Veils hiding and revealing the ultimate face of God, raining down *into the* human's *embrace* more flowers and more stars and more worlds and more songs and more loves and more prayers. Because its old prayers fly low, as pigeons *with tied legs* afraid to ascend to the unchanging heaven, whose *roof becomes* more and more *distant*. And God's new prayers must be mixed with those of humans, the worn. To begin *the great leap from* his *heart*, like a rainbow which, although struck by the great *bullet*, will not succumb to death's *vertigo* and plunge into the abyss.

Lord, elevated on humility's pedestal, the destitute, heed us. Seekers of Your worthiness, from the worthlessness of our trial, do not turn the grace of Your face away, the supplication of the unworthy believers, do not overlook. With the help of Your angels, make us worthy to accept the terrible strike of the sword. Heed the *humble psalms, accept* the humble song of our heart, heal the pain of our soul. Enlighten our higher intellect, let us recognize Your glory.

Prayer's power is infinite, the poetess says. And the soul knows how to radiate it properly, the mouth to pronounce it, the heart to spread it, for heavens to stop and hear it, the miracle to be performed. During their transformations, demons to be admonished, to recognize that they are sons of God, people deluded, spirits which even copper rocks become to escape His fiery sword. His macrocosmic spirit's presence permeates the chaos, it acquires the aspects of His choice, with predominant His own choice against the liking of people who, by their choices, His grace appropriated and His mercy kept prisoner within the bottomless depth of the abyss.

Heed, the one who under Your sovereignty holds the destination of our desires. We have suffered through the fallacies of our small egoes, which Your ego have ignored. An ancient prayer from the breasts of the world towards God is emitted. Time prays, the human pleads, the power of His grace the poet invokes. God, the beginning; God, the Life; the miracles of Creation within eternal chaos.

Lord, the Creator, the humans' guide is the Supreme. His favor into obstacles transforms, the desert becomes, an abyss which the human spirit must traverse. All intelligent beings the Word of His infinite wisdom evangelize and the prisoners of the abyss hope on the ascent to save His universe. Inside the human soul, His mercy is infinite. All fields of the spirit it permeates and through transformations to which it submits the form, to His unchanging face he uplifts and saves it. Path of the becoming, the imaginative road of the human, is bathed in the path of His light and through prayer the lost is cleansed of sins.

The power of prayer the poetess teaches; with the spirit of hymn-writers her spirit unites. And the entire universe the poet's prayer listens to and admires. God heeded me, that on the terrible pedestal of Your Word I reside and Your fiery *sword* that brings redemption I await.

KOSTAS MONTIS

NIGHTS

Well, they shall absorb something of your concern
the day, the traffic, your job, the friends,
and you will then be able to go
to a theater or nightclub or wherever.
But when they all come to an end
when theaters and nightclubs close,
and friends say goodnight,
and you must go home – what happens then?
You know that the cruel, unrelenting
concern, awaits you in bed.
You will be alone.
And then you will reckon.
Want to or not, everything will be laid down and reckoned with.
You shall be alone
and, from theaters and nightclubs defenseless,
and from your job and friends.
Concern will be awaiting you in bed.
It will surely come. – It is so certain of it, and it awaits.
It is at home, waiting for you.

(The songs of the humble life)

Cruel, unrelenting the universal concern, it pounds the day, oppresses the night, controls the planetary becoming, dominates humans, shackles their belongings – their ideas. It calls humans to account for their actions, balancing their individual and collective life, asking them to return what the sun gifted, what the sea donated throughout their life, those which previous centuries bequeathed to humanity. And this one, the chosen of choice, the finest of finest, a mere mortal, identical in mentality to the human kingdom, but at the same time representing all kingdoms, senses the weight of obligations, becomes startled by this realization and, panicking, makes for a conscious and unconscious flight. Many are the responsibilities, unbearable the irrevocable requirements. Prisoner among myriads.

Mastermind, dominating over the mind's vessel. Directing it at will. A vessel is earth, a vessel is the body, a vessel is its being, a world in light. A world of spirits, concepts, wonders; a mortal world, of eternity and immortality. A world human and divine. This is the only concern humans have, the poet says, which little by little absorbs them: *the day, the traffic,* their *job*, their *friends*. And humans, not wishing to be assimilated by their very self, resort to entertainment, trying to be set free of the fatigue of their responsibilities, ignoring their duty and seeking the complacency of their destiny.

A center other than that of the self does not exist and, when, due to errors caused by carelessness they are forced to return home, where all needs converge, concern comes, the poet tell us, to inspect – within the area's configuration – the readiness of the mind, the knowledge of life. There are many to which they have not tended. The greatest concern is that of the distribution of energies and forces of the soul throughout the world. The repositories were many and left unused. Every dark spot on earth could have received a portion of light's inexhaustible reserves; for each problem, a solution could have been found.

Concern asks of humans: "In the droughts of the century, have you become the inexhaustible source of earth, the oxygen of forests, the breeze of the sea, the ether of the atmosphere? In the losses caused by death, have you become the regeneration of life? For every *concern* that *awaits you*, have you become a concern higher even than myself?".

Concerns, in infinity's prompting, care for humans, serve them, working in their world so that people march on, evolve and create greatness. Micro-entities, which are arranged according to their will. Playing their perennial game, they beg to be recognized, to be seen as the hours of their time, as the moments of duration, parts comprising day and night, times comprising their century, centuries which the eternity of their existence constitute, for God's creation to appear brilliant amid the chaos of their spirit.

Oh, concern of concerns, redeeming communion with the ecstatic flow of angels, supreme life of immortals, consciousness of saints, the entity of the enlightened, having the responsibility for all existent, the nature of the holy spirit! Of this concern the poet speaks. With this concern humans reckon; with their conscience. For whatever they neglect to this they must answer to and obey. When from ignorance they are carried away, they drift, they wander amid their passions, but they always return to it. And when they do not, it comes to them. Supreme care, divine providence, guardian angel, true Word, self-evident divine glory.

Humans guide their vessel amid the ocean of the being of consciousness, which has designated them the only captain that can lead it to its destination. Their mind is affected by their travels, because it has initiative as a compass, the resultant of concerns, the most capable, which takes them wherever their desire commands. Until desire becomes love, as a divine attribute to be recognized, a spiritual nature that embraces all, a concern residing within every concern; to control the strong winds, the storms of passions which resist the course that will has set against spiritual expediency's target. Divine destination, whose intention life learns not to oppose, a concern which contemplates human concerns. The parts of its self it supervises, for these it cares.

When concern comes to humans, life itself comes, the poet says. With them it reckons its having. It cares for them and they feel love toward it. Whatever it does, it will find itself before them. This work, the days and nights, the entertainment and pain. It dominates them, it entertains them, it admonishes and comforts them, leaving them defenseless one moment, defending them the next. Bread and circuses, their life, insecurity and confidence. It is the good wife which always awaits their return, a mermaid on the ship's bow, the housewife directing their life through all forms of cosmic manifestation, rendering them responsible for the completion of the work they have been entrusted with. In free volition lies the reconciliation of aspects projected on them and the disclosure of the concerns arising from their action, a theatrical action, in which they must learn to consciously participate, to play the game of life just as well as the concern does.

PANTELIS BOUKALAS

ORIGIN

Grief extinguished him
as he failed to give meaning
to the fishermens' riddle.
 "Whatever we caught, we threw out"
they responded to his blind question.
"And what we did not catch
we brought with us."
These are the stories they say of Homer.
Seamen talked about their catch.
And about lice.
But he looked deeper.
The name of his art
he felt they were teaching him.
Once you conceive the rhythm
violently you throw it off you, startled,
lest you get burnt;
to dwell somewhere else,
a beggar of memory.
And within you
– you carry them, they carry you –
the poison of stray words festers.
And you die.
From your grief, they say.
Because you failed to unravel the riddle,
to let it bloom.

To lean under its shade
and be set free within the miracle.
Thus, the founder.
And thus, his grandchildren.
And great-grandchildren,
until the Great Crushing.
Deliberate prey to a Homeric issue
unreturnedly real.

(Wretched Signals)

The benevolent fishermen are the eternal mystics, but also the others, the cunning, they, too, initiate people to the secrets of the sea that is full of riddles. And all, unconscious and conscious observers, see the grief extinguish those who fail to give meaning to the recurring waves, which, after the lull, are created by the unrest of the heart and mind. Unrestrained cosmic desire, which eternally manifests the request for its prevalence on the world. Whatever humans conceive, whatever they can perceive, to comprehend as an answer *to* their *blind question*, they throw away. And what they do not comprehend and cannot appropriate, they carry with them until becoming enlightened. This is Homer's history all in all, the poet says.

Of their accomplishments the heroes speak, the seagoing seamen, of gargantuan monsters which their spirit catches, as well as others which they reveal, *the lice*, the devious mysteries, the subcutaneous, horrific secrets. Disparate ancient forces which compel humans *to look deeper*. They teach them *the name of the art*, seeking to familiarize them with the sun's rhythm, as, fearful that their body might become the dwelling place of fire, fearing they might get burnt, drive it away from them, forcing it to dwell someplace else. But, as eternal beggars of memory, within the unconscious they carry everything that for centuries have carried them.

The poison, which the mind did not manage to distill, *festers*. Stray concepts urge words to murder those not able to solve the riddle, to transform into a garden of sunflowers of knowledge. In their shadeless shade to lay, *within the miracle* of their perfected self to become free. To become the progenitor, the one from the origins. *And thus, his grandchildren. And great-grandchildren*, the coming races, *until* their *Great* perfection to crush, prey to become to the essence of the unborn, unprojected, true self. Essence of life and redemption, this is the spiritual reality of the *Homeric issue*, even beyond the Iliad and the Odyssey.

These are the humans, unique in their nature, contentious and good-natured, self-indulgent and tough, benevolent and cunning, mortal and immortal. Possessed of their dreams, rhythms, arts; decisively influenced by unrelenting thoughts. Now, in the New Age, the incorruptible assessment, made by the poet in agony, takes the gravity of the deliberate shortening of the *unreturnedly real*. Conscious action, before the inevitable Crushing that is imposed by the end of the century. Heavy is the legacy of the *Homeric issue*, which time keeps in its jurisdiction, as it carries the memories that carry humans and murder them with the poison of unprocessed words. And the grief of the world is an integral grief of the poet. A supreme guardian of memory, for centuries storing the treasures of knowledge on behalf of the race.

It is the riddle to be solved, spiritual fruits which the human spirit must tie. To realize the meaning of existence, to disclose the deeper meanings. Unconscious life has its own importance. It is divine providence which renders humans unable to give *meaning to the riddle* and to throw away whatever they catch. It incites them to carry whatever they cannot conceive. *To their blind question*, the entity with riddles answers.

The collective unconscious works on the behalf of people, and they, destined to process the stimuli with the aid of perceptions, delve into their being, to make knowledge of their respective Homeric cycle.

These age-old symbols, the fish, conceal innumerable secrets, the poet tell us, and make humans look deeper. They symbolize the end of a complete secular cycle which for two thousand years has taught the fine art of material and spiritual survival, enabling them to conceive the meaning of inner life, that which fearfully they tried to cast off. A purifying fiery rhythm forced them, for as long as they stayed in denial, to remain *beggars of memory*. And to record within them those circumstances which they carried and which carried them to the inevitable end of poisoning; a panacea of initiatory deaths, which from the beginning of creation has lead them to the mysteries of the eternal miracle's blooming. That which passes them to dianoia1, to the field of inner knowledge, from where they may – in possession of the history of their genealogical tree – enable the New Era to exist.

To this Era the Homeric question will be posed again. The law of retribution will work for those that will be trapped within the new cosmic cycle, will be enchanted by the dream, will become intoxicated by visions and through the abyss shall wander. And after the conquest of the other Troy, that of the technological Era, they will be recognized as a new Odysseus. And they will be called to carry out their Odyssey, falling *voluntary* prey *to an Homeric issue*, until the perfection of the universal world, the one beyond another, newer, perfective Era that is unreturnedly real.

---

* The term "dianoia" (coming from the Greek word 'διάνοια' which literally means "through the mind") means the oversimplification of ideas through the function of the Higher Mind.

RITA BOUMI-PAPA

IF I GO FOR A WALK
WITH MY DEAD FRIENDS

If I go out for a walk with my dead friends
    the city will flood with silent girls
    the air with the acrid scent of death
    the forts will raise white flags
    the vehicles will stop –
if I go out for a walk with my dead friends.

If I go out for a walk with my dead friends
    you will see a thousand girls with punctured breasts
    uncovered, crying
    "why did you send us to sleep so early
    in so much snow, uncombed, tearful?"–
if I go out for a walk with my dead friends.

If I go out for a walk with my dead friends
    the crowds in amazement will see
    how a lighter brigade has not stepped foot on earth;
    how a holier litany has not paraded
    a more glorious resurrection and bloodied -
if I go out for a walk with my dead friends.

If I go out for a walk with my dead friends
    the full moon, as a wedding flower will rise to adorn them
    within their hollow eyes, orchestras will weep
    their curls, the bandages will blow with the wind;
    Oh, then, many of remorse will die –
if I go out for a walk with my dead friends.   (A thousand slain girls)

If she goes *out for a walk with* her *dead friends*, the poetess says, in the silent procession of superb apparitions, pure visions, hallowed lives, which upon the altar of hate were sacrificed, barricaded within their forts, fearful are relentless times, the watchdogs of Hades, the *white flags* of peace they *shall raise*. And the vehicles carrying disunity will stop. The rivers of the world will also cease, the stars will halt amid their rotations, people will stop walking on the paths of the universe. Protests will be heard and the bare breasts of women who were not made worthy to nurture love will emerge punctured by the shame, the brutality and the ignorance of unloved men. *Uncombed*, *tearful*, the embittered brides, raised from their slumber will seek the culprit. And the harmony of their exquisite lament, a feminine grace, in all winds will diffuse, to activate the sea and the sea the sky and the sky the time.

Time slays the woman it is her unforgiving husband, her bloodthirsty lover. And then, by its own work it is abolished, the one that its dead nature gestates; its very own female substance. *An acrid scent* fills the air, girlish. It is the one whose buds did not bloom, a Word which in its virgin wombs remained silent; unblossomed hearts that they did not know, they did not enjoy the suns, to gestate them, to give birth to them, so as to become men in another heaven, that of infinity, beyond this miserable, unredeemed world. A world which learned to bury its children, to keep them in tombs, and is forced to listen to the protests of its dead aspirations, hopes waiting to be awakened through the compassion, the forgiveness, the grace of the tragically lost girls.

If the poet goes *out for a walk with* her *dead friends*, the dead of the entire world will rise. It will be a different *resurrection*, *glorious*, a moon's bloodied dance of the dead, reflected by its *orchestras* within *hollow eyes*. And music will accompany the *holy* and unholy *procession*, light-footed, ungrounded, unredeemed magic, devastation of the full moon, curse of the personality, a wedding complaint of a furious woman, which transforms death into illusions as she takes on a gruesome form and her curls become entangled with bandages to reveal the wounds; to become remorse, to slay the many who slayed beauty, the inner beauty, the grace of the divine power, of feminine love.

The woman-life, the woman-light, the woman-knowledge is a supreme field. Initiator of the male in the mysteries of universality, and yet she is not worshiped, she is not recognized; she is not protected from hate. Half, separative are humans, as a man he battles the nature birthing him, he degrades it, degrading his own being. He denies her the jurisdiction in mind and heart, and, under the pretext of needs created by the materialistic way of life, he disrespects the woman's deity and imputes the human passions to her. Claiming that the causes of his misfortune from her own nature originate, he leaves her exposed to war's hell, to the savage beast of devastation, to his lower self, so that she becomes prey of ignorance, she, who was destined to deliver him knowledge.

Supreme is the feminine human aspect, supreme is the male. In the field of morphic reality, his fate outweighs his spiritual nature. This fate is perceived as the one and only reality and the other is ignored, the essential one that which leads him to redemption, to release from earthly shackles. Along with the woman, the man is also slain; with the loss of life, the human is also lost. What is most valuable to him is lost, it becomes a ghost keeping him prisoner in the dream, a vision full of bitter memories, acrid scents, experiences of the lunar chain which are incessantly repeated keeping him a slave within the abyss of the lower mind and in the unredeemed heart's endless suffering.

The poetess delves into the drama, the drama of the human, the drama of the earth, the drama of time, the drama of the Word, into the poetry's drama. To the creation, to the feminine nature she refers to, in response to the injustice that is perpetuated and this reference of hers takes on the dimensions of infinity and records the drama of the universe. It is the injustice committed against the woman by the man, the injustice committed against the man by the woman; whether it is more or less by each party, it does not matter. What matters most is that the ignorance of the feminine nature's entity becomes knowledge, along with everything created due to this ignorance. The influences it exerts are infinite, grandiose, her presence irreplaceable, as that of man. However, in the relations between them the woman's effect is stronger, as she conceives the mind, gestates the whole and rebirths the world, keeping it in existence by nurturing the divine virtues, the supreme values which perpetuate the becoming of universality. Each person's life testifies to this universality, which is none other than the woman's life.

The poetess calls people to delve into the mysteries of woman's nature, by showing them the unique procession, perpetuated in the unconscious cycles of life. *If I consciously go out with my dead friends*, the poem suggests, it will be a revelation different both from that which happens daily in the world and from the other, the redeeming, the unique, which will bring an end to the dream. *If I go out for a walk with my dead friends*, death will be perpetuated beyond the limits of its own sovereignty. It will be resurrected in an unredeemed resurrection that will keep worlds captive in the chain of the permanent deadly imprisonment. The poetess invites the male aspect of the world to a revision, to a deep repentance for its impious behavior towards its own being, the feminine nature which rebirths it, nurtures it and destines it towards ultimate glory, a glory for which it was chosen by the creator of all.

TAKIS NATSOULIS

TONIGHT IT CAME

*Tonight it came
the lovely bird
above my sleep.
Its wings were open,
terrifying, threatening.
Slowly and rhythmically it repeated
as the returning wave:
"Now is the time, now is the time".
it plunged its beak
between my eyes.
My skin froze.
"Now is the time," it said,
"Now is the time".
I asked for a postponement,
I said I did not have time
the olives to gather,
to remove the garden's weeds;
I said I did not have time
to look at the stars,
and Freedom to look in the eyes.*

(Recollections)

When knowledge visits us, it knocks on the door of distinction and awaits the decision, the expression of truth, the presence of the soul to emerge of its own volition. Time transforms into a *lovely bird*. Knowledge is but death spreading its *terrifying wings* to cover the past with their shadow; to encompass it with the menacing but redemptive presence and, croaking, to plunge *its beak between the* human *eyes*, crying the great call to fallacy, so as to resign from its lie and succumb to truth. The shadow, through its own shadow, surrender to the light.

"Now is the time, now is the time", the poet says. The chills of fear freeze the skin and humans, clinging to the work of ignorance, request a postponement. They have run out of time, consumed in the dealings of earthly life, and the stars, they did not have time to look at. They did not think they had to delve into the heaven's absoluteness, in the immensity of chaos, where their being, the spirit of spirits, amid the heavenly Freedom treads. There, the poet eternally resides and overlooks the gardens from above, the roofs of houses and the perennial trees, the olive trees, watching his other self, the earthly, with the pretext of his work's need, the harvest of fruit, the uprooting of weeds and the completion of the roofs of uncovered houses.

Irrevocable is the imperative heavenly voice, it envelops the human demand. Its need has no power, no excuse is given. The dome is one, the roof of the house, of the universal temple, and the decoration, the harmony of the mind with the ideas radiating wisdom's light. Humans lie to time, finding pretexts and citing obstacles. It is the seeing and hearing of God, who bears their denials; and on the blessed hour calls them to abandon the futile preoccupation with the body's prison, where their spirit surrendered to the enchantment of nature, wanders within the realm of sensations and occupies itself with the human, earthly temptation.

"*Now is the time, now is the time*, to remember what you forgot," the voice of the Word is heard, and its every call is for a star, a person, a life, a presence, an idea, a feeling, a pleasure, a pain. Each call is for a memory tying humans to the chain of their coercion. As if they, humans, are responsible for the existence, the creation, made for people to mimic repeating at will the ideas of the universal mind, as, having chosen to reside on earth, they defend their rights and suffer.

Their only companion and savior in prison is death. It is the other face of God, that which, with His transformations claims His rights, teaching humans the impartial, wise justice of His cosmic law, so that His jurisdiction can be recognized. The great hour of death calls them to the awareness of eternity. Centuries are their thoughts and ideas when referring to the entity. Who builds a house consciously, considering that, as they place tiles on the roof, they partake in the perpetuation of the existence of the firmament? And who, when gathering olives, believes they collect fruits from the great tree of existence, so that light, eternity is born within them through the blessings of God?

Unconsciously do humans live their life. They overlook the magical acts of the becoming. Their spirit does not participate in the mysteries; of the universal initiatory process it does not partake. They refuse to recognize the miracle that is revealed constantly before their eyes. And the death of morphic life is the redemptive punishment imposed on them, the great calling for the realization of their true nature.

The poet is the only one who knows, who possesses the drama and envisions it as a *lovely bird*, giving glory to death, as its other aspect is God, the Word, who calls humans to see earth from the heavens, to take the poet's place and look closely at the stars, *to look Freedom in the eyes*, to direct the destination of their being. Each realization humans make is also the death of a cycle which came before and which leads to perfection, to which their own actions consciously and unconsciously urge them.

In the poem, with the *lovely bird* the poet tells us of the procedure performed by the human entity itself on the human field of vision, so that it can open up and allow distinction to deepen. He likens the bird to the angel of death, so that humans may familiarize themselves with it, accept God's will, pass into a greater union with their entity and thus continue to evolve. It is the power of their attachment to earthly matters which makes them stall, avoiding to deal, – in person, face to face – with the irrevocability of their destiny. And they plead for an extension on the grounds that they want to delve into the stars, *to look Freedom in the eyes*, something which they unconsciously avoid doing although having been given the opportunity, and which, with the aid of death, they will then be forced to realize in the continuation of their universal life.

GIANNIS NTEGIANNIS

FINAL ADVENTURE

When, burdened with futile experience, bitterness
 He returned to the island with the birds and dolphins,
They did not wait for him; they had denied him
People, child, woman, homemade gods,
And no one cared whether the shame
Of Achaeans he had washed away or if
Polyphemus he had defeated, Circe.

He was not too old
To fight with a bow and spear,
For the devious enemy to set traps,
But when glum and sad
For the pointless slaughter, the destruction,
The number of tears shed
Where he passed from.
Shivering, a secluded corner he wished for
To lean, but there was no
Home to accept him, or fire
The numb thought to warm,
A stone his fatigue to lay.

His cracked raft he took again
And in the vastness disappeared.
....

But the Sorcerer Poet, the one standing
Outside the circle of decay, of Time

And the indomitable human spirit is the same,
But the Sorcerer Poet into the eyes casts
A beam of enchanting dreams and dazzles them
The legend's cloth he weaves, which he embroiders
Stars, birds of Longing, with sunbeams,
Amid the ocean, he establishes
Islands, the refuges of castaways,
With a chosen essence, he shapes
The holy form of Penelope,
The plunderers he beats, the sin, and raises
The indestructible era, Odysseus,
Who, until the final hour stood
Cunning, proud, brave.

(The first and only choice)

Of the warriors who went out to conquer nations, to subdue people, of those who either succeeded or failed – it does not matter – who all have one face and one faith, one ideal, that of the family they leave behind and think of and keep in their hearts; of the many who are this one, of him, the poet speaks, *Odysseus* who returns.

He is the great conqueror, the one who plundered the mind and heart of the world, the resourceful ruler, the relentless monster, filled with the nostalgia of returning to the place from where he started, where his Time had stopped. He had left them guarding his heart, but *they did not wait for him, they had denied him*, the poet says; *people, child, woman,* even *homemade gods*, ignoring the feats he accomplished during his long return. In the reckoning of his futile cycle the remorse, the sorrow, the grief for this *pointless slaughter, the turmoil*, for the rivers of blood and tears that follow him like ghosts, as their souls, parts of his own great soul, claim his destination.

A tragic hero upon earth; beyond the world his role lies. *He is not too old to fight with a bow and spear*, so no *stone* is given on which *to lay his fatigue*. *A secluded corner* where he may silence his shivering, *a home to accept him, a* hearth his *numb thoughts* to *warm* – does not exist.

The world against the destroyer defends itself. Slaughtered by him, yet it does not surrender, although its own destruction it has authorized him to carry out. The hero is one aspect of divinity, the catalytic aspect of humans in their triune nature, that which brings destruction and devastation in the creation and maintenance, in vanity and complacency. The world is vain, complacent amid the works which enslave its soul and keep it prisoner within its personality's coercion, in the enchanting splendor of the form's beauty. The slave complains, the prisoned unconscious of humanity rebels creating cause for war. And he perpetuates the reason for his existence, under the pretext of those which his ignorant representatives project as excuses for the ignorance pervading them.

It is the impulsive spiritual force that overwhelms the wrongly structured family, and, in its expansion, the society, humanity itself. The internal conflict of the soul with its aspects becomes manifested within the social arena, seeking the faces that will utterly express it. These assert their rights, and their great heroic soul, their resultant, is the hero Hercules, the hero Odysseus, who has assumed the task of freeing himself, letting personality trace the necessary cycles, while following it to the – parallel to its own – evolution.

Odysseus is every pioneer in the work of evolution and the faces of his environment resist, oppose the ideas, his work. He exceeds his Time and handles their own Time. He lets them guard his heart so that they see his visions within it, which are their visions, his desires which are their own desires, the plans of his resourceful personality that is their own personality and the great single vision of their soul, which is the vision of his own soul. A silent, secret agreement is made between them, that he shall be the great liberator and role-model. It is agreed that they may react and blame him, because they are the same ones whom in his campaigns he fights. Their own fortresses are the city of Troy which covets the wooden horse, opening the gates to accept the Trojan horse, unconsciously having the knowledge of what hides within its depths – within their own depths.

For a thousand years, him, the helot – who represents the spirit and soul of the universe, the form and personality – *the Sorcerer Poet* places him, as being his own self, on *his cracked raft*. On it, he disappears within *the vastness* of his shipwreck and returns from it, untamed *outside the cycle of decay*, as the immortal soul that knows no fear. Because it has the ability to cast the beams of its *enchanting dreams* on death, blurring it with its legends, as it embroiders with the rays of its light the wonders of the endless Iliad and Odyssey on the heavenly dome. *Amid the ocean*, it raises its universal shipwreck, to establish it in the essence of the sacred form, which the centuries of the future will have to worship, of the holy entity that will merge all forms and souls of its universal being, as the timeless Odysseus, until his *final hour* will prove to be the great redeemer.

In the face of this supreme deity, societies will establish the family of the future, utilizing all past experiences, unifying them in the one and only, which will not be the result of futile experience. All experiences will refer to the entity, the conscious destination of the universal world, which, on its own volition evolving, will seek the cause of those occurring, the knowledge that will bring the requested peace, firmly working towards conquering it.

ZISIS OIKONOMOU

WHY I REJOICE TODAY

United I was born, with the wonder of the world
a drop in the water of the eternal
where the earth dreams and the soul breathes in its decay.
How did I find myself at such a precipice?
Imperceptibly I shall fall, without heroics.
Not within the chaos of Nothingness.
Nor into the utmost pitfall of the Ego dying.
The soil of mother earth is adequate
for a blanket and a mattress
nourishment of plants which fed you
ultimate abode of the present moment
watering you in the timeless duration
water of the bright ocean
which has dried up in its unfathomable original darkness.
In such future deprivation
objects dance
of the vertigo, which has broken out.
No resistance, give the hand
song of life
hymn of the unsupported love
I am nowhere
and you rejoice, you rejoice
hosanna, hosanna, to the creatures of the world.

(Fair Silence)

Humans – miracle of the world – united with God they are born, *a drop in the ocean*, a cell of the eternal body *dreaming* of the universe. And their soul *breathes their decay*, as, imperceptibly and *without heroics*, they fall into the precipice of the only question raised by their entity on the Ego, death, Nothingness, chaos, from which sprang mother earth. The soil nourishes humans. It is enough to become their blanket and mattress, the residence of every moment, until the ultimate presence.

Timeless duration, with *the water of the bright ocean waters* the spiritual sprout that time within the garden of earth's heart cultivates and exudes from its unfathomable original darkness, the inexhaustible. The human heart – the heart of the universe – is emptied of desire. To deprivation it is subjected and its objects of desire move to the invocative *dance of vertigo* which breaks out despite resistance. *Song of life* which gives its hand to unsupported love, to realize, to know the nowhere, the bliss of the absence of humans and exclaim *Hosanna, Hosanna*, that they are the creature of creatures in the spectrum of their world.

The poet celebrates union. "Hosanna in the highest, blessed is the coming in the name of the Lord". Inherent is the entity, God, in chaos, "which art in all places and fillest all things", and is yet not recognized by all. A resident in its dynasty the Ego, humans, by the projection of their cosmic existence are enchanted and by its futile faith are misguided. An innermost sun of the *brilliant ocean* is the poet, with the essence of his existence he illuminates the vast darkness of the Ego, belying hopes for the perpetuation of futile time, that keeps it imprisoned in the courtships of the unsupported, unrealistic work that resists the surrender leading to its being made void.

He is the poet who consciously becomes this cosmic Ego, while simultaneously remaining the irremovable essence of things. This dance of all, the eternal song, *the hymn of unsup-*

ported love, giving its hand to hold on to the other, the inner self, to accept it, to realize that, although it is in everything, yet it is nowhere apart from joy, in the bliss of the essence where all creatures in their ontological state reside; even though they are covered by *the soil of mother earth*, although they have the harsh nature as a mattress, that which nourishes them, that which is the *ultimate abode* of eternity, present *in the timeless duration* which perpetually by its own forces is illuminated *within the chaos of Nothingness*, where, as a supreme hero, it has chosen to fall imperceptibly. And it wonders how it found itself before *such a precipice, dreaming* of the breath of its soul, *its decay*, like a *drop* in the ocean of primordial planets, as a molecule of fires' matter – of the sun's miracles.

The essence of things resides in the mind, the poet tells us, within the sunlight darkness converges. *Hosanna, of vertigo* the outburst in the presence of *the brilliant ocean* which is absorbed by its *unfathomable original* darkness, the ultimate light. The deprivation of the future bows to the poet's revelation and the dance of universes ritualizes within the miracle of his presence. Eternal song which catalyzes the resistances, a redemptive chant of love which accepts its fallacy and escapes death's trap, the decay repeated with the breath of the soul, its desire for existence, for heroism within the futility of chaos, of Nothingness.

I, the Word declares through the poet's mouth, the *united with the wonder of the world*, the born and unborn. The fire of fires, the water of waters, the dream of dreams, the soul of souls. The planet of planets, the body of bodies, the breath of breaths, the precipitated hero, the penetrating chaos. The question and the answer, the creator of traps for the redemption of death. The mother earth, the soil that covers bodies, the food which nourishes them, the *ultimate abode*. Presence of timeless duration, brilliant ocean, original, an unfathomable entity which to deprivation subjects its times. Perpetual dance, divine vertigo, resistance to futility's power. Song, praise of praises, the eternal soul that rejoices and welcomes the descent into Hades and the return of creatures to its perpetual world.

I am the Word, the light, the failed eros, love, eternity, the nowhere of all, the Nothingness and everything; I – the joy, the eternal bliss, the soul and body of the perpetual becoming.

KOSTIS PALAMAS

THE TWELVE WORDS OF THE GYPSY
(excerpt)

Oh, forge the earth anew in molten flame;
With taintless virtues and with lofty crimes
Ring on your anvils with brave hammer-blows,

Leap over every barrier wall. Oh give,
give to your mules swift-soaring wings like those
which urge the broom-sticks that the witches ride.
Unbounded, unpartitioned is the world;
And where the spreading continents have end
begins the oceans' tide.

Whatever peaks you scale, you ever find
that from their summits other peaks are seen
and other landscapes beckon from afar.
And when you shall have stormed the highest peak
then shall you find, like always, that you stand
below the lowest star.

(The twelve words of the gypsy)
Translated by T. Stephanides & G. Katsimbalis

The poet talks to nature, to the horses and its intelligent beings – the humans. Great-breather sun, its spirit and its fire are the furnace which melts the crimes and blooms the good parts. Ringing *on anvils with brave hammer-blows*, humans shape their world, according to the requirements of God's will, which are always relative to the inclination of their soul. Worthy and capable is their own will, too; free and unhindered as the poet's, standing up to all subordinate realms, it processes the divine Word by forging it, endowing it with its dearest forms. That their spirit may take on the dimensions of infinity; to thrive in the mind; to be perfected in knowledge; the drama of their life to be redeemed.

The poet – a great spiritual leader – educates the humans within the macrocosmic field of God. He guides them, so that they may *leap over every barrier wall*, to exalt the instincts, symbolized by mules, over the castles built by time in self-defense. There, the heart's values hover, the forces of divine love, the appeals of the earthly soul. And they protect the world, keeping it vast and compact, unique in its pure nature, unharmed in the firmament of the supreme God's magnanimousness, a spiritual universe where natural land ends and the oceans of ontological quest *begin*.

Whatever peaks you scale, the poet tells the suns-giants, you ever find that *from their summits other peaks are seen*; other huge giants, even taller than the stars, who enchant God himself and intoxicate Him, so that His will is delivered to the will of another, seductive world; so that the beloved humans reach its highest peak with His divine grace, to witness and admire His inconceivable greatness. To comprehend the endless miracle of His creation, such that, no matter how high thought, passion, or love may go, the creator's light will always be higher, to illuminate His human stars in all eternity, creations which must love and hurt.

The works of their toil to become a sacrifice, like sins which bloom and wither on the tree of knowledge of good and evil – concepts which symbolize immortality and death. These concepts the poet says must be worked on with the fire of desires, as they are beaten by the hammer – which symbolizes the mind – on the anvil, which is the human heart. There, the world is unconsciously being worked upon and the poet teaches humans to work consciously. United with the will of God, he knows the mysteries of the universe, as with his Socratic knowledge he holds his soul's–the world's soul– ever-flowing toil, intending to reach the perfection of its morphic expression.

'Tis the sins which must bloom again, the desires which must be perfected and become love. For this reason, the docile mules must perform their service, they must carry the burden, the drama of personality, and, overcoming the barriers of protection, of defense and attack, symbolized by the stockyards, to lay it on the mysteries of transformations. There, the service performed for purification receives its wings; the offering, symbolized by the broomsticks, which the *witches ride* – freedoms earned when people have carried out their work, so that the world has the opportunity to maintain its unity within the vastness of eternity. A perpetual cycle, in which *the continents have end* and *the ocean's tide* begins, where *the ocean's tide* ends and the *continents* begin.

The continents which, with their solid ground, symbolize the stability of humans, their confidence, their faith in ideas. The seas symbolize their turbulent mental visions, which travel them through the vast field of their existence, through which they explore their inner and outer world; by the revelations of their works to be initiated into the deeper knowledge of their being and thus be able to unite their will to the infinite will of God. Human glory to be conquered, a unique freedom which experiences love.

The gypsy symbolizes the universal soul, which to the passions of personality resists, showing its love, its profound interest in the human drama. It suffers so that people overcome the impasse of ignorance, in which they deliberately found themselves, the chaos to which their desire urged them, as they followed their dream, which enchanted and entrapped them in their abysmal passions.

    A gypsy who must work, care, and supervise the drama of his grief. A Greek soul, a universal form; on chaos he focuses, as Hephaestus in God's furnace, to process and forge his spiritual world *with brave hammer-blows* of the mind upon *the anvil* of the Christ-like heart; with the primordial fire, the sun's unique power, shaping his world again and again, to its perfection leading it above and *below the lowest star*, to exonerate it.

I.M. PANAGIOTOPOULOS

THE WINDOW OF THE WORLD

33

Somewhere there is an afternoon sky.
There, the heron walks, pecking the cloud.
It seems as though autumn draws near.

Now I shall talk about your autumnal hair,
about your autumnal face.
The time is right, to look at your hands
to tell you about toil,
about quiet love,
about affection,
to tell you about the human,
to forget about fever.

To talk to you once more,
before nightfall.
Because nightfall will certainly come.
Without hope and without remorse.

Somewhere there is an afternoon sky.
It opens its leaves, it combs the golden locks by the river,
it sends the cloud to the heron.
Its eyes are childish,
inquisitive.
They are full of swallows.

Take the final swallow,
let it sleep in your hands,
without hope and without remorse.

Let it sleep in your hands.
The swallow is the twilight,
the ailing light,
that obliquely falls onto the window.

By this light
the oblique
we shall pave the ultimate path.

Somewhere will shall stand,
one will leave,
we shall say goodnight, we shall say thank you.

Thank you for what we have endured,
thank you for the love, the desire, for hope, the remorse,
thank you for those we looked at together,
for those we talked about,
thank you for the friendship,
thank you for the daughter,
for the boy,
thank you for the dead children,
for the daughter who left,
for the boy who is no more,
thank you for what still remains, for the vigilance,
 for the tenderness, for the sorrow, for the effort,
 for the courage, for the condemnation.

Thank you for the human presence.

         (The Poems of I.M. Panagiotopoulos)

When the sun reaches its peak, when the spirit is uplifted and the light realizes his entity, the afternoon heaven of heavens is revealed to the poet, as a person heading towards perfection. *It opens its leaves, it combs the golden locks by the river, it sends the cloud to the heron* and all realms are uplifted. *Its eyes are childish*, the poet says, *inquisitive, full of swallows*. These, for centuries have foreseen the spring, not this earthly one, but the other one, the occult, the divine.

To end all hope of external life and eliminate the need for repentance, humans must let *the final autumnal swallow* – that which foresaw earthly spring – sleep *in* his *hands*. Because this is *the twilight, the ailing light that obliquely falls onto the window*, and, with this light, humans must pave *the final path* in the myriad streets, where both selves timelessly stand and one always leaves. And when they say *goodnight*, when they say *thank you*, one thanks the other for all those he endures, for all those poet must deal with.

Whenever people say *thank you*, for their human presence they are grateful. This includes the processes of the universe, the desires and hopes, the undertakings and realizations, the deadlocks and efforts to escape to the external, but also to return to the internal, to the one, the unique. It is there where the friendships, the gazes, the conversations, the human aspects are driven; it is there where they return; the extensions of their being, which were left to become women and men, daughters, boys, alive and *dead children*, that had left, died and did not exist; and were reborn, to become the enduring *vigilance*, the *tenderness* of sadness, the *effort* and *courage*, the *condemnation*. Human presence in perpetuity, that transforms its futile cycle into an essential one; a cycle of which time prides itself with the *childish eyes*, an *afternoon sky*, a sun shining within the recollection of the heron, a symbol representing the other entity of humans, the earthly, which is surrounded by the cloud of their desiring life's emanations.

God is the beginning and end of each cycle and the human entity was destined to consciously reach the highest tiers of existence through gratitude, as it learns from the poet to thank for every single thing, whether great or small, good or bad, pleasant or sad, painful or painless, for its happiness and for its suffering, for everything that happened within the infinite and infinitesimal, within its microcosmic and macrocosm self.

In the poet's vision, as an *afternoon sun*, God is revealed with a human face, surrounded by the clouds of his existence, with *childish eyes, inquisitive*, filled by all springs and autumns. These, like the last, unique, *final swallow* of ineffable time, come to sleep in human hands, to rest, to end the cycles of the heron, the fish-eating bird. For *twilight* to pave *the ultimate path*, to stand, to say *goodnight* to its being, to thank the earth, the day, the light, the sun, the dreams which stood by it, the essence of its being that will greet it, welcoming it. There, the ageless acquaintances, humans and their divine nature, will talk of the sun's endless travels. Their Word will be a *thank you* for every rotation, for every aspect a truth, for every dream a life in the abyss, for every desire a regret, for every hope a saga.

Somewhere there was *an afternoon sun*, the poet tells us. There, the heron walked, pecking the cloud, knowing that the final autumn approached. Life, *your autumnal hair*; love, *your autumnal face*; God looked at your hands. In these, the toil of your quiet love has been written, your affection towards humans. The entity invited you to forget the fever. Before total serenity came, once again it talked to you of the absolute certainty and of hope's redemption, because only then is remorse exhausted, immaculate mysteries take place and the *human presence* is magnified in all its glory.

Humans learned to say *thank you* and their gratitude uplifted the universe to the Supreme, because, since the dawn of time, lava has thanked the fire which gave birth to it, as did the stone to lava, as did the plant kingdom to minerals. The animal kingdom extolled the plant kingdom. The human kingdom accepted the animal kingdom and praised God *for* its *human* presence, for the ultimate blessing of His creation, for the endless love and wisdom in which it apprenticed, for the inconceivable dimensions of His being, for the happiness of truth, which brought an end to its misery's drama, redeeming it for all eternity.

PANOS PANAGIOTOUNIS

CONFESSION TO MY SON

My son, through the window
the sun of your beauty comes.

Think that your father
is no owner, nor contractor
nor retailer, but faces life
as an upright straw that rises
on the morning rays of fairy tales.

Full of faults and outbreaks and
always, always alone – a twig
in the gurgling rivers of the world.

His verses were read, both here and elsewhere
and they said he is just a poet
painting sunflowers on the walls
listening to the time as it creaks
in the land's trees, in the grandmother's
white dew.
Without success, he traverses
the streets, with a loaf of hot
bread in his hands.

My son, a distant star you are
for your father, coming
and going. You should know that

your old man is a portrait
passing, at breakneck speeds,
of our times,
but, if he was reborn,
again he'd do the same,
the same mistakes.

He'd have the same faults,
He would sow verses, with his shirt

he would wipe the bronze sun
and he'd always be a man who wrote
poems, a farce in his land,

but now, more composed
about the world's events.

But I will always love you
because, in the mirror of life, you are
my new, tender face…

(Illuminated Aegean)

The poet confesses. In his confession, his tragic faults, his outbreaks, are his substantive verses, inherited from the myth of life. With these he faces it; with these he embraces it.

Always alone, a twig – I say each poet is a giant tree trunk – *in the gurgling rivers of the world*, which form the oceans of despair, he raises his spiritual stature. He rises and spreads to the forests of the planet, to the states and the plains, to the fields, as the *rising straw*, guiding the morning rays of fairy tales, from the lowest of their fall, to the highest of the endless chaos, to be reunited with the heavens, to be integrated into glory, the knowledge retained in the abyss, as it becomes human destiny.

His lyrics are read here, in this world, but they are also read elsewhere, beyond it, in the other dimension. From there, inspiration comes and comes again, giving him the strength to *paint sunflowers on the walls*, listening *as time creaks*, as his spirit, without seeking earthly success, passes between the *trees of his grandmother-earth*, like *white dew*. And his body is *a loaf of bread* for the hungry.

His son is none other than his continuation, and his verse, redemptive, states: *My son, through the window the sun of your beauty comes*, through the only window of the abyss. And it is as if he says to him: "My son, you are that sun! You are the other sun, the one beyond, the deliverer of knowledge, the eternal son of poetry of the uncreated light, the poem of poems, the spirit of spirits, the saint of saints, the great Poet".

The poet creates, projects, births and rebirths himself. In his journey, he is the star that comes and goes, so that he may see the beginning of his morphic manifestation, the manifestation of the amorphous world, as *a portrait distant, passing, at the breakneck speeds of the times*. He states that, *if he was reborn, he would do the same, the same mistakes.* He would embody the tragedy of the world, because his faults are the components whose resultant becomes his greatest asset. His divine fate is to sow verses and, with his clothes – his shirts – the bronze suns to wipe, preparing, as the wise alchemist, the coming of the other sun, the one beyond, which *comes through the window*, to liberate them, transmutating them into his pure uncreated knowledge.

Despite them saying that he is *a man who writes poems*, a *farce in the abyss*, in other words. He will be confident, certain of the great event, full of infinite love, because, *in the mirror of life* his *new, tender,* sun-blooming face will always be mirrored.

The poet knows this truth and addresses it, calling it to return and pass *through the window* like a luminescent sun, penetrating the abyss of his soul, the world's soul. And it tells him – innocent and immaculate as he is – to recognize his work, to attire his mind, ideas and visions, so that the world may see that the poet *is no owner, nor contractor or retailer* of the spirit's concepts. He *faces life* and is the blessed straw of ideas and emotions, which with their seeds knead the body of God, the bread from which all eat, to feed the spirit of mortals everywhere, of the forsaken, whose faults and outbreaks he bears, saying that they are his own, as they – solitary twigs – are confounded *in the gurgling rivers* of senses and are lost.

Only he is the one destined with his verses to transmutate the descending, abysmal Word of their soul into poetry, painting his poems, like sunflowers on the walls, to show them the path, as they, weak – *trees of the land* – fearfully hear the creak of time, lost in the mishmash of the chaos of their emotional and intellectual world. The *white dew* of the grandmother-earth, symbolizing human wisdom, does not cover them, as wisdom they have not gained. And time creaks above and inside their heads.

Without worldly success is the poet destined to march. It comes and goes, body within bodies, the body of bodies. And the portrait of his existence, *passing at the breakneck speeds* of times, remaining an image unseen by external eyes and a constant challenge, forcing its continuity to delve, to accept the projection, which is the tragedy of the manifestation, to see its true dimensions and redeem it.

He tells the sun of his beauty that, in this land, and in any land that has not yet realized his destiny, poems are a *farce*. Yet he remains calm. It is the stance of the poet who loves the world, since through it each time he reflects his tender, rejuvenated face, rebirthing him, renewing him.

GIORGOS PANAGOULOPOULOS

RECEPTION

Prepare yourselves, our President descends
from heaven, with his God tuckedunder his arms
both smoking the latest brand of death
they laugh at the reception
at the one with the crutches
and at the blind man with the harmonica

our ruler and God abreast
ambitious always, and crooks
with a recommendation to all
"Love each other"
gifting a knife to everyone

and then the place fills with armies of angels
miners, builders, professionals
faces with a wide smile
or a wide hat
people in love, who have come to loathe
the April roses

I have no entry permit
but I shall find the chance
let's say a dead fly, or something
which will pique their interest
to call me

like an insect, and myself drunk
for light and debauchery

but I carry a hatred
and when they descend, flooded with the fragrances
of the dream
I shall spit on them
with sordid agony
for my planned defeat
all these centuries

but they descended, dizzy with power
the president approaches, smiles
he shakes my hand, calls me his friend
I am his
I grab a flag and wave it

and then God is near me
tall and handsome
and I feel so insignificant
and I shall die
I look at him, speechless, respectful
and in awe
have mercy on me, my God, have mercy on me
I cry at him.

(Final flare)

    We exist and so do the others, the poet says, those who commit crimes, violating all that is sacred and holy, as they *descend with* their *God in* their *arms,* smoking the *latest brand* of death, from the position we have placed them or they have placed themselves. We usually laugh at their position and the reception we give them, because we know they are our crutches.

Vulnerable are our choices in time. We choose our rulers, and this is our damnation – their damnation. *Ambitious and crooks*, we love each other and, to the *armies of angels*, like *lovers who have come to loathe the April roses*, we – miners, *professionals, faces with a wide* smile – *gift* them *a knife*.

Subjects and leaders, we laugh at the *reception at the one with the crutches, our blind* self who enjoys playing the harmonica, to appease God into giving him *an entry permit*. An opportunity to transform from a human being into *a dead fly* or anything else *that will pique* his *interest*, so that he invites it to the symposium for insects intoxicated by light and debauchery. In this orgy, the dream – flooded by hatred and anguish – smells the vulgar fragrances and spits on its very existence for its *planned defeat* unto the centuries.

The elected ascends and descends into his dream of pandemonium; a defeated president, and in the vertigo of his power, spreading smiles, he chooses his friends in turn – his own people. And they take courage, waving the flags which bear his emblem. This is when *the* true God, *tall and handsome*, appears, so that they may see their insignificance and – full of *respect and awe* – may die. And before this death sentence, to which everything irrevocably is submitted, as the poet is everything and everyone, he exclaims: *"Have mercy on me, my God, have mercy on me"*.

The poet is destined to accept his positive and negative aspects, with which he alternates and plays. They are the forms which humans acquire for their transformations, so that they may escape the reality which forces them to accept their tragic self. And the poet sets the theater, so that the tragedy he is writing may be played. He becomes the deus ex machina, wearing the president's mask. To demonstrate that the God to whom people cling is but their own creation that anyone may hold under their arm, he performs his pleasant yet unpleasant role, laughing at the reception of the viewers, thus expressing the ritual of life and death, so that blind people may see again, as they still play their romantic harmonica supported by the crutch of his existence.

He, their ruler, is but a substitute of the true God. An ambitious crook, in whose face they see their own self, *gifting* them *a knife*, which symbolizes the power of their weakness, so that they become able to wield power against the inclinations of their soul, symbolized by angels, and the other aspects, those of the personality still undominated. These are expressed by the miners – the subterranean roars of their instincts – who become the *professionals*, the *builders* with the *wide* smile. In love amid their fallacy, their own creations they loathe, because, they do not recognize them as God-pleasing works, despite being *the April roses*.

And the poet continues. It is the role of roles. He, the supreme insect, the insect of insects; the conscious superego of human beings, which on every chance – whether having an *entry permit* or not – penetrates the unconscious to elicit the concealed hatred, the despicable, flooded with the *fragrances of* their *dream*. It forces their *sordid agony* to confess defeat, planned amid centuries for their existence, its existence, as it is also its own defeat, the defeat of its external ego, their ego, which insists on playing with God, laying forth its own power, challenging His dominance, which is the pure essence of life, of ideas, of concepts and things.

The tragedy ends. His defeat is evincible. He consents. The *dizziness* of *power* mutates. This president, the strong personality, hoping to make the poet his own, reaches out in a final attempt, and calls him a friend. With this premise, the banner of the ego, the flag with the emblems is subjugated, waving while saluting the presence of the true God. And the insignificance dies.

He is the one persuaded to seek his redemption. He has become tired in time. His games have all failed. He became a poem and was revealed. His lie became a truth, merging with the light. His micro-intellectual conception was absorbed into the intellect. He was the poet who knew unconsciously, and consciously became aware of his entity, because He who created him was the One who accepted and greeted him. He is the master, the ruler who abolishes him, so that he may recognize in himself the true God – whose substitute he enjoyed creating – and say: *"Have mercy on me, my God, have mercy on me"*.

KOSTAS G. PAPAGEORGIOU

FROM "THE FAMILY TREE"
(excerpt)

XV

But it stayed there
a wasted breath
with no teeth or hair
laying face down in the sea, suckling
the salt, whilst
a dim sun dozed upon it
slowly rowing as if
in a timeworn painting

with a few broken oars.

And maybe it was, or it wasn't the wind
which suddenly lifted everything
the guests, the trees
the tables, the food,
except the head of the bull which they cut
with its open eyes upside down
and the rain
weighing down on their shadow.

And my mother weeping
for our silverware
which the dead stole

on their ascent.

(The family tree)

The breath of the Word, the human breath, the breath of life, the wasted breath of cosmic eternity, the poet says. *Suckling, face down in the sea, with no teeth or hair.* Absorbing the salt, the essence of existence. It seems like an idea, a painting, a sun. Rowing in his imagination, and the oars – his hands – surrendered to the wind, are left to ascend on his spirit, dreams to be exalted, to hand over their life to him. During the symposiums, to which the entities are invited with all the realms, to be transferred to the other, non-breathing dimension, leaving behind the remembrance of the torrential rain which weighs them down. A magical symbolism of the unresolved passion of instinctual life, which has been imprinted on a *bull's head* and all the mysteries of the upcoming cycles of existence in its inverted eyes will once again be read. They will claim the privilege of breathing, as their mother will continue grieving for the silverware, symbolizing the agatho[1], which times will appropriate, because their fate is to come and go, partaking of the planetary symposium as both dead and living.

The earth breathes, the human breathes, time breathes with the breath of the One. The sun, from the idea of its existence takes life. By inhaling and exhaling, its being it recycles. Generations upon generations are created in its exhaling. A sun and the human amid infinite suns, which in eternity realize the affinities. Even a single life contains the cycle of cycles; and a single idea is capable of revealing the truth, the tragedy of existence. The sea conceals the secret of life. It is the breath living on its breath.

When the physical substance is lost, there is the time of the other dimension, whose body seems like a shadow but is not, like a supplication which is not, like a fantasy that

---

[1] The term "agatho" out of the Greek word «αγαθό» is used to mean all that is beyond the duality of good and bad. It is the Entity, the Whole, the Monad.

imitates the mind that created it, without being either that. It appears like a human who sprang from a source lost in the depths of its unfathomable being and lets its remembrance exist, like a sun that once existed, millions of years ago, with only its light remaining, to travel into the chaos among the other, existent and non-existent suns. An idea of some worlds, eternally traveling as a testimony of an irrefutable life which is oppressed by its own light amid the unredeemed darkness. In this tragedy, the purpose of infinity is one, to restore the form to the idea, to restore the idea to the immaculate mind, to restore life to love. An internal function, whose secret is known only to the poet.

A wasted breath is life, which has *hair and teeth*. A myriad bodies of archangels and demons grinding and assimilating its cycles in a dream where existence constantly feasts in the perpetual flow of time. The existence of demonic conception is always a substantive factor, a presence of imaginative grandeur, recycled in all seasons, which, in the confrontation with their entity, lose their value. And humans remain an idea of the past, foretold in their future time, the liberating effect of the return of the dead, aspects with which they had lined the body of the internal life.

Shapes, objects, colors, shells are all subject to what the wind is, to the spirituality it symbolizes, to the dim, distant sun's light. A sun which rows to the other side of its oceanic world, urging the range of creation to withdrawal and all beings to an ascending course, after they have suckled the essence, the salt of all oceans. Ascending, to extinguish the pain of the ancient mother for the stolen symbols they appropriated, returning the intransigence of their dreamlike existence to the source of all.

In the multidimensional presence of the Being, mega-cycles of exhalation to their own inhalation confess their drama. And the mega-cycles of inhalation in the other, the unborn breath, hope for merger, for forgiveness given by the magnanimity of the Being of visible and invisible universes to that part of Himself that was externalized.

Humans, a miniature of the Word, the miracle of their cosmogony they preach and, indecisive before Him, before the final surrender, they scatter amid alot, subject to the inscrutable power of their lower nature. They surrender to it and are not complacent until atonement for the severed *head of the bull* with the *eyes upside down*, a remembrance of a period of the cosmic, zodiac cycle, which also symbolizes the other seasons. To stop the rain of the dreamlike cascade from weighing down the shadow; to fly to it, to open its wings, to disappear in the absolute, within the timeless time, the shape to erase.

KAITI PAPADAKI-KARAMITSA

DECOMMISSIONED SHIP

You are, you use to say,
a decommissioned ship.
At the depths of the sea
your anchor rusts.
Pitch black, you stand
as a seaworn rock
and you accept the untamed waves
as eternal fate.
Within your innards,
the desolate silence resides.
And the still engines,
stopped hearts.
Your portholes, dull
from salt-water tears.
The seagulls dread you,
indecisively hanging around
lest, on one of your ledges,
their flight to rest.
You are, you use to say,
a decommissioned ship.
Stokers I wish to bring,
your engines to set in motion.
To go on journeys
even short ones.
Up to where

a strip of land can barely be made out.
From your innards,
the desolate silence to embark.
That the sun may warm the portholes,
their salty tears
to dry.
The seagulls, unafraid
to follow you
and myself, a seagull, joining them
joyfully admiring you upon the waves,
in your slow-moving journey.

(barbiton)

There are eras when time decommissions its needs, subsides and, as a disarmed ship, is left to the depths of the sea. Its *anchor rusts* and it becomes a *seaworn*, pitch black *rock* that stands *as eternal fate*, trying to tame *the waves within* its *innards* with its *desolate silence*. It deactivates the engines, its days and nights, wanting to stop the desires, to weaken its impulses, which from *the portholes* of pain gaze at the seagulls, which dread it and seek on its body to find a ledge to rest. And awaits for its other times to come, to bring a crew to lift it, urging it to even *short journeys, where* its future will *barely be made out*. For *the desolate silence to embark* and its *salty tears to dry*. The *seagulls, unafraid* to *follow* it, and one, the largest, the leader, which always had time's course on its mind, to follow joyfully, looking at the slow-moving ship on its journey.

The poetess becomes the fatigued time. It stops a bit, allowing its human parts to rest, its mind to pass into the *desolate silence*. To immobilize the engines, so that the heart may stop pumping pain, the blood of the earthly fire, which seeks catharsis, to find a way out into the sun's light. To turn desires into love, after passing from the passions of wandering to the universal life.

Time is an Argonaut, with the bodies of its bodies it struggles to be vindicated, to carry out its mission. And it gets tired, discouraged, before reaching its destination. Its own dark aspects battle it, removing its power, the will for knowledge and, to the extent that it agrees to illuminate them, they once again stand by it. Knowledge makes its presence known and, gazing at the seagulls, with its wisdom leads it, rousing it, to develop its will, forcing it to its eternal cycle, where the starting points for beginning and return are many. The fighters do not cease, the times do not end, the necessities of life have no end.

Humans tire, the body is discouraged and dizziness overwhelms their being. It is difficult to learn to love, to await, to dominate over powers, to manage your spirit. The need of others for their own satisfaction calls you. Frustration and pain, inactivity and decay, a cascade of powers, the volition of evil, which incites to flight. And the human resistance, a passive reaction, a resignation, an abandonment of visions and ideals.

It is the poetess, experiencing in her body the tragic reality of life and the dream becomes frightened. Time is left to the free will of humans. Wisdom, as a helper, stands by amid the confusion and ensures the continuity, offering hope, help, in the remaining strength.

It is humans who hurt and were forsaken. They asked to be excluded from responsibilities. They extinguished the mechanisms of the mind and the desiring heart deliberately stopped working, joyously refusing to beat. Even the seagulls, the poetess says, symbolizing the ideas, refuse to return, dreading and *indecisively hanging around.*

A human trait is the denial of the earth, when to self-denial it refuses to pass. They are called to give themselves to their work; a supporter of all to become, time which acquires consciousness and so from its own being is completed in the recycling of eternities that, as years, days and hours, worthily represent its existence, teaching humans that this is their nature, the perpetual need for existence, completeness and bliss, which, however, without a fight will not be given to them. It is their favorite, which chose them and supports them in their travels. It is the processes of their evolution, their own course on the path. Excitement, thrills, frustrations are its strengths, emotions transformed into joy and pain. An irresistible magic that enchants and misleads them, guiding them again, as the only wisdom, to the freedom of the spirit, where the soul is redeemed of the *sea depths*.

Poets have the gift of uniting. They experience pain and time as a state amid the reality of the spirit, which is trained and suffers. Daily witnesses to the becoming, they withstand the deadlocks and without protest invoke their testimony, placing the world's harrowing cries on the entity, by its glory to be healed. Carriers awaiting the redeeming within the world's passions, they oppose fate and blame it. They refuse to give in, surrendering their beingto become prey to the false needs of the chimera, which claims to be the enviable goddess, an actress in the theater of ignorance that derides knowledge.

The everyday people that suffer, the demigods of eternity which are in bliss, the spirits of earth, the archangelic fields of infinity are the poets. They live and experience the drama, with their work giving substance and meaning to life.

DIMITRIS PAPADITSAS

THE WINDOW

I say again, I am alone
As a single human footprint in the woods
I am alone, as a finger on a hand
Whose other four by the machine were taken
If I were a droplet, I would have been extinguished in the bowels of a
thirsty land
But I am no droplet
I am a tiny stone, perhaps precious
Which the weather turns to sand
And I see its shape and glow
And its hardness
And its weight becoming sand
I say again
In my heart dwells a prayer
But it abides
Now that there is no mouth, if only I had a knife wound on my side
Like a delicate girl
the prayer to emerge from it.

(Parentheses)

God, the unique irrefutable proof of the existence of all, the poet tells us. The lonely footprint of the anchorite-poet leaves a deep imprint in the woods, as, passing through time, he seals the presence of the one, the unique Being, whose entity through His infinite aspects into the absolute he emancipates. *Alone as a finger on a hand* – fingers symbolizing the five fields of the mind – which assimilates the other four into his essence, passing them through the universe that, as the great, unimaginable, cosmic machine, with His will's command works for the power of His uniqueness.

A droplet is the human spirit in the vast ocean of aquatic fires, a droplet which, in the bowels of the eternally *thirsty land* is extinguished and transmuted. It becomes a *tiny, precious stone*, by time to be turned into sand, sand of light, that is scattered in chaos and acquires the shapes of soft suns and the hardness of planets. There, through humans the creation represents the infinite forms of life, whose gravity is once again weighed against sand.

This immense weight does not lose even a grain of its volume and, within the poet's heart, becomes the one prayer towards the One which dwells in the depths of infinity. For infinity to acquire a mouth, a human Word, to become the Creator's sword which, by *stabbing* the human *side, the prayer to emerge from it like a delicate girl* embracing the boy, lovingly caressing and kissing. Because, as long as God was alone, His nonexistence contrived the existence, so that, playing with His creation, He would have company in His loneliness.

In His loneliness, he chose the human company, and His Word became hermaphrodite music, the poet's harmonious prayer, hardness and tenderness at a universal level of cosmic rotations, beauty of the divine Grace. Grief alternates with naivety and naivety with knowledge, as the poet, cynical in human matters, contests the mind's projections with other projections. He sneers at his fate's nature, whilst at the same time cherishing its impotence, transforming it into hope, to bring life's redemption, like a girl, which, by the power of her prayer, from the side of divine vision is projected, to gestate and nurture the continuity of his human existence. To repeat the words *"I am alone"*, giving the dimensions of his loneliness the meaning of ontological loneliness – that of the One, the complete in oneself, which is externalized in the woods of nature's vastness, of human nature, which delivers its spiritual destitution to the mercy of the absolute One.

To the one principle of One – symbolized by one finger of the hand – are the other four forces of His morphic expression subjected, personality processes which shape the becoming and which by His will are ruled, as they become prey to time that defines the human being's spiritual evolution. This follows the law of the sacrifice of the ego, which to the offer, to its exhaustion in this evolution – which is also its redemption – is forced.

The life of personality is hard, shapes and flashes its light is, imponderable dust is *its weight, a small precious stone* on the podium of the poet's heart. And yet, it is not even a single droplet of blessing to saturate the land's thirst. Unquenchable is its thirst and the poet in its abyss does not stand. Orpheus descends, his Eurydice calling with his prayer's song, with his love to take her to the suns; so that she may create, as another soul, the holy bodies, the imperishable, sacred concepts in his life's dream, where all projects are perfected, are redeemed within her essence. Because, the soul, as a mechanism is incited by the love of the form; it is subjected to the processes of personality and is forced its own of aspects to devour. For this reason, the poet wants it having no mouth and invokes the intervention of its horizontal radiance; to enter his side and emerge from it as his conscious feminine substance, a hermaphrodite delicate creature, a universal prayer to eternity's cruel and unbearable sorrow.

THANASIS PAPATHANASOPOULOS

SUMMER TIME

The Summer Memory of Takis Papatsonis

*I remember when I was sent to the water fountain
to fill the tin trough,
on an August noon, when stones were scorching hot.*

*And as I walked in the glow, I envisioned
that I had been removed from my body and time.
I hovered; being and non-being.*

*Although I could clearly make out the pandemonium
of frogs on the troughs, and of cicadas
on the shady plane trees.*

*Until I reached the plant cave
within which the fountain gurgled,
and I opened my trough's lid.*

*I had not yet regained my vision
in that cool shady world,
when I approached the stony handful.*

*And I stopped in awe, not fear
blurrily watching a whip snake
with a slender dotted body.*

*The reptile gleamed, as it lay
on the green velvety lichen
and jubilantly drank from the refreshing water.*

*It seemed as a forgotten friend
or as an ancestral god, fallen
which inalienably maintained
all its natural rights.*

*Could I have crushed it,
flicking the slimy stone onto its body,
or bashing my trough's lid
to frighten it?*

*But the snake, although aware of me, did not stir
in preparation for a disgraceful flight.
The dignity it perhaps had once been taught,
had by now become second nature.*

*And after cooling itself, only then
did it slowly make its way to the exit,
turning its head towards me
in the shape of a gentle salutation.*

*It had behaved as a nobleman – courageously,
before a potential threat.
And after moving far enough away, only then
did I place my vessel beneath the fountain.*

My turn, you see, had come.

("EFTHYNI" (RESPONSIBILITY) Magazine)

In the eighth month, symbolizing the union of humans with the world, the poet places the completion of the cycle of souls within bodies. And the chaotic glow is revealed within the courageous spirit of the cicadas, the snakes *and the frogs on the shady plane trees*, where life, hovering in its universal body, seeks its clear gaze, to find the source from which its existence flows.

The life of the plant cave gurgles, and, in the revelation of its mystery, awe overwhelms humans, as they face the symbol of fire that represents and dominates them. This is the *forgotten friend* and enemy, the *fallen* angel lying *on the green velvet*, jubilantly drinking the water of the earth, maintaining his *inalienable natural rights*.

The will of humans was always steadfast. From the onset, they could have displaced the serpent, this fallen angel, *flicking the slimy stone onto its body*, or frighten it, making it express its reaction through flight. But they did not; they did not want to kill the snake and thereby remove from their back the energy that runs along their spine and elevates knowledge to the head.

This force is what the serpent represents. Taught by a prior knowledge, overpowering, a divine dignity offered by the creator, it does not consider moving, *in preparation for a disgraceful* flight. It is *second nature* in humans to respect the dark lord, to let him quench his thirst and proudly turn his head *in a noble salutation*, since the possibility of having to offer his turn has now disappeared. Faced with the power of their own nature, humans pretend to be frightened. They put forward the fearsome symbol of their fate, the fallen wisdom, as if destitute, stigmatized and alienated; crawling like a threat that scares them, troubles them, forcing them to flee outside *body* and *time*; to remain hovering, with blurry vision within the world of shadows.

The dream gleams; a reptile lying in a velvet heavenly world, as it satisfies its thirst through God's *stone handful*, appeased in the eternal *summer time* of earth. And humans, full of memories for their imperfect creations, the substitutes of nature, tread through their life, trying to ground their spirit to the scorching stones, as it hovers in the vastness, enchanted by the idea of flight from the painful reality of drama which forces them to accept the consequences caused by their free will.

They are prisoners of the dream of unsolved, benevolent-making, cunning spiritual forces of their existence. They occupy themselves with their harmonization attempting, through their works, to reveal the deeper reason for the sufferings plaguing them, forcing them to a perpetual compromise with fate. Their only enemy resembles a *forgotten friend*, the other self, the unconscious. It *inalienably* maintains *its rights*. It demands the recognition, the awareness of its existence by humans, who contain it as the sole holder of the mysteries of the world, as in themselves they are contained within the Unit, with the absolute will of the creator.

The *slender body* is marked by the sun's spots, hiding under the shady tree, while its spirit, through the human spiritual majesty, rising to the higher branches, seeks to be released, trying, amongst the pandemonium of sounds and shapes that spring from its perpetual transformations, to distinguish the pure, substantive Word. The message to awakening causes awe and fear, while the motionless body, as an earthly, carnal provocation, is not *prepared* to attempt *a disgraceful flight*.

The hidden meaning of the poem refers to the memory of this primordial impression of the wise choice. An impression that was lost and must be repeated with the stimuli received by humans in everyday life, as they are manifested in the performances, in the projections of the mind, which, permeating nature, shows its presence with the images and things that symbolize it. The serpent – a dominant force – was chosen to symbolize the libido that runs through the human spine as the eternal exponent of instinctual life. This dictates to humans the desire for existence and dominance on the world where they found themselves ruled by an amorphous God, whose secret they are called to realize, awaiting their turn after the threat imposed by the will of the dark spirit.

Dignity itself is unconvinced, like second human nature, it refuses to submit. That is why divine providence drives it to find its exit from their head, like an inner mind, a lord diffusing his essence in the universe, so that, when the fear of form is long gone, humans may fill the vessel with the immortal water.

NIKOS PAPAKOSTANTINOU

WHO CAN
(excerpts)

XXXII

Who can
as the dawn rises
the curtain of the night
and the candles of the sun will brighten
the stage of life,
play his small role
with inspiration, craftsmanship and honesty
and with such compassion,
which allures
both Mind and Thought
of his grand Viewer and Critic,
of the One,
who asked for this show to take place?

XXXIII

Who can
as Noah
– before the world is wiped out by the flood
which flooded all creation –
bringing to peace beneath the roof
of his mortal ark
anything crawling, leaving, flying,
or stagnating, sticking or sinking,

to keep alive the concept of the human,
until seeing
by the window,
the white dove returning
with an olive leaf?

(Who can)

Under the dominance of lower nature, humans succumb to their passions. The *flood* of lies and passions, of the ego's desires, overwhelm *all creation*. The tragic result – which by its actions caused the dark past – is inevitable. They are unable, *on the stage of the great Viewer and Critic*, to perform the role given to them, *with inspiration, craftsmanship and honesty*, and thereby perish. Mental endurance has disappeared; they have lost their spirituality.

The poet seeks in his century, *with compassion which allures Mind and Thought*, the contemporary Noah – *before the world is wiped out by the flood* – who, amid the humble ark of himself will salvage the concept, the essence and practice of "human". In the theater of light, each time *the curtain of the night* is raised, *who can* consciously play his ontological role and convey the messages which save *all that crawl* and *leave*, taking the place of compassion upon the window of existence?

When the inclination of the soul is expressed, the spirit is transformed into a dove and offers an *olive leaf* to those who stagnate, become stuck and sink into the swamp of their *mortal ark. The candles of the sun* perpetually *brighten* the earth. It is the dawn that provides day with the strength to shake off the burden of the night; to play its role, interpreting the will of humans, which is shaped by their choices in life.

In the grand show, pure spirituality is the only redeeming choice. The dark currents converge on the annihilation of earth and the flood of individual needs overwhelms the mind of humans. Prey to the egoistic perception of life that they have, they are unable to head towards the redeeming mountain of conscience and elude the drowning brought by the lack of inner breath. When properly applied, the result of life's rejuvenating function is that humans receive within them the world, cleanse it within their heart and mind and deliver it, clean and untainted, to their Lord and God, surrendering their spirit to Him.

But who knows, the poet asks, who possesses, *who can*, who wants this tradition, tradition of the Holy Fathers, wise and enlightened, to continue partaking to the mystery of divine inspiration, to find the observer's honesty so as to judge his own actions? A crucial question and a crucial response which will be offered by the respondent. He is asked to shoulder the responsibilities of the world as if they are his own and answer for them. He is the night and dawn, and in the theatrical play he is the redeeming outcome of the performance.

The world is interpreted at will; life is interpreted at will. At will the high and low tide; at will the flood of ideas, of emotions, of knowledge brought by catharsis, which come as a response, depending on what humans attract from the center of their existence. An action of power is their every thought, determining their evolution. A supreme need to learn how to think correctly; of the mind and heart to guide towards the truth, to life's duty, which is the absolute interest for those occurring in the world.

Imperfection is a given, a consequence of heaven's and earth's nature. Inevitable is the lack of support from those finding themselves in ignorance. The evolution of the world, perfection, is the work of humans. They learn to think, to exist, to live, to taste the completeness of their being. Life is a school, and, their discipleship, by the appeal of their soul is determined. When the will of personality is aligned with the entity's will, the realization comes that each person is a Noah, who has been given the ability to salvage parts of his existence from the inevitable deluge. The spiritual self is activated, it awakens and undertakes its responsibilities. *With inspiration, craftsmanship and honesty, it allures the Mind and Thought of its grand Viewer and Critic*, and with His blessing performs its work on earth. *From the roof of its mortal ark* – the field of the mind – interprets the passions that crawl, those that sink the higher concepts into the waters of ignorance and bring within them punishment and purification.

The poet calls humans to the track where opposing forces balance, where the imbalances created by the irrepressible outflow of their negative thoughts and emotions are aligned. With the biblical example of Noah, humans are initiated to the absolute interest for the outcome of life. Encouraged by nature in the early stages of their development, in their first steps, in the early years of the awakening of senses, appetites, of thirst for gain and saturation, they hurry, they wish to satiate time, unconsciously seeking the closure of their cycle. They are carried away by the gallop of unbridled instincts. Their course is ignorance and knowledge comes late. As a guardian, the Creator's love punishes them so that they may realize the ultimate, and demands the vindication of His divine Word. The debt must be repaid in full. The care of His absoluteness is the seamless flow of perfected Life.

He is God, who, as Noah, resides in the ark. He saves His creation from the devastating flood which, His divine wrath, as a divine economy of His cosmic harmony, has imposed. And humans become His servants, His beloved Sons, fragmented by the winds of the storm which their passion for Life has created. They are overwhelmed by benevolence. Their prospects are all a divine blessing. The will of the Word is the Law, the path of union, the truth of wisdom. A tireless servant of God, in sins residing, the universal order invoking. Sinless is the Lord, to his invocations he responds and His world saves!

NIKOS PAPPAS

THE FINAL WALK

*It is not that we close our eyes
that we lose the tender light
that the remaining
fill our pillows with precious tears
nor shall we say that elegies of laments
might be heard
and perhaps justify us,
nor do I imagine your evening loneliness
is of any bitter importance
when you cannot find anything
that interests you
in an entire day
such an ending is an inevitable
mourning, which makes you feel
that, amid the world,
you are the last passerby,
the privileged, who stayed to promote
what others did not have the time to
mainly (this mainly, of course)
when you have to count
the miles you cross
knowing they are the last remaining
of a wonderful walk that cannot take place again...*

(New poems from the third elegies)

People close their eyes and leave, the poet says. Oh, providence of divine grace, the supreme destination of those remaining – the privileged – is to remain and promote *what others did not have the time to*. A supreme mission, a care which travels through the tormented distance in the vast field of the realm of the earthly mind and the emotional sea, in the field of sensual, sensory existence. Of an existence oppressed by pain, as the last remnants of the world resist, refusing to move towards their superior destiny. They express their inhibitive intentions, with their argument being that of a final *wonderful walk*, saying that it cannot *take place again*, it will not repeat its cycle in futility, a cycle holding the planetary tumult hostage in the sun's relentless need.

A passerby is the poet, an observer of sense, from the universal body of cosmic nature he measures the revolutions of time and is not surprised. He remains neutral to the result of chimeric expressions, which makes him feel that he is the last of the withdrawal, the one with the privilege of completing the sensory and cognitive processes which *others did not have the time* to complete. And from him, the only remaining, the ultimate operator, they seek redemption.

He knows well of the sacramental ritual, which must take place before the great voidance and he consciously participates in it. His Word predated the procedures of spirit and the manifestation of the physical body of the universe. When the human shape emerged, he knew it would not matter if the *elegies of laments* that would be heard of the cosmic drama would vindicate humans, who, driven by the impulse of a happy life, would have wanted to find everything interesting. Only the poet has the power, when in the great day of light, the mourning blooms before his eyes, marking the end of an unavoidable life forcing him to bear the responsibility and remain loyal to the promise he made, to wait until even his final self, the ultimate, is promoted to the essence of the absolute.

The great mystics, the masters of the race, the enlightened beings, those who were blessed, although privileged by the mercy of the entity, do not abandon the world. Situated in another spiritual dimension, they remain as guards and stand by the human course, until the cycle is emptied of every fallacy, so that humans break their mental shackles and are released; so that they are redeemed by the enchanting caress of the tender light, they do not leave the repositories of their tears, the precious gems of knowledge, on the pillow, where they placed ignorance, when they involuntarily closed their eyes, choosing to dream the duration of an uncertain joy. It was a dream destined to lead them to the elegies of pain, until they come to love day and night, to consciously cry over their lost love; to accept the abyss, to purify, to make practice what the redeemer of the world taught.

Many are the feelings humans have, infinite, and the ideas of their pain are eternal diamonds which adorn the chaos of their being. Passersby of their world, the first and last rhythm, harmony, whose exquisite sound resonates with that of the universal Word. The human spirit is unable to follow the music. Only the spirit of the poet can, on his return to the pure being, hold the meaning of existence, and, by interpreting it, promote the elegies to the other side. Lamentations, which will be heard as praises, so that humans are vindicated, perfected in the glory of the universal spirit.

It is not that we close our eyes – that is a given. Death, the wild darkness, deprives humans of *tender light* and the irreversible process of metastasis is perpetual. The external light loses its meaning and the *elegies of laments* induce *tears*, *precious* ransom for the bribery of justification. These all lose their value within the *bitter meaning* of loneliness, and, before the *inevitable mourning* from which the nature of the world is overwhelmed, they move towards the inevitability of its continuous mutation from body to spirit, from spirit to essence, from essence to light, from light to darkness, from darkness to existence, from existence to non-existence. The story of *a wonderful walk*, which, in itself has the privilege of never being repeated.

The poet delves into futility, into its need to exist. It is that which acquires shapes and bodies and is given spiritual substance, to exist and have the ability to assimilate its chimeric estrus and be assimilated by the essence of its being, with the presence of humans sealing the state of its vanity. A miracle of miracles occurring for the glory of God, so that the glory of humans is equated to it, as they accepted to be born, to exist, to be happy, to hurt, to win and to lose, to hate and to love, to grow old and to die, making the final walk. Thus, they cannot be reborn from where they will find themselves; to exist again and to be forced to cry, to listen to the *elegies of* their *laments*, to be subjected to their loneliness, to depend on the light and darkness and to be forced to die, so that they find themselves in this world once again. But such to be their universal walk, so wonderful, complete, that it would not have to *take place again*, after having returned to the omnipotence of their own entity.

T.K. PAPATSONIS

THE STONE

*When, in summer, the time comes for cooling winds to blow
at once to dispel the sovereignty of the heavy sun,
coming from the sea, suddenly lashing at it and, from a mirror
motionless, bring its shivering momentum and illuminate it,
– again, this large flaming Disc
remains the center of the entire surrounding world.
It isolates everything in its contemplation.
It holds the scepter of the Day and the World.
It shakes the reason in the breath of its shimmer.*

*And, as Night falls, so silent and mystical,
on the same, altered Shore,
where the sandy beach constantly changes its boundary
to the lines of the unresting wave,
who colors this blurry Moon, with its proud,
dead color, but the Sun itself? And although
just two or three hours ago, it prepared such a flaming
retreat somewhere below and out of the world, with fanfare and scarlet colors
and vanished, it always knows, even hidden, to send something
to remind us of its eternal presence.*

*Something hidden is contemplated these hours within the human,
which, like a Sun or Moon has perched*

in the midst of the soul, and gives it
the glow of a darkness that does not alter
from the intellect of God or the shattering of the Church.
A tendency for the good and the imperturbable. A Love
and an embrace to all those surrounding it. Without discrimination or preference,
without overshadowing, without decay or waste.

Without discrimination, except – my God – for one; of that heavy,
sharp Stone, you promised some people
weighing on their chests at night, so heavy, so suffocating,
so hopeless and loving. That which, if ever released,
would be succeeded by the tomb's lasting stone.
So sovereignly, so obsessively has it been placed there forever.

("AVGI" Newspaper, Pyrgos)

Heavy is the Stone which covers the mysteries of the soul, keeping the magnificent Sun's congregation in the tomb. An immaculate chest which is burdened by the sins of the universal World. The earth holds the largest share in the gathering of shadows. The Sun, imperious, plays its games from high above, concluding with humans on ephemeral life and the volatility of their external nature, which is allured by the magic ploys of the Moon. And Day and Night are tormented, trying to determine the limit of the waves of cosmic light, where their time is altered, as power, endurance, which *never rests*, shifts the borders of its dominion.

Summer time comes with the cooling winds, *the sovereignty of the – heavy* as a *stone – Sun* is dispelled. In the mirrors of nature, shivers and impulses are illuminated; *the motionless* agitates *the sea*. The entire world is *a Disc, a flaming* God, which, with its *scepter isolates the reason in the breath of its shimmer*. The occult, in the innermost is contemplated, and, *whether Sun or Moon*, the Word of darkness is one, a glow that does not change. The time of the great shattering, of the sacred passion.

The congregation of infinity has a tendency *for good, for the imperturbable*, where Love embraces decay and redeems it in the intellect of the divine heart. *Such a flaming retreat somewhere below and out of the world, with fanfare and scarlet colors*, as God, unseen, reminds all of *his eternal presence*. Always sending His preparation's Time *into the midst of the soul, without discrimination* in His *silent and mystical Night,* to support the despair of humans, removing the burden of their earthly existence, which is succeeded by *the tomb's Stone*. This, persistently and sovereign, awaits to hear the redeeming Word, which, *with fanfare and scarlet colors* will give the command to be released, for the century's deceased to emerge in resurrection.

When, in the flaming fields, the wind *marks* the broadness of *the soul*, the form is cooled and the sovereignty of the burden is persuaded to lighten the toil of its own sun. *Coming from the sea*, the omens suddenly come to celebrate through their reflections. The liberated forms scatter luminescence – the flares of the redeemed mind – which, focused on *the center of the entire surrounding world*, isolating *everything to its contemplation*, controls itself with the law of its -authority, lest it scatters its magic and the realm of foolishness is overthrown by reason and takes shimmer under its rule, requesting that human radiance be extinguished.

This is the benefit that the conceivable being receives from God. It sees its world, its Sun. The Sun may see itself, even when lost, when immersed in the distances of night, relenting to the Moon's demands, which claims its color, to keep the Sun dead within the glory of its pride. A wave that refuses to rest on the steady line of a sandy beach unaltered in the boundary of the silent eternity of infinity. Transcendent being with flesh and bones, to live and to realize the importance of the radiance, of the blowing winds, of the meaning of waves, the blows received by the sea, when, as the Sun, it becomes involved in the process of shivering momentum, which draws its egoistic presence from the mirroring of its substance, the projections of its divine mind. Because, it, hidden beyond the time of hours, sends its presence to remind the wakefulness of the century, the glowing *soul*, the message *of Church*, the teaching of love, a testimony of confession, the poet's honest confession. An apposition of the forces of the essence, for the elements of all to partake of the divine sacrament of Love. *A tendency towards the good and the imperturbable*, which indiscriminately embraces all those surrounding it, elevating human humbling to the absolute, to the redeeming field of all, a consciousness coveted by ignorance from the tomb of its tomb.

Raise your heavy Stone, human, free your chest, and, in the scorching summers, draw courage by the compassion of coolness. Become *the large flaming Disc* and with the power of your scepter isolate your logic. Shake it with the breeze of shimmer. And when *Night falls, so secret and silent upon the Shore*, altering the blurriness of its face, taking the paleness of the Moon, become *the Sun itself*, demand your absolute rights. Consider the power of the inner mind and with the glimmer of your radiance blare, to disperse the fire amid *the eternal presence* of infinity. There, enthroned *amid the soul*, become as Themis, contemplate the Moon's innermost, *the glow of darkness that does not alter*; since, you, the Sun, are fed by darkness and forever bloom.

The coming of summers are humans, the poet says. Humans are the time, the wind, the coolness; they mark the dissolution of the sovereignty *of the heavy sun* – the lower mind, of reason. Humans are those who arrive from *the sea*, as it *receives the lashing* of radiance from the externalization of their cognitive functions. *They are the sea* of passions; they are the power of harnessing. They are the essence and the mirroring, the projection and *the motionless shivering of its momentum*, the phosphorescence of the irrepressible intellect of the flaming Disc. *They are the center of the entire world, they are the Disk,* the shaking of the universe in its recognition.

We delve into the meaning of the poem, verse by verse. We delve into the human sense, idea after idea. Frontier by frontier, line by line, the desiring wave does not rest, as the sandy beach, symbolizing the cosmic field of the shaken life, is influenced by the blurry prejudice offered by the Moon – the personality. And there remains the need for union with the spirit, with the Sun, as the essence of its existence, hidden within human depths, waits to raise the Stone from the chest of its tomb and be released.

EVANGELIA PAPACHRISTOU-PANOU

EXERCISE IN ENDURANCE

To exercise in the ascent,
yet tasting the vertigo of the fall.
To be caught up by the sobs.
To be enveloped by the rivers, carrying,
in their living waters,
the matutinal signs of your blood.
So, you sit on the bank and think:
who are the "seeing that were born
with the sign" and hope?
Stones, born supporting our homes;
refusing to say how leaves died in the autumn,
and how, after their fall,
life does not emerge, transforming
the sedated sperm into a dew-covered branch.
The Lord sealed their offer,
when they, humble and homeless,
ran through crossroads, leaving
a pleading tear against death.
They, with hopes of a "common resurrection",
were silently reaching the bedside of the sick,
hearing the joints of the moribund creak
as the chills of death lay upon them.
Their body will peacefully be buried,
because they dearly loved; they dearly held vigils, they dearly...
Hunched over the warm autumn soil

the ode of resurrection awaiting
to emerge from the decomposition of vegetation.
An exercise in endurance is love,
as death follows the warmth of life.
An exercise in endurance is, for us, their absence,
because they held a vigil, forestalling our death.
Deep in the night, we hear their song
overflowing from the sweet wine of the Eternal.

(The clay eyelids)

The entire universe is in a constant, perpetual *exercise in endurance*. It exercises in the ascent and tastes the vertigo of the inevitable fall, as *the sobs* of rivers *catch up with it*, those which refuse to die, carrying *their living waters that bear* within them *the matutinal signs* of its fiery blood.

The poetess sits *on the bank*, thinking and wondering: *Who are those "who see* this miracle, *who were born with* the poet's *sign* and continue *hoping*?". Eternal stones are the celestial spirits, born to lay the foundations, to support our homes – which in their entirety constitute the cosmic house – they refuse to reveal their secrets to the uninitiated, to talk about the purpose of death, to state why *life does not emerge* from the *sedated sperm* of nature's spirit, so that the transformation of their soul takes place within the vigilant gray matter of God and becomes *a dew-covered branch*.

The Supreme seals the offer of those integrated into service, as they run, *humble and homeless, through the crossroads, leaving their pleading tear* to confront death. They, the living souls of time, *have hopes of "a common resurrection"*, as they silently reach *the headrest of the moribund sick*, whose joints creak, while *death chills* permeate them. *Their body will peacefully be buried, because they lovingly held a vigil, hunched* over a season's soil, waiting for *the ode to emerge* as new vegetation *from the decomposition*.

An exercise in endurance is love, which the entity feels towards itself, *as death follows* its *warmth*. An exercise in endurance is the acceptance of the absence of its aspects and forms, as, although dead in its manifestations, it holds a vigil *forestalling* their *death*. *Deep in the night* its *song* is heard, *overflowing from the sweet wine of its Eternal* self, of the vineyard that offers its juices, for people to taste and awaken their dream, a vision of the entity that is perpetually exercised.

Thought is exercised in emotion and emotion is exercised in love. The dream is exercised in the abyss and the abyss is exercised in hope of catharsis from eternity. All its beings mimic the entity. In their infinite exercises, its exercises they admire, the endurance of its strength, of their strength, the quality of life which brings completeness, the death of the becoming and its resurrection, while at the same time they desire to taste *the vertigo of their fall*. And the heavenly sobs, catching up to the beings, envelop them with their living, fiery waters, *the matutinal signs of blood*, for the entity to receive the communion of its existence and to be initiated into the deepest meaning of the exercise, which imposes on its members itself, until they learn that in reality they are *the seeing ones with the sign*, the spiritual and physical *stones*, which were created to support its house.

They refuse to talk about the knowledge of death, the giants of the spirit. They are deliberately silent, because they are aware of the danger lurking when mysteries are not exercised with due reverence. Upon the existence of themselves and their other irrevocable parts – the sleeping deceased – they project the exercise, the lesson of perpetual endurance. Because they, foolish amid their conscience, live and experience the dream of seasons recycled by the centuries, giving birth to flesh and letting it rot, since it is a sin of their body, a wreck of the soul.

The poem is filled with the spirit of the exercise and the sacrifices it entails; it conveys the message of erotic endurance, of love. By law *death must follow the warmth of life*, the warmth of exercise, as life itself is the exercise of exercises performed by all our members, those of earth and those of heaven. Necessary processes, recreated by feelings and ideas, as they compete with their very existence to prove themselves – and so they must – worthiest before the challenge of the spirit, whose purpose is the great awakening, beyond the cycle of life and death, beyond the perception the world has of the resurrection.

Thus, *the ode of resurrection* takes on its great, glorious significance. It becomes the matutinal, divine song, chanted by all stars together which, inextinguishable reside within us and exercise us in divine and human love, forcing death into following the radiance, the light, the glow, the human warmth – *the warmth of life*. An *exercise in endurance*, for humans to learn to hold a vigil, forestalling their existence, listening to the chanting *in* their *deep night, as it overflows the sweet wine* of the one and only eternal Ascetic – the Entity itself.

GIANNIS PATILIS

FROM THE "WARM MIDDAY"

Middays in Attica!
Large pots of light
White stones.
You left me with the few
With the least possible.
There is no fear
Only harmony.
The convoluted life
Has been untangled.
In two simple lines.
A belt was unbuckled.
The beautiful buildings
And the awnings
The shiny cars.
Now and then, some greenery
Above-ground, lest I step on it.
A small, stationary cloud.
And mountains
Great petrified winds
Surrounding the apartment buildings in Attica.
This is what it has all come down to.
To so much light
Which, all together, gives us
A bright darkness.

Yes! I work at middays.
An inspector.

I oversee the light
The sky, the apartment buildings.
In case anything has diminished.
Many apartment buildings, many people.
Many bodies, many wounds, many cigarettes.
Many sorrows.
You should go into the light.
I am looking out for
the light.
When I too will die.
Someone else
Will continue.

(Warm midday)

The poet, an inspector of light, love and power. Darkness and light, both equal to God. In *harmony, the convoluted life* is untangled. In the *large pots* of ancient tradition, the repositories of wise kingdoms are kept, savings of the essence of civilizations; and, although already limited, still only a scattering among them are capable by their presence to render fear nonexistent.

The poet intends on unbuckling the belt of the two lines encircling the prejudices, which must be dissolved. They are primordial monsters, in basins they reside, transformed into *beautiful buildings* and *shiny cars*, allowing the meager, unique nature of times to linger from above, painted on floral awnings. The poet untangles the Gordian knot of human relationships, resembling a *small stationary cloud*, which is analyzed in petrified winds, in the mighty *mountains of Attica*, which have always existed.

From the onset, the volumes of juxtaposition have existed in the agonizing contemplation of decay, which preaches the glory of sepsis while singing about how it ends up in the light. *Bright* is the *darkness* in which the poet constantly works, overseeing the productive processes taking place, as he unbuckles the belt of the greatest witch of all – of life. From its retained passions, spring the desires which hurt the bodies. The cigarettes fool the sorrows, so that nothing will be diminished of *the sky*, of *the apartment buildings*; and all end up in light again, the light which causes the death of humans, for its supervision to be replaced by the more experienced knowledge of the hierarchy of the spirit, which the blessed inspectors are graced with receiving, those who were named poets, and indeed, poets they are.

In *the Attica middays*, when the sun is at its highest, the volumes of light are encouraged. *White stones* placed by the hand of God, mountains of intellect, gigantic pots into which the sun stores its past and future. In these sun's history is kept. They are so rich that, with their meager offerings to humans, with their presence alone they are capable of expelling fear, giving them harmony, so that they may untangle life with their knowledge. Allowing knots to be untangled *in two simple*, parallel *lines* which, left on their journey through the universe, converge, are consolidated and again form the light. And all is light, the poet says, all is love, energy, which makes life distance itself from its drama. A cohesion of concepts, of wonders in the insurmountable chaos of brilliant darkness. An altar preaching the divine, to deify the beings, to break the spell placed by the needs of demonic moments, as they joined the spirit of time, so that humans may acquire a conscious entity, the existence in the self-existent divine altars.

Time is bathed by light, a sky wishing to acquire a body and dwell on earth. And it becomes the volumes and shapes, *the apartment buildings, the cars, the petrified winds*, the hills and towering mountains, aimed at giving people their being. To deliver the senses inherited from infinity, their dreams, their desires, their wounds. So that people in turn may give the sorrows that they have undertaken to uphold, the wounds they swore to heal, the cigarettes they smoke, without any part of the dream diminishing, to integrate them into the programming of the earth. Under the supervision of the poet, the earth has an obligation to stand by the work of light, which nourishes and grows it in its other, etheric life, the greatest concern of God, the unique human heritage.

The poet is the most rational, the most pragmatic, the most down to earth, because his mind deals with the entire world; as middays, when the glory of moments culminates, they acquire the importance of the great pots of light, which, as *white stones* land, to establish the dynasty of the human spirit, whose poverty, blissful – as it is content with few – redeems, loves fear and its Word becomes harmony. It frees life, which is transformed *into simple lines*, graspable, to be followed by thought, emotion, reason, to enter the beautiful buildings, temples, where the liturgies take place, the rituals of the gods, where people are taught of their rights, where they apprentice in the mysteries of the mind, for centuries to thrive, for bodies to be healed, to finally reach the light. Even the stars that have been tied to life will pass into the light, becoming earthly light.

Great winds, petrified, wandering in their universe, around the apartment buildings of some very familiar gods, familiar people, who shine their cars, while their awnings protect them from the heat and rain. And their evolution reaches its peak, because among them live poets who have the strength of mind, the kingdom of knowledge and they perform miracles. They build the future of love; they construct the future of light; they oversee and foresee; they look death in the eye and its darkness reaches light; for they know that all is light.

The volumes and shapes are but the light, guarded in the pots of the mind and heart, the story of God, the beginning of humans and the end of the century.

LAMPROS PORFYRAS

DON'T CRY

Don't cry, don't say that you have nothing left here.
You have the passing storm up in the mountain,
the dawn, far in the sea and the day
down on the plain, and olive trees and the bustle of the city.

You still have the poor sheltered shore,
into which, as dusk comes, the rocks, the piers fall;
the houses, the old fisherman, patiently rowing;
don't cry! you have there – behold – all our life. All of it.

You still have it there, with its silent and innocent serenity,
with its sweet smile, its carefree beauty,
with its shadow; its shadow slowly erased
by the dusk and the night's sea breeze...

(Collective works)

Humans cry for their life, for their own life. And if they have crossed the boundaries of themselves, they grieve for the lives of others as well. They ache and complain, as they realize that there is nothing left in their world, in the social space in which they exist and work, shaping with the chimera their vain deeds. And they dissolve with *the passing storm*, which leaves its markings on the mountains, trails that lead to the sky's clear balcony, from which a person can oversee *the sea down below*, to see into the dawn of a new day, into *the bustle of the city*, the fruits of the olive trees that shine.

Don't cry, the poet advises humans, *you still have the poor sheltered shore*, into which, as the cycle of life closes, the dreams of the world fall as rocks. You still have the piers, along with those who sought shelter, and all the houses and *the old fisherman*, who symbolizes your wise self, *patiently rowing. You have there all your life*, the entire universe. *Silent and innocent, serenity* with *its carefree beauty*, as a shadow's shadow erases one another, *as dusk slowly erases* itself and night erases the sea breeze, the seductive wind of the earth's breath.

This sacramental life is what is left, the poet says, when the shadows are erased, the delusionary selfish ideas of appropriation, the inexhaustible "wanting", the endless desires of the ceaseless searching *in* the chaotic *plain*, where the fruits of the toil shine like dreams. And they leave the light of their radiance, to remind a world that passed and was lucky enough to climb the mount of high perception, where physical coercion ends and the emotional needs of the psychological sphere of earth stop. Because knowledge is the one chosen to rule the dream, when humans decide to leave their complaint, to sacrifice it; so that their crying may become laughter, passions to be equated with intellectual neutrality, bliss to become the life of the entire earth.

It only takes a conception of a poetic moment, a flare of the mind, to enable humans to see the meaning of the life oppressing them, as their spirit strives to be freed from the illusions keeping them captive in pain, making them cry like children for the inevitable losses caused by the decay that their morphic and mental presence in life is subjected to, during the evolutionary processes.

Nothing is lost, the poet says. Humans gain in value, in entity. Their experiences are all transmuted into the absolute.

The sophisticated mind coexists with its inner being and is arranged in its flows, so that it becomes the conductor of pure essence towards the plain of true fruitfulness of the spirit. There, the experiences gained from pain are utilized, and being free can cope with the cycle of a glorious life, where the shadows of the background do not misrepresent the image of their living work – their own self. Dreams, ideas, feelings, desires and passions to the One they lead, to the ideal, to the perfect, to their completion, to redemption, to justification of life. And this is what humans must see.

For this reason, the poet who knows advises them not to cry, passively letting themselves be carried away by the currents of weakness, of helplessness; to stop being overwhelmed by the insecurity caused by the complaint, which leads to clouded minds that are unable to recognize the benefactions of the blessing which stems from their very nature. They were meant to be the owners in the perpetual becoming of their world; by evolving, to be able to evolve what surrounds them, as they learn to accept their cosmic destiny. This, through loss makes them wise; to have the ability to row, as the great fisherman leading their selves and others to the one and only substantial existence of the supreme being, where nothing is lost and where every being finds itself amid its uniqueness.

That is where the mountains are, and the seas, the plains, the olive trees, the harmony from *the bustle of the city* and *the poor sheltered shore, into which piers fall* and fade. There, amid the *silent and innocent* serenity of life, in its smiling and *carefree beauty*, the dream goes to erase its form, as, in its essence, the soul of the world unfolds and all unite with the owner of their being, to be redeemed, to be illuminated within their entity.

The poem speaks of the truth of perpetuation of the form within the amorphous and of the perpetuation of the amorphous within its human, universal self.

MANOLIS PRATSIKAS

QUESTIONS

Friend,
you who preceded us, neglecting the consequences
with a silent twilight of frustration on the neutral flowers,
with an indifferent final line of the face.
Give us some news, some knowledge.
Are there hopes, dreams in your lands?
Are sins being recorded? Is the soul burdened?
Do childish smiles bloom? Is blood red?
What does the sky say?
How scared we are of this move...
Friend,
You who preceded us. Are you content?
Did you ever complain? Do you have this right?
Do they deny it of you, counting on the non-existent sweetness of your eyes?
Can we possibly escape? Can we hide somewhere?
Are the supplications, the prayers, the means heard? Are they allowed?
Friend, help us.
The time has come for protests, for denial.
Perhaps we might accomplish something. An omission perhaps, an abandonment.
Just show us the way. Can you do it?

(Travelogue)

Through the entity's time do humans travel. In the *silent twilight* of frustration, they recede, leaving the *neutral flowers*, which symbolize their perfection, to represent their dreams upon earth. *Indifferent* is the *final line of* their *face*, like the first, the original one, leaving the promise of news, of knowledge, the one which with a question answers the eternal question:
– *Are there hopes, dreams?*
– Are there visions?
– Are there gods?
– Are there people?

The weight of the soul is the recording of human works. When *childish smiles bloom*, the heavens laugh, and, at the sight of blood, the scarlet dream of the Word by the beauty of its wonders is enchanted. The movement of fear from one cloud to another is but the path of the matutinal for the revelation of the dialectical power imposed by cosmic law.

The questions posed by humans during their life do not remain unanswered by the poet. They are all analyzed by him, the other self, the superior – by the timeless Socrates. It is customary for limited questions to be answered by other, expanded ones. A challenge by the macrocosmic self to the microcosmic counterpart, amid the endless cycle of self-existence, to become aware of the idea that created them and to expand, uplifting the parts of their fall, as they are subjected to the charm of chaos. The protest is the inalienable right of both the blissful and the miserable. The former objects, inquiring about the status of the latter, while the latter asks about the status of the first.

Non-existent is the *sweetness of* the *eyes*. The morphic frolics are unable to juxtapose their sweetness onto the emptiness. Denial and traction in the field of inevitable convergence are one and the same. The meaning of one in the concept of zero is included and vice versa, the poet suggests. Existence cannot escape non-existence, nor can non-existence escape its own existence. And everything, *the supplications, the prayers, the means,* are both heard and not *heard, are allowed* and not allowed, depending on the necessity that determines the choice of each individual. And the only one who can help in this selection is their friend, their own self. Time is eager *to protest, to deny.* The "maybe" of hope is the superlative of an omission for its own abandonment and of the abandonment for its omission.

Both easy and difficult is the way which the oriented points to, so that the disoriented self may find the path. Of its own volition, the ascent, of its own volition, the fall. The fall asks the one preceding it – the ascent. It follows in its footsteps. It is possessed by agony and, dominated by doubt, its own faith disputes. Faith precedes, predating consequences and, in the *silent twilight* of its own self, frustration surrenders, to the symbols of knowledge it places indifference, into which it plunged by its own initiative. The human face becomes the face of God and the human face hopes to realize the perfection of God. Its knowledge informs ignorance and ignorance seeks to please the supreme knowledge-holder.

Decision and practice, practice and result, question and answer – one and the same. A universal question which, as a sun is consumed, emitting its questions to the questions posed by chaos. The answer is the result of the question itself, it emanates from it as another question and returns back to it.

– Who are you?
– What are you?
– Where are we going?
– Where are you going?

Perpetual is the journey of self-search. The self asks its aspects and the aspects ask the self about their identity. And the answer is self-induced; a question that is constantly expanding, repeating itself.

The poem, though entitled "Questions", is nothing more than answers posed in the form of questions. Those preceding, *neglecting the consequences with a silent twilight of frustration on the neutral flowers, with an indifferent final line of the face*, while remaining a great question mark, at the same time offer *news, knowledge*. And they are the same ones that ask themselves, in this world or the other where they reside, if *there are hopes, dreams,* if their own selves exist. But, since they ask, they exist, in whichever dimension they might be, even if this is their imagination, up or down, high or low, in the recordings of sin, in the weightlessness of the soul, in the blooming *childish smiles*, on *red blood*, in the sky which they ask and by the same question the sky answers back, as the clouds move, symbolizing emotions and thoughts, pleasure and bitterness, or fear of their own movement.

A protest of pleasure for discontent and of discontent for its own misery. A denial which in itself is the prerequisite for the success of the abandonment of the ego within its ontological self. A brilliant, clear, easy path, always disclosed by the entity to its own self.

YIANNIS RITSOS

FROM "THE MOONLIGHT SONATA"

Let me come with you. What a moon tonight!
The moon is kind – it won't show
that my hair turned white. The moon
will turn my hair golden again. You will not understand.
 Let me come with you.

When the moon is full, shadows grow larger within the house,
invisible hands pull the curtains,
a faint finger writes on the piano's dust
forgotten words – I do not want to hear them. Hush.

Let me come with you.
a little farther down, as far as the brickyard's wall,
until the road turns and
the city appears, all concrete and airy, whitewashed in the moonlight
so indifferent and immaterial
so positive, as if metaphysical
that you can finally believe you exist and do not exist
that you never existed, that time and its decay did not exist.
Let me come with you.

We will sit on the ledge for a while, up on the hill,
and, as the spring breeze blows upon us
we might even imagine we can fly,
because, many times, even now, I hear the noise my dress makes

as the noise of two powerful wings beating,
and when you shut yourself within this flying sound
you feel the tight mesh of your throat, your ribs, your flesh, and so,
tense within the muscles of the sky-blue wind,
within the robust nerves of height,
it matters not whether you are coming or going
nor does it matter that my hair has turned white
(this is not my sorrow – my sorrow
is that my heart too does not turn white).
Let me come with you.

I know that everyone walks alone in love,
alone in glory and death.
I know. I have tried it. It is of no use.
Let me come with you.

(Moonlight Sonata)

When the moon is full, the shadows grow larger and the past returns, the poet says. *The moon* turns *hair* golden, *invisible hands pull* the veils, *forgotten words* are written in dust, the heart is enchanted by the music that the terrible *time* played and then left, abandoning its audience amid the heartlessness of the ancient house.

The poet talks to the entity. It tells it he is its soul and form, its female and male aspect and pleads it to take him with it. Yet he does not deny his habits, with those he wants to follow it. He uses the brickyard to show that he agrees with the continuity of life in the concrete cities, the ethereal, the whitewashed – cleansed – despite the moonlight's supervision – the glamor of personality – that no matter how much it tries to give substance to its projects, they, as creations of God himself, resist the coercion of materialization and lose their mass, become immaterial within their own matter, formless within their own form. There, the exact science meets metaphysics – its transcendent reality –, uniting form with its essence, so that humans may finally believe that they exist and do not exist, that they *never existed* and in fact *time and its decay* never truly existed either; to be able to consolidate in their mind the theory of redemption, to act on it, building its house with earthly bricks, the house of the eternal all, which passes through the changes imposed on it by the necessity of the formation of the formless.

The poet talks to it, to his supreme thought, to the superior relationship, the theory that does not surmise its world, the one which realizes the dream, the great soul of his soul, the great form of his own form, the only one able to understand him and heed his pleas; to justify him, to redeem him so that he is deified by the gentle blow of the spring breeze, by imagination's flight, by *the noise* of its *dress*. A perfected woman, a little girl with the boy, her mature husband, they sit united on the highest ledge of the observer and protect their ontological field while overseeing the perpetual game, which, within *the sound of the two powerful beating wings*, hides *the noise* of the restless, human, divine heart.

A hermaphroditic divine being which feels the tight mesh of its throat; its ribs, its flesh, tense *amid the muscles of the sky-blue wind, within the robust nerves of the height* of its own entity, which, wherever it may be going, whatever it may be doing, whether coming or going, it *matters not. Nor does it matter* whether its *hair has turned white*, if its *sorrow* is the sorrow of a man who loses his youth and of youth which loses its man. What *truly matters*, the poet stresses, *is that* the human *heart does not turn white*, that it does not follow the lonely *love to glory and death*, that tries and finds that nothing is beneficial, if not passing through deprivation to which eternity subjects its body, so that personality is forced to seek the one and only truth of its entity; to plead in the mysteries of its nature, to initiate it to the uniqueness of its united life.

All poets refer to the entity. They acquire its aspects; they unite with its essence. They become seekers of its truth, and upon it – upon God – they place their hopes for the success of the vision of cosmic existence that desires that they, its lovers, follow its will. Only the exalted poets have the grace to unite with it, which is why its presence is familiar to them. They shape it in its vast, invisible being, they play with it, they find ecstasy. Their passion is its passion and they call its form their form. Woman and man have one purpose, that of union, of truth, of the love life which is not afraid of death, as its knowledge is its glory. They know that it is of no use for the sun to remain separated from erebus, matter from spirit and spirit from essence.

Supreme are the secrets of poetry, magical words, verses that shape the character of the earth; verses of the soul, of form, of personality, verses of love; weighty proposals, dazzling flares, tales of the primordial, universal drama; melodies that soothe the pain, dissolve the confusion, atone the calamity; the power of spirits within God's love.

Let me come with you. A universal request coming from the depths of the being, passing from sensuality to thought, from thought to idea, from idea to mind, from mind to entity, from entity to itself. Let me live, let me exist; to bear the sky, my being, my life, my time, my decay, the concept of my presence.

Pleading, invocative is the need, to the love of light it prays. The kind-hearted moon calls for compassion from the benevolent ruler of prudence, surrendering to the glory of his grace and splendor, so that the life of its love marches in parallel to the life of its death. A life lonely, glorifying, unique, human and divine is the poet's life.

BIANKA ROMAIOU

MOSAIC PIECES

Your thought,
a glow, a bird's fluttering
a flower, filling my heart
with pollen.

The hands are more beautiful
when returning from tenderly wandering
over the body.
They expel barbarism.

When tightly holding a beloved hand,
you feel your heart writhing
in its grip.

All my small desires
were fulfilled with great interest.
Time multiplied "the Thirty
pieces of silver".

The chest is tight for the deep
breath of the imprisoned.
For the earthquake of emotions,
and the lighthearted words,
which dissolve as they make
the blood red hot.

(Requiem)

Thoughts pollinate the desires of the heart. Glittering flashes are the imaginations, they mold the body of desires, breathing emotions into it. The visions of poets are the fluttering of birds, sun flowers, offering their pollen to earthly hearts, to fertilize desires, to be gestated, to be born in love.

Long is the path of uninitiated bodies in their carnal wandering. How can they dispel the ferocity of senses within human barbarity? The sensual hands *are more beautiful* in their hedonistic quest and their magical functions, after the sacred erotic orgiastic catharsis, bring purification. In the greeting of recognition, when the heart explores the heart, the expectation vibrates, *writhes in* the *grip*, anticipating the fullness of human love.

As time passes, desires increase the interest imposed by treason, as humans deny the destination of their nature. And the debt of "Thirty pieces of silver" grows, as, within the valuation of passions, multiplication has no ending. The chest of desiring life contracts, the spirit of the *imprisoned* suffocates, preparing *for the earthquake of emotions*. Light-hearted are the words of temptation, they are destined to dispel, the poetess says, in the fiery blood of the being.

The unbridled power of thought, is urged towards orgasm by the mind, which the will of the ineffable world dictates and its essence with the startles of flares as pollen scatters, to fertilize ideas, which, as flowers project the triggering force of nature, seeking ratification by humans; to rule their dreams, the elegance of the body, the grace of the spirit. To become the beauty that will dispel the barbarity of dark, unconfessed instincts of the visceral, unrestrained life.

It is the heart of life that seeks its very heart, as its beloved hands, the human hands, tightly grasps with its other hands, the invisible ones, trying to feel their writhing in its grip. To feel the pulse, to check its quality, and, experiencing the jolt, to reach the depths of the source from which the unknown springs, to place it under control, to dominate it. Holy is the purpose; the containment, the harnessing of spiritual forces that determine the evolution of humans, of the vital fires flowing through veins like blood and stubbornly attempt to be freed, to be released from prison.

The great problems of life are its small desires that are paid with interest, as, passionately proclaiming the expediency of their existence, are held accountable for the earthquake of emotions. They cause *the lighthearted* thoughts and words, which rekindle blood and are then dissolved, leaving the human expectation for happiness unfulfilled. *The small desires* are those which must become knowledge, because, as they increase the human demands, they multiply the punishments of death in chaos, by fooling the senses and misleading them. Time becomes the key factor of the long, evolutionary process of the produced spiritual disorientation.

Life is dragged into the prison of its body. The breathing shortens, its chest contracts and the *deep breath* cannot be achieved. Only with the acceptance of the irrevocable ontological will on the part of humans can the power of the spirit penetrate the depths of the soul, to appease the instincts, the underground impulses, and carry out the necessary combustions for the assimilation of descending fires.

The thought of each human is a *glow, a bird's fluttering, a flower, filling* their *heart with pollen*. The thought of the mind, the spiritual self, which externalizes its power as light, is a sun symbolized by a flower and which by its fiery pollen fertilizes the heart of the earth and learns to love its bodies. On the return from their tender wandering, it welcomes them and with its *beautiful hands* cleanses them, expelling the embarrassments caused by lower thoughts, as they did not merge into the light. To erotic harmony they did not wish to surrender and the desires of the people with *tight chests* were left writhing in the grip of hands, imprisoning their breath and becoming prey to earthquakes caused by emotions.

Light-hearted are thoughts and words. *They make blood red-hot* and *dissolve*. Desires become knowledge in the perpetual current, which, with its power, makes the new redeemed thoughts revolve around the mind that creates them and illuminates them, as the earth rotates around the sun.

SAVINA

BLOOD DONATION

Deep, in my final soil, angels with dark circles
under their eyes – my weary guardians –
with troublemaking wings plow my land.
Embers; consumers; flayers; squashed truths;
vertigo poems which are still clay...

They walk deeper, angels with bloodied feet
– my companions on the cliffs –
they look on with eyes as lakes, stifling the rough sin,
the sad, envious say. Thus, I learn the truth...
It moves ahead and hides or they hide it, deeper,
where darkness breaks, in the center of my forehead, there
the ancient cosmic light that passes
– angels in white, my companions in the carefree –
which moves on and knows, featherweight, among the innards
heart and bones, as a wound about to heal,
they allow a second eternity
my faith, which is also called chaos
The wreck saves itself
as the ticking sound saves the clock
as babies save innocence
as the unknown saves imagination
as the stone saves the shadow
I gain from what is lost...

(Contact lenses)

Deep, on the first and *final soil*, the white and black angels line up, as the first preach God's paternity, and the second claim it for themselves. The latter, the rulers with *dark circles under their eyes*, the torturous wing-bearers of confusion, the *weary consumers* of the great mother's grace. *Vertigo poems which are still clay, squashed truths* their unfulfilled projects are. And the embers remain, the unassimilated remains created by the great retained fire in the depths of the darkest desires of humans, who seek to be born into the light; to repent, for their souls to shine, their romanticism to acquire substance in the eyes of bright angels, to spare the mercy given to them as panacea on earth, so that they may be saved and stop throwing themselves off cliffs.

Rough, unappeased is the sad, envious pulse of the heart of humans. *Angels with bloodied feet* are the armies of desperation, which in the agatho[1] of the revelation are redeemed. The sins commit suicide in the deep lakes of their eyes. The hopes of false life drown, and the truth is revealed. The drama of the poetic soul becomes knowledge, nature learns of itself, of the one which *moves ahead and hides*, the eternal woman, but also about those who *hide it, deeper*, on the Cyclops' forehead, who, either male or female, the power of his reign is one, that of the most ancient cosmic light.

Great healers are the *angels in white, companions* of feminine ecstasy, they move and dissipate their weightless aura among the innards, the heart and bones, healing the wounds of the entity, allowing it with faith to repeat its existence in chaos as *a second eternity*. And *from what is lost*, the shipwrecked time will gain itself, poet's *innocence* will gain *innocence*, *imagination* will gain its *unknown* destiny, and the petrified light will absorb its shadow into itself.

---

[1] The term "agatho" out of the Greek word «αγαθό» is used to mean all that is beyond the duality of good and bad. It is the Entity, the Whole, the Monad.

Deep within the earth's tomb, humans recycle their fantasies, formulating their agonies into hopes and their hopes into dreams, trying through mental processes to release the desires which are to blame for the coercion of their death. Horrible angels are the rulers, guardians of the unfulfilled orgasm that causes *dark circles under the eyes*; using their wings they scatter riots in hell, plowing erebus, to sow the *embers*, the *squashed truths* which are consumed by flayers. To unrestrainedly increase the vertigo of passion, *poems which are still clay* and seek for the poet to take them to glory.

Deep within the poet's being, the *bloodied feet* of fallen angels determine the course of the envious and the rough sin of her company. And it precipitates into the abyss, to drown in the lakes of its own voluptuousness. Thus, life learns the truth of this woman-witch, the voluntarily punisher of lies, which always hides behind and ahead of the events – the happenings. This unacknowledged protest that comes to the surface, even though it is *hidden deeper* in the forehead by her beloved angels, eternal lovers of her nature, which worship her, protecting her from even their own sacrilegious gaze.

Knowledge contemplates on the soul. Light rests on infinity's consent, as the two large opposing currents converge – ignorance and wisdom – and end up between the two eyes, depositing there their positive and negative charge, so that the universal eye remains inextinguishable; to diffuse its inner light, accompanied by the angels in white, and, passing through the body of eternity, to heal with its faith the wound of chaos. For the shipwrecked universe to be saved from its own shipwreck, as the heart's pulse saves the love, as the breath of the young child saves the holiness of the wise, as the unexplored unconscious saves the dream and as the mineral realm saves the shadow of its density.

Unbridled is the human, undominated is pain. An imaginative woman is the vertigo of the lunar personality and the knowledge of the solar soul. Fear and erebus is coercion. Essence is the ending of activities in the becoming, in the voluptuousness of winds, poems are the works of light and the weakness of humans becomes the temptation of angels, divine beings of the idea, visions of the soul. Guardians of the mind, of the abyss are those having knowledge, divine advice, they stand by humans. Of their own volition the fallen indulge in desires and wear the earthly body.

Ascending is the inclination, to the house of the heart it returns the Word and love, an erotic act of deification, it bears the sins, restructuring the conditions of existence of the eternal all. Self-disciplined humans, within the house of the body they evangelize to themselves, alongside the angels, the spirit's supreme works, *poems* of the supreme God.

GIORGIOS SARANTARIS

COME, JOY WILL BE DIVIDED...

Come, joy will be divided among us
We, the people without touch
Dream of a holy skin
And with haste we light up our attention
From a non-existent forest, we chop firewood
For use against the enemy
And for the lovely fire of conservation
One with the elements

At one point, everyone's veins are opened
With tenderness, the soil lies
And blood receives the instincts
It hunts the invisible soul
The inconceivable life leaves it
But its embrace is warm
A kiss hiding the truth
The universe grieves at a distance

The heart knows no borders
It does not bathe under a tap
Beneath a mountain
Gazing has no ending
It lasts as long as the shepherd's song
Now that neither the plain ends
And whether sunset or moon
One is the music's tune

(Poems, fourth volume)

Between the sun and the earth, the entity contemplates on the division of its bliss into joy and sorrow. It is humanity which, in its physical existence, is governed by touch, but as an intangible, sophisticated principle does not have this need. As if *a holy skin*, its own *skin* life dreams of.

The study lights the brazier, sacrificing the attachment humans have to the ephemeral. Through the *forest* of non-existence and existence, their notional bodies are cut, symbolized by the trees, and humans become a burnt offering to appease the most ancient of gods, an enemy and friend, who also maintains the other fire, that *of conservation against* the elements opposing eternity.

The veins of temporal humans are destined to be opened and in this timeless bloodshed *the soil lies with tenderness*, the body of eternity, which struggles to accept the instincts of its totality as it tries to hold on within the chaos, insisting on hunting the invisible greatness of the soul of its own inconceivable life, which constantly leaves it. And the embrace of the earth with the sky, as the entity alternates its roles, declares the meaning of the universe's existence, which, surrendered to the carnal *kiss hiding the truth*, is unable to distance itself from passions, grieves and continues hurting, because it has not learned that the heart of the entity knows no boundaries. *It does not bathe under a tap*, but is a water fountain itself. *Beneath* the *mountain* of its desire, from its earthy field, the *gazing has no ending* and it knows this. Its duration is the eternal *shepherd's song* and its *tune*, the musical life manifested through the primordial conception and interpretation, a symphonic performance of the infinite.

Time is divided, it grows, it multiplies and becomes self-removed. It is the feelings and ideas of the mind, holy dreams, sacred visions, studies carried out with care and destined for its safekeeping. Its time conserves it in existence. The emotional and mental sensuality, manifested with time as its carrier, is but an endless forest. The existence is the identity of its non-existence, whose expediency lies in the preservation of the integral whole, fire which, with its elements perpetuates the beauty of the form, to ground the concept of touch to reality: "The finger set upon the imprint of nails". This is the reality, the poet says. That of the divine being with the *holy skin*, the immaculate, proof of immortality, which alone is opposed to death and transmutes fire to the eternal fire of the pure spirit, which spiritualizes the creation, by burning and transforming time.

Futility is realized, it opens its veins to the tenderness of the earthy falsehood. It is the blood, the radiance flowing through the universes, what accepts *the instincts* hunting *the soul. The inconceivable life leaves*, as veins have been opened, seeing that its *warm embrace* was but a kiss hiding the truth. And the truth is that of the fleshless, inner heart, the love of which has no boundaries, since it *does not bathe under a tap* – the fountain of the water element symbolizing the outpouring of emotions – because it knows well that, from the foothills of the mountain, the gazing of the chimera *has no ending*. Equal to God is the song's duration in the valley of bliss and joy, the field where sunlight is divided into the magic of the moon, symbolizing ignorance, and to knowledge, which is the inner light, when the day is deliberately equated with night and is delivered to music's single tune, the indivisible of the shepherd mind and the divisible of the time of emotions, of unfulfilled love.

The power of life is joy and sorrow, which have not realized their carrier and cannot be expressed, the poet says, they have no feeling of touch. They are left to dream of it as the Golden Fleece, which must be mastered with the study that brings knowledge, distinction; to be able to see and realize the nature of the *non-existent forest* which is where the roots of the being emerge. And so they may grow up, to be sacrificed in the fire that burns against time, the one responsible for maintaining the beautiful fire of the unappeased need for the form, which is composed of the elements of totality.

Humans are this form, "for dust thou art, and unto dust shalt thou return". *With tenderness* they *lie* in their repeating cycles, accepting into their new cycle the blood with the instincts of the invisible soul, which is hunted by the mind as a life that leaves. Their *warm embrace* embodies the cause of their universal grief, the tragedy of their existence. The one and only truth of their freedom is betrayed by a kiss.

The timeless sun becomes temporal, the one without boundaries, that, like a fountain lets its light flow and fire becomes water, so that knowledge is analyzed into ideas and emotions, a spiritual mountain symbolizing the world; a world which, from the center of its existence, gazes at the chorus of its projections, enjoying the musical duration of its Word, apprenticing to the meaning that duality has within its uniqueness.

GIORGOS SEFERIS

THE FORM OF FATE

The form of fate above the birth of a child,
the revolutions of stars and the wind, a dark night in February,
old women with remedies climbing the creaking stairs
and the dry branches of the grapevine hanging bare amid the courtyard.

The form above a child's cradle, of a fate wearing a black headscarf
an inexplicable smile and downcast eyelids and breasts white as milk
and the door that opened and the storm-tossed skipper
who threw his damp cap into a black chest.

These faces and these incidents followed you
as you unraveled the thread for the nets by the beach
even when, while sailing with the wind to your stern, you gazed at the pit
of the waves;
in all the seas, in all the bays*
it was with you, and it was a difficult life and it was joy.

Now I know not to read below,
because they chained you, because they pierced you with the lance,
because, one night in the woods, they separated you from the woman
that was fixedly staring and did not know how to speak,
because they deprived you of light, of the open sea, of bread.

How did we fall, comrade, into the burrow of fear?

It was never written in your destiny, nor in mine,
we never sold nor bought such merchandise;
who is it that commands and kills behind us?
Never mind, do not ask; three red horses on the threshing floor
trampling on human bones, blindfolded,
never mind, do not ask; wait; the blood, the blood
one morning will rise like Saint George the rider
to stab the dragon with the lance over the soil.

(Collective Works)

* The reader must bear in mind during the following analysis that the Greek word for bay is also used for the bosom («κόρφος», pronounced korfos).

Above the birth of a child, the resultant of all forms, *the form of fate*. As the universe whirls, the wind – the spirit – in the dark night of duality, symbolized by the second month, February, becomes the old women, the past seasons, climbing the creaky stairs, holding the remedies of their immeasurable wisdom. These are the magical secrets of the Creator, secret elixirs of nature that offer their power to *the dried completely bare, branches of the grapevine*, to open their eyes, to grow leaves, to blossom and to tie the fruits of communion. To offer them to the perpetual, so that it may drink their juices, so that life is initiated through the black-headscarf-wearing *form of fate* – form of the world – through the *inexplicable smile* of the soul, *the downcast eyelids and breasts as white as milk*. With them, the soul nurtures its spirit and flesh, the skipper, and opens the gate to him, so that he may throw – an act of desperation – *into a black chest* – the coffin – *his damp cap*, wanting to renounce the responsibilities for the evolution of life, the stairs, that creak in the ascent of the multifaceted fate which traces his long course.

These faces and these incidents, the poet says, follow the mariner, *as* he unravels the soul's thread *on the shore*, crafting the nets of need. Life sails downwind through the seas, focusing its eyes on the pits *of the waves, in all seas, in all bays*. With it, all faces, visible and invisible, that constitute the hierarchy of the spirit and help it withstand the difficulties and pain, the joy and the bliss.

The unattended aspects of life bind the human being with chains, with its own chains, and pierce it *with their lance*, its own *lance*, separating man from woman and woman from man within the night, in the heavenly woods, which they transform into hell, causing them to stare fixedly in despair and are thus unable to read the scriptures. By depriving them of *light, of the open sea, of bread*, they submit them to a test, letting them fall along with their companions *into the burrow of fear*, so that they all become aware and see that those written are not of their own fate, that they did not negotiate, they did not sell and buy *such merchandise*; and so, to seek the one who *commands and kills behind them*.

They are not discouraged. They ask and learn of *three red horses which are on the threshing field, trampling their bones, blindfolded*. The poet urges them to surrender, not to ask, to wait until the radiance of blood is released. To become the blessing's morning, Saint George the rider, who will *stab* the earthly dragon *with his lance*, as it is the one recording *those written in their fate*, commanding and killing behind them.

The poet struggles against the life of his century, refusing it, and claims his own life with unrelenting determination. He does not want fate as a leader. Humans themselves must be theleaders. They must take the elixirs into their hands, the magical secrets of life, and with the knowledge of prudence, to analyze *the inexplicable smile of fate*, to drink the pure radiance from its breasts, as they are the travelers, the great skippers, the humans. The poet advises them, admonishes them to stop throwing their countless worries – which are symbolized by the damp cap – into *the black chest*, letting them become buried by the century.

Thefaces that follow, he wants them toobey and to reveal the incidents which open the pit of abysmal waves. Because these are which constitute the power of the soul, as it, ruthless and cruel, refuses to illuminate with its wisdom the turbulence of personality before it succumbs. So that humans are forced to delve deeper, to read the secrets, to know how hell and heaven, woman and man, will be united within the night of the vast woods that symbolize the spectrum of creation.

The poet invites humans to learn to read, to indulge in the scriptures, to accept the teaching, so that the chain of causes, which keeps them shackled and pierces them with lances, breaks. God deprives humanity, which is His wife, of the Word, *of light, of the open sea* of the spirit, the essence of the body – the bread, the manna – letting it fall *into the burrow of fear* and become prey of the century, which determines its fate, selling its merchandise to the one who kills it and purchasing it from him again.

It is the dragon of desire which binds the eyes of the three red horses, which symbolize the reversed triune human nature, and commands them to *trample the bones* of humans, spreading death. It is the power of blood, of life's fire, which is directly ruled by the will of the man-eating dragon. And it is the will of humans, symbolized by Saint George the dragon-slayer, which must emerge and be imposed upon the century, the poet says. To stop the scourge, the fate, from dominating over humans, being the driving force of the life flow. Their form to attend their birth, as an image and likeness of their own entity, which defines the rotations of the stars and planets and the wills of the earth's winds by the calendar of their divine will, so that they are able to realize the duality of their nature, in its form and essence, the uniqueness, and thus ascend, as the entity, the stairs which will not creak. The eternity of form, wearing a white headscarf, free of the penalty of time, will offer its essence, letting it flow into the grapevine of God, so that its branches do not wither, do not hang bare amid his courtyard.

And humans drink the immortal wine and the immortal milk from the breasts of the mother of all, while the gate of her heart remains open, so that their spirit passes through it and grows within God's immense vineyard, where the thread which makes the nets of fallacy no longer becomes unwound. Sailings will not take place for futile quests that force *eyes* to focus onto the *pit* of despair. *The form* will be accompanied by its infinite forms, redeemed *faces*, holy as suns, and difficulty will transmute into bliss by the love of *Saint George, the rider upon the poet's horse.*

AGGELOS SIKELIANOS

BECAUSE I DEEPLY PRAISED

Because I deeply praised and trusted earth
and did not spread my secret wings in flight
but rooted in the stillness all my mind,
the spring again has risen to my thirst,
the dancing spring of life, my own joy's spring.

Because I never questioned how and when
but plunged my thought into each passing hour
as though its boundless goal lay hidden there,
no matter if I live in calm or storm,
the rounded moment shimmers in my mind,
the fruit falls from the sky, falls deep inside me.

Because I did not say: "here life starts, here ends,"
but "days of rain bring on a richer light
and earthquakes give the world a firmer base,
for secret is earth's live creative pulse,"
all fleeting things dissolve away like clouds,
great Death itself has now become my kin.

(Lyric Life)
(Translated by Edmund Keeley and Philip Sherrard)

Praised is the Word – the earthly and the solar – of the poet, who reaches their roots, his own roots. From there *rises the spring* of his inspiration and acquires *the secret wings*, not those of flight, but the ones raising him to a rotating dance, becoming the earth and, around the earth, becoming the sun. And in the silence of his silent sound, where the spring of the universe quenches the thirst of the suns, he swears upon his faith never to question *how and when* his mind itself will be during his plunge, on each passing hour, the silence as well as the uncountable tumult, the creation's rhythm, a hesychasm of fair or bad weather, a downpour amidst a tempest.

The harmony, each rounded moment's goal to become the fruit which, as rain *that falls from the sky*, as his spirit's fruit, falls inside him. Fruition without end, without beginning. Light the days rain down and the earthquakes give the world a firmer base in the secret pulse shaped by the earth. The ephemeral clouds dissolve, as death, having no more to say and do, becomes the poet's great *kin*.

Earthquakes shake the earth to its core and lava ascends, surging towards the sky, relieving the sphere of its burden, the retained stubbornness of its angers against time *giving the world a firmer base*. Time never ponders the concept. *A live* hidden *pulse*, shaping *the fleeting*, into the perfectly round, inner meaning of the mind, immersing its thought into the everflowing, rooting it in the immensity; so that humans seek the truth in the seismic vibrations of their mental and emotional world, motivated by the message of the poet, inviting them to take the place of lucidity. By dissolving the clouds of death, it will turn them into kin, fellow travelers, fellow dancers, in the sacred ritual of the boundless goals of summers and winters, circles followed by the *rich light*.

Life, breath, spirit, all are flight, and, for their own thirst, the poet cares. His heart a spring and those who believed in the desperation he calls, in the threat of death, in his love, to quench their thirst, because they did not experience the force hidden in the *live pulse* of the earth's heart, their own heart, the live *dancing spring* of the cosmic fire, bliss surging from the sky like eternal joy.

Because they did not *deeply praise*, they did not believe in earth. And, in *flight*, they *spread their secret wings*, seeking another spring to quench their soul's desire, avoiding the rooting of their mind in silence, after questioning *how and when*. Their thoughts plunged, into *each passing hour*, not *as though its boundless goal lay hidden there*, so as to protect themselves from the tempest, the hardships of life, not wanting to accept them, prefering only fair weather. But, as the poet says, spiritual fruit without this admission, a fruit, *falling from the sky*, as blessed rain, does not exist, since *here life starts, here ends*, as earth exists in the sky, in the universe, shaped by the hidden, terrible earthquakes, the pulses that give a firmer base for the evolution of its own Word.

The earthquake, the poet – the initiated – experiences, the turmoil taking place within the human being's psychological world. Realizing in it a sacred blessing, an opportunity for consolidation. He invites humans to accept it, to regard death as kin, as *a dissolving fleeting cloud*, releasing the fumes created by the rain, a symbol of a life shaped by desire. This life of desire drags its nature's rich light, like the eternal *day of rain*, to the boundless goals of its will.

Humans are called to question their carefree penchant for flight, to make it bow to the knowledge that will give it the poet's visible wings, the restless ontological power, symbolized by the planet's etheric field. This is the only spring that can quench their insatiable thirst for the unified, the deeper life. That which, as the mind descends into silence, gushes from the heart, becoming the eternal *dancing spring of life*, their joy's bliss.

ILIAS SIMOPOULOS

A RIVER OF STARS

It was the dawn
Coming through the window
With two myriad colors
It was the floodlit sky
Fine-woven lace
With two million stars
It was the land, it was the sea
It was the last whistle of the ship
At the dock

* * *

Fleeing from the threat
Of mediocrity
We raised the anchor
For fearless journeys.
In our wanderings
Amid the oceans of the Night
We had no compass.
Yet
as a talisman we kept
In the very depths of our being

A stream of songs
A small river of stars.

(Poetry-First volume)

It was the dawn; the one, primordial idea that was *coming through the window with two myriad colors*, the start of the dual world, which became a *floodlit sky*, a *fine-woven lace with two million stars* – the visible universe. *It was the land, it was the sea*, the dwelling place of people, the provision of suns. *It was the last whistle of the ship at the dock* – the desire of the one, the warning of the Word.

Chased by their mediocrity, humans raise *anchor for fearless journeys*. And, as they whirl in the oceans of their eternal night, where no compass can determine the broadness of their being, *a stream of songs, a small river of stars*, determines their course. It shows them the way of the mind and heart in the perpetual cycle of dawn and night, of the land and sea, where they endlessly wander in order to find themselves.

The anchor symbolizes retention, the halting of power, the deliberate constraint humans bring to their evolution. An inevitable providence, justified, for the hardships to which they are submitted by their own power, as it is guided from their fate's innate compulsion to the exploration of the nature that leaves them prey to the vast *oceans of the Night*. There, the only compass is the pure mind, their talisman, which they keep in the depths of their being. *A stream of songs*, the poet says, *a small river of stars*.

How many the talismans, how many the beings, how many the people, the countless songs, the rivers, the light of infinity, the ideas of the mind, its plans – *fine-woven lace* on which their multidimensional nature has been recorded. Their spirit, *the floodlit sky* in the endless night. And from *the window*, the only opening of the senses, pours out *the dawn with two myriad colors*. It is the uniqueness of their being which, with the first and *last whistle*, signals the great alternations of their journey.

Human beings were born to be poets, to envision their world, to interpret it with verses, visualizing the unexplored of creation, the happenings in their cosmic cycle. And this is their great interpretative skill, poetry. A window – the frame of their soul – through which the *myriad colors* of dawn that is born flow in, as the devastated emotions emerge to trace their cycle amid the wandering of the day. To become, when nearing its end, *the floodlit sky*, so that the *two myriad colors* transmute into *two million stars*, which, in their conclusion, are nothing more than the land with the sea in the vast ocean of the cosmic night, there where the poet wanders without a compass, because he does not need it.

His compass is his own verses, his own ideas and feelings. His ideas are autonomous; inextinguishable lamps of all that is, poems of his soul, fiery bodies of his spirit with the self-luminous light. They send their song to his reflective of light feelings, to the creations of his personality, which sounds like *the final whistle of the ship at the dock* of the harbor where the Word has chosen to ground the weariness.

Unstoppable is the flow of rivers. The poet knows. The galaxies do not cease their revolving. The universe does not stop the existence, perpetual is its journey into chaos. Humans do not cease thinking, being tormented, living. The desire for life dictates to them the will to continue wandering. Their only expectation is the understanding of the cause that gave birth to dawn. Their only care is the understanding of the need for the existence of a floodlit sky. Their last hope is the knowledge of their world. Their only redemption is awareness of the Word, symbolized by *the whistle of the ship at the dock*, where they stop and are forced to cast anchor and to raise it again for new, *fearless journeys*; for new, fearless explorations.

A wandering is every idea, every state of mind, every human thought. A darkened sky is their spirit, which, with the new opportunity that rises every morning, becomes a radiant day, a promising idea. A brilliant sky in their night, a *fine-woven lace* that enchants them with a million sparks, with a million new ideas, visions of the universe, as their ship is ordered by the desires that threaten them to set sail, urging them to overcome mediocrity and to consciously become the superior of daily life. To be uplifted above the human traits, the common; to become the benevolent giant, who in his talisman hides the bright songs, the promises for happiness of his world, who, without a compass – the direction of the mind – wanders *amid the oceans of the Night* of sufferings and miseries. *A stream of songs, a small river of stars* is the path of wisdom. A spiritual leader is the poet, with his magical verses leads the world, initiating it to the mysteries of life, of redemption, of poetry.

The entire poem is but the narration of the path followed by creation; an epic realized by the wise, by the perfected, by those who travel *the oceans of the Night* of the chimeric life without a compass, with esoteric knowledge as their only aid. With it, they transmute threat into desire, to overcome the mediocrity to which common humans are limited, who do not refer to the starry sky, to hope, to the faith that allows the union with the essential nature.

A stream of songs, a small river of stars is the path, says the poet in his message. Humans must be permeated by optimistic thoughts and ideas and thus receive the blessing and support of the entities, the illuminators of all.

TAKIS SINOPOULOS

LANDSCAPE

Bare rocks; Strike them – no water resonates;
just a funnel opening with the wind;
soil, lower down, and light of a golden colour
and above, the lost forest we sought,
and below, the dry bridges, the cypresses
immersed into limestone.
White on black.

Together we go, with only our thirsty touch,
into the deep green – and ink-colored further down –
shinny thickened salt; we go there
where the poisonous vegetation blackens.
The wind, a tyrant in the day and at night a tyrant,
Anoints itself with light, digging incessantly.
Together we go; further down we shall shout
and awake naked, and shall be
swans and wild pigeons, bare
in the white day.

(Borderline)

Bare rocks in the desert; the eternal, vast retreat, where only the hand of the novice ascetic makes the holy waters, the retained Word, resonate from the depths of essence. And the human being lays astounded before the religious painting, the Byzantine ode, a form diffuse amid its golden light. The wind's funnel is the passage into the soil. Earthly life below, and higher up, the colors of golden wonders that succumbed to their nature and became *the lost forest*.

Dry are the roads bridging the distance between white and black. Limestone boulders are the ancient graves, cypresses standing guard, motionless seekers, the explorers of the forest of knowledge we have lost. And *touch* is left *thirsty*, a clumsy caress, touching the curvatures of the mind *into the deep* green of the plant kingdom, where the poet, with the *ink-colored shiny thickened salt*, creates the lyrics of the essence – a panacea against the *poisonous vegetation*. To placate the *tyrant wind* that *incessantly digs* into the bowels of the days and nights of the sphere, in order to successfully conclude its dealings with the light.

There, the poet invites us, *further down,* always *together further down*. In the Hells to shout our Word, with our protest to force it to transform. Naked, to uplift the destitution of our being. *Swans and wild pigeons*, the spirit of all, to illuminate the beauty of life in the immaculate, undefiled, white, eternal day.

A landscape of the soul, a landscape of love, a landscape of light is the landscape of the spirit. A *white* vision *on* a *black* background, which travels the endless realm of the mind. A tormented sphere, soil is its body down below, and the sun high above, magnified in the colors forming the transcendent gold, as the wind, which symbolizes the power of the spirit, opens the way to the lost paradise.

The inner roads, which bridge the gap between low tide and high tide, between darkness and light, must become accessible. The contrasts that create friction must be leveled out. And the *thirsty touch*, on behalf of the senses, must absorb the *ink-colored shiny salt*, so that, through the form, the essence may return to its essence. The unification of the plant and the mineral kingdom must happen, the animal kingdom to must join the human kingdom, kingdoms whose existence is symbolized by the swans, the naked people and the *bare wild pigeons*, so that the *white day* will shine, transmutating its black background into golden uncreated light. The world's light evangelizes the grace of God, and, by surveying the kingdoms of His creation, supervises the humans.

The poet shepherds the concepts. Rocks, naked ideas, savage in their nature, which by the saints are harnessed, to allow the water of life to spring, to flood the desert, so that the spirit overflows the earthen body. For the colours to be united within the golden colour of the light's aura. For humans to be freed and to seek their Creator. To become harmonized with their nature, to accept it and recognize within it the miraculous soil, from which their body was created. This body is the quality of the spirit that enabled their soul to be magnified in the chaos, increasing with its frictions the broadness of universal consciousness in the light of the mind, representing the greatness of the Creator in all its glory.

This is the course of humans, the course of the planet. A landscape is the earth, a landscape is the universe, a space in which humans learn to envision the world, and on the proper evolution of the envisioning their perfection depends. It is to the outcome of this envisioning that the poem refers to. Further down, the poet says, life must be immersed, tension must be grounded down below, the worldly nature of the wind must be settled, must be humbled. Instincts must not shout alone; the soul must also shout. As an undivided music, the Word shall be heard, its harmony shall awaken the universe. Life laid bare, liberated. The tame shall grant deification to the wild.

A ritual of the winds and of the waters with the grace of the spirit's light, an earthen vigilance on a golden star. *There,* the *thirsty touch* will be satisfied, taste will be satiated, smell will be scented, hearing will receive, vision will be able to see its gaze.

Oh, blessing of poets, great grace, divine revelation amid the destitution of the earth. Their poems a prayer, a spiritual contemplation, an ecstasy. A dance of celestial bodies in God's magnanimous poem. Gratitude is the praise on the verge of silence.

KOSTAS M. STAMATIS

EXPERIENCES

Both believing in cooperation
together we took the long road;
but there, at the crossroads, suddenly,
we decided, each to follow
our own fate.
You set out for the places where the sun comes out
and with your hands sought out its light.
You experienced almost by touch
the mysteries of heaven.
I remained here, at the crossroads,
with a torn opinion and experiences,
a beggar of passersby, a sign of the winds.
In this bustling place
I felt thick the abyss of darkness
filling me with frost and hatred.
I experienced in Hell the menace of the night.
Now I believe more in cooperation;
If ever we two meet again
we shall have to exchange, you'll see,
such rare and so different experiences.

("The melody of the human comedy")

At the depth of time, at the depth of the self, at the depth of the being, there are two worlds, the poet says. Two worlds which believe in cooperation and, by mutual consent, take the path to the exploration of their being. In the triunity of their nature they decide, *each* for their *own fate*, taking turns claiming wisdom's middle path. As if one has been designated as the underworld and the other as the upper world; one as the earth and the other as the sky. And the one who chooses the sky has the sun as their companion, knowledge and spirit as their guides. Whereas the one of the earth is the divided of the experiences, a beggar of powers, of the energies of the soul spread over the fields and subfields of the abyss; a *bustling place*, the poet says, of the beings of hatred, of fear, of atrocities. Prey of the darkness, of ignorance, whose kingdom cannot be abolished, if no agreement is concluded between the one and the other world, the one and the other person, for the exchange of these rare and different experiences, acquired by each person during the long discipleship in the Entity of the One.

Superior to the powers is the superego, the resultant of the cosmic becoming, it delves into the study of the multi-natured existence, using as its carrier the natural world. A sensual body that lives, works and, through the senses, tastes and enjoys life, having the capability to choose, as to the species that are externalized with the morphic alternations, and the mental, psychological processes of the presence of the being. Nothing hinders the agreed cooperation between the two parties except for free will, which entitles each one to differentiate their stances, to change the original Word's plan and to deviate from the purpose to which they were pledged, thus prolonging the process of completion for the time required for this very completion. An extension necessary, justified by the cosmic evolution, as, without the processes it entails, the psychological and ontological regions which seek the catharsis would remain unexplored and which have been defined as an abyss.

To these so *rare and different experiences* the poet refers to. These constitute the meaning of existence and are necessary in the becoming of the universality to carry out the plan, whose main purpose is the perfection of the being; a divine plan devised by the creator himself. Destined are the superhuman beings to work towards the success of this purpose. They are the servants of the divine will and comprise the hierarchy of archangels and saints, who assist within all realms of cosmic expression and especially the human one, for the glory of the Supreme Being, whose individual parts seek the awareness of their nature, which is His nature.

The mysteries of heaven and the torments of Hell are the sacred and profane matters, which the wise and saints have addressed over the centuries, partaking in the high cosmic chorea as conscious parts of the Word, voluntarily subjected to its grace and glory, completely surrendered to the creator's love. And this chorea is recognized within all humans; through them it is analyzed and studied; it is inherent within them, and they are inherent as the center and at the same time the periphery in the expressed absolute of all.

The poles are separated and reunite, unifying their contrasts, the two in one and the one in all. Body and soul, spirit and mind, love and hatred, the eternal bipolar currents. Spirits of infinity that divide the universe and, for the sake of their education, disorient humans and their facets. Upward and downward tendencies that radiate their fire; a spiritual power that eternally flows from the source of the universal mind, the Mind of God, the omniscience of His inconceivable life, the life of the Supreme Being, which in human form, the resultant of kingdoms, as His perfect indication has been projected.

It is the higher and lower self, a benevolent angel and a demon angel, God and human, donor and recipient the One, the existent. A dualistic wailing, as the necessity of His absolutism exists. He endures those which arise from Himself, and, crossing the distances of His infinite being, He withstands His dynasty's fever, the fiery Word, appointed to illuminate and serve the bustling *abyss, the menace* of His Hell.

This is the nature of the being, the poet says, the solar and the human one. Greatest is the former, engaged in the work it has entrusted to humans. The latter is worthy of the powers of the former, and, learning to recognize the being of both as the nature of the universal being, it becomes unified with it and is freed.

MARO STASINOPOULOU

THE UNICORN
(excerpts)

I

Hatching wind,
tempest of light,
a long, attractive line of blossoming trees
– archangelic figures –
recomposing the green.
The New Era
emerges from the hills and descends
with large, silent gaits,
as a thin straight line of water
or a lump of honey,
soon it will conquer the indolence of Nature,
It will stand, sunlit, amid All.
The blood of Beings and the blood of things
around them
will lurk, enticed, to imprint
what was happily loved,
in a riot of colors.
The mild light will no longer have its place here.

Amid the ecstatic silence
there it is,
the first Unicorn is born.

III

Beloved universe.
All, in the green age of tender leaves.
Vast deserts were filled with seashells.
Conducive imaginations with the sound from gurgling waters
and salty flavors.
All Beings reside in God's hand
satiated and happy,
The World is one,
 playing the blithesome blind man's buff
beneath the trees,
the drowned swim in euphoric rivers.
Beloved universe.
A sky with unrivaled moons.
I gather them in my pouch
like a great miracle
as Life, up to now has been measured
with dark mirrors,
the inexperience of shapes
and life-long rights.

VI

A damp canopy of trees
in their most fruitful time,
the day spurts fragrantly from the branches.
With it, agile archangels
the adolescent unicorns,
the gallop of Good,
a whirlwind of inconceivable and thriving beauty.

The uniform things,
the wasted vigor,
the anathema and fear
do not belong to the transformed Time any longer.

(The stigma and the Unicorn)

Within the cosmic egg, God hatches His spirit, the wind. And it becomes the vast ocean, the *tempest of light, a long, attractive line of blossoming Beings, archangelic* presences, who, from the peak of their nature, compose the earthly heaven in the *New Era*. From the depths of the centuries comes the new entity. From their spirals it descends quietly, straight, aquarian, vertical in its essence, accompanied by the flocks of its saintly spirits, to conquer the indolence to which Nature is subjected, and sunlit to stand amid the universes, in the centre of its centres.

This is the inner entity, the benevolent maker of synthetic power, whom the desires of ancient life expect in order to capture their *riot of colours* in its absolute love. Uncompromising is the entity, happy, intrinsically complete, it does not accept *the mild light* of the world. Here, in the existent, are the centuries of ecstatic silence. A Unicorn is the first omen, its beloved universe that is born.

The poet fills the vast deserts with the powers of green *tender leaves*, with the imaginations of seashells, where the depths of the oceans, the conducive sounds with their gurgling, become the *salty flavors* of *waters* in her Word, for oceanic Beings to drink and become satiated in joy. *A World* that ascends and becomes earthly in the heavenly *hand of God*, while playing like a *blithesome blind man's buff beneath the trees* of the dark forest with the tragedy of its own existence. *A sky with unrivaled moons* is the strength and *the drowned* swim *in* the *euphoric rivers* of their beloved universe.

The poet gathers the miracle in her pouch, a great dream that life measured, as, in the *dark mirrors* of the life-long inexperience of shapes, she reflected her experience, in order for her to be the fruitfulness of the damp canopy, *the day* that *fragrantly spurts from the branches*, with the synergy of the agile angels. People will become adolescent Unicorns, as they surrender themselves to the gallop of Good, a whirlwind of beauty in their inconceivable thriving nature. And the uniformity of things, the wasted physical strength, the anathema of fear, will *no longer belong to the transformed Time*, the one which touched the concepts, caressed the chaos and enclosed its essence within the treasury of the untransformed.

The Unicorn symbolizes the agatho*, the eternal source of the miracle, God's magnanimity, from which the human existence emerges. An ancient symbol which was given to reveal the potential for the unification of the bicornuous, luciferian mind, whose radiance is divided, ending in the downward flow that is lost in the abyss, in the unconscious of the universal action. It envisions its redemption and juxtaposes its positive visions on the respective negative ones, so that its already shaped world becomes troubled and follows the ascent, driven by the urges dictated by the pleadings of the descent.

A Unicorn is each poet, a savior luminary, calling humans to a stand, to their own strength of positive envisioning, to the one-horned feat, which loses the limits of form and disperses its aura, as it is encircled by the dark forces so as to absorb them into the inner celestial equator, redeeming with the sanctity of its virginity, the ferocity of the World's demonic aspects. Archangelic is the future of humans, multinatured, dazzling. Their blood being fire, purifies the flesh, leading their spirit to a divine-erotic feast. And the mildness of light, sinning to a great extent, repentant, radiates the gloriousness of the uncreated.

Wisdom is the wreath, the ever-blossoming of All. And people learn to love, to deepen, in the essence to delve and to celebrate. Infinite are the possibilities of feelings – of the waters. The mind's essence is knowledge that frees the eyes, letting the century gaze upwards. *The New Era* is established when the Beings are spiritually nourished and *beneath the trees* they consciously reenact the dance of the universe. The drowned are resurrected and from the rivers of water they swim into the rivers of fire.

A New Era. An aquarian that irrigates the deserts, quenching the thirsty spirits and the armies of angels, brigades of civilizations, will prove to be the initiators of synthesis, ecclesiasts of the mind, spiritual leaders of life, supporters of humans. And they, agile, within the agatho[1], traversing the century of their adolescence, will refer to the maturity of the spiritual Word, helping kingdoms to finish within the sunlit devoutness of All. There, *the indolence of Nature* surrenders to the radiance of the luminous cascade of Good, to the gallop of the Unicorns, the benevolent spirits of infinity, fleshless and incarnate Beings which give the mount of initiators the ability to transform the human into a Unicorn and the Unicorn into the entity of the human being.

---

[1] The term "agatho" out of the Greek word «αγαθό» is used to mean all that is beyond the duality of good and bad. It is the Entity, the Whole, the Monad.

PANAGIOTIS E. STAVRAKAS

AND IF!

There are moments I doubt
as my lifetime's reckoning,
if you – ever – existed!
I doubt that night
(which in my dream I saw tonight)
t h e n !
when all chanted around life's Hossana!
if it was you, and if some silky curls,
and if some brown hair
caressed my face.
And if, And if, And if, And if,
and if we met and when,
at life's crossroads
and our gazes met...
There are moments I doubt
my lifetime's reckoning
if I even truly existed!
... He!...
that now, with truly how much sorrow now,
I inscribe these few verses.
....

There are moments I doubt!...

(Life's Chart)

Life has doubts about its life. The poet has doubts. Their life is his. His life is theirs, the doubts'. They exist only to realize their non-existence, his non-existence, in the existence of a reality that only imagination projects as an image of the mind, as a theory given to him so that he may stay the course towards the materialization and dematerialization of his ideas, apprenticing in the ultimate truth of their essence.

And, in every century, doubt deepens. He doubts about *that night*, the primordial, the one, of its cosmogony, which is relentlessly repeated in his desiring heart, as it struggles to feel, to smell, with all the senses of its bodily fever, to be able to believe, through the nature of the mind, in the miracle of its being. *Then! when all chanted around life's Hossana!* in the birth of the Son of God that symbolizes the birth of the universe, which is intended, through the doubt of his existence, to be spiritualized. To pass into the absolute realization of the non-conscious and to be diffused into the beyond, from which the poet draws inspiration and fantasizes beyond the limits of his imagination, beyond the images and shapes, the form of nature, as its girlie *silky curls* try to caress his face, to convince him that he exists.

Mystifying is existence; mystifying is non-existence. Between the two great paths, the middle one is the worthiest of all. It is this one that the poet has been journeying on for centuries. And when he follows one or the other, he does so, to have the converging currents intersect upon himself and seek the causes of their disorientation, as these entities were separated from their essence, a movement of an unprojected immobility, which decided to create its imaginary world just so that it can wonder whether or not it exists. Since then, there are times it doubts, the poet says, when making *a lifetime's reckoning, if* he *truly* ever existed within it; if he was existent or nonexistent.

Only he can form such concepts, as his reference is always to the entity, because it is poetry, which takes form into everything. And his poem, his existent and non-existent work, the lyrical creation of his heart, is his seal in time, as it changes and takes into its variations the forms of the Word, *with sorrow* inscribing his *few verses*, *moments* of doubt but also of faith in a controversial encounter at the crossroads of parallel paths, the center of his self, in and around of which his world revolves with dizzying speed, his spirit, the eternal poetic soul, living the dream of existence and non-existence.

The world dreams of his world. The poet lives the dream consciously. His tragic fate, his intended glory, to be guardian of this dream, analyzer of the spectrum, to convert with his imagination the non-existent to existent and the existent to non-material. Unseen, invisible, ineffable the works of his jurisdiction – all are poetic.

And *there are moments* when he doubts, as he makes his *lifetime's reckoning*, *if* her *hair* was *brown*, and if their *gazes* ever *met*, as this abyss of existence he walked, another abyss, that of non-existence. Because, he is the witness of her dream, a poet counting the doubts of her being in the reckonings of her life in order to make her a work of perfect completeness, a poem of an existence on the way to the mysteries of life, accepting the non-existence of her astral, egocentric spectrum, whose visible lines only he can change into invisible with the power of his sorrow, since she is his supreme beloved!

As life acquires knowledge, eros becomes greater, redeeming the dream in his own love and his doubt dies, to be resurrected into an undying faith that saves. And he is the light in her darkness, he is the darkness in her light. He shines like a momentary sun, a shooting mind that surrenders to his being's essence.

The clear mind walks along the path, inscrutable, unaffected by the need of the false truth. From its birth, it was divided of its own volition, endlessly multiplying. It became a spectator of nature, which in its chaos manifested, and allowed its life as its image to exist. As a division in its own duality it was distributed, seeking in itself the beginning of its existence and the end of its non-existence.

Outstanding strength is doubt, as a mental principle that shines with reflected light, attracted by the source that created it, and, surrendering to it, realizes that it derives its existence from the pure nature of the mind. In the grace of everything resides the tumult of its drama. Bliss is the harmony of the glorious return and the heavens celebrate in the universe's work. Doubt is the conceit in the sorrow of uninitiated life. In the love affair of the mind with its projections, the poet's extent dominates the light through allegories.

STAVROS STAVRIDIS

PREGNANT NYMPH

*The pregnant nymph
beneath the veils of clouds
inhales the oxygen of the forest,
about to give birth.*

Serpents, scorpions and flower-winged insects in agitated motion.

*Her living waters erupt and scatter
and move towards the river bed.*

*The cries of her labor pains
penetrate the canyon canals,
they pierce the gills of fish,
And plant shells in the sand.*

*The bearing nymph travails.
The unshaded smile
soars.*

*As a new mother, she will return
Fondly leaning her neck
to the humble beings of torment.*

*Appeasing passions
gifting self-oblivion*

and transformation.

(The period of Promise)

A pregnant nature is the human heart, the woman, the earth herself, nourished by her own oxygen. Ideas and dreams of her desires is the temptation, a forest of clouds her forest. The serpent of mysteries, with *flower-winged insects* and *passions*. A holy motion is the flow of rivers. Scorpions journey on the path toward heaven. *Her living waters* are *the cries of her labor pains* which penetrate her, and the vibration of her pain reaches the gills of her oceanic beings and pierce the human lungs. Incessantly is her creation's birth repeated. *Unshaded* is the *smile* of her complete satisfaction, commanding self-sufficiency, journeying through her infinity's ocean. There, she transforms her labour pains into seashells that become the principles for glorious civilizations, which penetrate the canals of the universal canyons where *the humble beings of* her *torment* lead their lives. Passions are perpetuated and people are in need of her aid, of the help of the nurturing womb-heart. She is the supreme mother, the gift of transmutation, a saving transformation, to whose greatness when all nature returns, from the depths of the abyss it is redeemed.

The poet appeases passions. The world is initiated into self-oblivion, the dream is transformed and becomes a human. Its nature is constantly pregnant, a nymph covered by the veils of emotional and mental processes of the male Word, who impregnates her with his lusts. She is a heart, giving birth again to his desires transmuted into love, to redeem the pain, to give travail wings, to fly, to be resurrected. And the stillness which received motion, the inertia that acquired a rhythm, to become a harmony which journeys in its bliss. There, her *living* currents erupt and *scatter*, and become the rivers of fire, waters transmuted into light. And *the cries of* her *labor pains* become odes, they become psalms that fill the channels of the entity, musical conductors of the canyons, with the seven-note pulse which deifies the world, uplifting the passion of the mystery into an unshaded blissful smile.

This coerces life to *fondly* lean its *neck to the humble beings of* its *torment*, to support them throughout their lives, until they are perfected.

The poet becomes the Word, the nature, the woman, the existence, the eternal life. Pregnant is the ascent and redeems the descent. The births of the spirit are the only of essence, they are the deeper meaning of transformation on the mountain of exaltation of ideas, of mental concepts that structured the sphere, so that the chimera has a body and a reason to exist. This is the human body, and its heart, the universal heart, a *pregnant nymph* gestating and birthing the mind, as it is surrounded by *the veils of clouds*, which from the unassimilated passions of the world emanate. Life inhales the outcome of its nature, and, until self-consciousness arrives, rebirths it into new cycles. The serpents, which symbolize the inferior ideas, acquire wings, are uplifted, and humans, from their bounds to symbols are released. *The gills of fish* are pierced, and expanding, reach the perfection of their evolution – the human lungs. Aquatic and land-dwelling, earthly and heavenly is lust, it passes into self-oblivion and its ignorance into spirituality is transformed.

These universal cycles which the poet speaks of, are parts of the Word, spiritual beings that evolve humans and are evolved by them. The *pregnant nymph* of the universe, the feminine aspect of the being, becomes the *bearing nymph*, which gives hope to life and meaning to existence. The seashells in the sand are but the spiral galaxies of the universe, which as travails are born upon the earth. And time travels, it transforms into humans and is magnified. Its will is ordered to the will of the universal Word. Since the origins and throughout the evolution of the species, God appointed humans as the regnant of His vision. They are the potentiality of conclusive transformation, the exception of the universe, the glory of His spirit.

An initiate is every poet, initiating the world to the truth of God, pointing out the immediateness of life to humans, talking about the unique values of everyday life, which the chimera appropriates and uses to subdue them. Rebellious is the son, invoking the compassion of the Entity, the great mother. The bearer and holy new mother, who fondly nurtures him, to indulge in the mystery of form, to learn from the *agitated motion* and the *cries of labor pains*. To overcome his saga, to reach the woman's heart, to unite his desire with the love of her entity, the world's desire to be transformed into eternal love. In the dark channels of human consciousness, illuminated pathways are etched. Radiating sun, the earth gestating the Word, it births the Man-God and in His glory the universe is deified.

MICHALIS STAFYLAS

EVRITANIA
(excerpt)

The calloused hands of my brothers
– thousands of hands –
rise to infinity
holding a bouquet of hopes
or are empty of hopes,
as they unite to raise
their mountains higher.

The horsemen run to and fro
upon the torched hills
they hold a dove up
in their hands
they hold a young child up,
they hold their anguish up
embroidered on a white cloth
in which they wrap their meager portion of bread.

My swallow, my kind swallow
you knock on spring's door
you bring the joy of life
and you open up the leaves of our heart
to the warm sun.
Come, swallow of expectation
with your beak to embroider
a sign of joy

on the torn shirt
of my brother
a sign above the place
of his heart
which beats yearning
a day without rain,
a good day...

(Evritania)

Thousands of bodies, *thousands of hands*, millions of heartbreaking cries *rising to infinity*. Dreams full and empty of hopes, bouquets made of suffering, of ruined lives. Giants are the poet's brothers who wanted to raise, to throw the *mountains higher* than their nature, to release them from the chaos of their fate. *Upon the torched hills* of earth, human spirits dominate over their instincts to subjugate the chimera; horsemen of temptations run and *hold up* the vision of the new generation *in their hands*. A white dove, a child to grow up, to lift their agony, to turn it into a flag, a truth *embroidered on a white cloth*. Panhuman is the request to increase the *meager portion of bread*, the spiritual and physical nourishment, to satisfy humanity's hunger.

As Apollonius of Tyana, every poet knows the voice of birds and speaks the language of humans with knowledge. He invites the swallow, symbol of eternal spring, the one who knows the destination of life, the leaves of the universal heart to open. Its messenger to bring the light to human hearts. With its beak to embroider the sign of expectation on the brotherhood's humble shirt – the glorious shape of the indefatigable heart, sealed by the patience of the great effort for a day without complaint and tears, *without rain*, for a day without death, for a day of eternal justice.

The poem is a tribute to the pain of Evritania, to the pain of the entire Greek land, chosen to nourish the wise, the fighters of truth against the dark forces of all eras. Children of the great mother who become martyrs for their ancestors' and descendants' work, a work of the land and sky, which seeks a way out amid the dead-ends of humanity. A worthy continuator of tradition is the Greek spirit, raising the panhuman vision higher through its faith for the realization of the earth's ideals. An unsurpassed participation in the cosmic work through the offering of its unique civilization, which continues to struggle in the forefront in order to ensure the material and spiritual goods – essential supplies for the evolution of all humankind.

Great is the contribution of poetry, of literature, arts and sciences. Unimaginable is the splendor expressed through Greek writing, so that all people may prepare the earth's fruition. The forces of the universal soul converged to materialism and the defiance of the dark aspects, by reversing the Word of the wise and with the choices of refusal, led time to hopeless despair. The only hope is the path of the spirit, the return to the source, from which belief sprang in the ontological force that shined and illuminated the times, as they were finding their way in the darkness, seeking their glory within the knowledge of the human spirit.

For centuries has the universal symphony been dominated by the Greek rhythm, the supreme of beauty and harmony, serving the necessity of the being and continuing to serve it with its contribution to modern civilization, where its presence is needed now more than ever. The poet, referring to Evritania, conveys the message of the constant battle humans must fight, so as to uplift themselves above the instinctive material needs, which diminish the bread of humans and deprives them of the opportunity for spiritual evolution.

The dove, symbol of the Holy Spirit, illuminates the path of those baptized in faith, for the tormented people to find their salvation, those who have lost the tree of their inheritance and were left unprotected before the destructive fury of unredeemed times. Redeeming is the saga of spiritual leaders and their followers become witnesses to the union of people with the spirit of the New Age that raises their hopes higher than the mountains of obstacles and thus relieves earth of its burden. It replaces their territory with the expectations *of the heart, which beats yearning a day without rain, a good day,* which will come to redeem the human divide.

KOSTAS STERGIOPOULOS

INSIGNIFICANT MOMENTS

The insignificant moments, when recalled,
are solitary lights, sparkling at night
on distant mountains and desert ridges.

As if they did not happen; as if they did not exist.

You can recount them, as a love tale,
but you cannot transfuse their flavor and pulse.

The insignificant moments, suddenly overwhelm you.
But the cruelest part is to forget them.
Sometimes they emerge from oblivion,
and then submerge again forever.

Irreversibly.
(You once liked that word.)

Along with ourselves there,
how many we left to be buried!
And now we see them on the street and do not recognize them.

The insignificant moments restore
that which they had drunk from your soul.

(Midnight sun)

Insignificant words, insignificant acts, insignificant things surround humans in their *insignificant moments*. Only memory is significant and that, amid the insignificance of the world, is lost. And beyond, in the vastness of space, *solitary lights*, pale, millions of stars sparkling in the nights, so that the insignificance of the being may gaze at them from the peaks of mountains and the *desert ridges* to be consoled by imagining that all these *did not happen, they did not exist*, they never took place.

This is the wrong belief of humans. Because how is it possible for an important cosmogony to consist of insignificant elements that comprise the whole? Even though its resultant, humans, while recounting this *love tale*, cannot transfuse its flavor and its pulse, as they are overwhelmed by the concepts of the story – which is their own story – a story made of infinite, alleged, *insignificant moments*. It is this belief that divides them and makes them forget the emergence and submergence of their world, when they, through their own oblivion rise and precipitate again into the bowels of their seeming insignificance.

Forever? Irreversibly? "How much that word is liked", the poet meaningfully says. As if all this is happening in a dream and the other aspects of humans do not exist. And, under the influence of their ego, they seek to prove that only they are important and that everyone else is insignificant, nonexistent, dead, because they and all that is reminiscent of them are those which frighten them. For that reason, they do not recognize the passersby in the street. They are the ones left to be buried amid the depths of their memory and they are the same who return from eternity as insignificant timeless moments, existences which *restore that which they had drunk* from the greatness of their soul.

How well does each poet know infinity! In their insignificance, they recognize their universal nature – the significant one. Its story is read in the events of human life, in the dramatic moments of their existence. These constitute their being. They keep returning to memory, to remind them of the greatness of the entity, which from nothing composes the becoming, to perpetuate the miracle of the existent, which from its own non-existence springs, weaving with the unique moments the polysemy of the being.

Time transmutes the moments, humans transmute time. Idea of a unique moment, a unique moment their every idea. Behind the apparent world hides the other, the substantial one. Behind those characterized as *insignificant moments*, hide the others, those which created the molecules, the parts of existence, the spirits which drink from their souls' energy, so as to return it again, the poet says. Perpetual is the cycle, infinite, a daily ritual repeated evermore through human emotions, thoughts and actions. A significant ritual that with absolute consistency is carried out by the alleged *insignificant moments*.

Every moment is an idea, a situation, a detail that encompasses all knowledge, the all, the significant. It is of this every moment that the poet tells us of – the all that repeats itself. This overwhelms humans. Cruel is the fate that makes them repel the all and forget about it, attracting it again, to emerge from their own oblivion. And then again to submerge into the irreversible, which they like and cannot avoid, as they are the soul, the source from which, through their own power, the world quenches its thirst and is nourished, for life to return again to the life of the One. To realize and understand that they themselves are the moments in time, existent and non-existent, hopes of the universe, which overwhelm them, asking them to stop burying them. To recognize them as prominent memories, significant and insignificant, as never before, transcendent components of their own resultant, micro-entities constituting the power of the One, the eternal memory of the most significant, unique in its nature, the most comprehensive miracle of miracles, which transfuses its single dream to the other miracles, to their dreams.

Pulse and flavor are not perpetuated, if humans do not become the conscious rhythm, the harmony of the consonant wailing of repentant ignorance, a multilevel of those considered insignificant moments that integrate their being into their complete self. Infinite is the all, of its personal moments it is composed. With these it expresses its being, and humans are called upon to recognize its value, giving each of their personal moments its own value, a transcendent reality that starts from and returns to them. This is the nature of the being, the poet says, and the entity does not question those defined as *insignificant moments*, considering them different from the significant ones, thereby separating existence from its existence.

KOSTAS E. TSIROPOULOS

6ᵀᴴ OF ROMANOS THE MELODIST

*A ceiling of the golden hall is the sky
on their bodies
unopened wells their souls, trembling
accepted the myrrh of the hours
and weaved in time's territory
the beauty of their form
so that they are touched
to the depths of their unwatered root
and become a den
of one another's body
of their passion the intense sweetness
weaving a scarlet wing-bearer
the night to set ablaze
withering their fragrant words
while the wisdom of their flesh
molded
engraved images of memory
of mysterious chemistry
the communion
then the essence the transcendent
sow on a bridal bed
new words, divine songs
with the nostalgia of the allotrope dawn
the beautiful bodies suffering.*

Hail God of the bodies the loom's warp
deep myrrh of the mystery
which sprouts words full of dew.
Hail Graceful Mary
of creation the virtuous golden clavicle.

(Mystery)

The sky of the spirit, *the sky* of the soul, the sky of the body are the *ceiling of the golden* bridal *hall*. And the *souls, unopened wells in time's territory*, acquire the fragrance of myrrh, trembling, and weave the hours with their chimerical beauty's glamour. Life is *a scarlet wing-bearer*, experiencing the magic of its bodies, realizing *to the depths of their unwatered root*, the light, *a den of passion* within *the intense sweetness* of all. *The night* of centuries *is set ablaze*, the *fragrant words* of the world wither in the gloom of the flesh. The body's wisdom remolds *engraved images*, and memories in the testimony of its *mysterious chemical* communion are recalled, and *the transcendent* sow *the essence* on bridal beds. And the seeds of the divine Word are *new words, divine songs* on the pain of the beautiful bodies, so as to maintain *the nostalgia of the allotrope dawn*.

Hail Graceful Mary of creation the virtuous, words full of dew you sprout, deep myrrh of the mystery. Hail God of the bodies the loom's warp.

Every poet becomes Romanos the melodist. The soul of beautiful bodies contrives the pain, and from the experiences of the flesh to the transcendent fields rejoices. The coherence of religious devoutness has disappeared from our era. The poet pulsates, vibrates with and throughout his entire body, the bodies of bodies, to the holy participation. Above them *the sky, a ceiling of the golden hall*, and the wells of the souls open, so that the one who is coming to pump out the water of life, offering it to be drunk by those thirsty for light. The passion of bodies will be redeemed and the power of love will become kindness. The material world, the earthen, will be spiritualized, it will glorify God.

Hail Mother of bridal chambers of the uncreated all. Hail the one worshipping the essence. Hail the shining grace of the becoming of the forms. Hail Womb of the immortals, the one bearing the myrrh of spirits. The poet is the hymn-writer of all. His reference to the Superior of the universe, to Graceful Mary, of spirit and matter, of body and soul the life-giving source. Song of Songs is the becoming, the miracle of the cosmic presence, the mysteries of Your universes we see, that You, in Your Omnipotence, are God.

The poet suggests the transmutation of passions into a sacred erotic act of a deliberate participation. He invites the world to consciously take part in the cosmic ritual of deification, with threads of light to weave the wing-bearing archangelic glory of heavens, and be clothed in it. The beauty of souls and bodies to emerge and through the fiery glow to set *the night* ablaze, *the fragrant words* of its flesh to wither. Abandoning *the intense sweetness* of passion, to be uplifted to the wisdom of the sacred memory, where, being an engraved illustration of the essence, at the sacred altarpiece of the cosmic temple, with its radiance will brighten the bridal time.

Within and above the bodies, the sky penetrates the souls, flooding them with the myrrh of the holy spirits who reside in it, and they receive the blessing. They perceive it as a divine gift for the conservation of the beauty of form, and, in *time's territory*, with the threads of radiance weave the resplendent beauty. *To the depths of* the *unwatered root* reaches the supreme spiritual sun, whose power unites the soul with the form, to create the wing-bearer of the forces of light, who sets the night ablaze and withers the gloom of the dark spirits. And the flesh becomes the Word, a universal communion, so that humans may participate in the perpetual liturgy, which renders the spirit immortal in eternity.

The heavens on earth, the human in the universe. The eternity in the spirit of God, the knowledge in the human mind. There, memories are engraved, multidimensional images that formulate the glory of God in its entire splendor, the spirit of whom contrives the human perfection.

Hail bridal night of the spirits, hail radiating glory of miracles. Wisdom is the praise of all. Bodies cleansed, partake in the holy spirit. In the communion of the heavens, of the earthen realm the drinking, that the coming of the forces of God in the infinite harmony of uncreated light.

ANTONIS FOSTIERIS

NOTES ON THE COMING DAY

To ignite poems, to burn words, to chase away
　the voracious serpent which draws near. And which hisses.

To cut the curls of memory to the roots. What do I
　need them for? Bald should the present remain, bald
　and slimy. As an elderly baby.

A fool to become. An idiot and an imbecile. Oblivion
　with its soil to cover the relics of yesteryear. To become
　a tomb of days. To blossom above the tomb again
　and to wither. Without crosses the tomb, and without
　herein lies. That is very important. Lest I forget it.

I should forget it. It is the only way I will remember it.

To sleep with eyes wide open. To see the defeat
　of light. To see and know that I am imagining. To
　leave the horses of senses, and the carriage
　now motionless to continue its endless journey.
　As, I have said, the journey will be endless. And as the carriage
　is I.

To learn that I am not. With passion to think that I do not
　exist. Because if I existed, of course, I would not think. (Why?)

To eavesdrop on the quiet of nothingness. To hear
  the deep snoring, the snorting of time. Not to be frightened
  – and not to rejoice.

To write poems with only a single word. (Which?).

To change and stay the same. (Who?).

To clean my mind of the blood, to wash
  the dead of History.

To devise plans for the past.

(The Will and There of Death)

In the processes of fire, universes – entire poems – disintegrate. The words constituting the Words of their existence burn, and which exist solely to welcome the *voracious serpent*, for whose sake they suspect they have been created. They cannot withstand its nature, their nature, the hissings of their own rotations, and perpetually seek their self-destruction. The serpent symbolizes the energy following the thought-forms of humans which originate from the creative Word, keeping them prisoners to the chain of their work, without being able to rid themselves of the consequences of their eternal act. And then comes the poet, the redeemer, with the other body of the Word, that which records memories and tastes the cosmic psychic pain.

The curls symbolize the knowledge of civilizations, depicted in ancient statues. In the energy processes of the universe, the poet distances himself from the past, and the present is left naked, *bald and slimy, as an elderly baby,* without the beauty of hair, which symbolizes ancient wisdom. Symbols for the poet to always remember the rhythm of the ashes – of the energy – that remains of the incessant processes of fire. And time is left alone. Oblivion covers the relic, which was once God, who was knowledge. A tomb to remind people of the perpetual blossoming of body and spirit.

With eyes wide open, it consciously sleeps; light observes its defeat. It knows it is imagining. It has the knowledge of the stillness of the inner mind in the *endless journey* of senses, because it is the carrier of the universe, the carrier of the Word, the carrier of the poet. It is the spirit that learns the meaning of its non-existence but also the necessity of the specific mind, the point of thought-processes, which take place in the relentless becoming of the externalized all, as it avoids inner peace, tranquility, and takes a liking to the joy derived from sleep, from deliberate flight when faced with the threat that its own chaos projects. And the poet is the one who tutors the spirit to not rejoice and to not be saddened unnecessarily, so that it does not become frightened. It seeks the one concept of the pure, devoid of thought mind, the intrinsic act of the essence. Only this can cleanse the *mind of the blood*, so that the dead of History can be purified and begin to devise the *plans for the past*, which is always the present and will always be the future.

The Being exists, abides and lives. It is the nobody-self and it is all. It is the presence of light in the presence of darkness. It is the movement in stillness. It is the stillness in rhythm. The center of things is the human, the beginning and the end of the ontological becoming. Perpetual action that recycles its existence in the fire which springs from its being, assimilating it, dematerializing it and reprojecting it as the uniqueness of the Supreme One.

The poet wonders about his roots. He devises the *plans for the past*. He returns. In it lay the answers. Inextinguishable is the fire burning him. With passion he contemplates existence, with passion the non-existence. The great (Why?) dominates. The answer lies in the quiet of the mind.

The human terror and joy are the great obstacles that must be overcome. The entire Word is *only a single word*, one being, which, while constantly changing, still remains always the same. It is the Word of every person, of every poet, the universal Word, the Word of becoming. This is the meaning of things. The serpent that comes hissing, ready to devour the essence, to assimilate it and be assimilated by it.

From its commencement the effort of humans has been banished even by their own being, a self that renounces the self, passing into unconscious oblivion. The poet seeks the conscious one, delving into the decision and the will. He becomes the courage, the heroism that is required for the return to the depths of the unconscious, to achieve his transmutation to a superconscious. The *plans for the past* must be devised. To consciously make the return to the unconscious, to penetrate the subconscious layers which raise pretexts, seeking to halt the passage, fields alternating in the seasons, recording the legend and the history as the unique existences which are acknowledged in the Word of creation, in its morphic and psychic expression.

The *(Why?)* and the *(Who?)* are questions that cannot be answered, if humans do not go beyond appearances – the poet knows this well. Creation itself lays difficulties for humans, until it realizes the point of its ontological existence. Its creations are the shells covering it. Only the fire is that which burns the form, transforming it into ashes, into energy. Civilizations must be cut from the root from their own memory. External knowledge is not enough. The present must cease to be lined with its past, in order to reveal the absolute truth.

What the poet characterizes as slimy, is the false, the despicable. The entire past, as it has not passed into consciousness, looks like *an elderly baby*. Knowingly he becomes *an idiot and an imbecile,* to show that the unconscious forgetfulness, the unconscious oblivion, is merely a flight that covers with *its soil the relics of yesteryear*. A tomb, on which the world blooms and then withers and is left with no identity. Humans must decide to consciously forget, because only then will they remember. To wisely release *the horses of senses*, so that their carriers are able to continue *the endless journey* in absolute stillness. To learn, to know that they are not, that they do not exist, and, placing the inner ear to the quietness of the absolute being, receive the answer to the great Why.

GIOTA FOTIADOU-BALAFOUTI

SARAH...

On Melidoni street, at the Museum
I found you again Sarah...
The gray Auschwitz uniform
made teeth clench.
Nothing need be said.
Bitterness to the bone.
The dark history was written in the stripes.
Your ring, Sarah, with the yellow stone
as a rambling sea, told me plenty.
Do you remember?
When we played the brides
yellow marjorams were our wreaths.
On your school uniform, a yellow star
was jabbed in by ravens
you stubbornly stomped your feet
like a snake the yellow star stung you.
Do you remember? We changed uniforms then.
The black ravens did not let you bear fruit
they deprived you of this soil too.
They turned you into soap-powder.
Their dirt to wash.
As a seed of fire in the blackened ash,
your ring was hidden, Sarah,
to speak at Melidoni street,
at the Museum for centuries to speak.

(Literary New Year 1991)

A deep memory is the past, a deep memory the world, the relations, the friendships, the fraternal cries, those which were caused by the friction, the inevitable conflicts between humans and the invisible wall built by ill-tempered fate, to stand as an obstacle to their spiritual development. They are knocked down by the shock waves of their own repulsion for their negative aspects in the unexplored past, where they cannot be self-disciplined and therefore tame the dark, inscrutable, instinctive forces of their nature. Their past actions keep them enslaved, prisoners of their sins, in the bowels of the hell of the uncontrolled instincts and the animalistic mind. They are submitted to the difficulties caused by unbearable pain, a punishment imposed by the cosmic law, to maintain the balance of the cosmic becoming, which, despite any human will, urges them to the path of evolution of immaculate time. There, the universal feat is magnified and the human glory, as substantial, immortal life, shines from the inextinguishable light radiated by the soul.

A panhuman vision of perfection is the universal celebration, and, until the achievement of the work, many are the hecatombs, infinite, for the sake of the realization that must come with the acts of the intentional and unintentional fighters. Perpetrators and victims alternate their roles, and the tragedy of the Word, reaching its peak, gives its place to the absolute consciousness, so that its respective redeemed self can emerge. Centuries are consciously at work, resisting their unconscious being, horrendous aspects, monstrous; and the torures, holy and sacred, gruesome and unholy, serve only one purpose, that of the realization of the nature.

The field of pure intellect is misunderstood and becomes insanity in the reflection of its essence. Humanity's choices are those which irrevocably determine the path of its course. A deep emotion overwhelms the becoming, it becomes passion, and for the balance of all, the inextinguishable sun acquires the dimensions of infinity, that which existed before the creation of the world, the inner, the unborn, the one which contains the seeds of its manifestation. Invisible, human archetypes, which potentially bore the secrets of deification, and sought as universes to be expressed, for the vindication of the world's existence. And they became the aggressors and the victims of the becoming, which the birth of its dream imposed on them.

Such a mystery is human nature, cosmogonic, primitive, from its origins inscrutable, demonically spectacular, prey to its abysmal soul, a mystery destined to seek salvation in the depths of its own being. A relationship, a kinship is the memory, a friendship whose foundations are suspended in the vastness, thus holding the world within its own chaos. Maintaining the rhythm of its orientation so as to not be lost in the depths and widths of its unconscious life.

Tragic is the drama of the poem's heroine, a drama of millions of people; the world a Museum, and there the currents intersect, *on Melidoni street*, which symbolizes all roads leading to the inevitable end, to death, to the sources of inspiration, from where life springs, taking the forms which laid their being, the experience of their pain, to recycle them, in the state of some other ignorance to make their nature knowledge.

Outgoing life, resultant of a previous solar system, delivers its wisdom to its torch-bearing carriers, its own aspects, begging for atonement of their prior and future sinful life. It is aware of the shortcomings of the imperfect, external nature of which it is possessed. Prone is life to selfishness, to divisiveness, to its preference to one race over others, it suffers because of the choices it fancies making. And it leaves behind it intractable problems and unpaid debts, which its perfection anticipate for their payment. It changes the forms, it dies and is reborn. It trusts its being to the respective races and generously offers its teaching.

Great is the Jewish race, equal, as the others, to God. The esoteric tradition says that the teaching of Kabbalah is that of the previous solar system. Our present solar system was initiated into the knowledge of universal life and shouldered the enormous task of the unified life. Many are the pros and cons of this feat. The allocation of responsibilities is not just a human task. The common mind fails to conceive the functions of the cosmic law and to give a solution to the universal problem. The only path is that of love, taught by the great Spiritual Leader, that of apology, of reparation of the error committed by every race. It is the path of the merger of the opposites into the single panhuman race of all spirits, colors, bodies, into the one body of one mind, of one God, the unique, that which always existed, exists and will exist for all time, to oversee the state of His omnipotence. To protect life from the dangers it faces due to the errors it is forced to commit, errors caused by the shortcomings generated by its desire, as, through it, it seeks to be renewed in order to exist. The tragedy of life the poet contemplates, experiencing the woes of humankind's passions.

Life keeps in the memory of its pain the events that result in an uneven rhythm. It aggregates the hatred accumulated by centuries, and which it asks of humans to accept, to open their heart, to quench their thirst at its source, to be purified in the waters of its love. To be magnified within the mind, to spread, to pass into infinite wisdom. There, *the dark history* to forget; *the sea* to stop rambling. *The brides* that leisurely played, *the wreaths* that were worn, the school uniforms which became the grey uniforms of *Auschwitz*, the clenched *teeth*, the *bitterness* which reached into *the bones*, *the ravens* which jabbed the madness into the tormented mind, the *soap-powder* that purified an era's impurity, to pass into eternity's archives.

And to be recorded as unavoidable human errors, which in the future realizations must, as tragic failures of the past, from the Absolute seek forgiveness, so that they may be merged within It.

ALEKOS CHRYSOMALLIS

YOU CAN

*Kiss
the stone,
even if grass
does not grow on it.*

*Kiss
The sweaty hand,
the weary hand,
which supports
the stone,
the heavy stone
lest it roll away.*

*Kiss
the wave,
the angry wave
and if it soaks you,
do not care.*

*Kiss
the soil,
The hard soil,
which the end of life
covers,*

*as Hades' ghost
joyfully scoffs.*

*Kiss
the winds,
the frigid winds,
the night shadows,
and the fire.*

*Kiss
the human,
the anyone, the every human,
wherever you find them.
You can...*

(Stone Clay)

The poet embraces the stone, the eternal, the universal, and initiates us into its infinite, fiery secrets, those of the lava that was created by the others, of mystic fire, whose spiritual existence was established before time, composing its body's forces, in order to acquire ever-molding cohesion so that it may withstand the decay of its molecules, and through its transformations adapt to chaos, as, like the matter of infinity, it was assigned for God to use in building and reconstructing His cosmic temple.

His is *the weary hand* that humans must embrace, the poet says. The hand which supported existence, the heavy heritage, and holds it with the invisible power, *lest it roll* beyond the boundaries of its essential nature. A sample of reverence and gratitude, a thankful recognition of the supreme miracle of the creator, whose existence the glory was revealed, a contribution to human existence, the provider of forces. The ocean of oceans, whose fiery spirit, mutated into aquatic waves, wets the human beings, as the saltiness – the quintessence of salt – penetrates them to the bone and reaches their soul.

And the poet does not care, he contemplates the blessing, he kisses the wave and prays, urging humans to pray to the unfathomable power of all. To embrace the sea which gave its glory to earth, to the soil, so that the beginning and end of the beings of life take place, the birth and death of humans, the force that reveals them, gives birth to them and covers them. Let abyss scoff at their struggle, they are the sacred spirits of the winds that will carry the embraces. They are the archangels which will carry the fiery kiss of the soul to *the frigid winds*, in order to rekindle, to awaken their spirit, so that *the night shadows* kiss *the fire* – the sun. This is every human being, who is able to see their radiance everywhere, with their rays to embrace the century. This personified wind, the morphic wave, the earthen God, an entity exposed to the scoffing of its demonic nature. It is the one battling the darkness, the endless night, its cosmic existence.

Humans embrace their nature and kiss it, but they do not yet know of the rejuvenating power hidden in the kiss of love. They do not know of the holy sacrament of the breath carried to the lifeless, since with their kiss they animate them, unconsciously imitating their creator, who first gave life to them by instilling His spirit into them, and *the hard soil* became the living, the soft pulse, a divine, supreme vibration of love and light, the final miracle of creation.

Kiss, to initiate and be initiated, exchanging the fire of life. Resurrect your deceased, dead dreams, those which you underestimated as parts of yourself. Do not care if you are exposed to the relationship of necessary dependence, if you are shaken by the emotion from the passions of desire. Your cleansing kiss, a rose of veneration, will uplift you – *do not care* – up to heaven, to become light, the sun, with your rays to bend down and kiss your own soil, *the hard soil* from abandonment, that which covers the ill-advised life.

Kiss the winds, sun-human, warm the freezing cold of the erebus, embrace the dark *shadows of* your *night. Kiss* your *fire*, revitalize the fire of mother-earth. Kiss her son, the human, yourself, your every aspect, wherever it may exist. As the eternal spirit of life, *you can...* everything... Kiss life!

Every poet is an initiate, holding the secret of deeper communication, the miraculous mystery of the kiss. The wind kisses the earth, the sea wave kisses the stone, the soil kisses the dead and the dead, learning to embrace the elements, as they scoff at them, are released from Hades. The days kiss the wind, the frigid spirit of centuries and it kisses the nights. The shadows become familiar with the fire and kiss it. And it gives birth to the dreams which shape the worlds, so that humans can live from the kiss.

The poet invites humans to the magical ritual of kissing, to the sacred relationship of the union of the consciousness of spirit and matter, of soul and form, of form and God, of image and essence. The power of the kiss governs humankind, it defines relationships, it predetermines the outcome of the evolution in the union between people. The attraction it exerts is the driving force that encourages them to continue their life, since, by transferring through kissing their love to one another, they become connected through the bonds of kinship, of friendship, of sexual union, and specifically of marriage.

Life finds religion, and the embrace of holy images uplifts humans to the divine and equates them to the supreme. This religious embrace the poet refers to, he applauds it, he suggests it. Life is magnified with the kiss from the human being to the entity, the essence and the presence of God.

POETS' BIOGRAPHIES

KRITON ATHANASOULIS*
He was born in Tripoli in 1916 and died in Athens in 1979. He studied for two years at the University of Athens Law School and worked at the Athens Notary Association.

His work can be divided into two periods, corresponding to the three basic turning points of his creative effort. In the first period (1940-1946), which includes the collections "Cain and Abel" 1940, "The State of the night" 1943 "Oh my sweet springtime" 1944, the verses are distinctive for their social content. In the second, marked by the issuance of collections "The song of the five winds" 1947 "Hotel the World" 1956, his reflection acquires an existential character. In the third period of his creation (1957-1976), which includes the collections "The boar" 1963 (Prize of the Twelve) and "My little universe"1969 (National Poetry Prize), his poems express the need to reconcile his personal vision with a world that appears to be opposing it and emphasize his faith in the power of panhuman love.

He also wrote the essays "The poet Rigas Golfis" 1957 "Pages from my personal journal" 1958 and "Poetry today" 1972, as well as the play "The other of the beautiful solitude" 1969.

ARIS ALEXANDROU
It is a pseudonym. He was born in Leningrad in 1922 and died in 1978 in Paris. He belonged to the left political movement and underwent persecutions and imprisonment until 1957. He then lived in Paris and was greatly influenced by the European literary atmosphere.

His works: "Even this spring" poems 1946 "Barren line" poems 1952 "Straightness of roads" poems 1959, "Poems 1941-1971" texts 1972, "Bluntly 1937-1975" essays 1977, "The hill with the fountain" scenario 1977, "The box" novel 1974, with which he became well-known.

Apart from his poetry and prose work, Alexandrou is also a successful translator. He translated Dostoevsky, O'Neil, Steinbeck, Faulkner and Malraux. He is considered a notable and important figure in modern Greek literature.

MANOLIS ANAGNOSTAKIS

Born in 1925 in Thessaloniki. He studied medicine at the University of Thessaloniki. He lives in Athens.

He published the poetry collections "Seasons", "Seasons II", "Seasons III" and then collected version of these poems in 1971.

He wrote reviews in the volume "Anti-dogmatic" and the volume "The Additional". They were followed by the poetry collection "The margin" and lastly by the poetic work "Postscript". Editor of the journal Kritika from 1957 to 1961.

TASOS G. ANAGNOSTOU

Born in Athens. He studied Law and Philosophy. He collaborated with many newspapers and magazines, with poems, narratives, essays, historical and aesthetic articles, etc.

Poetry: "Uplifting", "Music of winds," "Night of the rain", "Stone Time", "On the borders of the large shadow", "Inner wind", "Flesh of the soul", "The other of the hidden flash", etc.

Prose: "The absence of the sun."

Critical study: "The stalemate"," Consciousness of chaos", "Emigration to zero".

Translation: Poesie (Traduzione di Felice Mastroianni).

His works were translated into Italian and French and were awarded International Prizes: "Salvador Dali", "Giuseppe Ungaretti", "Pablo Picasso", "European Senate", "French Revolution", "American Freedom", the "Athens Award", etc.

He is a member of the International Association of Literary Critics, the National Society of Greek Authors and chairman of the Philological Association Parnassos. He has been included in the most prestigious encyclopedias and anthologies, both Greek and foreign.

TAKIS ANTONIOU

Born on March 5, 1932, in Agrinio. He studied Theology at the University of Athens and continued his postgraduate studies for five years at the Faculty of Philosophy at the University of Munich, in the departments of Philosophy and Byzantine and Modern Greek Literature. He has a Doctorate in Philosophy from the University of Athens.

His plays and poems were translated and published into English, German, Polish, Swedish, French, Dutch, Italian, Romanian and Spanish. His philosophical essays and treatises in German along with essays and critical notes in Greek were published in various literary and literary journals.

The "Cycle of Death and Birth" in music composed by Theodoros Antoniou, was presented in a world premiere by the Boston Symphony Orchestra in January 1981, in Boston. Another world premiere of the work by the same composer with poetry by T. Antoniou "Epigramatta", was presented in Chicago, on April 1982. The same composer has written the "Revolution of the dead." as a Byzantine musical drama. This medieval anti-liturgy has the title of the homonymous poetry collection.

ELENI ARGESTI

Contemporary poet prosaist. Born in Piraeus. She lives in Athens. She worked at the Ministry of Finance.

Eleni Argesti appeared in literature in 1964, with the poetry collection "Gray State". In 1965, she gave her second poetic collection "Grey state, series II". Followed by: "Sorrows at the docks" 1969 "Dull portholes" 1972, "In the cracked mirror" short stories 1973, "The songs of gallantry and death" poetry collection 1974, "And... they tied up this man ..." short stories 1976, "Pikranthoi" poetry collection 1982, "Erotic" poetry collection 1983, "Monologue with Time" poetic 1984.

Eleni Argesti still works and contributes to literature.

ELENI VAKALO*

Born in Istanbul, 1921. She lives in Athens.

Poet, critic and historian of fine arts. She studied archeology at the University of Athens and specialized in the History of Art in Paris. She taught for a while in secondary education but later professionally devoted herself to the "Vakalo School of Decorative Arts" which she founded with her husband, painter Giorgos Vakalo.

She appeared in literature in 1944 with her poems in the journal "New Letters".

Poetry collections: "Theme and variations" 1945, "Memories of a nightmarish state" 1948. "In the form of theorems" 1951. They were followed by collections with composition poems comprising a broader section. This section, which includes six poetic compositions, was published under the title "Before lyricism" 1981. Her poems have been translated into many foreign languages.

Other works: the poetry collections "Genealogy" 1971, "Of the world" 1978 and the essays "Introduction to painting themes" 1960, "Twelve lessons on modern art" 1970, "The meaning of the forms" 1975, "Rhythms and terms of European art" 1980.

As an art critic, Vakalo wrote (1949-1974) the relevant column in the newspaper Ta Nea and published critical studies on Greek painters in magazines, mainly in the Zygos.

TAKIS VARVITSIOTIS

Born in Thessaloniki, 1916. He studied law but dealt with poetry and literature. He collaborated with several literary magazines in Thessaloniki and Athens.

Poetry: "Leaves of sleep" 1949, "Epitaph" 1951, "Winter Solstice" 1955, "Alphabet book" 1955, "Birth of sources" 1959 (honored with two awards), "The veil and smile" 1963, "The metamorphosis and Autumn Suite" 1975," Summary", vol. I 1980 (consolidated version), etc.

Translations: Baudelaire, Pierre Reverdy, Paul Eluard, Mallarmé, Pablo Neruda, etc.

Studies: "Poetry and poetic Themes of G. Sarantaris" 1958, Federico Garcia Lorca "A passionate of instinct" 1964.

Poet Takis Varvitsiotis was awarded the First National Prize for Poetry, the Poetry Prize of the Athens Academy, the Ourani Prize, etc. He represented Greece in World Conferences and received significant honors, such as the Fernando Riello International Poetry Prize at the United Nations (New York 1988) and the title and the medal of Knight by the Ordre des Arts et des Lettres of the French Ministry of Culture 1989.

KOSTAS VARNALIS

Born in 1883 in Pyrgo, Bulgaria, and died in Athens, 1974. He was a poet, prosaist and essayist. He studied Classic Literature at the University of Athens and became a Doctor of Philosophy. In 1919, he went to Paris with a state scholarship for postgraduate studies in Modern Literature and Aesthetics. He served as a Greek teacher of Primary and Secondary Education and professor of the Higher Education Academy of Athens.

He issued his first collection of poems "Honeycombs" in 1905. Followed by: "Symposium", "Dionysian hymn", "Orestes", "The Pilgrim" 1919, "The light that burns" 1922, "Slaves and besieged" 1927, "Free World" 1965, etc.

Studies - Prose: "Solomos without metaphysics" 1925, "The true apology of Socrates" 1931, "Living People" 1939, "The Diary of Penelope" 1947, "Dictatorship" 1956, "Of Solomon" 1957, "Attalus the Third" 1972, the play "Wrath of the people" 1975, "Literary memoirs" 1980.

He also translated Aristophanes, Euripides, Xenophon, Sophocles, Cornelius, Moliere, Racine, Flaubert, etc. His writings are included in American and European anthologies of modern Greek literature, while individual publications of his works were repeatedly issued in the Soviet Union and almost all countries of Eastern Europe. In 1959, Varnalis was awarded the Lenin Prize for Peace.

GIORGOS VAFOPOULOS

He was born in Gevgelija, Yugoslavia, in 1904. He attended lessons of the Mathematical School. He worked as a journalist and then as Director of the Municipal Library from 1939 to 1963. He worked as Director of the "Macedonian Literature" and member of the group which published the "Macedonian Days".

Poetry: "The roses of Myrtali" 1931, "Offering" 1938, "The Floor" 1951, "The great night and the window" 1959, "The poetics" 1970, "The New Satirical Gymnasiums" 1975, "The selected" 1977.

Prose: "Autobiography Pages", "The Passion" 1970, "The Resurrection" 1971, "Travels and Parentheses" I, 1973, II, 1975.

Theater: "Esther" 1934.

He served as General Secretary of the first National Theater of Northern Greece. He received the Excellence Award of the Municipality of Thessaloniki, the first National Poetry Prize, the K. and E. Ourani Foundation Award by the Academy of Athens, of which his is a corresponding member. He is also an honorary professor at the Philosophy Faculty of the Aristotle University.

NTINOS VLACHOGIANNIS

Born in Vrachati, Corinth, in 1910, and died in Athens, 1992. He studied at the Law School. He worked as a journalist in the Eleftheron Anthopon and made his career at the Bank of Greece until 1965. He moved to Paris for five years and there excelled in poetic contests by Associations, Companies, the French Academy and the Goncourt Academy. He reached the forefront in 1925 and his persecution peaked during and after the occupation, with imprisonment, dismissal from his service, exile etc.

His works: "Smoke of the charging" 1960, "Flute instead of trumpet" 1964, "Matins in the storm» 1967, "Pipeau Contre Trompette" 1966, "Aube dans la Tempete" 1968, "Poemes" (anthology) 1968, "Witnesses of silence" 1973, "Footsteps on rice paper" 1982.

Essays: "Argyris Agrafiotis" 1965, "Two bucolic poets" 1967, "Deep incisions in the poetry of T. Ritoridis"1982, etc.

Translations: "Flowers replanted by friendship" 1969 and "Written on the skin of the heart" 1975.

Short stories: "Stories from Vocha" 1970.

Anthology issues released with his poems in English and Arabic. His work was presented in Greek, French, English and Slovenian TV. He was translated into French, English, Slovenian, Polish, etc. anthologies. He received the National Literature Prize.

EVANGELOS V. VOGAZIANOS

He was born in Syra, where he finished the historic High School and was imbued with the teachings of the island's great cultural tradition. There, as a child, he began his spiritual creation with verses and novels published in local magazines. At just seventeen, he passed the exams of the Law Faculty of the University of Athens and later served as a lawyer. He worked at the National Bank.

At the same time, he studied classical singing with the unforgettable professor of the National Conservatory Ourania Oikonomidou and appeared as a soloist (lyrical-dramatical tenor) in the country's greatest complexes, in free melodrama and on the radio. At the same time, he continued his literary events in Athens, where he collaborated with the "Journal of Poets."

He has published the poetry collections "Season Mort", "Lost as sea", "Androniki of Tribulation", "Iliothesia", "strongly", "In single file".

VASOS I. VOGIATZOGLOU

He was born in S. Ionia, Attica, in 1935. He originates from Sparta, Asia Minor. He studied medicine at the University of Athens and specialized as a pediatrician. He has published eight poetry collections: "Danae" 1966, "In the constellation of Virgo", "The Exiles" 1969, "The Expected" 1972, "The Murder of the warrior" 1974, "The Survivors" 1975, "Tracking" 1977 and "The Stigma" 1988.

Alongside Poetry, has studied History and Folklore of Asia Minor Hellenism. In this context, he has issued: "Pisidia of Asia Minor" 1978, "Presences" 1979, "The neighborhoods of the non-believers" 1981, "Sparta of Asia Minor" 1978 and "The surnames of Asia Minor" 1992, "The faces of Janus" (aesthetic study) 1991, "Bible Psalms" (translation) 1992, "Bells of the Almighty" (Mount Athos, 1992) and "Jonah's Word" (critical study) 1993.

His work has been translated into Romanian and Polish. He has participated in numerous conferences and workshops on the Minor Asian Culture and has given many lectures on the same subject. For his work, he has been honored with eight first prizes and honorary certificates. He is a regular member of the Society of Greek Writers, the Greek Society of Medical Writers, the Greek Society of Christian Literature and the Association Onomastique Grecque.

NIKIFOROS VRETTAKOS*

He was born in 1911in Krokees, Laconia, where he died in 1991. He worked as a journalist and published his first poems in 1929, entitled "Under the shadows and lights." His entire poetic work until 1976 is gathered in two volumes with the common title "The poems" 1981, while and the poetic compositions "Prometheus and the play of one day" 1978, "Liturgy under the Acropolis" 1981, are published separately, as is his subsequent poetic collection "The prominent planet" 1983.

His prosaic works include:

"The naked child" novel 1939, "The wild beast and the storm" chronicle 1945, "Two people talk about world peace" 1949, "Suffering" autobiographical notes of New York 1969", "In front of the same river" short stories 1972.

He was honored three times with the National Poetry Award (1940, 1956, 1983) and in 1977 with the Academy of Athens Award for his poetry collection "Afternoon sunflower" 1976. Moreover, in 1981, the Sicilian Arts and Letters Society awarded him the ASLA International Prize. His works have been translated into thirteen languages and distinct volumes of poems have been published in Germany, Switzerland, France, Holland, Russia, Bulgaria, Italy and Turkey. He joined the Academy in 1987.

DIMITRIS GAVALAS

He was born in Corinth, 1949. He studied Mathematics and Cybernetics and free studies on Depth Psychology. He is involved with education.

He first appeared in literature with the poetry collection "Studies" 1973. It was followed by "Movement to the limit" 1974, "Progression" 1975, "Delos" 1976 synthetic poem, "Internal incest" synthetic poem 1977, "The city with the ineffable" 1978, "Elegy" 1979, "The extroverted" 1980, "The poetry of the secret water" 1983, "The face of happiness" 1987, "Simple songs for an angel" 1988, "Photolysis" 1989.

He also published two essays, "Internal dialectic to Maria Nephele of Odysseus Elytis" 1987, and "Psycho-cybernetics and Politics" 1989. His works are included in numerous anthologies and literary magazines.

NIKOS GALAZIS

He was born in Tirnavos, 1912. He appeared in literature in 1929, in the newspaper Democratis of Mytilini. Since then, he has collaborated in literary magazines and newspapers, provincial and Athenian, in all kinds of written word.

He served as a captain in the war against the Germans. His experiences from the war, his wounds, his participation in the protection of others, influenced his literary work, which, as he says himself, is autobiographical. He was awarded the Golden Bravery Medal.

His works: "The pipe of my father" novel, 1948, "The Italian hill" antiwar novel, 1961, "The Return of the Argonauts' theater 1961, "Poetry 1970", the "Adventure" short stories, 1975 "With the step of the goose above the corpses" poetry, "Theater" two volumes, "Visual Arts" two volumes", "Lalilo" poetry, 1992, etc.

STELIOS GERANIS

A literary pseudonym of Stelios Panagiotopoulos. He was born in Piraeus, 1935, where he died in 1993. He went to the Panteion University, where he studied Political and Economic Sciences, which he was forced to abandon during the German occupation. He offered his services to the cultural sectors of the national resistance organizations. He was involved in journalism and worked in encyclopedic and anthological publications. He worked as a director and chief editor of literary magazines.

He first appeared in literature in 1944 with the poetry collection "Transitions". It was followed by: "Path to the Light" 1949, "Wind in the swamp" 1951, "A dying time" 1955, "Pathology" 1960, "A bloodied psalm" 1963, "I rediscovered Poetry" 1993, etc.

In 1975, he was awarded the National Poetry Prize for his collection "My small wonders", the Dionysos Award of the Salichli city in 1992, the honorary medal of the Municipality of Piraeus and the Arts and Letters Society, the Award of the Kostas and Eleni Ourani Academy, 1992.

He worked as Secretary and Vice Chairman of the Society of Greek Writers and Chairman of the Society of Arts and Letters in Piraeus.

DIMITRIS GERONTAS

A poet and essayist, member of the National Society of Greek Authors and the Greek Association of Literary Translators. He was born in Athens, 1934, and lived for a significant part of his life in Thessaloniki, mainly during the postwar period. He is a literature graduate of the University of London. He has published seven poetry and essay collections, and regularly collaborates with large literary magazines and has given a series of lectures on literary and philosophical subjects.
Essays: "Correlations - Modern Greek and Western Word" (1963).
Poetry collections: "Poems 1952-1972" 1975, "Poems II 1973-1977" 1978, "Poems III 1978-1982" 1983, "The Poems Accumulative version and later poems" 1989.
Gnomikos Logos: "Reflections and Aphorisms" 1986.
Translations: "Great Moments in English Poetry" (anthology with translations, introduction and commentary by the same) 1981.

ILIAS GKRIS

He was born in 1952, in Bischini, Olympia, and for the first 17 years of his life resided in Krestena. He finished high school in Athens and studied economics at the Higher Industrial School of Piraeus. He has been working as a journalist since 1975. He is a member of the Journalists' Union of the Athens Daily Newspapers (ESHEA). He has also worked in television and radio.
He appeared in literature in 1977 and, by 1993, had issued five collections of poetry, one collection of prose and one extensive prose piece. His work has been published in many literary and art magazines: "New Breakthroughs", "Why", "Observer", "The tree '" Instead", etc. He is a member of the Society of Greek Authors.
His works: "Ravaged state" poetry 1980, 1984, "The unsweetened" prose 1980, 1983, "At the bridges of the world" poetry 1982 "Hostile landscape" poetry 1983, 1985, 1991, "Lethargic world" poetry 1987, 1991," The eye of the asylum" prose, 1990. "The efesos of horses" poetry 1993.

NIKOS GRIGORIADIS

He was born in Korifi, Kilkis, 1931. In 1946 he moved to Thessaloniki, where he finished high school and studied literature at the University. He has been living in Athens since 1959. He worked as a professor at various provincial schools, and at schools abroad. He retired in December 1992, with the rank of school counselor. He is one of the founding members of the Association of Authors.
Poetry: "The depth of lekythos" 1963, "Sampling I" 1981, "The garden and the gate" 1982, "The weights and measures" 1983, "The absence and the word" 1985, "Shadows" 1987, "The unseen within us" 1988, "Boustrophedon". The constitution of life" 1988, "Flora Mirabilis". "The pot and the lamp"1992.

Other works: Several books on reading literary texts, the teaching of language and the art and technique of writing. His poems are included in several anthologies.

OTHON M. DEFNER

He was born in Athens, 1953. He is a scion of the old Bavarian family of Defners. He graduated from the Athens College. He is a regular member of the National Society of Greek Authors.

He has published the following poetry collections: "Atlantis" 1979 "Queen of Lydia" 1982, "Madrigalia" 1984, "The Thyamis" 1990, "Stichira ldiomela" 1992 and "A Night Flower for Morpheus" 1993.

He received the Ourani Poetry Prize (for young writers) by the Academy of Athens.

ARIS DIKTAIOS

A literary pseudonym of Kostas Konstantourakis. He was born in Heraklion, Crete, 1919, and died in Athens, 1983. He was a poet, essayist and translator, studying at the Law School of Athens until WWII. During the occupation, he lived in Crete and in 1945 moved to Athens, where he became involved with journalism and radio. During 1960-1965, he worked as a director of the new editions Fexi.

Poetry: "Twelve nightmarish vignettes", "The poems 1934-1965" (1974), the collection "Voyage to Kythera" 1980.

Essays: "Seven human figures" 1961, "Poetry theory" 1962 (Second National Essay Prize), "Open accounts with time" 1963, "Seekers of a face" 1963 "Homer, the epigram, the inscription, the writing" 1974.

Translations: Goethe, Dostoevsky, Hölderlin, Nietzsche, Rimbaud, Rilke, etc. He issued anthologies on foreign and Greek poetry and prose. In 1956, he was awarded the First State Poetry Prize along with Giannis Ritsos. His poems and essays have been translated into most European languages and Arabic.

APOSTOLOS DOURVARIS

He was born in Serres on December 1931 and died in Athens, 1993. He finished high school in Thessaloniki and graduated from the Law and Philosophy at the University of Athens. At the same time, he also worked in theater and journalism.

The stimuli he received while reading at a young age were the reason for his eventual love and deep involvement with Greek folk literature.

These investigations led him to folk illustrator S. Christidis, whose life and work he has extensively dealt with.

At the same time, he wrote poetry and published the poetry collection: "By His Own Hand".

NIKOS EGGONOPOULOS*

He was born in Piraeus, 1910, where he died in 1985. He was a painter, stage designer, poet, and one of the most important representatives of the surrealist movement in Greece. He studied painting at the School of Fine Arts (1932-1938). He carried out free studies in Italy and Munich. He was a faculty-curator and then appointed professor at the School of Architecture of NTUA.

Engonopoulos lived his childhood in Istanbul, with this period leaving indelible memories on both his literary and illustrative creations.

Poetic works: "Do not talk to the driver" 1938, "The clavichords of silence" 1939, "Bolivar" 1944, "The Return of the birds' 1946 "Eleusis" 1948. A cumulative standardized version in two tomes of his seven collections of poems in 1977, and the work "In the valley with the roses" 1978, which includes translations of: Dante, Baudelaire, Lautréamont, Lorca, Mayakovsky, etc. The edition includes twenty color paintings by Engonopoulos and one drawing. His poems have been translated into numerous foreign languages.

ODYSSEAS ELYTIS

A literary pseudonym of Odysseas Alepoudelis. He was born in 1911 in Heraklion, Crete. He studied law at the University of Athens and attended literature courses at Sorbonne. As an Art critic, he represented Greece in many International conferences, while he also worked as a radio program director. From 1952-1960, he was a member of the Group of Twelve (Committee for awarding literary prizes), etc.

Poetry: "Guidelines" 1940, "Sun the first" 1943, "Axion Esti" 1959, "Six and one remorse for the army" 1960, "The Fotodendro and the fourteenth beauty" 1971, "Maria Nefeli" 1978, etc.

Essays: "Open papers", "The painter Theophilos", "The Magic of Papadiamantis".

In 1976, he presented the book "Second writing" with translations of foreign poets.

Elytis is among the finest modern Greek poets with worldwide recognition and radiance. He received the Nobel Prize for literature in 1979. His works were translated into many foreign languages. He belongs to surrealists, such as Embeirikos, Engonopoulos, Antoniou and Seferis.

ANDREAS EMBEIRIKOS*

He was born in 1901 in Braila, Romania and died in Athens, 1975. He was a poet, novelist, psychoanalyst, and introduced surrealism to Greece. He studied Economics in Switzerland, Literature and Philosophy in London and Psychoanalysis in Paris. In 1931, he returned to Greece and from 1935 onwards devoted himself exclusively to literature and psychoanalysis.

Poetry: "Chimney" 1935, "Inner land" 1945, "Oktana". Prose-form poems

1980, "Ai geneai pasai i i simeron os avrion kai os echthes" 1984, etc.
Prose: "Written the Personal Mythology" 1960, "The Great Eastern" unpublished novel. Also unpublished is the section "The talismans of love and of the chariots", "White Whale" poem, "The City" poem.
Translation work: He has translated the "Four little girls" by Picasso and published the study "A case of a neurotic obsessive idea with premature ejaculations" in the Revue Francaise de Psychanalyse 1950. His study of "A case of unconscious homosexuality" remains unpublished.

GIORGOS THEMELIS*

He was born in Samos in 1900 and died in Thessaloniki in 1976. He was a poet, essayist and playwrighter. He graduated from the Philosophy Faculty of the University of Athens and worked as a literary teacher in Thessaloniki, where he settled in 1930. He also taught at the Drama School of the National Conservatory of Thessaloniki.

His substantial contribution to Modern Greek literature began with his collaborations (poems and reviews) in the journal Makedonikes Imeres (1932-1939) and in the journal Kochlias (1946-1948). The net poetic contribution, however, began in 1945 with the publication of the poetic collection "Nude window" and since then his presence in Literature continued unabated. His collections issued up to 1968 were gathered in the publication "Poems, I and II" (1969 and 1979). They were followed by another eight collections with newer poems, from which the "Ars poetica" 1974 and "The Biblical" 1975 stand out.

Essay work: "Our newest poetry," 1963, "The last judgment" 1964, "Our new poetry", "General views" 1967, "Cavafy's poetry" 1970, "The Solomos among us" 1970, "A monologue on poetry" 1975, etc. He translated Aeschylus, Sophocles, Baudelaire, Chekhov, Ibsen, Ionesco, etc. He was awarded the Second National Poetry Prize in 1956 and the First in 1962, and in 1960 he was awarded by the Municipality of Thessaloniki.

DIMITRIS IATROPOULOS

He was born in Athens in the 40s. He studied Theater and Film in Athens, while taking History of Art and Philosophy lessons in Germany. He was a program director for Greek State Television, a magazine Editor, reporter, producer of television films, etc. He lives permanently in Athens and works as a columnist for the newspaper Ethnos, as a book critic with the magazine Eikones and teaches commenting and vignette at the Homer Journalism Studies Center.

Poetry: "Apology" 1963, "My era" 1966, "Third coming" 1967, "Fundamenta" 1969, "Rhesus" 1983.

Monographs: "Bolivar" 30 Years of Engonopoulos 1972, "Georg Trakl" Sebastian in the dream, 1971.

Essays: "Concise Chronography Handbook" 1991.

Theater: "Sun and Rain" KEA Theater 1976, "Journey to the Planet of the Toys" DIANA Theater 1978, etc.

Songs: Lyrics for approximately 600 songs with 80 Greek singers and 50 composers.

Television: He has written scripts and directed shows- features for television.

Awards - Distinctions: Prize in the National Poetry Contest for Peace 1963. Prize in the National School Poetry Competition 1966. First Screenplay Award at the 40th World Experimental Arts Festival, Brussels 1967, Special Prize at the Ithaca Theater Festival 1976. He was also awarded prizes and honors for his songs, etc.

CONSTANTINE KAVAFY

He was born in Alexandria, Egypt, in 1863, where he died in 1933. He studied English Literature and Ancient Greek Literature at London and Alexandria. He worked as a clerk at the Irrigation Department of the Ministry of Public Works in Egypt.

From 1886 onwards, he began writing poems and publishing them in magazines. He published two poetic collections with the same title "Poems" in 1910. Since then, he began printing his poems on individual sheets which were later bound in volumes, always under the title "Poems". The entirety of his poems that Cavafy published and recognized is 154 along with the "On the Outskirts of Antioch", published for the first time since his death with the issuance of his Collected Works in 1935.

He is considered one the leading poets of modern Greece.

In Greece, he became known in 1903 with a presentation made by Grigorios Xenopoulos. Besides, English novelist E.M. Foster was the first foreigner to introduce Cavafy to the international audience in 1919. He was awarded the Silver Medal of the Phoenix. His work was translated into English, French, German, Dutch, Catalan and Italian.

NIKOS KAVROULAKIS

He was born in Karanou Kidonia, Chania, in 1917. He fought in Albania and took part in battles with the 80th Infantry Regiment near Tepelene, 1940-1941. After the collapse of the front, he traveled to Athens and lived through the terrible famine of 1941. In the spring of 1942, he arrived in Crete and joined the resistance. After the war, he continued his studies and received a Literature degree from the University of Athens. He was appointed professor and in 1964 published his first book on the teaching of Modern Greek. He then wrote the books:

"The roots of Rizitika Songs" 1967, "The reckless" novel 1976," Language, rhythm and poetry" 1981, "In Minoan Crete in 1460 BC" novel 1987, "The diptych" poetry 1989, "The path of the Mousouron" 1991, "Malispap" 1991.

Besides these, he also published many articles in newspapers and magazines. He was elected member of the Society of Greek Authors since 1981.

EKTOR KAKNAVATOS*

A literary pseudonym of Giorgos Kontogiorgis. He was born in Piraeus, 1920. He studied Mathematics at the University of Athens and has since worked as a private teacher.

He appeared in literature in 1943, when he issued the collection of poems "Fuga". It was followed by the collections: "Diaspora" 1961, "The scale of stone" 1964, "Four-digit" 1971, "Four-digit with the seventh chord" 1972, "Narration" 1974, "Laestrygonian Street" 1978, "Ia perpetuum" 983, which also received the Second State Poetry Prize.

He also translated the "Love Poetry of Joyce Mansour" 1975.

ANTONIS KALFAS

He was born in 1956 in Katerini, where he still resides. He studied Political Sciences in Athens and Modern Literature in Ioannina, while attending post-graduate courses in the Theory of Literature and Communication at Konstanz.

He has published the poetry collections: "Extent of emotional age" 1980, "Champions of short distances" 1985, "Notes on innocence" 1992.

He is engaged in literary research and book reviews, and is a regular contributor to the Diavazo magazine. He works as a Literature teacher in secondary education.

GEORGOS K. KARAVASILIS

He was born in Athens, 1949. He studied Political Science and Theater next to D. Rontiris. He now works as a journalist at the Secretariat General of Information and Communication.

Poetic works: "The writing and the knife" 1970, "Blood Culture" 1973, "Idypathi" 1976, "The Secret rooms of the Tower" 1978, "Poems (1970-1980)" 1980.

Essays: "The rule of the game" by Jean Renoir 1977, "The woman of the waters in Lyric Poetry" 1977.

Translations: August Strindberg, "Easter - Pariah" 1970. Paul Éluard, "Poems" 1971,1978,1982, Tristan Corbière, "Poems" 1972. Pierre Louis, "The woman and the puppet" 1978, 1981. Charles Cros "Fantastic actions" 1980. Ivan Turgenev, "Spring showers" 1980. Théophile Gautier, "The dead mistress' 1981. "Leaves of Twentieth Century French Poetry" 1981, Acques Cazotte, "The devil in love" 1983, etc.

GIANNIS KARAVIDAS

He was born in Mikri Gonitsa, Ioannina, in 1934. He served education for 25 years. In 1965, he officially appeared in literature with the poetry collection "Sparks in marble". They were followed by many others: "Footprints in the black and white" 1971, "Exit diary" 1973, "Poesie" 1977, "The other sun" 1978, 1991 "Intersections I" 1981, "Intersections II" 1985, etc. He also wrote several studies, numerous articles and critical notes in newspapers and magazines.

Studies - essays: "The poet Phoivos Delphis" 1972, "Lily Iakovidou, the

poet of youth" 1978, "The poetic path of Vasilis Krapsitis" 1984, "The Dialectics of peace in the poetry of Georgos Kouloukis" 1990, etc.
His poems were translated into Italian, French, Polish and Hungarian. Giannis Karavidas is chairman of the Society of Greek Authors.

OLYMPIA KARAGIORGA

He was born in Alexandria, Egypt, 1934. He studied Sociology at the American University of Cairo and English and American Literature and Creative Writing at the University of Standford in California. He published short stories, poems and studies in American academic journals.

In 1959, he moved to Athens and began working as an English teacher. At the same time, he attended Dramatic Art studies at the Christos Vlachiotis School.

He appeared in Greek literature with the poetry collection "Thousands of faces of fate" 1961, "The loudspeakers" 1966, "The great wave" 1974, "Who" 1985, and received an honorary place at the Athens Municipality contest. He published the study of "Virginia Woolf, a great unknown" 1981, "Nijinsky - Journal, testimonials, his life and death" 1982.

His translation work is extensive: "Caligula" by Albert Camus 1965 and 1977, "Duende" by Frederic Garcia Lorca 1970, "D.H. Lawrence - Twenty Poems" 1972, the essay by Oscar Wilde "The soul of man under socialism" 1984.

DIMITRIS I. KARAMVALIS

He was born in the capital of Cameroon, Yaoundé. He studied Law and Journalism. He works as a lawyer at the Athens Supreme Court.

He is involved with poetry, essays, critique, studies. He has written short stories and a one-act play. He has composed more than four hundred songs (his own lyrics and music - self-taught). His works have been translated into French, English, Italian, Polish, etc. He has translated poems by Giorgos Sarantaris and four modern Cameroonian poets from French.

Poetry: "At the fronts of times" 1978, "Evidence" 1980, "The autopsy of the waves" 1981, "Small Fires" Haiku 1982, "Way Out" 1984, "The words of lightning" 1987, "Aimassousa recording" 1992, etc.

Texts: "Five texts on the poetry of Gratsia Spyrou Depounti" 1990. There is also a large unpublished work in poetry, essays, studies.

He publishes in prestigious literary journals, and produces television and radio programs. He is a regular member of the National Society of Greek Authors, the Philological Association "Parnassos", the Greek Society for Philosophical Studies, etc. He has received over forty distinctions or honors in literary, poetry, drama and essay competitions.

DIMITRIS KARVOUNIS

He was born in Athens, 1937. He emigrated to Africa, Johannesburg, where he studied Sociology. Before leaving for abroad, he issued two poetry collections: "Respect my concern" 1961 and "Inconsistent Agreement" 1963.

After his return to Greece, he published the novella "The Decay" 1988, the poetry collection To Fengrisma 1989, the short stories "The Crypt and The Nest "1989 and the novel "Lillian" 1990. With poet Dimitris Kakalidis, he also wrote the poetic work "Alaloum and Hallelujah" issued in 1989.

ZOI KARELLI

A literary pseudonym for Chrisoula Argiriadou, sister of N.G. Pentzikis. She was born in Thessaloniki, 1901. She studied music and was a poet, essayist, novelist.

Poetry: "March" 1940, "Age of death" in 1948, "Time Fantasy" 1949, "The Ship" 1955, "Tales of the garden" 1955, "Contrasts" 1957, "The midnight mirror" 1958. "The Poems I" and "The Poems II" 1973 (cumulative versions).

Theatrical plays: "The devil and the seventh command" 1959, "Suppliants" 1962, "Orestes" 1971, etc.

Essays: "On doubt" 1958, "The ultimate in Claudel's work" 1959.

In 1956, he was awarded the Second National Poetry Prize and the French distinction of "Academic Palms".

NIKOS KAROUZOS*

He was born in Nafplio, 1926 and died in Athens, 1990. The poet began studying Law and Political Sciences at the University of Athens, but without finishing them. He first appeared in literature in 1949, publishing a poem in the magazine O Aionas Mas.

The first collection of poems by Karouzos was "The Return of Christ" 1954. It was followed by: "New Tests" 1954, "Point" 1955, "Twenty poems" 1955, "Dialogs" 1956, "Poems" 1961, which gathered the collections of the seven-year period from 1953 to 1960, "The Deer of the Stars" 1962, "The sleeping bag" 1964, "Penthimata" 1969, "Bandage for small and large discrepancies" 1971, Overgrown Chasms" 1974, "A descendant of the night" 1978, "Poems", 1979, which gathered the collections of the seven-year period from 1969 to 1974, "Possibilities and Use of speech" 1979, "the Zeal of the meta-relevant with errata" 1980 "Monolektismoi kai oligolekta " 1980, "Poems," 1981, which gathered his work from 1961 to 1980, "Faretrion" 1981 "Earth-proof tomb" 1984.

He has also published the essay "Metaphysical impressions from life to the theater" 1966.

GIORGOS CARTER

He was born in Corfu, 1928. He studied theater at the Drama School of the National Theater and Painting at the School of Fine Arts.

In 1959, he studied television in Vienna and later, with an Italian State scholarship, in Rome.

He was a director of Television in ERT-1 and the first director of Television and Radio in ERT-2.

He appeared in literature in 1944. To date, he has issued twenty-two books (poetry, essays, etc.) and seven discs with historical documentaries and specials on literature and theater. His collections entitled "A tempo" and "Il grande Gaos" were printed in France and Italy, respectively. His poems, also translated into Italian, French, German, etc., have been included in foreign literary satires and anthologies.

He has given lectures in Greece and abroad and has participated in international conferences. He wrote the theater critique column for four years in an Athenian newspaper and now writes TV critique in the Eikones magazine. He has participated in committees, such as for the Greek Film Festival and in television and poetry contests.

He is a member of the Society of Greek Authors, secretary general of the Union of Theater Critics, member of the Panhellenic Cultural Movement and of the International Theater Institute. He was also president of the Artistic Committee of the National Theater and a member of the Radio & Television Broadcasting Council.

He is cited in in several encyclopedias, biographical dictionaries and historical books on Greek literature.

CHRISTINA KARYDOGIANNI

She was born in Athens. She studied law at the University of Athens. She has been involved in literature and painting since her school years. She lived for many years in the former Belgian Congo (Zaire) and collaborated with Greek magazines of S. Africa.

she returned to Athens, where she printed the poetry collection "Kari" in 1966, in memory of her son and bequeathed the homonymous annual award at the National Technical University. It was followed by the books: "Pilgrimage" poetry 1968, "For a better Hades" Theater 1971, "Deadalic course" poetry 1976, "Law Draft" short stories 1978, "The Pain exceedance" theater 1982, "Young Centaurs" short stories 1984, "Athens in the streets of the spirit" essay study 1986, "20th Century-the twilight of Titania" poetry 1988.

She has been honored with Greek and foreign awards, such as: By the Lutece International Academy, Gold medal, Paris 1977. Cavallieri per l 'Europa Silver medal, Milan 1978, the Academy of Letters and Arts of Perigord, Bordeaux 1990, etc. Her Poems are published in Greek and foreign magazines.

She is a member of the National Society of Greek Authors and other spiritual and cultural associations.

STELLA KARYTINOU

Born in Athens. She studied Law at the University of Athens and Vocal Music and Theory at the National Conservatory. Concerts followed with important appearances at the music and the National Broadcasting Corporation.

She made her career at the Bank of Greece. She is a member of the National Society of Greek Authors.

She became involved with Literature since she was a student and published in newspapers and magazines. In a short story contest in 1967, proclaimed by the Honorary Bank Director and Academic Mr. X. Zolotas, her short stories "The best gift", "Love" and "Temptation" were awarded by a committee of Academics Ilias Venezis, Thanasis Petsalis-Diomidis and poet Minaw Dimakis. In 1964, the Womens Literary Team awarded her work "Wings" (Poetry for children), and in 1965 her work "March" was awarded by the Philadelfeian poetic contest. She was a regular contributor to the monthly banking magazine Kyklos, from 1961 to 1969.

MICHALIS KATSAROS*

He was born in Kyparissia, 1919. As a young man, he became involved with political movements of the Left and during the occupation he was active in the resistance. After the end of the war, he settled in Athens (1945). He was a member of the editorial team of the magazines Themelio 1947 and Stochos 1950. In 1975, he published the magazine Systima, whose material he wrote almost entirely on his own.

Katsaros appeared in literature in 1946, with the publication of a poem in the magazine Elefthera Grammata. His first collection of poems, "Messolongi", was published in 1949. It was followed by: "Against Sadducees" 1953, "Plateau" 1956, "Textbook" 1975, "Rehearsal and odes" 1975, "Clothing" 1977, "Alphabet book, poems A-Z" 1978, "Names" 1980, "3M-3M = 6M" 1981, "4 Maginot" 1982, his prose texts "Pass-Lakis-Michelet" 1973, "the Chronicle of Morea" 1974, "Contemporary brochures" 1977, "The articles of free communards" 1978, "The state employer" 1978.

Poems by Katsaros have been set to music by Mikis Theodorakis, A. Kounadi and G. Markopoulos.

CHRISTOS KATSIGIANNIS

He was born in Athens, 1930. He studied at the Panteion Higher School of Political Sciences, which he left to study theater. He first appeared in theater in 1954 and dedicated himself professionally to it until 1973.

His issued books are:

Poetry: "The Permitted" 1972, "The Permitted II" 1977, "Un-illuminated and voiceless moments" 1980, "Time of Apnea" 1987, "The flowers of silence" 1989, "Poems 1972-1992" 1993, etc.

Theatrical plays: "Improvisation Exercise" 1971, "The Ark" 1973.

He also wrote essays and translations.

His poems have been translated and published in Hungary, Mexico, Brazil, France and Italy. References to work are included in encyclopedias, anthologies and in many newspapers and magazines in Athens and other cities. In 1991 the University of Naples released the book "Christos Katsigianis - poesie", translated and commented by Professor Konstantinos Nikas.

MITSOS KATSINIS

He was born in Arcadia, in the Village Kerasitsa, Tegea, in 1918. He finished the Pedagogical Academy in Tripoli and settled permanently in Athens in 1945.

He was a collaborator in several literary magazines and newspapers, dealing with all kinds of written word. He is, however, a legitimate, polyphonic poet. He praises peace, freedom, and social justice. He has fought against violence and war. The author's work amounts to 36 published books, some of which are:

"Scattered arias" 1939, "Altars of freedom" 1943, "Bloody Songs" 1947, "Poor loves" 1953, "Blue Songs" 1956, "Crucified Cyprus" 1956, "Peace" 1961, "Mournful symphony" 1963, "Resistance to the haze" 1976, "The red river" 1978, "Stone ship" 1979, "Good Morning soldier" 1980, "The Peace doves" 1981, "Peaceful" 1985, etc.

Mitsos Katsinis was won the first International Poetry Award in Italy in 1983 and the first Poetry Prize by the National Society of Greek Authors in 1985. His poems were translated into French, English, Italian, Bulgarian and other languages.

MANTO KATSOULOU

She was born in Patras and has lived for the past 30 years in Piraeus. Once she completed general education in Greece, she studied English Literature and Sociology in England. She worked as an English teacher and as a translator. Now she has retired from work and is fully engaged in literature and especially poetry.

To date, she has published ten poetry collections, a collection of short stories and one essay, while a large part for her writings remains unpublished. Her work has been recognized and she has received honors in Greece and abroad.

She is also involved in painting and she illustrates her own books. She writes literary and social articles and chronicles in newspapers and magazines.

KOSTIS KOKOROVITS

A literary pseudonym of Konstantinos Kokorakis. He was born in 1911 in Spetses and comes from a family that was involved in the 1821 revolution, heirlooms of which reside in the Spetses Museum.

He first appeared in literature in 1931, with a foreword by Pantelis Horn. His second poetic book was prefaced by Grigoris Xenopoulos,

Miltiadis Malakasis and Nikos Veis. He has published six collections of poetry, one chronicle book and one with essays.

He has given numerous lectures for "Parnassus, the "Archaeological Society", the "Society of Friends of the People", the "Piraeus Contact" and for provincial Cultural Centers. His poems have been published in many magazines and newspapers—Greek and foreign—and his poems have been included in numerous Greek and foreign anthologies—translated. Several encyclopedic dictionaries refer to him.

He is a member of National Society of Greek Authors, a member of the Union of Journalists of Regional Press, he was speaker of the Ministry of Education in Modern Literature, at the Education Department and as a professor of History of Modern Literature in Theater Drama Schools. His poems have won awards in France and have been translated into French, Italian, English, Hindi, Polish, Turkish.

TAKIS KOLIAVAS - MOLIOTAKIS

He was born in Molos, Fthiotida, in 1926 to native parents.

From an early age, he worked as a journalist in the provincial press, writing daily chronicles, comments, articles, verses and book reviews.

In 1961, he moved with his family to Athens. He worked as an executive with a large commercial and industrial company until 1991 when he retired. So far, he has given nineteen multipage collections of poetry in traditional artistic form. He appeared in literature with his first collection "Return from the country of dreams" 1966.

His poetry has been awarded four times in national contests, while, in 1985, he won the prize for poetic speech in the "Parnassus" contest. His collaborations have been published in literary magazines and newspapers and references to his poems are included and presented in poetic anthologies, biographies, encyclopedias and literature stories.

As to prose writing, he has given the narrative book "Memory and Writing" 1987, with more to follow. The chronicles and articles are also a creative pastime for the poet.

He is a regular member of the Hellenic Literary Society and the Union of Journalists of Regional Press.

GIANNIS KONTOS

He was first published in 1964. He has issued poems and texts in various magazines and newspapers. In 1973, he received the Ford sponsorship.

He has been translated into the main European languages. Also, in 1978, two selections of his poems were issued in English; one translated by Giannis Goumas entitled "Mercurial Time", and the other translated by Giannis Stathatou entitled "Danger in the Streets". In 1984, he published his book "Bones" in Danish, translated by W. Gjertov P. In 1986, his book "The bones and other poems '72 - '82" were published in the US, translated by James Stone. In 1989, the "Bones" were also

issued in Germany, translated by Mars Geraldi and Gunnar König.
He also worked in Radio for a number of years. In 1980, he released an album with poems set to music by composer Nikos Kallitsis, entitled "Attempt". He has written texts on contemporary Greek painters. A selection of his poems was issued in April 1992, entitled "When over the city, a drum is heard", in a limited number of copies, illustrated by Dimitris Mytaras.

TASOS KORFIS

It is a pseudonym for Tassos Robotis. He was born in 1929 in Corfu. He finished high school in Patras, moved to Athens in 1947, and worked as a Navy officer, reaching the highest ranks.
Short stories: "Travel without polar" 1952 (honored with the Efstathiou prize, of Cyprus Letters), "A deserted house" 1973, "Patrognosia" 1984, Second State Prize for short story.
Poetry collections: "Diary" 1963 "Calendar 2" 1964, "Diary 3" 1968, "Handiwork" 1977, "Pafsilipa", "Sonnets and haiku" 1987.
He also edited works mainly by traditional poets of the interwar period, such as Mitsos Papanikolaou. "The Poems" 1966, 1979, by Anastasios Drivas, "A bundle of sunrays on the water" 1978, "Translations" Kaisaras Emmanouil 1981.
He issued the studies: "Romus Philyras" 1974, "Nikos Kavadias" 1978 (prize by the Ministry of Mercantile Marine), etc.
Translations of foreign poets, such as: "Lustra" by Ezra Pound 1977, "Poems of William Carlos Williams» 1979, 1989, etc.
Since 1978, he has been editing and publishes an annual poetry anthology entitled "Voices".

GIORGIS KOTSIRAS

He was born in Athens, 1920. He studied Law and Political science at the University of Athens and practiced law until 1965, when he was appointed a notary until 1986, when he resigned. He was honored by the state with the FirstClass literary writing. He has been nominated several times as a member of the Committee for awarding literary prizes and book market until recently.
Poetry: "The Land of the Lotus Eaters" 1948, "Sentinels of Silence" 1949, "The Conversation with Sisyphus" 1958 State poetry award, "Anatomy of a Crime" Group of 12 Poetry Prize 1964, "The "Alpha" of Centaur" State poetry award 1975, "The poems" cumulative version, poetry Prize by the Athens Academy 1980, "The Mythology of Persons and other poems" poetry prize by the K. and E. Urani Foundation 1989, etc.
Translation: Giovanni Guareschi "Don Camilo" 1954, Albert Camus "The Stranger" 1955, F.G. Lorca "The House of Bernardo Alba" 1957, 1969, Dante Alighieri "The Divine Comedy" 1987, Greek Association of Literary Translators Prize 1988.
He has also written plays, essays and studies. He has been writing the critique column in the Efthini magazine since 1982.

CHRISTOS NIKOMOU KOULOURIS

He is a poet, novelist and essayist. He was born in 1924 in Lamia. He appeared in literature in 1942 with collaborations in magazines and newspapers. He has been the director of the Nea Skepsi magazine since 1961. He is a member of the Hellenic Literary Society. He was awarded the 1968 Poetry Prize by the Womens Literary Team, the 1971 National Narrative Award, etc.

Poetry: "Morning Start" 1943, "Northern Lights" 1946, "Iolkos" 1948, "The Melancholy of Daedalus" 1952, "The Courage of Waves" 1955, "The Direction of the Evening" 1962, "The Rope Ladder" 1964, "I sing of spring"1967," Secret Scripture "1974,"The Earthly"1975, "Evening Archipelago" 1978, "Brass" 1983 "Desires" 1986, "The children of captain Odysseus Columbus" 1987, "The inhuman Lake" 1989.

Prose: "The Fan of Spring" 1949, "The Legend of the Sea" 1952, "Solitude" 1963 "In our own Earth" 1969, "The Kumara" 1970, "The Unknown Day" 1976, "The Hidden Flame" 1977, "The bitter Grape" 1979, "The Reporter" 1980, "The Pavement" 1990, "The Delusion" 1991.

Critique-study: "Zacharias Papantoniou" 1953, "The War in Pindos and our Poets" 1954, "Takis Doxas" 1956, I.M. Panagiotopoulos" 1959, "Unforgettable and Forgotten" 1960, "The Lyrical and Prose Word" 1961, "Writers of our Time" 1965, "Forms and Reflections I" 1971," Forms and Reflections II" 1973.

LETA KOUTSOCHERA

She was born on March, 1945, in Ziria, Achaia. Her first painting teacher was Spyros Sokaris in Patras.

Studies: Design and Stage Design at the Vakalo School (Athens). Interior Architecture and Furniture Design at the School of Fine Arts in Stuttgart, Germany.

Group exhibitions: Terpsithea Cultural Center (1978), P. Faliro Cultural Center (1979), "Aquarius" Art Gallery (1981).

Individual exhibitions: P. Faliro Cultural Center (1978), Art Gallery in "Plaka" (1979), "At Govostis" 1990.

She has issued three poetry collections. Her poetry has been awarded and translated into Hungarian, English, Italian and Russian. She has been teaching at the Athens TEI since 1981.

She was in charge of stage design and costumes for Albert Camus' "The Just", performed at the "VICTORIA" Theater.

GIANNIS KOUTSOCHERAS

He was born in Ziria, Achaia, in 1904. He studied Law and Political Sciences in Paris and Athens, where he worked as a lawyer. He became involved with politics and was repeatedly elected as a municipal councilor of Athens and Minister.

He published the works "Contemplations and Echoes" 1942, "Blue breaths" 1949, "Greek Nights" 1954, "The supper of Bethany" 1959,

"Jordan the Ever-flowing" 1960, "Leaping Smoke" 1961, "Mark the Gentle" 1964, "Aphaia" 1964, "The lyrical chronicle of the Mother" 1969, "Silence and cry of the sea" 1987, "Hellenic" 1980, "the Golden fleece" 1981, etc., many of which were translated into French.

Presentations of his poetic work in many cities of Greece and honors (medals, honorary citizen, honorary teacher, etc.). Abroad: Paris, Rome, Hamburg, Hannover, Cairo, Stockholm, Brussels, Sydney, Tokyo, etc.

His poetry has been set to music. In 1985, he was awarded the Grand Rrix d 'Europe and Monnaie de Raris released his personal Medal in 1988.

D.P. KOSTELENOS

He was born in Athens in September, 1932, and has been living in isolation in Ermioni for several years now.

He studied Law, without ever getting a degree, and foreign languages.

He worked from 1958 to 1969 as a journalist in Athenian newspapers, throughout that time maintaining his book review column. His first poetry collection was released in 1950, without ever appearing in bookstore showcases.

Since then, he has issued the following: "Excerpts from Achilles' Lament", poems, 1972, "The poems of the closed horizon" 1974, "What is a novel" essay, 1975 "Biographical Encyclopedia of Greek Literary Writers" 4 volumes, 1976, "History of Modern Greek Literature" 1977, "Great poetry anthology from Homer to today" 6 volumes, 1980, "Poems of Ermioni" 1984, "107 quatrains and other poems" 1991.

DIONYSIOS KOSTIDIS

He was born in Astakos, Akarnania, but grew up and lived in Thessaloniki and Athens. He is a member of EEEL (National Hellenic Literary Society). He received the first Prize for Short Story of the Hellenic Literary Society (Veropoulos) for the year 1990, for his book "Anhydrous earth".

He was an administrative judge and reached the rank of president of the Court of Appeals. He withdrew from the judicial service in 1989.

His works: "The night which passed" novel, "Days and nights of Stratos Davis" novella, "Anhydrous earth" collection of short stories," Civil War Diary" testimony, "The concealed and the occult" essay, "A thripta" poetry collection, etc.

VASSILIS I. LAZANAS

He was born in Corinth. He was a graduate of Law of the University of Athens and Doctor of Philosophy from the University of Tybingen. He made his career as Director of the National Foundation for the Deaf and as inspector of the Ministry of Health and Welfare. He was a poet, essayist, scholar, translator. Distinctions:

1. Academy of Athens Award for his book: "The Roman Elegy" by Goethe 1972.
2. First State Prize for his book "Fr. Hölderlin, the brother of the ancient Greeks ..." 1985.
3. Award by the "Greek Society of Christian Literature" for his performance in ancient Greek, Latin and German literature and his respective translations (1991).
4. Gold medal by the city of Corinth.

MARIA LAINA

She was born in 1947 in Patras. She studied Law at the University of Athens and lives in Athens.

She has issued six poetry collections: "Coming of Age" 1968, "Beyond" 1970, "Landscape Change" 1992, "Punctuation marks" 1991, "Hers" 1985, "Rose Fear" 1992.

Theater plays: "The clown" theatrical monologue 1985, and "The reality is always here" in three acts 1990.

Reviews of her work were published in many newspapers such as the Nea, Eleftherotypia, Vima tis Kyriakis, Avgi, etc., and also in literary magazines, such as Diavazo, Epikaira, Poiisi, Endeftktirio, etc. The poet has been included in many Greek and foreign anthologies, such as that of Renos Apostolidis, Estia, "The generation of the 70s", etc. She is a member of the Society of Authors.

TASOS LEIVADITIS*

He was born in Piraeus, 1921, where he died in 1988. He was a poet with significant action in the Left area. He began Legal Studies, which he never completed. His first poems were published in magazines Elefthera Grammata 1946 and Nea Estia 1947.

In 1947, he was arrested due to his political views and was displaced to Moudros, Makronissos and Agios Efstratios in 1951. In 1952, he published two poetry collections: "Battle at the edge of night" and "This star is for all".

He was one of the founders of the Epitheorisi Technis magazine (Christmas 1954), of which he was a regular contributor, while also appearing in the columns of the newspaper Avgi as a poetry critic.

His collections are: "It is windy at the crossroads of the world" 1953 (First Prize Warsaw Festival), "The Man with the drum" 1956, "Symphony No. 1" 1957, "The women with the equine eyes" 1958, "Cantato" 1960, and "25th Rhapsody of the Odyssey" 1963. All his works are incorporated in the volume "Poetry" 1965.

Other works: "The last" 1966, "The pendulum" 1966 (collection of nine short stories), "The devil with the candlestick" 1975, "Violin for a one-armed man" 1976, "Euthanasia manual" 1979 (First National Poetry Prize), "The blind man with the lamp" 1983, and" Violets for a season" 1985, etc.

His works have been translated and included in foreign anthologies. His lyrics have been set to music, mainly by M. Theodorakis.

STATHIS MARAS

He was born in Athens, 1929. He took part in the national resistance and for this reason, although still a child, was displaced to the Middle East. He studied Law, without getting a degree.

In 1950, he printed three poetry collections, worked with magazines and published translations of Spanish poets. His poems were also translated into Italian ("Cinzia" 1959). Since then and for about twenty years, he devoted himself to the study of philosophy, sociology, psychology, and literature.

The result of this work was an Introduction to Art and Literature, I Filothrini Diathesi ston Anthropo kai ton Poioiti and a large set of distinct but interrelated studies, which envelop the entire New Greek Literature, combined with the overall socio-economic and aesthetic Greek life (with ramifications to the international arena) from pre-revolutionary times to the present day. Four of these studies - on Varnalis, on Kazantzakis, on the poets presented up to 1920, on the "Matter of the Woman" - have been released by Kastaniotis Publications.

MELLISANTHI*

A literary pseudonym of Ivi Kougia-Skandalaki. She was born in Piraeus, 1907, where she died in 1990. She was a poet and translator. She studied French and German literature in Athens, as well as music, dance and painting. She periodically worked as a journalist in Athenian newspapers and was a permanent collaborator of the E.I.R. during the decade 1945-1955. She also worked as a French teacher.

Poetry: "Insect voices" 1930, "Prophecies" 1931, "Burning bush" 1935, "Return of the Prodigal" 1936, "Human shape" 1961, "The Barrier of Silence" 1965, "The New poems" 1982, etc. In 1965, the first cumulative edition of her poems was released, the "Election, 1930-1950", in 1975 the second, "The poems, 1930-1974", and in 1986 the Third, "Journey, poems 1930-1984".

She has published her theatrical work for children, "The little brother" 1960 and has translated poems by Robert Frost, Pasternak, Longfellow, Eliot, Brecht, etc. In 1985 she released a selection of essays entitled "Allusions" as well as the volume "Matins the coming" with 36 studies on her work and bibliographic information. Melissanthi has been awarded the Praise of the Academy of Athens 1936, the Second National Poetry Award 1965 and the First National Poetry Award 1976.

KOSTAS MONTIS

He was born in 1914, in Ammochostos, Cyprus. He studied at the Pancyprian Gymnasium of Nicosia, followed by Law and Political and Economic Sciences at the University of Athens. He served as professor and

employee. He worked as a journalist. He attained a high-ranking position at the EOKA.
He dealt with prose and poetry. His work depicts the historical, political and military events of contemporary Cyprus
His works: "Camels" short stories 1930, "Minima" Nicosia '46, "The songs of humble life" Nicosia '54, "Unknown Man" 'Nicosia' 62, "Poetry" Nicosia '62, "On beloved Cyprus" Nicosia '69 "Anthology form the "Moments" Athens 1978, etc.

PANTELIS S. BOUKALAS

He was born in Lessini, Messolonghi, in 1957. He studied dentistry at the University of Athens. He works as a publishing proofreader and editor. His writings were first published in 1979 in the magazine O Politis. He was a daily columnist for the Proti newspaper and for the past three years for the Kathimerini newspaper, while also writing the third page of the book reviews.
He has published the following poetry collections: "Algorithm" 1980, "Evdokia's excursion" 1982, 1993 "The inside Panther" 1987, "Ruinous Signals" 1992.
In 1991, he published his own translation from ancient Greek of the "Epitaph of Adonid" by Vion.

RITA BOUMI - PAPPA

She was born in 1906, in Syros, and died in 1984 in Athens.
She studied Pedagogy in Italy and for a time was the director of the Syros Kindergarten and Nursery. At the same time, she also wrote poems. She married poet Nikos Pappas and settled with him in Thessaly and then in Athens. During the German occupation, she engaged in resistance activity.
Her works: "Songs to Love" 1930, "The pulse of my silence" 1935 (First Honor of the Academy of Athens), "Athens - December" 1945 (First National Resistance Award)," Ritorno in Ortigia" 1949 (International Syracuse Award) "A thousand killed girls" 1963, "The magic Flute" in 1964 (first Prize Womens Literary Team), "Morgan - John - The glass prince" 1976 (First National Poetry Prize), etc.
She also wrote prose, travelogues, encyclopedic texts and also issued magazines. She translated works of poetry, novels and plays, and together with N. Pappas, she issued the "Global Anthology of Poetry" 1953. Her works have been translated into many foreign languages. The poet was honored with over eleven awards and honors in Greece and abroad.

TAKIS NATSOULIS

Born in Athens. He graduated from the Panteion School, Athens Law School and the Drama School of the National Theater. He worked as an actor in many Athenian Theaters and played in many Greek films. In

1952, he was appointed to the EIR (ERT 1) as an announcer and later as head of Radio and Television.

He released the magazines Efthimos kosmos and Radioreportaz. He is the founder of Cultural Associations in Amarynthos, Evia, and of the newspaper Ta Amarynthia and Amarynthiaka Nea. He collaborates with many magazines and newspapers and is a member of the Union of Journalists Regional of Press. He has written book reviews for many literary magazines and newspapers.

His poems have been translated into Portuguese and he is a member of the "Centro Cultural". His writings are significant and his folklore publications are unique in Greece. His works have been published in various anthologies and he has collaborated with the encyclopedia YDRIA, offering numerous folklore entries.

He has been honored with many awards and special distinctions. He is a member of the SEI, a founding member of the Hellenic Association of New Literary Authors, where he served as chairman, etc.

GIANNIS NTEGIANNIS

He was born in Chalkida. He became involved with literature from a very young age. At the time, he published a few poems in Athenian magazines. One of his short stories was awarded in a contest by magazine Neoellinika Grammata by D. Fotiadis. He later published four books with lyrics, the "Hourglass" 1961, the "Afternoon" 1963, the "Return" 1978, the "Prologue to any future happiness" 1981.

He meanwhile published articles on literary and language issues, in newspapers and magazines. He is more interested in prose. He published the "Trial" 1991 (five editions) a history book, the "Parallel Seasons" 1991 short stories and the "Parade" 1993 novel.

ZISIS OIKONOMOU

He was born in Skiathos in 1911. He was fluent in Italian and German, and served as an interpreter in the war from 1940 to 1941. He researched issues related to Indo-European languages, psychology, sociology and politics. He wrote poetry, essays and plays. Today he lives in Skiathos.

Poetry collections: "The saga of non-noble metals" 1934, "The world in its setting" 1935, "Recovery" 1935 "Landscapes" 1936, "The earth's prayer" 1938, "Oceanic" 1939, "The accompaniment of the wind" 1945, "At the crossroads of time"1946, "To the pure self" 1953, "Cloudless silence" 1976, "Poems 1934-1953" 1977.

Essays: "The stay of the one who left" 1938, "The confession of humiliation" 1944, "Reflections on music and poetry" 1946, "Fate and word" 1948, "Nihilism and spiritual revolution" 1978, "Culture of death and Vital quickening" 1982, etc.

Theatrical plays: "The bottom floor" 1947, "Dead Zone" 1947, "The Haunted House" 1948, "The return of the prodigal" 1948 and "The long journey" 1948, etc.

KOSTIS PALAMAS

He was born in Tripoli in 1859 and died in Athens in 1943.
He was a poet, critic, journalist, novelist, playwrighter, and academic. He was a leading representative of the so-called "1880s generation".
Poetic works: "My Homeland's Songs" 1886 "Hymn of Athena" 1889, Award on the "Filadelfeian Poetic Race" of 1892," The eyes of my soul" 1892, "Iamvoi kai anapaistoi" 1897 (music by Manolis Kalomoiris) "Tomb" 1898, "Oi chairetismoi tis Iliogennitis" 1900, "Still Life" 1904, "The twelve words of the gypsy" 1907, "Flute of the King" 1910, etc.
Short stories: "Death of the lad" 1901, "Trisevgeni" 1903.
Critique: on Solomos 1901, Andreas Kalvos, etc.
In 1925, Palamas was awarded the State Prize of Arts and Letters, and, in 1926, year of the establishment of the Academy of Athens, he was one of its founding members, while in 1931 he became its chairman.
His work was translated into French, English, German, Italian, Swedish, Spanish and Yugoslavian. He died in 1943, during the German occupation.

I.M. PANAGIOTOPOULOS

He was born in 1901 in Aitoliko and died in Athens in 1982.
He studied at the University of Athens and later on worked in Secondary Education.
Poems: "The book of Miranda", "Lyrical plans", "Alkyoni", "The Zodiac cycle", etc.
Novels: "The seven sleeping children" (First National Novel Prize", "The two and the night", "Starlight", "Chamozoi", "Captives".
Short stories: "The ring with the fairy tales", "Human thirst", "Flamingos", etc.
He also wrote travelogues, essays, a brief history of Greek Literature and had numerous collaborations with newspapers and magazines. His works were translated into many foreign languages.
He was awarded the Palamas prize for his work "Kostis Palamas". In 1956, he received the First State Prize for Prose. In 1976, he was named Honorary Doctor of the Faculty of Philosophy of the University of Athens, for his literary and philosophical contribution to Greek Literature.

PANOS N. PANAGIOTOUNIS

He was born in Kalamata. His general studies began and ended in Athens, where he moved with his family from a young age. He studied Law at the University of Athens and serves as a lawyer in the Supreme Court. He then enrolled in the Department of Economics and Political Sciences of the University of Athens. He studied directing and received a director's diploma. He is a poet, scholar, playwrighter, anthologist. He published about fifty books in literature. He wrote poetry, essays, histories of literature, plays, etc. His poems were translated into English, Russian, Egyptian, Polish, Portuguese, etc.

He is a professor in Higher education schools on directing and theater, where he teaches Greek and world history of literature and theater, as well dramatology.

He has participated in many conferences in the East, Far East and West, where he represented Greek Literature. His main works.

Poetry: "Testing hours" 1955, "Always Dawning" 1957, "Concert of Solitude" 1959, "Open Window", "1960, "Nuclear Test" 1963 "Epitome I" (1950-1970), "The white room" 1979, "Dionysus Sufferer" 1980, "Illuminated Aegean" 1983. "Beavers" 1987.

Theater: "Three one-act plays", "A Murder in the dream", "Dionysus Sufferer" (Satiric drama 1988), etc.

GIORGOS PANAGOULOPOULOS

He was born in Pyrgos, Ilia. He studied Law, practiced it for a few years and then became involved with trade.

He issued: Ten poetry collections: "Reveille" 1961, "Escape" 1971, "Sack" 1975 "Everything I did not say" 1978 "Alternation between vigil and dream" 1980, "Futile Game" 1981, "Senses which do not decide" 1983, "Something a bit more", "Last flare" 1989.

A volume of short stories entitled "Shift" 1972 and the novel "Towards the exit" 1974.

Theater: "One-act plays" in 1970 and the three-act play "The Bridge" 1979.

He also worked on theater critique and has published many critiques on plays in newspapers and literary magazines, as well as theater essays. His prose and poems were translated in France, Italy, Poland, Romania, Bulgaria, Sweden, Germany and the US. He is a member of the Hellenic Literary Society and the Union of Theater and Music Critics.

KOSTAS P. PAPAGEORGIOU

He was born in Athens, 1945. He studied Law and Literature. He was jointly responsible for the annual publication Katathesi '73 and '74. Since 1982, he has been publishing and managing the magazine Grammata kai Technes.

Poetry collections: "Poems" 1966, "Collection" 1970, "Epi pygin kathisai" 1972 "Sketching" 1975, "The family tree" 1978, "The killed blood" 1982 "Below in sleep" 1986 and "Sewn mouth" 1990.

Narratives: "To Giotapato" 1977, "Of all Saints" 1992. Studies: Notes on the "Three Hidden Poems" by Giorgos Seferis 1974, suggestions on the "Moonlight Sonata" by Giannis Ritsos 1981.

His poems and other works have been translated into several languages. A section of his collection "Sketching" was set to music by Thanos Mikroutsikos and released on disc in 1983, while individual poems were set to music by Nikos Tatsis and recorded on a disc released in 1978 entitled "Erana".

KAITI PAPADAKI - KARAMITSA

She was born in Nicosia, Cyprus. She lived for several years in Egypt. She now lives in Athens. She studied piano and taught music. She is engaged in poetry and prose.

She issued the following books in Athens: "Shooting stars" poems 1973, "The second-created" short stories 1975, "June Seven" short stories 1977, "Oleanders" poems 1979, "Portraits" short stories 1981, "Internal dialogs" poems 1983, "Sunflowers" short stories 1985, "Flame and Ashes" poetic versions 1986 and "Varvitos" poems 1988.

Her poems and short stories were translated into Arabic by Doctor Naim Attia and were published in Arabic anthologies. Her writings have been included in literary magazines in Greece and in various anthologies and encyclopedias.

She is a regular member of the Hellenic Literary Society. In 1993, she was awarded an honor for the short story "Fence with jasmine" from the book "Portraits" in the Greek-Turkish contest "Abdi Ipekci". The story was inspired by and dedicated to Cyprus.

DIMITRIS PAPADITSAS*

He was born in Tripoli in 1922 and died in Athens in 1987.

He studied Medicine at the University of Athens (PhD). He was trained in Orthopedics in Munich. As a physician, he worked in many provincial cities and in 1976 moved to Athens, where he offered his services to an institution for the disabled.

He appeared in literature in 1943 with the publication of his poetry collection "The Shaft with the phorminx". It was followed by: "Essences I" 1959, "Essences II" 1961, "Poetry 1, 1941-1963" 1963, First State Poetry Prize, "In Patmos" 1964, "As Endymion" 1970, "Poetry 2, 1964-1974" 1974, "Enantiodromia" 1977, "Dyoeidis logos" 1980, First State Poetry Prize, "The disembodied" 1983, Award by the Athens Academy, "To proeortion" 1986, etc.

His poems have been translated into many languages , while the following translations have been published: "Ivan Goll" Traumkraut 1959, "Orphic hymns" 1984 and "Homeric Hymns" 1985, in collaboration with Eleni Ladia.

In 1983, he published the "Os di esoptrou", a selection of thoughts, quotes and drawings by the poet.

THANASIS PAPATHANASOPOULOS

He was born in Perista, Nafpaktia, in 1937. He studied Law in Athens and serves as a judge. His first poetry book "Roumeliotika" was published in 1960. To date, he has published 15 poetry books, essays, folklore studies, short stories, translations, etc.

Poetry: "The Angel of Fire" 1971, "With light and death" 1977, "Supervision" 1979, "Hercules burning" 1984, "Poems" Volume I 1987, "Poems" Volume II 1988, etc.

Essays: "Encounters in the area of our Modern Poetry" 1971 "Literary Studies" 1980, "G. Athanas" 1991, "Notes" 1992, etc.
Folklore: "History and Folklore of Perista" 1967, "Folklore studies" 1980, etc.
Prose: "Test" short stories 1981, "Depths" short stories 1986, "Laocoon kai alla Diigimata" 1990, "The square" chronicle 1940-1950, 1991.
In 1990, his great epic poem "Digenis Akritas" was honored with the Award of the Academy of Athens. In 1993, his narrative "The Square" received the first State Chronicle Award, while his poetry collection "Narratives" won the "Ipekci" prize on the same year.

NIKOS D. PAPAKONSTANTINOU

He was an actor, writer and professor of Speech Training. He played in the National Theater, the Free Theater, the D.P.TH. of Agrinio, in Film and Television.
He taught Speech Training at the school of the National Theatre, at the Piraeus Association and other Drama Schools.
He published translations of works by Wilde, Pushkin and Solomon, his poetry collections "Who can" and "Shooting stars" a historical monograph, two plays and his literary work "Speech Training".
In 1989, he completed the construction of the stone Theater Setta in Evia, a miniature of Epidaurus, his contribution to the Greek people.
He died in 1993.

NIKOS PAPPAS

He was born in Trikala, 1906. He studied Law at the University of Athens. He married poet Rita Boumi in 1936. She started practicing law in Trikala and Athens until 1968 when, due to the military dictatorship, was forced to resign. From the first year of the occupation, Nikos Pappas with Rita Boumi joined the progressive national resistance organizations and wrote poems about it. These views were underpinned by his aesthetic theory on Composite Realism in the magazine Filologiko Chroniko in 1943.
He published the following books: "Futile words" 1931, "Prisoner Angels" 1939, "The blood of innocents" 1945, "Four-timed night" 1946, "Five past twelve" 1959, Second State Award, "The heroic rose"1964, First State Prize "With all and with none" 1965, "After the 21st..." 1974, etc.
Along with Rita Boumi, he issued the "Global Anthology of Poetry" and the in 1976 the "New World Poetry Anthology" in four volumes, again with Rita Boumi, and, lastly, the "True History of Modern Greek Literature (1100-1975)" 1973.
He published poems, essays and critical studies, he gave numerous lectures and participated in conferences (Germany, Romania, Bulgaria, Yugoslavia). He was a member of the Board and Chairman of the Hellenic Literary Society. His poems were translated into all major foreign

languages and were recorded in world-class journals. He received the Award of the Academy, and the Ourani prize in 1980.

TAKIS PAPATSONIS*

He was born in Piraeus, 1895, where he died in 1976. He was a poet, essayist, translator, academic, and introduced free verses in modern poetry. He studied Law and Political Science at the University of Athens and Political Science at the University of Geneva. He worked as Secretary of the Ministry of Finance, vice president of the Board of Directors of the Emporiki Bank, General Secretary of the Ministry of Press, etc. He appeared in Greek Literature with translations in 1909 and in 1913 published his poems in the Acropolis newspaper.

His works: "Election I" cumulative edition of poems in 1934, "Urse Minor" 1944, "Election II" 1962. He also issued two travel books with impressions and reflections, "Exercise in Athos" 1963 "Moldovlachika tou mythou" 1965. He systematically addressed essays and left an extensive translation work. He collaborated with literary magazines and the newspaper Kathimerini.

In 1963, he was awarded the First State Poetry Prize.

EVANGELIA PAPACHRISTOU - PANOU

She was born in Agionori, Corinth, in 1923. She studied at the Naturalistic Faculty of the University of Athens. She studied Theology, Philosophy, Literature. She has published until now eighteen poetry collections and seven essay volumes.

Poetry: "Conversations with Heaven" 1950-1970, "Crystallization" 1974, "In the shadow of the vineyard," 1976, "The Flapping of the Archangel" 1979 "Blackberries as shooting stars" 1981, "The clay eyelids" 1986, "Surveilling Collection" 1991, etc.

Essays: "The Christian Experience by C. P. Cavafy" 1974, "Behold I ..." Essays on Odysseas Elytis 1980, "The revelation of John" 1983, "The Meaning of Night in poetic word" 1988, etc.

She received many awards in Greece and abroad. Her poems were translated into French, Hungarian and Romanian. The entire poetic collection "Blackberries as shooting stars" was translated into French, issued in 1985, and received a diploma and medal from the Academy of Letters and Arts of Perigord in the city Bordeaux. She was also awarded first prize for her book "Biblical vineyards, Votryes" from the Christian Literary Society. Laimos Prize (1991) and Gold medal of the city of Corinth by the City Corinth, etc. She is a member of the Hellenic Literary Society.

GIANNIS PATILIS

He was born in Athens, 1947. He studied Law at the University of Athens and Literature at the department of Byzantine and Modern Greek Studies of the Faculty of Philosophy at the University of Athens. He

worked successively as an employee of OPAP, at the post office service, as an encyclopedias editor and translator. Since 1981, he has been serving Secondary Public Education.
Poetry: "The Little one and the Beast" 1970, "But now be careful! ..." 1973, "For the fruit" 1977, "Coins" 1980, "Non-smoker in a smoker's country - Poems 1970-1980" 1982, "Warm Midday" 1984, "Grafeos Katopron" 1989.
Since 1986, he has been publishing and managing the literary magazine Planodion.

LAMBROS PORFYRAS*

Literary pseudonym of Dimitrios Sypsomos. He was born in Chios in 1879 and died in Piraeus in 1932. When he was still young, his family settled in Piraeus, where in 1894 he published his poem "Sorrow of Marble" in the Asty newspaper. For a period, he studied Law at the University of Athens.

He devoted himself to poetry. For his literary work, he received early favorable judgments by eminent writers such as K. Palamas, P. Nirvanas and M. Mitsakis. The only book Porfyras printed while alive, was the "Shadows" 1920. Posthumously, with the care of his brother, a second collection was published, "Musical Voices" 1932, which was awarded the National Letters Medal. Finally, in 1956, G. Vallettas edited a consolidated version of his work, which included translations of English and French poets.

MANOLIS PRATSIKAS

Literary pseudonym of Margaritis Papadopoulos. He was born in Athens and has resided permanently in Patras since 1954. He has written poetry, prose, drama and essays.
Poetry: "Small margins" 1965, "Travelogue" 1968, "Quest" 1984.
Essays: "Approaching Kafka" 1985 First Prize - Award for best essay of the year, Hellenic Literary Society.
Prose: "11 Short Stories" 1962, "Peter No. 2" collection 1964, "Barren line" collection 1966, "The eviction" novel 1971, "The Protest" collection, Second State Award 1976, "Thursday's diary" collection 1982, distinction by Literary Writers, "The increasing God" novels 1990, etc.
Theater: "4 one-act plays" 1973, "Balance Game" 4 parts 1980, "Theatrical - 2" 1988, etc.

GIANNIS RITSOS

He was born in 1909 in Monemvasia, Laconia, and died in Athens in 1990. He worked as an actor and director and as an editor at Govostis publications. He underwent persecution for his leftist ideas during the period of Metaxas, after the end of the civil war, and finally during the dictatorship.

In 1934, he released his first collection of poems entitled "Tractor" and the "Pyramids" in 1935. In 1936, he published the "Epitaph", which was later set to music by M. Theodorakis. In 1937, he printed "The song of my sister", in 1938 the "Spring Symphony" and in 1940 the "March of the Ocean". Other works: "Old mazurka of rain" 1943, "The man with the carnation" 1952, "Vigil" 1954, "The Moonlight Sonata" 1956, which won the First State Award for Poetry, "A woman by the sea" play 1959, "The window "1960, etc. His poems have been translated into many foreign languages.
In 1975, he was declared a Doctor of Philosophy at the University of Thessaloniki. In 1977, he was awarded the Lenin Prize.

BIANCA ROMANOU

A literary pseudonym of Niki Kollarou. She was born in Tinos and studied at the local School of nuns.
She issued eleven books, two of them novels. Her first two works were awarded the first prize in the Filadelfeio Contest. The Hellenic Literary Society awarded her book "Study on crooked line", along with D. Giakos. The Athens Municipality also awarded her the Medal of Wisdom of Goddess Athena.

ZOI SAVINA

Born in Athens. She studied drawing and decoration in Florence. She presented (Milan '82) 34 poets on the Grafic Olimpia di Milano (Nuovo Poeti Greci). She writes essays, fairy tales, poetry, translations.
Her works: "Shades" 1979 poetry, "Without Archangels" 1980 poetry, "townships" 1981 poetry, "Acrobats" poetry 1983, "Witches" 1985 (bilingual) Poetry Award by the Hellenic Literary Society, "Contact lenses" 1989 poetry.
Translations: Mimo Morina "Poiemata", Leopold Sedar Senghol "Words adorable to the heart and when heard", etc.
Her poems have been awarded and presented in magazines, anthologies, newspapers, radio (Greece - Italy - France - Mexico - Poland - Belgium - Brazil, etc.). Her work "Witches" was translated into six languages.

GIORGOS SARANTARIS

He was born in 1908 in Constantinople and died in Athens, 1941. He was a poet, philosopher and essayist, one of the most important scholars and modernist poets of the interwar period. In 1912, he moved with his family to Italy, where he lived until 1931. He studied Law at the Universities of Bologna and Matserota, from where he received his doctorate. In 1931, he came to Athens, joined the army with the declaration of the Greek-Italian war, but fell ill with typhoid fever and was transferred to Athens, where he died aged 33.
He appeared in literature with collaborations in newspapers and magazines in Italy. He first appeared in Greek literature in 1933 with the

publication of his short story "Martha's Life."
Poetry: "The loves of Time" 1933, "The Heavenly" 1934, "Stars" 1935, "Letters to a woman" 1936, "C.P. Cavafy" single-paged text 1939, "To friends of another joy" 1940.
Philosophy: "Contribution to a philosophy of Existence" 1937, "The presence of Man" 1938 and "Logic Essay as a Theory of the Absolute and non-Absolute" 1939.
He has many unpublished works in reviews and essays on known writers such as Dostoyevsky, Goethe, Dante, Hugo, Baudelaire, Tolstoy, Hamsun, Shakespeare, etc.

GIORGOS SEFERIS

His real name was Giorgos Seferiadis. He was born in 1900 in Izmir, Minor Asia, and died in Athens, 1971. In 1914, his family settled in Athens. He studied Law in Paris. He worked as an attaché of the Ministry of Foreign Affairs, a vice consul and consul in London and as embassy counselor.
Poetic works: "Turning Point" 1931, "The Cistern" 1932, "Book of Exercises" 1926-1937, 1940 "Ship's Log Book" I 1940 "Ship's Log Book" II and III, 1944, 1955, "Three secret poems" 1966, etc.
Essays: On Cavafy, Kalvos, Palamas, Sikelianos, Dialog on Poetry Eliot, Forster, Stravinsky, etc.
Translation work: Significant translations on Greek and foreign works.
He was the central figure of the literary generation of the '30s. He was honored for poetry and his overall work with the Palamas award 1947, with the Foyle award in London 1961, with the Nobel Prize for Literature 1963. His work of become known through translations in many languages.
Honorary titles: Honorary Doctorate in Literature at the Universities of Cambridge (1960), Thessaloniki (1964), Oxford (1964) and Princeton (1965). Honorary member of the American Academy of Arts and Sciences (1966) and member of the Institute of Advanced Studies of the Princeton (1968).

ANGELOS SIKELIANOS

He was born in 1884 in Lefkada and died in Athens in 1951.
He was a poet and scholar, recognized as one of the greatest poets of the 20th century in Greece and Europe. In 1901 he enrolled in the Athens Law School, which he abandoned to devote himself to the study of ancient poetry. In 1907, he married American intellectual Eva Palmer, who would aid him in his various scholarly endeavors, and, in 1940, Anna Karamanou.
Poems: "Alafroiskiotos" 1907 "Delphic Hymn" 1910, "Victory celebration I", "Dithyramb", "Prayer", "Mother of God", "Venus Urania", "Song of the Argonauts", "Easter of Greeks", "Victory celebration II", "Acritic", etc.
Prose: "Rodin," "Periklis Giannopoulos", "Speeches to the best",

"Delphika", "The Eleusinian Testament", etc.
Poems by Sikelianos were translated into French, English, German, Italian, Russian and Swedish. He was nominated for the Nobel Prize in 1946 and 1947. The Sikelianos couple was honored by the Academy of Athens with silver medals for the implementation of the Delphic, with the direct purpose of making Delphi a "global unifying center of humankind."

ILIAS SIMOPOULOS

He was born in a village of Arcadia and came to Athens as a child.
He is a graduate of the Law School and the French Institute. He speaks French, English and Russian. He took part in the Albanian war and the national resistance. He has collaborated with several literary magazines and newspapers with book reviews, aesthetic studies, literary feuilletons, etc.
He has also released to date fourteen poetry collections "Salute to the first sun" 1946, "Arcadian Rhapsody" 1958, "Evidence" 1968, "The notebook of the earth" etc. Also, released in Paris, translated by Goston Henry Aufrere, were the "Sixth command" 1961, "The wounds and windows" 1988, by the Jean Grassin house and the "Anxious" issued by the poet. "The roses of Jericho" 1970 were released translated in Italy. His poems have been translated into many languages and have been included in numerous foreign anthologies.
For many years, he served as chairman of the Society of Greek Writers and later of the Hellenic Literary Society. He has participated in many international conferences and for many years was a member of committees for awarding plays, literary books, etc.

TAKIS SINOPOULOS

He was born in 1917 and died in 1981 in Pyrgos, Ilia.
He was a poet – one of the most important of the first postwar generation – translator and book critic. He studied medicine in Athens, where he worked as a doctor until the end of his life. He took part in the civil war and was involved with the resistance during the dictatorship, experiences that influenced his poetic work.
Although he dealt with poetry from a very young age, he only published his first poetry collection in 1951, entitled "Borderline". It was followed by the collections "Songs" 1953, "The acquaintance with Max" 1956, "Eleni" 1957, "Borderline II" 1957, "The night and the counterpoint" 1959, for which he was awarded the State Prize for Poetry, "Funeral supper" 1971, "The Chronicle" 1975, etc.
In 1978 he published his prose work entitled "Nychtologio" and in 1964 the essays "The poetry of poetry". His study on G. Seferis is also remarkable (1961). He translated French, mainly, poets and essayists, such as G. Apollinaire, P. Éluard, E. Pound, etc.
His poems have been translated in Italy, England and Germany.

KOSTAS M. STAMATIS

He was born in Vrachati, Corinth, in 1935. He studied Political Sciences in Athens and Law in Thessaloniki, without getting a degree. At times, he managed various magazines and has been publishing and managing the magazine Pagosmia Synergasia since 1983.

To date, he has printed:

Poetry: "The abduction of the shepherd's daughter" 1961, "In the Cave of Pan" 1966, "The Sound of human comedy" 1981, "Poemes" 1982 (French), the novel "Great Storms" 1989.

Essays: "Bucolic poetry" (Antiquity) 1974, "Homer the Bucolic" 1978, "The Fantosmagoria of inspiration in the poem", "The Poet and the Crow" by T. Ritoridis" Rome 1980, etc.

Translations: Carmelo Laureta "Poems" 1985, Franco Calabrese "Salty bread' 1989 novel, etc. His works were translated into English, French, Italian, Spanish, Yugoslavian, etc. His work was included in anthologies in Greece and Italy. He received numerous awards in Italy and India and is a member of several international academies as well as the Hellenic Literary Society and Greek Folklore Society.

MARO STASINOPOULOU

She was born in Athens. She studied Law. To date, she has written the poetry collections: "Evangelizations" 1978, "Days without borders" 1980, "The light which travels" 1984, which in its Italian translation received the special prize of the Calabria Academy and the Medal of Lokron, and the "Weavers" 1987. Also, the novel "Revolution" Also, in two editions, 1981 and 1982. She collaborates with newspapers and magazines in Greece and abroad, mainly with poetry and essays, and rarely with short stories. She has given lectures in Athens and the province and has at times made radio shows for ERT-2 Radio. She is a co-publisher and director of the literary newspaper Sychroni Skepsi in Athens.

She is a member of the Hellenic Literary Society (and member of the Committee of Public Relations of the same Society) and of the Academia Culturare Del 'Europa, in Rome.

She has taken part in literary conferences in Europe (Italy, France, England, Turkey, where she was awarded the "Dionysus" prize, and in Eastern Europe (Poland, Yugoslavia).

Her writings have been translated into Italian, French, English, Polish, etc., and have been published in literary publications and anthologies of these countries.

PANAGIOTIS E. STAVRAKAS

He was born in Messolonghi, 1912. He studied Law at the University of Athens, which he left after the third year, because of the difficult circumstances of the time. He has resided in Ilioupoli since 1951. His first book "Life Cycles", a poetry collection, was published in 1981. To date he has published ten collections of poetry and six studies.

Poetry collections: "Trilogies" 1983, "Contrasts converging" 1984 "Courses" 1985, "Courses II" 1986, "Ripples" 1986, "Song of songs "1987 "Hope wanted"1988 "Prose-song" 1990 and "Life Chart" 1992.
Studies: "M. Malakasis, the man, the poet, his era" 1989, "I. Gryparis, the man, the poet" 1989 "Messolonghi - D. Solomos - Zakynthos" 1990, "K. Palamas" 1991, "T. Agras" 1992, "K. Varnalis" 1993.
His works were translated into French and Italian. The "Hope wanted" (Le recherche espoir) received the Grand Poetry Prize at the 19th international contest by CIPAF France. The "Song of songs" (Le cantigue des cantigues) received honors by the SOCIÉTÉ DES POÈTES ET ARTISTES DE FRANCE (1990). An anthology of all nine poetry collections was published by the INSTITUTO UNIVERSITARIO ORIENTALE DIPARTIMENTO DI STUDI DELL' EUROPA.

STAVROS K. STAVRIDIS

He was born in Agrinio, 1943. He studied English Literature at the University of Athens. He is a poet and short story writer. He has published reviews and essays in newspapers and magazines. HE writes the book presentation column for the Emvolimon magazine.
Poetry: "River and City" 1976, "After physics" 1978, "The promised period" 1989. His poetic work was presented at the 13th Poetry Symposium in Patras by professor-critic Michalis Meraklis.
Short stories: "Of the Stone and of Love" 1991. The collection's two novels have been selected TV adaptation.

MICHALIS STAFYLAS

He was born in Granitsa, 1920. He studied at the Law School of Athens. He made his career in the government as inspector of the Ministry of Transport. He participated in the national resistance.
He first appeared in literature in 1950 with the essay "Nazim Hikmet" and continued with the publication of studies, reaching fifteen in 1992. He also published two collections of short stories, four novels, two poetry collections and a play which excelled in the first theater contest (1962) of the Ministry of Education.
He is the director of the Pnevmatiki Zoi magazine, while previously directed the magazine Neoellinikos Logos, and the magazine Thessaliki Estia for for eighteen years. He also published the Encyclopedia Gigantes tou Pnevmatos (ten large volumes prefaced by I.M. Panagiotopoulos) and continues the issuance of the Diarkis Istoria tis Neoellinikis Logotechnias (Continuing History of Modern Greek Literature) that presents all who publish books, along with their bio-bibliographical details.
He is the administrative counselor of the Hellenic Literary Society, the International Society of Literature Critics and a member of the PEN-CLUB. He participated in International Congresses of intellectuals in Berlin, Damascus and Marseilles.

KOSTAS STERGIOPOULOS

He was born in Athens, 1926. He studied Literature at the University of Athens and received a doctorate from the University of Thessaloniki. He worked in private education, as a lecturer at the University of Athens and as a Professor of Modern Greek Literature at the University of Ioannina. He is a poet, essayist, critic.

Poetry: "The landscapes of the Moon" 1955, "The shade and the Light" 1960, "The dawn of the myth" 1963, "The risk" 1965, 1972, "The landscapes of the Sun" 1971, "Eclipse" 1974, "Half of the voyage" 1979 "Change of lighting" 1984, "The midnight sun" 1991. Also, cumulative versions "The Poems I" 1944-1965, (1988) and II 1965-1983 (1992).

Reviews and literary studies: "The effects on the work of Karyotakis" 1972, "From Kalvos to Papatsonis" 1982, "In the area of our old Prose" 1986, etc.

Short Stories: "First Separations" 1947, "Closed Life" 1952 novel.

He was awarded the Second State Poetry Prize in 1961, the First State Poetry Award 1993, the Critical Study and Essay Prize of the Twelve in 1963 and the First State Award for Study and Essay 1974.

His poems have been translated into 10 languages, including French, English, Italian, German, etc. They were published in magazines and anthologies abroad.

KOSTAS E. TSIROPOULOS

He was born in 1930 in Larissa. He studied law in Thessaloniki and History of Art in Barcelona and Paris. He is the founder and director of the annual publication Christianiko kai Symposio and publisher the magazine Efthini. He has been an associate of ERT, magazines and newspapers, for a number of years.

Poetry: "Conservatory for lonely voices" 1962, "Between nights" 1964, "The angels" 1977, "Holy Week" 1980, "Eros - Sleep - Death" 1984, "Mystery" 1988, etc.

Essays: "Word on passions" 1963, "Secret Supper" 1965, "An autopsy of the time" 1966, etc.

Narration: "The Ghosts" 1967, "Distant Lonely Moon" 1972, "Scylla and Charybdis" 1990, etc.

Travelogues: "African Diary" 1964, "Spanish Study" 1966, "American Human-Geography" 1977.

Art History: "Introduction to Byzantine Decoration" 1970, "Romantic painting - Byzantine Painting" 1980.

His books have been translated into Spanish and Italian, and he has translated poems and texts by Jose Ortega Y Gasset, Federico García Lorca, Antonio Machado, etc.

He is a regular member of the Hellenic Literary Society and the PEN CLUB, secretary general of the House of Fine Arts and Letters. He has been honored with the Fexi Award of the Twelve, the State Essay Prize, the First State Novel Prize, the Ourani Award by the Academy of Athens, the Prize by the Society of Christian Letters and the First Prize by the Translators Association.

ANTONIS FOSTIERIS

He was born in Athens, 1953. He studied law in Athens and History of Law in Paris.
Poetry collections: "The Great Journey" 1971, "Interior spaces or the twenty" 1973, "Poetry within Poetry" 1977, "Dark Love" 1977, "The will and there of death" 1987, 1990, etc.
Translations: "Advice to a new poet" by Max Jacob 1984, "Time of the murderers" by Henry Miller 1978, "Poems" by Boris Vian 1982.
He managed the annual publication Poiisi for seven years. He composed the conversation volume with fifty writers and artists "In the second person" 1990. He has been producing and directing the literary magazine I lexi from 1981.
His poems have been translated into many languages, they have been published in magazines and newspapers and have been included in Greek and foreign anthologies

GIOTA FOTIADOU - BALAFOUTI

She was born in Veria in 1932. She worked at the local notary office - land register. She has lived in Athens since 1973. She officially entered the publishing sector with her poetry books "Stirrings" 1973 "With the white birds of the sky" poetry 1986.
Novel: "Never again" 1979, 1980, "Leave the book, bring milk" 1983, 1984. This book was awarded the Prize M. Lountemis by the Hellenic Literary Society. An excerpt from the book "Never Again" has been included in the manual for the 4th grade of elementary school I glossa mas. She was also awarded the first prize of the Spiritual Hearth Takis Tranoulis, "Without Vindication" 1988 "We the Vlachoi" 1991, etc.
Children's writing: "All the animals together" 1985, etc.
Her poetry was translated in Italy, France, Portugal and was included in many anthologies. She is an honorary member of the association "Panagia Soumela", a member of the Hellenic Literary Society, the Greek Children's Book cycle, the Folklore Association of Museology and a member of the International Writers and Artists Association.

ALEKOS G. CHRYSOMALLIS

He was born in Elaiochorion, Kalamata, in 1929. He lives in Kalamata. He followed the stage of the Secretariat of the Courts from where he resigned with the rank of Secretary of Appeals. Today, he is a regular contributor to the newspaper Messiniakos Logos and Nestor and the Radio Station Super. He is mainly involved with poetry, historical research and book reviews.
Poetry: "Rose petals" 1962, "Christian Pulse" 1973 "Stone soil" 1976, "Voices" 1985.

Novel: "Forgive me" 1954, "The Gods groan" 1957. Historical studies: "Ilias Chrysospathis, o protos Maniatis Filikos" 1977, "The silken of the Nuns Monastery of Kalamata" 1984, "The path of self-denial" 1992, etc. He received an honorary distinction with a medal by the Development and Cultural Congress Mani 1990, First Prize for Poetry with the poem "Mother, sweet mother" 1991, an honorary diploma by the Pan-Messinian Federation of the USA and Canada 1991, and a prize by the Writers Committee "Goddess Athena" for his contribution to Greek literature.

*From the Pagkosmio Viographiko Lexiko by Ekdotiki Athinon SA.

BIBLIOGRAPHY

VITSAXIS VASSILIS: The Reflection and Faith Volume I and II ed. Estia Bookstore. Athens 1991.

BUESS LYNN: Numerology for the New Age. De Vorss and Company. California 1987.

CHEIRO: Cheiro's Book of Numbers. Prentice Hall Press. New York 1988.

COOPER D. JASON: Understanding Numerology. William Collins, Sons and Co. Ltd. Glasgow 1990.

WILLIAM WESTCOTT: Numerology. Fiery World. Athens 1983.

PETROS GRAVINGER: The symbolism of Tarot. Library of the Sphinx. Athens 1966.

DRAYER RUTH: Numerology: The Language of Life. Skidmmore - Roth Publishing. Texas 1990.

ALIKI A. BEILI: The Rays and Initiations Volume I and II. Greek Goodwill Unit. Athens.

PETER OUSPENSKY: The symbolism of the Tarot. Fiery World. Athens 1983.

SCHWALLER DE LUBICZ R.A.: A Study of Numbers. Inner Traditions International Ltd. Vermont 1986.

SEPHARIAL: The Kabala of Numbers. Newcastle Publishing Co., Inc. California 1974.

SCHURE ED.: The Great Initiates. Cactus 1982.

STEIN SANDRA KOVACS: Instant Numerology. Newcastle Publishing Co., Inc. California 1986.

TATLER JOHN: The Cycles of Time. Prism Unity. Australia 1990.

VAUGHAN RICHARD: Numbers as symbols for Self-Discovery. CRCS Publications. California 1985.

YOUNG ELLIN DODGE and SCHULER CAROLANN: The Vibes Book. Sammuel Weiser, Inc. New York 1979.

MEGAS SEIRIOS PUBLICATIONS
English Editions

The Concealed Lotus of Manifestation
Fallen Paradise Holy Matter
Logos the Third
a poetic trilogy by Dimitris Kakalidis (bilingual edition)

Incentives I & Incentives II
poetic collections by Dimitris Kakalidis (bilingual edition)

The Revelation of the Entity
by Dimitris Kakalidis

The Wisdom of the Poem
by Dimitris Kakalidis

Spiritual Healing,
A human potential in theory and practice
by Klairi Lykiardopoulou

The Master [1],
First Concepts – First Experiences
by Klairi Lykiardopoulou

The Path from Fear to Fearlessness
by Ioanna Dimakou

Individuality Unity Monad
by Klairi Lykiardopoulou

Seeking... from Alpha to Omega,
Synthesis of Science and Philosophy
by Mina Gouvatsou-Karekou

I Will be Here (poetry)
by Paraskevi Kostopetrou

- **Small Temples on a Wave** (poetry)
- **Fiery Notion** (poetry)
by Vassiliki Ergazaki

Experiences of a Spiritual Healer
by Kiki Keramida

...And the Shadows Became Light
by Klairi Lykiardopoulou

You can Open Your Eyes Now
by Ade Durojaiye

Greek Editions

Dimitris Kakalidis
- The Wisdom of the Poem
- The Wisdom of the Short Story

Poetic Trilogy:
- The Hidden Lotus of Revelation
- Fallen Paradise Holy Matter
- Logos the Third

Poetic Collection:
- Incentives I
- Incentives II

- The Revelation of the Entity

Klairi Lykiardopoulou
- Woman - Exploring her Position and Role in Society
- Man - Exploring his Position and Role in Society
- Couple - Exploring its Position and Role in Society
- Spiritual Healing, *A human potential in theory and practice*
- The Master [1], *First Concepts – First Experiences*
- The Master [2], *The Awakening of the Soul*
- The Master [3], *Processes of the Mind*
- The Master [4], *Accomplishment – Spiritual Healing*
- The Knowledge of the Educator
- The Power of the Woman
- Man and Money, *A philosophical study of their relationship*
- Individuality Unity Monad
- The Family Circle
- The Sacred Task of the Soul
- The Heart of the Earth, *Imaginary Short-stories to give Light to our Planet!*
- The Diachronic Master [1], *Seeking the Knowledge in simple thoughts and deeds*
- The Diachronic Master [2], *Discipleship in the Eternal Truths*
- The Diachronic Master [3], *The Power of Love*
- The Diachronic Master [4], *Our Hidden and Apparent Self*
- ... And the Shadows became Light

Dimitris Karvounis – Dimitris Kakalidis
Alalum and Hallelujah (poetry)

Dimitris Karvounis
- The Crypt and the Nest (and other stories)
- Lilian
- My Spirit Crucified (poetry)
- The Eternally Collected (poetry)

Ninon Dimitriadou-Kampouri
Fear Not, Day is Breaking! (poetry)

Ioanna Dimakou
The Path from Fear to Fearlessness

Kiki Keramida
Experiences of a Spiritual Healer

Petros Panteloglou
The Road I Chose
A Professional Driver's Path to Spirituality

Mina Gouvatsou-Karekou
Seeking... from Alpha to Omega
A Synthesis of Science and Philosophy

Vassiliki K. Ergazaki
- Small Temples on a Wave (poetry)
- Fiery Notion (poetry)
- For the Flowers to Sing (poetry)

Dionisis Dimakos
Flows of Reflection and Heart (poetry)

Paraskevi Kostopetrou
I Will be Here (poetry)

Ade Durojaiye
You Can Open Your Eyes Now

www.ingramcontent.com/pod-product-compliance
Lightning Source LLC
Chambersburg PA
CBHW050118170426
43197CB00011B/1623